Investment Treaties and the Legal Imagination

Investment Treaties and the Legal Imagination

How Foreign Investors Play by Their Own Rules

NICOLÁS M. PERRONE

OXFORD
UNIVERSITY PRESS

OXFORD
UNIVERSITY PRESS

Great Clarendon Street, Oxford, OX2 6DP,
United Kingdom

Oxford University Press is a department of the University of Oxford.
It furthers the University's objective of excellence in research, scholarship,
and education by publishing worldwide. Oxford is a registered trade mark of
Oxford University Press in the UK and in certain other countries

First Edition published in 2021

Impression: 3

Published in the United States of America by Oxford University Press
198 Madison Avenue, New York, NY 10016, United States of America

British Library Cataloguing in Publication Data

Data available

Library of Congress Control Number: 2020944791

ISBN 978–0–19–886214–7

DOI: 10.1093/oso/9780198862147.001.0001

Printed and bound by
CPI Group (UK) Ltd, Croydon, CR0 4YY

Preface

I discovered international investment law by accident after reading a 2002 decision of the Argentine Supreme Court. A foreign investor had requested the court to rule that a measure taken by the Governor of Salta (one of the 23 provinces of Argentina) violated the Spain–Argentina investment treaty. This dispute occurred before the string of ISDS cases brought against Argentina in relation to the 2001 economic crisis; it was not even an ISDS case. As a law student, interested in the interface between law and economics, I was fascinated by the fact that an international treaty was actually reshaping the relations between investors and provincial and federal authorities. Through the years, as my interest for international investment law grew together with the number of ISDS cases against Argentina, my view that this legal regime was not only a means to resolve disputes but also a platform to shape relations and channel conduct persisted. So in my PhD I shifted the focus from states' right to regulate, which was the dominant approach back in the early 2010s, to foreign investor rights, property, and contracts. My aim was to bring to the fore the multiplicity of distributive and normative implications of investment treaties and ISDS, concerning states—but not just their right to regulate—as well as host populations, particularly, local communities. For the transnational lawyer I was becoming, international investment law was almost ideal as an object of study: private law, public law, domestic law, and international law all intermingled into complex and high-profile disputes with clear local, national, and global dimensions.

This book has been in the planning for some time, but its actual theme and structure are the result of an unexpected coincidence. I found that like me, the business leaders, bankers, and lawyers who promoted investment treaties and ISDS in the 1950s and 1960s had a great interest in the ability of this legal regime to shape foreign investment relations. Their interest was more than intellectual, of course, as they organized and networked around the premise that promoting foreign private investment—under a specific set of rules and expectations—was a top priority to advance their world-making project and resist competing visions. This finding gave the book its present historical structure, as my interest expanded from how investment treaties and ISDS shape foreign investment relations today, to investigate whether the current implications coincide with those envisioned by the norm entrepreneurs of the 1950s and 1960s. If this was the case, as it turned out to be, their world-making project could be used as a starting point to examine the political economy that investment treaties and ISDS have contributed to bringing about in the last two decades.

I should say from the start that I do not think international investment law does many things in and by itself. In most cases, there is a combination of social, economic, political, and legal factors shaping foreign investment relations. For those who defend or criticize this legal regime, then, I believe that the local, national, and global context should be taken as seriously as possible. I have attempted to do that here in my analysis of crucial ISDS cases in Chapters 5, 6, and 7.

The journey of this project began at the end of my doctorate. I remain thankful to Andrew Lang and Ken Shadlen for their open-minded approach to my PhD supervision, which allowed me to explore ideas even when the time for finishing the dissertation was running out. Thanks to this 'extra' time, I discovered the legal realist and socio-legal approaches to property and contracts, which continue to inspire my work. For this discovery I am also grateful to David Kennedy and the Institute for Global Law and Policy, where I encountered the writings of Wesley Hohfeld, Morris Cohen, Robert Hale, and Karl Llewellyn as well as the more contemporary contributions of critical legal scholars such as Joseph Singer and Duncan Kennedy. I am also thankful to Robert Wai and Horatia Muir Watt for many conversations about investment law and transnational law during Institute for Global Law and Policy events. More recently, I have had the privilege to work with Peer Zumbansen, who has also been influential in my thinking on transnational law.

The third intellectual pillar of this book relates to my long-held interest in political economy, particularly the political economy of development in Latin America. My understanding of the relationship between investment law and development changed markedly during and after my doctorate. In this respect, fruitful exchanges with Areli Valencia on the case of La Oroya were crucial. Although the article we planned remains to be written, my research moved away from the typical conception of international investment law as a two-actor structure (i.e. foreign investors and host states) to embrace a more pluralistic approach. My thinking also gained enormously from a workshop with local communities, which I co-organized in Bogotá in 2018 with Jimena Sierra and Federico Suárez, and from a recent research trip to the Páramo de Santurbán with Lorenzo Cotula and Brendan Schwartz. A very special thanks to those local leaders who shared their experiences and struggles with us.

This book would not have been possible without numerous enriching encounters with fellow academics and their work. Like most intellectual efforts, this contribution is inherently collective. It has been written against a background of scholarship that I admire, has inspired me, I agree with, and I disagree with—this last category being as important, if not more, than the others. It is impossible to do justice to all these encounters here. Two people must be explicitly mentioned, however, as they have been central to my academic journey through conversations, discussions, and collaborations. David Schneiderman was a generous examiner in my PhD defence; I have never regretted that the examiner proposed by my supervisor was unavailable. David became a demanding reader of my early drafts, for which

I am thankful, and later also a mentor and co-author. My thinking has also benefited from many discussions and collaborations with Lorenzo Cotula, to whom I am especially grateful for his careful—and fast—reading of draft versions of the Introduction and Chapter 1. Aoife O'Donoghue and John Linarelli also deserve credit for their advice on the book proposal, as well as Tomaso Ferrando for suggesting the title everybody liked, and Jenifer Evans for the fantastic editing work.

I had the useful opportunity to present and receive comments on important parts of this book at research seminars held at Warwick and Edinburgh Universities during 2019. Celine Tan and Andrew Lang were magnificent hosts, and James Harrison and Rafael Lima Sakr provided important comments. My analysis of the norm entrepreneurs of the 1950s and 1960s benefited from an exchange with Quinn Slobodian at Queen Mary University in London, where I was invited to participate in a launch event for Slobodian's *Globalists*. Juan Pablo Scarfi was also generous with his time and expertise in history, as I struggled to make sense of the role of the business leaders, bankers, and lawyers in question. Lastly, but not least importantly, I am indebted to the librarians at Harvard Law School, the John F. Kennedy Presidential Library and Museum, the World Bank, and the US Library of Congress for their help. Librarians, I found out, are among the nicest people in the world. I am also thankful to Lauge Poulsen, Andrea Leiter-Bockley, and Todd Tucker for sharing their archival research.

This book project coincided with difficult circumstances, both personal and public. I am deeply grateful to Nicole Selamé Glena for her support throughout these last months, including her large dose of patience. She also deserves credit for insightful comments, discussions, and the excellent German translations.

Este libro está dedicado a mi mamá

Un párrafo es infinitamente injusto para con su esfuerzo y dedicación

Valparaíso, July 2020

Contents

Table of Cases

CASES

ISDS CASES

Let investors unite

Hermann J. Abs

List of Abbreviations

BIAC	Business and Industry Advisory Committee
BITs	bilateral investment treaties
CERDS	UN Charter of Economic Rights and Duties of States
CUP	Cambridge University Press
ECT	Energy Charter Treaty
FET	fair and equitable treatment
FITs	feed-in tariffs
FPIC	free, prior, and informed consent
GATT	General Agreement on Trade and Tariffs
ICSID	International Centre for the Settlement of Investment Disputes
IACtHR	Inter-American Court of Human Rights
ICJ	International Court of Justice
ISDS	investor–state dispute settlement
JRP	joint review panel
MNCs	multinational corporations
NAFTA	North American Free Trade Agreement
NIEO	New International Economic Order
NGO	non-governmental organizations
OECD	Organisation for Economic Co-operation and Development
OUP	Oxford University Press
TRIPs	Trade-Related Aspects of Intellectual Property Rights
UNCTAD	United Nations Conference on Trade and Development

List of Abbreviations

Introduction

A Legal Imagination

In October 1957, Hermann Abs was invited by *Time* and *Life* magazines to discuss 'The Safety of Capital' at the International Industrial Development Conference in San Francisco. He was introduced to the audience as the person whom German politicians Konrad Adenauer and Ludwig Erhard asked for advice on international finance, and as director of Deutsche Bank. Abs spoke to 600 business leaders from 56 non-communist countries about the 'superior importance of private capital exports'. International aid had been crucial in reconstruction after World War II, Abs conceded, but it could not promote widespread and sustained international development. This was a task for foreign *private* investment—the kind of investment that 'cannot develop in a straightjacket of government control'.[1]

Abs thought foreign investors had reasons to be worried. They had been treated unfairly or discriminated against in Iran, Egypt, and Indonesia, he felt, and were also subject to everyday 'cases of indirect interference with their rights'.[2] Essentially, foreign investors wanted to remain in control of their businesses. Abs encouraged his audience to contribute to international development, but only if states would do their part and implement international rules to safeguard capital, including international arbitration. For this problem he had already planned a solution. Abs and his Society to Advance the Protection of Foreign Investments had prepared a proposal for a multilateral convention, what he called 'a Magna Carta for the protection of foreign interests'.[3] He presented his Magna Carta to the audience, asking the assembled investors to unite behind it.

After the San Francisco conference, Abs's Magna Carta was greeted by the *Financial Times* in the UK and the *New York Times* and *Time* and *Life* magazines in the US.[4] In an editorial, *Life* wrote that the US had done little in this area, but that 'financing the "new revolution of expectations"' required more foreign private investment, and 'Abs's scheme, it seems to us, is one good way to promote it'.[5] The

[1] Hermann J. Abs, 'The Safety of Capital' in James Daniel (ed.), *Private Investment: The Key to International Industrial Development: A Report of the San Francisco Conference, October 14-18, 1957* (McGraw Hill 1958) 69–77, 69, 70.

[2] Ibid., 73, 72–3.

[3] Ibid., 76–7.

[4] Arthur S. Miller, 'Protection of Private Foreign Investment by Multilateral Convention' (1959) 53 American Journal of International Law 371–8, 374–5 (footnote 25).

[5] *Life Magazine*, 'Editorial: A good idea for foreign investment', 28 October 1957, 34.

Investment Treaties and the Legal Imagination. Nicolás M. Perrone, Oxford University Press (2021). © Nicolás M. Perrone.
DOI: 10.1093/oso/9780198862147.003.0001

US Council of the International Chamber of Commerce shared this view, having urged the US government earlier in 1957 to implement 'an energetic program of bilateral investment treaties with those friendly and underdeveloped countries which need and want private American investment'.[6]

In the post-1945 period, many business leaders, bankers, and lawyers supported Abs's Magna Carta or similar proposals. This coalition of people raised the alarm about the perils faced by foreign investors, and organized themselves as a group of norm entrepreneurs[7] to promote international investment protection. This objective, crucially, was also relevant for their broader, longer-term goal. Indeed, they regarded foreign investment as essential for securing Western liberal values. In 1958, Abs stated that his Magna Carta was necessary for banks to 'perform [their] essential economic and even political function, without which the economic order of the West cannot be maintained'.[8] In the same year, American Bar Association head Charles Rhyne told the American Bankers Association that lawyers and bankers would 'make a great contribution to world peace by developing world law to govern foreign investment'. International investor rights would expand 'the old and enduring concept of the rule of law to new frontiers'.[9]

Clearly, the recommendations from Abs and professional associations such as the International Chamber of Commerce envisioned international investment protection not only as an end in itself but also as a means to resist competing ideas, namely state economic intervention and communism, promoting their own world-making project.[10] The legal imagination enshrined in the resulting documents reflected a world in which foreign investors could control their investment projects for their own benefit, for the survival of the free enterprise model, and, ideally, for the promotion of international development. These were initiatives of like-minded European and US business and legal figures, all white males, aimed at strengthening foreign investor rights and minimizing state economic interference *by making the rules of the world economy.*

Many of these norm entrepreneurs had started contributing to the making of international investment rules in the inter-war period, and put forward several concrete proposals from 1945 onwards. Significant initiatives came from the International Chamber of Commerce in 1931 and 1949, including its opposition to the rules on foreign investment included in the charter of the International Trade

[6] Ellsworth C. Alvord, Letter to Theodore Francis Green, Chairman, Senate Committee on Foreign Relations, 30 July 1957, in The Joint Committee on Internal Revenue Taxation, Legislative History of United States Tax Conventions (1962) 191, 189–91.

[7] Cass Sunstein, 'Social Norms and Social Roles' (1996) 96 Columbia Law Review 903–68, 929.

[8] Hermann J. Abs, *Proposals for Improving the Protection of Private Foreign Investments* (Institut International D'Etudes Bancaires 1958) 15.

[9] Charles S. Rhyne, 'World Law to Protect World Investment' Speech before the American Bankers Association, New York 1958, in Society to Advance the Protection of Foreign Investments, Convention on Investments Abroad with Comments, Speeches and New Literature, Publication No. 3 (Bergisch Gladbach, J. Heider 1960) 61–7, 61.

[10] Nelson Goodman, *Ways of Worldmaking* (Hackett Publishing 1978) 6.

Organization, which was ultimately rejected by the US in 1950.[11] Abs stands out for reviving the subject of international investment protection with his 1957 Magna Carta, and later joining forces with Hartley Shawcross—the general counsel of Royal Dutch Shell—who was working on a similar project with a group of international lawyers. Together they addressed some criticisms and drafted a new treaty proposal in 1959.[12] The resulting 'Abs-Shawcross draft' never became a treaty itself, but its provisions—including foreign investors' direct right to arbitrate disputes—pervade the more than 3,000 investment treaties that are in force today.[13]

Evaluating the achievements of the norm entrepreneurs is not straightforward. In addition to launching various discussions and initiatives, they promoted the adoption of a multilateral convention based on the Abs–Shawcross draft, and lobbied states and international organizations to agree to this and other proposals. While many had powerful connections, some of their political efforts were more effective than others: no multilateral convention was ever adopted, and states, notably Abs's Germany, refrained from granting investors a direct right to arbitrate disputes for a decade.[14]

This book argues that the norm entrepreneurs for international investment protection did succeed in promoting a legal imagination about foreign investment relations, which consolidated in the 1990s, and that this imagination thrives in both international investment law and investment awards. History gives us several examples of property and contracts serving as platforms to rethink the organization of society. John Locke's 17th-century theory of property and Garrett Hardin's 20th-century tragedy of the commons are just two paradigmatic examples that remain influential even though their main premises have proved historically and socially inaccurate.[15] My claim is that the norm entrepreneurs in question accomplished something similar for foreign investment relations. They may not have achieved a multilateral convention, but Abs, Rhyne, Shawcross, and their allies did create a particular meta-language of international investment law that is still influential today. Irrespective of whether their empirical claims were, or remain, accurate, they crafted a *canon* of the imagination.

The concept of the legal imagination is fundamental to understanding the continuity between the endeavours of the norm entrepreneurs after World War II and today's investment treaty and investor–state dispute settlement (ISDS) practice.

[11] Abs (n. 8) 26.

[12] A. A. Fatouros, 'An International Code to Protect Private Investment-Proposals and Perspectives' (1961) 14 University of Toronto Law Journal 77–102, 86–8.

[13] See Rudolf Dolzer and Christoph Schreuer, *Principles of International Investment Law* (OUP 2012) 8–9; Andrew Newcombe and Lluís Paradell, *Law and Practice of Investment Treaties: Standards of Treatment* (Wolters Kluwer 2009) 22.

[14] Lauge N. Skovgaard Poulsen, *Bounded Rationality and Economic Diplomacy: The Politics of Investment Treaties in Developing Countries* (CUP 2015) 52–3.

[15] See Jeremy Waldron, *The Rule of Law and the Measure of Property* (CUP 2012) 27–41; Elinor Ostrom, *Governing the Commons: The Evolution of Institutions for Collective Action* (CUP 1990) 1–28.

I borrow the concept from Jedediah Purdy's work on property rights: he argues that influential authors such as William Blackstone and Adam Smith relied on property to develop a 'worldview'—a view about sociability and human coexistence. It is this worldview that he calls the 'legal imagination', the space in which our ideas about the limits and purposes of property take shape.[16] Purdy's thinking about imagination follows closely Charles Taylor's notion of the 'social imaginary' of our contemporary world, meaning 'the ways we are able to think or imagine the whole of society'.[17] For Taylor, imagining 'is something much broader and deeper than the intellectual schemes people may entertain when they think about social reality in a disengaged mode'.[18] It is about practice as much as ideas.

The legal imagination of the norm entrepreneurs is the product of both their theories and their practice—discussions, lobbying, and networking. Their ideas about international investment law matter, but so do 'the collation of those ideas'[19] in the larger frame of foreign investment relations. These individuals and associations did not launch a detailed plan to impose a world project or directly addressed the struggles between either the West and East or the North and South. Instead, they focused on certain problems related to international development that they, as practical people, had identified and for which they claimed to have good solutions.[20] Their legal imagination is their specific way of thinking about foreign investor rights and investment relations, regardless of their concrete proposals.

Fundamentally, the bankers, lawyers, and business leaders in question approached foreign investment relations from a global perspective. Their coalition was transnational, and their ideas were in line with the interests of global business, not of their home states or domestic business.[21] They believed that a global legal imagination could help to promote global capitalism.[22] Abs, Eberhard Reinhardt, and others spoke for international banks; Shawcross, Rhyne, G. W. Haight, and influential lawyers talked on behalf of multinational oil companies and the international bar. In many ways, these individuals and their clients embodied the

[16] Jedediah Purdy, *The Meaning of Property: Freedom, Community, and the Legal Imagination* (Yale University Press 2010) 4–5.

[17] Charles Taylor, *Modern Social Imaginaries* (Duke University Press 2004) 63.

[18] Charles Taylor, *A Secular Age* (Harvard University Press 2007) 171.

[19] Paul James, 'The Social Imaginary in Theory and Practice' in Chris Hudson and Erin K. Wilson (eds.), *Revisiting the Global Imaginary* (Palgrave 2019) 33–48, 41.

[20] See David Kennedy, *A World of Struggle: How Power, Law, and Expertise Shape Global Political Economy* (Princeton University Press 2016) 59, 90, 103.

[21] See Claire Cutler, *Private Power and Global Authority: Transnational Merchant Law in the Global Political Economy* (CUP 2003) 12, 180, 254.

[22] Dezalay and Garth observe that lawyers often work together with investment bankers and business consultants 'to extend their hegemony'. Yves Dezalay and Bryant G. Garth, 'Introduction: Lawyers, Law, and Society' in Yves Dezalay and Bryant G. Garth (eds.), *Lawyers and the Rule of Law in an Era of Globalization* (Routledge 2011) 1–16, 1–2. The role of lawyers has been recently highlighted by Katharina Pistor in *The Code of Capital: How the Law Creates Wealth and Inequality* (Princeton University Press 2019) 7–8.

emerging 'multinational man',[23] and they expected to be the primary beneficiaries of their proposals.

There was nothing essentially new in this global business perspective. The characters I discuss in this book were not the first, nor the only ones, to champion the international protection of foreign investment. Their way of thinking about the problem of foreign investment can be traced back to the work of Hugo Grotius in the early 17th century. In his capacity of counsel to the Dutch East India Company, Grotius supplied international law with influential legal doctrines about property, territory, and trade.[24] Another significant moment was the period between the two world wars, which saw numerous discussions, proposals, and cases concerning the responsibility of states for the treatment of individuals. As Hersch Lauterpacht wrote, the importance of this topic was paradoxical: while individuals were not recognized as subjects of international law, 'the great majority of cases which come before international tribunals have their origin in injuries to private interests as distinguished from general State interests'.[25]

Interestingly, the work of Grotius, the inter-war cases, and the proposals of the norm entrepreneurs of the 1950s and 1960s all share a high level of ambition. Grotius is recognized as a founding father of international law, while the cases decided during the inter-war period were ground-breaking in recognizing individual rights under international law and the internationalization of contracts. They have been described as 'practical' innovations 'equivalent to the caveman's discovery of fire'.[26] Building on these and other antecedents, the proposals of the norm entrepreneurs for international investment protection aspirationally used the language of a Magna Carta—the short-lived charter of rights agreed to by the king of England in 1215, and still held up in the West as a historic symbol of freedom and universal rights for merchants.

The main world-making idea of the norm entrepreneurs, however, was more specific and practical. They claimed that foreign investors should have a direct right to sue states before international arbitral tribunals without having to exhaust local remedies. This proposal was based on their everyday experience as bankers and lawyers. They hoped to see such dispute settlement mechanisms (i.e. ISDS) included in a multilateral convention resembling the Abs–Shawcross draft. Commentators at the time were unsure about 'the prospect of states accepting such

[23] Thomas Aitken, *The Multinational Man: The Role of the Manager Abroad* (Routledge 2012 [1973]).

[24] Martti Koskenniemi, 'International Law and the Emergence of Mercantile Capitalism: Grotius to Smith' in Pierre-Marie Dupuy and Vincent Chetail, *The Roots of International Law/Les fondements du droit international: Liber Amicorum Peter Haggenmacher* (Martinus Nijhoff Publishers 2013) 3–37.

[25] Hersch Lauterpacht, *The Function of Law in the International Community* (OUP 2011 [1933]) 115.

[26] V. V. Veeder, 'The Lena Goldfields Arbitration: The Historical Roots of Three Ideas' (1998) 47 International and Comparative Law Quarterly 747–92, 772.

a change'.[27] Aron Broches, general counsel of the World Bank, was cautious. In 1962, he argued that:

> it would be both unreasonable and unrealistic to advocate a compulsory international jurisdiction for disputes between States and foreign investors which would be available without the prior exhaustion of local remedies. This would in effect amount to extra-territorial status for all foreign investment.[28]

The World Bank instead proposed a model based on the 'consent' of states, whereby they would agree to arbitrate 'a specific dispute or a group of disputes'.[29] Under Broches' leadership, and after years of discussion, this led to the creation in 1965 of the International Centre for the Settlement of Investment Disputes (ICSID).[30] In the meantime, some states had started signing bilateral investment treaties (BITs) due to the lack of support for a multilateral convention. The first was signed between West Germany and Pakistan in 1959.

For the norm entrepreneurs neither the ICSID Convention nor the bilateral treaties were entirely satisfactory, for they lacked an ISDS provision. By the end of the 1960s, however, the ICSID Secretariat had convinced states to include ISDS clauses in their bilateral investment treaties;[31] the norm entrepreneurs had finally obtained something close to what they had lobbied and networked for—an 'extra-territorial status' for all the investors covered by the treaties. Describing the innovation, Jan Paulsson evoked the times of Grotius: 'Explorers have set to discover a new terrain for international arbitration', a world where

> claimant need not have a contractual relationship with the defendant and where the tables cannot be turned: the defendant could not have initiated the arbitration, nor is it certain of being able even to bring a counterclaim.[32]

[27] James Leslie Brierly, *The Law of Nations* (OUP 1963) 277. Cited in Nigel Blackaby, Constantine Partasides, Alan Redfern, and Martin Hunter, *Redfern and Hunter on International Arbitration* (OUP 2015) 443.

[28] Aron Broches, 'The Present Need for a Permanent Arbitral Tribunal' Address at the Institute on Permanent International Courts organized by the Minnesota State Bar Association, 13 June 1962 (Broches, M. Aron—Articles and Speeches (1951–1982)—vol. 1) (1651418) World Bank Group Archives, Washington, D.C., United States, 7.

[29] Ibid., 10. Until the 1990s, all the disputes resolved under the auspices of ICSID were contractual cases. See Dolzer and Schreuer (n. 13) 9–11.

[30] Taylor St John, *The Rise of Investor-State Arbitration: Politics, Law, and Unintended Consequences* (OUP 2018) 115–16. The President of the World Bank, Eugene Black, was highly interested in the project. See Eugene R. Black, 'Address to the Annual Meeting of the Board of Governors, September 1961' in ICSID, Convention on the Settlement of Investment Disputes between States. Documents Concerning the Origin and the Formulation of the Convention, vol. II, part 1 (World Bank 1968) 3.

[31] St John (n. 30) 183.

[32] Jan Paulsson, 'Arbitration without Privity' (1995) 10 ICSID Review 232–57, 232.

This 'adventurism', as Muthucumaraswamy Sornarajah has described ISDS, was followed by 'an avalanche' of creative interpretations of investment treaties.[33] The usual explanation for these unpredictable, sometimes inconsistent arbitral awards concerns the treaties' vague terms. Notions such as 'indirect expropriation' and 'fair and equitable treatment' (FET) are so broad that they require interpretation. They operate as standards, not rules.[34] The arbitration literature suggests that arbitrators, having no option but to interpret the treaties, may have had a more flexible approach than judges would have had in similar circumstances. Ole Lando notes that arbitrators often act as 'inventors', particularly when relying on general principles.[35] States were not entirely aware of this creative potential, as negotiators did not take it into account when signing investment treaties, and in some cases, more crudely, they did not actually know what they were signing. Not even the sophisticated US and Canadian negotiators of the North American Free Trade Agreement (NAFTA) could anticipate the inundation of interpretation.[36]

This book adds a new layer to the debate about the origin and evolution of international investment law and ISDS practice. First, it shows that the norm entrepreneurs of the 1950s and 1960s were aware that terms such as 'indirect expropriation' and 'FET' were ambiguous, and could be interpreted in various ways. For this reason, they gave equal weight to these provisions and to ISDS. They sensed that foreign investors' direct access to international arbitration was a fertile terrain for developing an international investment law consistent with their world project, while also providing a mechanism to resist increasing state intervention and economic nationalism in the Global South and the Global North. This task demanded global explorers, not locally embedded adjudicators. As Julian Lew has noted, the international arbitral community sees arbitration as 'free from the controls of parochial national laws, and without the interference or review of national courts'.[37] In this regard, it can be said that 'inventor' arbitrators have not been inconsistent; they have always thought about law in terms of *lex mercatoria*, occupying 'the space of imagination [...] for their own projects'.[38]

[33] Muthucumaraswamy Sornarajah, *Resistance and Change in the International Law on Foreign Investment* (CUP 2015) 143.

[34] Federico Ortino, 'Refining the Content and Role of Investment 'Rules' and 'Standards': A New Approach to International Investment Treaty Making' (2013) 28 ICSID Review 152–68, 154–5.

[35] Ole Lando, 'The Law Applicable to the Merits of the Dispute' in Peter Šarčević (ed.), *Essays on International Commercial Arbitration* (Martinus Nijhoff Publishers 1989) 129–59, 154.

[36] See Sornarajah (n. 33) 143; Poulsen (n. 14) 18–20, 66, 135; Ann Capling and Kim R. Nossal, 'The Rise and Fall of Chapter 11: Investor-State Dispute Mechanisms in the North American Free Trade Agreement and the Australia–United States Free Trade Agreement' Paper prepared for the Oceanic Conference on International Studies, Australian National University, July 2004, 26–7.

[37] Julian D. M. Lew, 'Achieving the Dream: Autonomous Arbitration' (2006) 22 Arbitration International 179–203, 179.

[38] Ralf Michaels, 'Dreaming Law Without a State: Scholarship on Autonomous International Arbitration as Utopian Literature' (2013) 1 London Review of International Law 35–62, 62. Veeder argues that the continuity between the ground-breaking awards of the 1920s and contemporary

Secondly, the book demonstrates that the norm entrepreneurs promoted an interpretation of investment treaties remarkably similar to the bulk of ISDS awards. They construed foreign investor rights and indirect expropriation in a broad manner, upheld the value of case-by-case analyses, and favoured the protection of foreign investors' reliance. As the first investment treaties were being signed in the 1960s, the norm entrepreneurs were discussing how their provisions should be interpreted, connecting the practical problems of international business and development with their conception of the solutions.

Today, the future of investment treaties and ISDS is under some reconsideration; the Working Group III of the United Nations Commission on International Trade Law is one manifestation of this.[39] International investment law has become one of the most controversial areas of international law, and civil society and some states have voiced serious concerns about investment treaties and ISDS. As we will see, the present critique is not markedly different from that made against the proposals of the International Chamber of Commerce, Abs, and the other norm entrepreneurs of the 1950s and 1960s. Those initiatives were found to be too favourable to foreign investors, concealing the costs and risks of foreign investment to host states and local actors. Unsurprisingly, the literature has debated why states signed up for this regime and the role international organizations played in that process, but has largely overlooked the substantial participation of business leaders, bankers, and lawyers in its evolution and development. Abs and Shawcross are sometimes described as two individuals on a sort of personal quest, rather than as the most visible faces of a broad coalition in favour of international investment protection.

In showing that these norm entrepreneurs crafted the present canon of legal imagination in international investment law, this book aims to highlight not only how they contributed to the law's progressive development, but also how 21st-century ISDS practice is still closely related to their world-making project. For those who favour making significant reforms to this international regime but still think that can be achieved without reconsidering its pillars, the fact that present ISDS practice reflects the norm entrepreneurs' vision of foreign investment relations should be more than just an anecdotal observation.

ISDS practice responds less to the rules and institutions and more to the international legal culture associated with international arbitration. See V. V. Veeder, 'Chancellor Wirth and the Mologoles Concession 1923-1927: The German-Speaking Origins of the ICSID Convention' in Christina Binder, Ursula Kriebaum, August Reinisch, and Stephan Wittich (eds.), *International Investment Law for the 21st Century: Essays in Honour of Christoph Schreuer* (OUP 2009) 377–405, 398–9.

[39] See UNCITRAL Working Group III: Investor-State Dispute Settlement Reform, available at https://uncitral.un.org/en/working_groups/3/investor-state (last visited 23 June 2020).

A. Escaping the 'straightjacket of government control'

In essence, the legal imagination of the norm entrepreneurs of the 1950s and 1960s was a response to state intervention in the economy. In the post-1945 period, the dominant views about property and contracts favoured economic planning in both the Global South and the Global North. States had a good margin to expropriate and regulate private property, and contracts could be renegotiated or adjusted to domestic public imperatives. The norm entrepreneurs found this concerning, particularly in the context of the natural resource businesses, which they themselves had stakes in, and decolonization. They insisted on the sanctity of private property and contracts, but also knew that much of this was just rhetoric. Shawcross recognized that states had a right to expropriate and regulate private property, and these public rights could not be annihilated.[40] The best option was to tame the state.

The norm entrepreneurs had two primary concerns: the practice of partial compensation and what they considered to be abusive regulation, including state attempts to reshape economic relations or create state economies. Addressing these problems, however, engendered new issues of different legal and political complexity. The notion of indirect expropriation, that is, measures equivalent or tantamount to expropriation, could capture cases of excessive taxation or cancellation of permits and licences. The norm entrepreneurs recommended that states refrain from regulating, but legally they knew such disputes were hard cases and it would be difficult to come up with a clear formula to distinguish legitimate from abusive regulation.[41] The doctrine of unjustified enrichment, which worked to limit cases of partial compensation, was not useful in cases of indirect expropriation.[42] States often do not get enriched through regulation.

But Shawcross and other international lawyers held a different view on the relationship between contracts and sovereignty. Irrespective of the law applicable to the contract, they argued that states cannot breach their commitments because they are bound by the international rule of *pacta sunt servanda*. As sovereigns, states enjoy a special status and can regulate and even expropriate property. But contracts can impair this status, placing foreign investors and states on an equal standing. Shawcross went as far as claiming that under international law states could not expropriate concession contracts.[43] The problem was that enforcing a strict interpretation of *pacta sunt servanda* is not straightforward. Contracts do not only serve to facilitate transactions—they are also embedded in a legal order

[40] Hartley Shawcross, 'Problems of Foreign Investment' (1961) 102 Recueil des Cours 339–63, 353.

[41] Society to Advance the Protection of Foreign Investments, 'International Convention for the Mutual Protection of Private Property Rights in Foreign Countries: draft' (1957) 12.

[42] See Christoph Schreuer, 'Unjustified Enrichment in International Law' (1974) 22 American Journal of Comparative Law 281–301, 285–9.

[43] Shawcross (n. 40) 352–4. Shawcross's views are discussed in Georg Schwarzenberger, *Foreign Investments and International law* (Stevens & Sons 1969) 161.

and a social context, where public law imperatives shape the content of transactions.[44] The norm entrepreneurs addressed this by claiming that these imperatives were inapplicable to investment contracts, as state obligations are governed by international law and this legal order calls for a stricter interpretation of *pacta sunt servanda*. Judges may still privilege domestic public imperatives, but the norm entrepreneurs expected international arbitrators to resist this impulse.

Internationalizing contracts was a useful strategy to tame states' right to regulate, but it did not resolve all threats to foreign investment projects, particularly situations in which no contract existed or the contract did not regulate the controversial issue. For the norm entrepreneurs, the challenge was to turn a transactional view of relations between foreign investors and states from the exception into the rule, and the solution they subscribed to was the protection of foreign investors' ability to rely on regulations in place when investments were made. They argued that the notion of fairness and the imperatives of the global economy required that foreign investors could legitimately rely on the assurances and representations given by states at the time of making the investment (their 'legitimate expectations'). This was an audacious interpretative move. It drew on international law and a strict interpretation of *pacta sunt servanda* to unplug foreign investment relations from domestic public imperatives and plug it into global business imperatives. If arbitrators were to interpret the facts of the dispute from a global perspective and in a transactional manner, those investors who had neither contracts nor assurances would also benefit from this approach.

Unless foreign investors could extract detailed contracts for every project, mitigating the sovereignty status of states required these two moves—*unplugging* and *plugging*. This way of interpreting foreign investment relations meant that a previously rather exceptional transactional model, limited to contracts and stabilization clauses, would become the dominant way of thinking about international investment law, one that recognized foreign investors' 'extraordinary citizenship rights'.[45] The investors themselves demanded this special treatment as protection from the political consequences of their projects, which can clearly have 'more impact on the lives of ordinary people than most generals and politicians'.[46] They sought rights that would not only enable them to make investment decisions but also ensure that states and populations would respect those decisions regardless of

44 Florian Möslein and Karl Riesenhuber, 'Contract Governance—A Draft Research Agenda' (2009) 5 European Review of Contract Law 248–89, 269–71; Hugh Collins, 'Regulating Contract Law' in Christine Parker, Colin Scott, Nicola Lacey, and John Braithwaite (eds.), *Regulating Law* (OUP 2004) 13–32, 13–14, 16.

45 David Schneiderman, 'The Global Regime of Investor Rights: Return to the Standards of Civilised Justice?' (2014) 5 Transnational Legal Theory 60–80, 70. Similarly, Cotula argues that this exceptional transactional model is becoming 'the dominant paradigm of government' in the global economy. Lorenzo Cotula, 'The State of Exception and the Law of the Global Economy: A Conceptual and Empirico-Legal Inquiry' (2017) 8 Transnational Legal Theory 424–54, 427.

46 Richard Barnet and Ronald Muller, *Global Reach: The Power of the Multinational Corporations* (Simon and Schuster 1974) 214.

the 'macroeconomic dislocations created by globalising policies'.[47] The premise, for Paulsson, is the separation of governmental policies that facilitate investment projects from the legal regime, which is 'purely instrumental': 'To be sure, using a good tool to implement misguided policies leads to poor results, but that is no reason to blame the tool.'[48]

In this legal imagination, focused on investment protection, there was never any place for foreign investor obligations. States could impose obligations through contracts, if they wanted, but the benefit to them of investment treaties—the *quid pro quo*—was seen to be an increase of foreign investment flows. In the 1970s, when the political landscape came to be less favourable to foreign investors, the norm entrepreneurs contemplated the possibility of foreign investor obligations but in a way compatible with the canon of imagination enshrined in investment treaties: they proposed the adoption of voluntary obligations in the form of *guidelines*.[49] In 1974, Gerrit Wagner, head of Royal Dutch Shell, was asked by a UN panel if the governance of foreign investment should move closer towards a model resembling a general agreement with rights and obligations on both sides. He replied that this would require a lot of analysis and discussion, but in the meantime, 'the ICC guidelines are to be recommended as providing a useful framework for initial consideration and discussion'.[50]

B. Grasping the legal imagination: a transnational law method

Making sense of the legal imagination of the norm entrepreneurs in question requires an analytical framework calibrated for an examination of the background ideas framing ISDS practice. In the late 1960s, Georg Schwarzenberger observed that Abs, Shawcross, and their 'united capitalist front' aimed to 'change the law as it suited them' and achieved this trick through devices which, 'by their very subtleness, exposed their authors to the charge of having been less than frank'.[51] We cannot then expect the legal imagination to be openly discussed in ISDS cases or policy debates about international investment law. Arbitrators and lawyers build on certain background ideas to argue about issues concerning procedure or the interpretation of indirect expropriation or FET; they rarely debate the existing canon

47 Jan Paulsson, *Denial of Justice in International Law* (CUP 2005) 232.
48 Ibid.
49 International Chamber of Commerce, '1972 Guidelines for International Investment' in UNCTAD, *International Investment Instruments: A Compendium*, vol. 3 (United Nations 1996) 279–91.
50 UN Department of Economic and Social Affairs, *Summary of the Hearings Before the Group of Eminent Persons to Study the Impact of Multinational Corporations on Development and International Relations*, ST/ESA/15 (United Nations 1974) 416.
51 Schwarzenberger (n. 43) 137–8. Also, Georg Schwarzenberger, 'Decolonisation and the Protection of Foreign Investments' (1967) 20 Current Legal Problems 213–31, 219, 223–5.

of imagination in the arbitrations. Irrespective of who prevails in individual disputes, ISDS always wins.

An approach oriented around the resolution of ISDS cases, for this reason, is not suitable for understanding the legal imagination involved. Indeed, practitioners are primarily interested in analysing ISDS as a mechanism to enhance rights protection, as opposed to a system effecting a worldview.[52] It is true that such 'mainstream' debates include broader questions, but, as Stephan Schill explains:

> One concern that exists irrespective of the professional socialization of writers on international investment law, however, is that much of the writing is done by authors who themselves are involved in investment treaty arbitrations. Although this ensures the practical relevance of the topics addressed, and accounts for the sensitivity for current concerns and the richness of practical insights, it also constitutes a potential obstacle for independent and clear positioning.[53]

A more productive focus might be the public law critique of the effects of investment treaties and ISDS on states' right to regulate. This literature relies on a public law approach to illustrate how such a legal regime undermines the ability of states to implement regulations in the public interest. Gus Van Harten's authoritative critique of ISDS argues that awards do not follow public law principles of adjudication and, more importantly, there is no assurance that ISDS arbitrators will conduct judicial review with the neutrality and impartiality of domestic judges.[54] Those who are more optimistic about investment treaties agree that ISDS is akin to judicial review, but believe that arbitrators can perform this function appropriately, respecting states' right to regulate.[55]

This focus is surely necessary to understand the legal imagination of the norm entrepreneurs, but the public law critique needs to be expanded to encompass the full dynamics of foreign investment relations. The norm entrepreneurs had clear expectations about the role and conduct of states in relation to investments already established in host countries, but their vision extended to the period before and after projects, as well as the connection between foreign investment relations and their world-making ambitions. They used the language of private property and contractual rights to shape conduct and expectations, concentrating on the ability of investors to calculate, plan, and organize the economy. A public law framework may be insufficient to analyse such rights, which are indeterminate, incomplete,

[52] Martti Koskenniemi, 'It's Not the Cases, It's the System' (2017) 18 Journal of World Investment & Trade 343–53.

[53] Stephan Schill, 'W(h)ither Fragmentation? On the Literature and Sociology of International Investment Law' (2011) 22 European Journal of International Law 875–908, 893–4.

[54] Gus Van Harten, *Investment Treaty Arbitration and Public Law* (OUP 2007).

[55] Catharine Titi, *The Right to Regulate in International Investment Law* (Bloomsbury 2014); Stephan W. Schill, 'Deference in Investment Treaty Arbitration: Re-conceptualizing the Standard of Review' (2012) 3 Journal of International Dispute Settlement 577–607.

and always require interpretation. Further, private rights and public authority are intrinsically related. It is difficult to understand states' right to regulate without considering foreign investor rights, and vice-versa. The public sphere of authority is shaped by the scope of foreign investor rights, as sticks in the bundle of rights, as much as by the relative strength of these private rights vis-à-vis public authority.[56]

Concentrating on foreign investor rights, moreover, reveals something that is implicit in the legal imagination of the norm entrepreneurs. These rights relate not just to states' right to regulate, but also to local values and competing rights. Foreign investment projects can affect the local community, meaning indigenous peoples, a specific group within indigenous peoples, or local residents who may be united by the impact of the investment but do not share a strong social identity.[57] The norm entrepreneurs omitted reference to local rights when they talked about the sanctity of property. Implicitly, this omission assumed the existence of *good* and *bad* property.

The place of local communities is key to the legal imagination of the norm entrepreneurs. Historically, their attitude to the issue was to ignore it, although some international lawyers did leave the door open for the internationalization of rights other than those of foreign investors. Since the 1970s, this latter internationalization has gained more support. Towards the end of the century, René-Jean Dupuy, Elihu Lauterpacht, and Francisco Orrego Vicuña, who contributed to the evolution of international investment law as scholars and arbitrators, discussed the international recognition of local rights in the form of human rights. They believed such a development was inevitable after the internationalization of foreign investor rights.[58] Indeed, international treaties and legal decisions have gradually recognized that local communities have some human rights related to the land where they live. José Alvarez claims that since the 2000s a new international property field is emerging from these different categories of the human right to property. They are not uniform, however; they rather represent a terrain on which various regimes, rights, and purposes coexist, including the rights of foreign investors and local communities.[59]

Inevitably, as Alvarez points out, these rights may enter into tensions not only between owners but also between owners and non-owners.[60] Addressing the tensions

[56] Joseph William Singer, *Entitlement: The Paradoxes of Property* (Yale University Press 2000) 6–9.

[57] Lorenzo Cotula and Mika Schröder, 'Community Perspectives in Investor-State Arbitration', International Institute for Environment and Development (2017), 1, available at https://pubs.iied.org/12603IIED/ (last visited 16 May 2020).

[58] René-Jean Dupuy, *Dialectiques du droit international: souveraineté des États, communauté internationale et droits de l'humanité* (Pedone 1999); Elihu Lauterpacht, 'International Law and Private Foreign Investment' (1997) 4 Indiana Journal of Global Legal Studies 259–76, 274–5; Francisco Orrego Vicuña, *International Dispute Settlement in an Evolving Global Society: Constitutionalization, Accessibility, Privatization* (CUP 2004) 53.

[59] José E. Alvarez, 'The Human Right of Property' (2018) University of Miami Law Review 580–705, 649–55. Also, Lorenzo Cotula, *Human Rights, Natural Resource and Investment Law in a Globalised World: Shades of Grey in the Shadow of the Law* (Routledge 2012).

[60] Alvarez (n. 59) 667.

between and relative strength of the rights themselves is complicated because they belong—at least in principle—to different international property law regimes. One strategy involves comparing the interpretation and enforcement of foreign investor rights in ISDS and local community rights in multiple international courts. But this has some limitations. It does not address the conflict directly, because in both instances the state is on the other end of the litigation. Further, it overlooks the fact that ISDS is equally relevant as a site of struggle for foreign investors and for communities. ISDS arbitrators have to deal with competing property rights, individual or communal, and make sense of often conflicting purposes and rationales. As tribunals increasingly have to deal with local community rights, at least indirectly, the question is whether their reasoning remains consistent with the abovementioned legal imagination or if we are instead witnessing a radical rethinking of international investment law.[61]

In view of this complexity, a more appropriate method to analyse international investment law is through transnational law.[62] Every large investment project involves different laws, rights, and rationales. Jeswald Salacuse insists that there are at least three legal orders at play here: domestic, international, and contractual. These laws are conceptually different and emerge from distinct sources, but are 'in practice interconnected and interactive in the application to specific investment transactions'.[63] Schwarzenberger similarly observes that a rule of substance was smuggled into the ICSID Convention, that is, applicable law (Article 42), and that by calling for the application of both domestic and international law it creates a problem that arbitrators must resolve creatively.[64] This situation of legal pluralism is further complicated once we account for local communities and their rights. In a study of the 2016 *Pacific Rim v. El Salvador* case, Robin Broad identifies three levels of analysis—the local, the national, and the global—each of which includes multiple actors, laws, and expectations.[65]

Additionally, a transnational law method can truly capture the legal imagination of the norm entrepreneurs for foreign investment protection. These individuals and their associations promoted audacious views about public international law

[61] Sornarajah argues that: 'If a shift does occur towards the recognition of the rights of people, the role of international law in investment protection will require radical rethinking.' Muthucumaraswamy Sornarajah, *The International Law on Foreign Investment* (CUP 2017) 69.

[62] As Zumbansen I understand transnational law to include the major premises and analytical tools of legal realism. See Peer Zumbansen, 'Transnational Law' in Jan Smits (ed.), *Encyclopedia of Comparative Law* (Edward Elgar Publishing 2006) 738–54; Peer Zumbansen, 'Defining the Space of Transnational Law: Legal Theory, Global Governance, and Legal Pluralism' (2012) 21 Transnational Law & Contemporary Problems 305–36.

[63] Jeswald W. Salacuse, *The Three Laws of International Investment: National, Contractual, and International Frameworks for Foreign Capital* (OUP 2013) 405.

[64] Schwarzenberger (n. 43) 144.

[65] Robin Broad, 'Corporate Bias in the World Bank Group's International Centre for Settlement of Investment Disputes: A Case Study of a Global Mining Corporation Suing El Salvador' (2014) 36 University of Pennsylvania Journal of International Law 851–74, 853.

and the sources of law rules, conflating private and public law as much as domestic and international.[66] They blurred these boundaries to allow the rules to evolve and consolidate, relying on a transactional view of foreign investment relations and a specific interpretation of contracts. In this sense, they were among the precursors of the shift from property to contracts that consolidated later in the 1990s in areas such as international business law.[67] Essentially, Abs and others aimed to *dethrone* the state from its privileged position at the centre of the law, including international law. It is not surprising, then, that some scholars have come to think of international investment law as a field in which corporations can act as lawmakers[68] or challenge the operation of the sources of international law.[69]

C. Overview

In this introductory chapter, I have presented the claim that the norm entrepreneurs for foreign investment protection played a primary role in shaping an imagination that remains a fundamental part of international investment law today. As we will see, the evolution of this legal regime has adapted to new circumstances while helping reproduce the world-making project of Abs, the International Chamber of Commerce, and others. We continue to play by their rules.

Grasping this legal imagination, its implications and its evolution, requires an analytical framework calibrated to the task. I have explained why an approach focused on the resolution of ISDS cases is not appropriate, and suggested that a public law approach has limitations. Foreign investment relations involve domestic and international law, and both public and private law, as much as issues that have remained silenced or actors who have been made invisible. For this reason, a transnational law approach appears to be the most appropriate. The next chapter builds on these premises to develop an analytical framework for visualizing the multiple ways in which foreign investor rights relate to foreign investment relations. It also explores how investment treaties and ISDS relate to these rights.

The rest of the book develops the substance of the argument. Chapter 2 introduces the norm entrepreneurs, their worldviews, who they considered to be their opponents, and how they expected ISDS arbitrators to interpret investment treaties. Chapter 3 examines some critical developments during the long 1970s,

[66] As I discuss in Chapter 2, Philip Jessup collaborated with the American Branch of the International Law Association, preparing a response to the questionnaire of the International Committee on Nationalization. Jessup is the author of the famous book *Transnational Law* (Yale University Press 1956).

[67] See Harry N. Scheiber, 'Introduction' in Harry N. Scheiber (ed.), *The State and Freedom of Contract* (Stanford University Press 1998) 1–11.

[68] Julian Arato, 'Corporations as Lawmakers' (2015) 56 Harvard International Law Journal 229–95.

[69] Jorge E. Viñuales, 'Sovereignty in Foreign Investment Law' in Zachary Douglas, Joost Pauwelyn, and Jorge E. Viñuales (eds.), *The Foundations of International Investment Law: Bringing Theory into Practice* (OUP 2014) 318–62, 319, 362.

when different imaginaries about foreign investment competed with each other. This discussion puts the legal imagination of the norm entrepreneurs in a broader context, examining how it addressed competing world-making projects and evolved to become stronger. Chapter 4 focuses on the 1990s and the emergence of ISDS practice. It shows that most tribunals approached investment treaties and disputes in a way that is remarkably similar to the legal imagination of the norm entrepreneurs of the 1950s and 1960s. The remaining chapters, 5, 6, and 7, change the angle of inquiry and provide a detailed analysis of some influential ISDS cases or groups of cases. They situate investment disputes within a broad account of foreign investment relations, which I compare and contrast with the storytelling and interpretation of the awards. These chapters show how international investment law has both evolved and stayed consistent, and conclude that the canon of legal imagination in this field remains, essentially, that of the norm entrepreneurs for international investment protection.

1
Foreign Investor Rights and Investment Relations

Investment treaties and ISDS serve not just to resolve disputes between states and foreign investors; the interpretation of foreign investor rights also helps structure foreign investment relations. This chapter leaves the norm entrepreneurs of the 1950s and 1960 aside, for a moment, to develop an analytical framework for examining how the rights of foreign investors can contribute to defining their role and relations with states and local communities. It discusses the type of rights that make foreign investment projects, their purpose, and different ways of looking at the interface between these rights, states' right to regulate, and social relations more generally. The rest of the chapter focuses on the significance of ISDS for foreign investors' rights. This particular dispute resolution mechanism has important implications. As Karl Llewellyn summed it up, not only is there 'no remedy, no right' but there is 'precisely as much right as remedy'.[1]

A. Foreign investments as a combination of rights

Foreign investment projects generally make use of a 'combination' of rights, rather than just one entitlement.[2] To extract gold, for example, a foreign investor needs more than a concession or a mining title; large mining projects also require surface rights, environmental and social licences, intellectual property, and so on. Investments in most economic sectors operate similarly. The rights involved in any multimillion-dollar investment project seldom match laypeople's imaginaries about property and contracts, which tend to think in terms of the rights and obligations over a house or sale of goods. Foreign investment is not about personal property or one-off transactions. The *Methanex v. USA* tribunal observed that foreign investor rights are about the 'managerial control over components of a process that is wealth producing'.[3] Most ISDS tribunals highlight this element. They define

[1] Karl Llewellyn, *Jurisprudence: Realism in Theory and Practice* (Transaction Publishers 2000) 63.

[2] Christoph Schreuer, 'Investment Arbitration' in Cesare Romano, Karen Alter, and Yuval Shany (eds.), *The Oxford Handbook of International Adjudication* (OUP 2014) 295–315, 300. Also, *CSOB v. The Slovak Republic* (ICSID Case No. ARB/97/4) Decision on Jurisdiction, 24 May 1999, para. 72.

[3] *Methanex v. USA* (UNCITRAL—NAFTA) Final Award of the Tribunal on Jurisdiction and Merits, 3 August 2005, Part IV, Ch D, paras. 16–17. Similarly, the *Chemtura* tribunal refers to an investment as an 'enterprise': *Chemtura v. Canada* (UNCITRAL—NAFTA) Award, 2 August 2010, para. 243.

Investment Treaties and the Legal Imagination. Nicolás M. Perrone, Oxford University Press (2021). © Nicolás M. Perrone.
DOI: 10.1093/oso/9780198862147.003.0002

foreign investment as the organization of various assets, for a certain period of time and assuming a risk, with the expectation of making an economic return.[4]

This functional distinction has deep consequences. Generally, property and contracts are structurally distinct from each other. Property is the creation of the law, it is rigid (as per the *numerus clausus* rule), and it generates relations between an owner and an entire community, including the state. Contracts, on the other hand, are the result of party autonomy and affect only the parties to the transaction.[5] This distinction works well when we focus on rights regularly traded in the market. Thanks to the standardization of property, people have good and reliable information about the bundle of rights they are buying and selling; this facilitates market transactions over, say, a house or a car.[6]

But the situation is quite different when it comes to large foreign investment projects. Such projects are rarely similar to each other; the rules governing them can vary from region to region, and sometimes the underlying legal titles cannot be transferred without the approval of the host state.[7] As a result, classifying foreign investor rights as either property or contracts can be tricky. Some fall in a grey area because property and contracts in foreign investment projects frequently refer to the same thing: control of resources.[8]

The scope and strength of the rights on which foreign investment projects depend derive from general laws, sectoral regulations, and, sometimes, specific commitments or contracts. Many foreign investment projects are governed by sectoral regulations, which cover central issues ranging from incentives to social licences. Additionally, foreign investors and states regularly bargain with each other to define the scope and strength of their rights. When negotiating an investment project, foreign investors and host states may agree on a specific bundle of rights in a contract; for instance, the host state may provide a stabilization agreement for tax or environmental conditions. State officials may also provide representations or assurances whose effects depend on whether reliance is protected. Overall, these contracts, commitments, and representations add to the rights defined by the legislation. Through legal planning (or interpretation) it is possible to make property out of contracts.[9] As the *Saudi Arabia v. Aramco* tribunal noted, 'the concession has

[4] *Phoenix v. Czech Republic* (ICSID Case No. ARB/06/5) Award, 15 April 2009, para. 114; *Romak v. Uzbekistan* (PCA Case No. AA280) Award, 26 November 2009, para. 206.

[5] Gregory S. Alexander and Eduardo M. Peñalver, *An Introduction to Property Theory* (CUP 2012) 2–3.

[6] Thomas W. Merrill and Henry E. Smith, 'Optimal Standardization in the Law of Property: The Numerus Clausus Principle' (2000) 110 Yale Law Journal 1–70.

[7] See, e.g., Peter D. Cameron and Michael C. Stanley, *Oil, Gas, and Mining: A Sourcebook for Understanding the Extractive Industries* (World Bank 2017) 47, 77, 79–80, 85.

[8] See Jeswald W. Salacuse, *The Three Laws of International Investment: National, Contractual, and International Frameworks for Foreign Capital* (OUP 2013) 167–70; Zachary Douglas, 'The Hybrid Foundations of Investment Treaty Arbitration' (2003) 74 British Yearbook of International Law 151–289, 197 (particularly footnote 219).

[9] Morris Cohen, 'Property and Sovereignty' (1927) 13 Cornell Law Quarterly 8–30, 11.

the nature of a constitution which has the effect of conferring acquired rights on the contracting Parties'.[10]

The content of these rights is another aspect that can raise interpretative issues. The majority of ISDS tribunals describe foreign investor rights as 'a bundle of proprietary, contractual and administrative rights', ranging from the right to enjoy benefits to the right to participate in relevant decisions.[11] But some arbitrators have also suggested that these rights represent economic value or expected benefits, which investment treaties protect.[12] From a legal standpoint, this second view is problematic. Value is neither a legal nor a normative concept. It is a calculation performed by market actors, based on economic, social, political, and legal information, to define how much money a rational actor would pay for a certain asset or assets. Here, the 'market cannot constitute the fixed point since it requires another point of reference, the legal one'.[13]

Investment treaties and ISDS practice protect property and contracts, as well as rights that escape clear categorization. Most treaties currently in force define investment as 'every asset', and although some agreements have narrowed down this definition, they still describe foreign investor rights quite broadly.[14] Some of the assets protected under investment treaties have a typical property structure, such as legal titles over land. Others may be more difficult to classify, such as incentives, licences, or permits. Lastly, there are assets that reflect a specific commitment or are contractual but fall within the investment regime thanks to a broad definition of investment or the operation of an investment treaty standard such as the umbrella clause. ISDS practice has followed the same principle protecting a broad variety of rights too, such as to compensation awarded through arbitration or creditors' rights in sovereign debt.[15] The arbitral definition of investment, like the treaty definition, is broad and flexible.[16] As we will see in Chapter 2, the norm entrepreneurs

[10] *Saudi Arabia v. Arabian American Oil Company* (Aramco arbitration) (1963) 27 International Law Reports 117, 168.

[11] *Generation Ukraine v. Ukraine* (ICSID Case No. ARB/00/9) Award, 16 September 2003, para. 6.1. Also, *ATA v. Jordan* (ICSID Case No. ARB/08/2) Award, 18 May 2012, para. 96; *Waste Management v. Mexico 2* (ICSID Case No. ARB(AF)/00/3) Award, 30 April 2004, para. 173.

[12] *Metalclad v. Mexico* (ICSID Case No. ARB(AF)/97/1) Award, 30 August 2000, para. 103; *Burlington v. Ecuador* (ICSID Case No. ARB/08/5) Decision on Liability, 14 December 2012, para. 397. This interpretation has been criticized, e.g. in *El Paso v. Argentina* (ICSID Case No. ARB/03/15) Award, 31 October 2011, para. 252, but ISDS tribunals have continued to look at profitability to decide, e.g., whether state measures were proportionate, see *Total v. Argentina* (ICSID Case No. ARB/04/01) Decision on Liability, 27 December 2010, para. 333.

[13] Christian Barrère, 'Judicial System and Property Rights' in Enrico Colombatto (ed.), *The Elgar Companion to the Economics of Property Rights* (Edward Elgar Publishing 2006) 129–53, 151.

[14] Jeswald W. Salacuse, *The Law of Investment Treaties* (OUP 2015) 174–84.

[15] *ATA v. Jordan* (ICSID Case No. ARB/08/2) Award, 18 May 2012, para. 125; *Abaclat and others v. Argentina* (ICSID Case No. ARB/07/5) Decision on Jurisdiction and Admissibility, 4 August 2011, para. 387.

[16] Salacuse and Sullivan note that investment treaties recognize 'that investment forms are constantly evolving in response to the creativity of investors and the rapidly changing world of international finance'. Jeswald W. Salacuse and Nicholas P. Sullivan, 'Do BITs Really Work: An Evaluation of Bilateral Investment Treaties and their Grand Bargain' (2005) 46 Harvard International Law Journal (2005) 67–130, 80. Similarly, Arato claims that investment treaties 'blur' the *numerus clausus* principle. Julian

of the 1950s and 1960s relied on actual business practice, rather than rigid legal categories, to promote such broad formulation and interpretation.

B. The purpose of foreign investor rights and investment treaties

From a public policy perspective, investment treaties and ISDS are meant to promote foreign investment flows, contributing to the development of host countries. This means-ends rationale is enshrined in the treaties themselves and in many policy documents. The international organizations that championed this idea in the 1990s, namely the World Bank and the United Nations Conference on Trade and Development (UNCTAD), touted the ability of such treaties to attract foreign investment inflows.[17] Yet the evidence supporting this premise remains weak. Empirical work on the relationship between protection and new investment flows has arrived at mixed conclusions, and no study suggests that the impact is significant, except for mining projects and resource-rich countries.[18] In forums like UNCTAD, many states have 'raised the question' of the performance of investment treaties in attracting new investment flows.[19]

International investment scholarship has paid less attention to the relationship between foreign investment and development, although it is a link that is also central to this legal regime. The ICSID Convention and investment treaties describe protection not as an end in and of itself but as a means to economic growth and development.[20] Again, however, the evidence is mixed. Some foreign investment projects benefit host countries, but others are problematic, with costs and risks outweighing the benefits. Foreign investment can increase inequality within host states.[21] Further, some economists argue that countries that have aligned 'the

Arato, 'The Private Law Critique of International Investment Law' (2019) 113 American Journal of International Law 1–53, 2–3, 11, 16.

[17] Lauge N. Skovgaard Poulsen, *Bounded Rationality and Economic Diplomacy: The Politics of Investment Treaties in Developing Countries* (CUP 2015) 71–99.

[18] Jonathan Bonnitcha, Lauge N. Skovgaard Poulsen, and Michael Waibel, *The Political Economy of the Investment Treaty Regime* (OUP 2017) 159–61, 207–10. Also, Joachim Pohl, 'Societal Benefits and Costs of International Investment Agreements: A Critical Review of Aspects and Available Empirical Evidence' (2018) OECD Working Papers on International Investment, No. 2018/01.

[19] The 2017 UNCTAD Annual High-Level IIA Conference: Phase 2 of the reform. Report available at https://investmentpolicy.unctad.org/uploaded-files/document/BoS%204_agenda%20and%20report%20back.pdf (last visited 19 May 2020).

[20] See Tarcisio Gazzini, 'Bilateral Investment Treaties and Sustainable Development' (2014) 15 Journal of World Investment & Trade 929–63, at 941; *Amco v. Indonesia* (ICSID Case No. ARB/81/1) Decision on Jurisdiction, 25 September 1983, para. 23.

[21] Liesbeth Colen, Miet Maertens, and Johan Swinnen, 'Foreign Direct Investment as an Engine for Economic Growth and Human Development: A Review of the Arguments and Empirical Evidence' in Olivier De Schutter, Johan Swinnen, and Jan Wouters (eds.), *Foreign Direct Investment and Human Development* (Routledge 2012) 70–115, 85, 94, 100.

interests of foreign investors with their national interests' have been more successful in achieving their development goals.[22] The overall consensus is that 'it depends'.[23]

In this respect, it is still worth noting the obvious fact that foreign investors 'do not do benevolence'.[24] Like all other investors, they seek economic returns. The relationship between foreign investment and development can therefore not be judged only by looking at contributions of capital or technology. Foreign investors expect to recover this capital plus a return. The impact of foreign investment on development depends rather on the effects of a project in the host country and local community, including job creation, linkages with domestic firms, and positive effects on business culture and domestic institutions. The key is how the foreign investor and the domestic economy adapt and benefit each other.[25] As we will see, however, the legal imagination contains little about how to maximize the development impact of foreign investment.

Instead, the rationale of international investment protection is to stabilize the expectations and increase the calculability of foreign investors. The reasoning follows the ideas of Jeremy Bentham, Max Weber, and Douglass North on the role of law in capitalist societies. The law should enable private investors to rationally calculate how to use their capital to make an economic return.[26] After investors sink their capital into a project, the law should also minimize potential demoralization costs—costs that could not have been rationally calculated—to maintain investors' confidence and encourage new investments.[27] As socio-legal scholars point out, property and contracts can serve multiple purposes in a society, from personal enrichment to enhancing democratic values or community life.[28] But, as we will also see, this is not the case for foreign investor rights, which interpretation has been primarily focused on enhancing calculability for foreign investors with the hope that this will lead to economic growth and development.

[22] Ha-Joon Chang, 'Regulation of Foreign Investment in Historical Perspective' (2004) 16 European Journal of Development Research 687–715, 711.

[23] Stephen Cohen, *Multinational Corporations and Foreign Direct Investment: Avoiding Simplicity, Embracing Complexity* (OUP 2007) 332.

[24] Adeoye Akinsanya, 'International Protection of Direct Foreign Investments in the Third World' (1987) 36 International & Comparative Law Quarterly 58–75, 58.

[25] Colen et al. (n. 21).

[26] Jeremy Bentham, *The Theory of Legislation* (Trübner & Co 1864) 111–12; Max Weber, *Economy and Society: An Outline of Interpretive Sociology*, Guenther Roth and Claus Wittich (eds.) (University of California Press 1978 [1922]) 162; Douglas North, *Structure and Change in Economic History* (W. W. Norton 1981) 21.

[27] Frank I. Michelman, 'Property, Utility, and Fairness: Comments on the Ethical Foundations of "Just Compensation" Law' (1967) 80 Harvard Law Review 1165–258, 1237. Whether or not these costs should be compensated is contested. See Jonathan Bonnitcha, *Substantive Protection under Investment Treaties* (CUP 2014) 95–7.

[28] Gregory S. Alexander, Eduardo M. Peñalver, Joseph William Singer, and Laura S. Underkuffler, 'A Statement of Progressive Property' (2009) 94 Cornell Law Review 743–4.

Foreign investors may welcome investment treaties, or find them unimportant to their business projects, but whether or not these treaties promote foreign investment or these capital flows contribute to development is secondary for investors. Their main interest lies in the means, not the ends. In the short term they want to maximize their economic returns, and higher calculability may serve this objective. For those few investors interested in the longer term, a category which includes our norm entrepreneurs, the relationship between foreign investment and development is salient because it helps to justify a world ruled by private investment decisions. The rhetoric of economic growth is materially significant for this goal.[29] Yet their primary interest remains to maximize their economic returns. This attitude is not inconsistent with their world-making ambitions because, as Anwar Shaikh reminds us, profit, not growth, drives capitalism.[30]

It is to these investors and their agents that investment treaties and ISDS make most sense. The means of this legal regime, rather than its ends, have defined the 'epistemological boundaries' of foreign investor rights and shaped foreign investment relations.[31] As ISDS practice shows, the developmentalist narrative in the preambles of the ICSID Convention and investment treaties has had few implications for the arbitral decisions, which have mostly been limited to an interpretation of the notion of investment—the so-called Salini test—which tribunals have generally rejected.[32] Arbitrators rarely consider whether an investment project and the regulatory framework were appropriate to promote sustainable development. The situation is different when we focus on the regime's role in enhancing foreign investors' calculability. Investment treaties and ISDS have not actually insulated investors from business risks,[33] but have functioned quite well when it comes to promoting private enterprise and liberal reforms 'from above'.[34] They have institutionalized 'a model of constitutional government' aimed at facilitating capital

[29] Shawcross was aware of this significance. Hartley Shawcross, 'The Promotion of International Investment' Speech before the Society to Advance the Protection of Foreign Investments, Cologne 1959, in Society to Advance the Protection of Foreign Investments, Convention on Investments Abroad with Comments, Speeches and New Literature, Publication No. 3 (Bergisch Gladbach, J. Heider 1960) 46–60, 60. Also, José E. Alvarez and Kathryn Khamsi, 'The Argentine Crisis and Foreign Investors. A Glimpse into the Heart of the Investment Regime' in Karl P. Sauvant (ed.), *Yearbook on International Investment Law and Policy 2008/2009* (OUP 2009) 379–478, 473.

[30] Anwar Shaikh, *Capitalism: Competition, Conflict, Crises* (OUP 2016) 206.

[31] Annelise Riles, 'Property as Legal Knowledge: Means and Ends' (2004) 10 Journal of the Royal Anthropological Institute 775–95, 789–90.

[32] For the Salini test, the definition of investment under the ICSID Convention requires considering the contribution to the host state's economic development. See Chin Leng Lim, Jean Ho, and Martins Paparinskis, *International Investment Law and Arbitration: Commentary, Awards and Other Materials* (CUP 2018) 210–30.

[33] *Maffezini v. Spain* (ICSID Case No. ARB/97/7) Award, 13 November 2000, para. 64; *Biwater v. Tanzania* (ICSID Case No. ARB/05/22) Award, 24 July 2008, para. 601.

[34] Razeen Sally, *Classical Liberalism and International Economic Order: Studies in Theory and Intellectual History* (Routledge 2002) 178.

flows, limiting state capacity in matters related to markets, and protecting economic policy from majoritarian politics.[35]

C. Foreign investor rights and social relations

Promoting foreign investors' calculability and spreading global capitalism comes at the cost of the autonomy and expectations of *others*. Theorizing private property as an *in rem* right avoids the social by focusing on relations between owners and things. Owners can exclude others from the use of their resources. Similarly, a narrow interpretation of contracts deals only with the contracting parties and the transaction, irrespective of their bargaining power or the effects of the transaction on third parties. These exclusions are significant for investors, increasing their ability to control, plan for, and invest resources.[36] Once we widen our perspective, however, to also concentrate on the social relations that ownership creates among people or how contracts affect third parties and a given society, the autonomy and expectations of other owners and non-owners can hardly be concealed.[37]

For those who support a strong conception of private property and contracts, dealing with these social implications often poses a problem. Take liberals and utilitarians, for example. Liberals focus on property as a means towards individual freedom,[38] while utilitarians, such as Bentham, define property as the 'expectation of deriving certain advantages from a thing which we are said to possess'.[39] Both positions are open to a similar criticism: that expectations as much as individual autonomy are socially interdependent and only make sense in a social context. Locke responded to this objection by including a proviso according to which private property works 'where there is enough, and as good, left in common for others'.[40] Utilitarians have addressed it by taking into account distributive concerns when measuring utility. Expectations, then, should not only facilitate individual economic returns but also promote social welfare.[41] This requires that economic decisions, such as a foreign investment project, produce a Kaldor–Hicks efficient

[35] David Schneiderman, *Constitutionalizing Economic Globalization. Investment Rules and Democracy's Promise* (CUP 2008) 2.

[36] Alexander and Peñalver (n. 5) 136.

[37] There is a tradition in private law and theory that looks at property and contracts as social relations. It includes legal realists such as Morris Cohen and Robert Hale, as well as critical scholars such as Duncan Kennedy, Joseph Singer, and Jennifer Nedelsky. See, e.g., Joseph William Singer, *Entitlement: The Paradoxes of Property* (Yale University Press 2000) 95; Duncan Kennedy, 'The Stakes of Law, or Hale and Foucault!' (1991) 15 Legal Studies Forum 327–66.

[38] Among a liberal tradition, there is a distinction to be made between a libertarian and a democratic self-government interpretation of Locke. Alexander and Peñalver (n. 5) 36.

[39] Bentham (n. 26) 111–12

[40] Alexander and Peñalver (n. 5), 39.

[41] Ibid., 13–14.

outcome, whereby the people who benefit are in a position to compensate the losers so they consider themselves not worse off than they were before.

Foreign investment may or may not promote social welfare or leave something for local communities, but it inevitably creates and shapes social relations. Foreign investor rights define the relations between investors, states, and local communities, determining 'who will adapt to whom' so to make the investment work.[42] Investment treaties and ISDS can contribute in various ways to this objective; these include silencing some social effects and making invisible some of the actors involved.

The consequences of large-scale investments, however, are often too significant to be silenced. To illustrate these consequences, particularly to non-investment law experts, I will rely on the *Pennsylvania Coal co. v. Mahon* case, which engendered the regulatory takings doctrine in the United States.[43] Pennsylvania Coal Company claimed to have the right to mine below the property of an individual named H. J. Mahon, and notified Mahon of its intention to make use of this right. Mahon took them to court, arguing that the 1921 Kohler Act prohibited mining coal in such a way that would cause the subsidence of any structure used as a human habitation. If the Pennsylvania Coal Company mined below the property, Mahon would lose his house. If the state banned mining, Mahon would keep his house but the company would not be able to continue mining there and future mining projects might be discouraged. The state intervened in favour of Mahon, prohibiting mining in these circumstances, but the US Supreme Court reasoned that this regulation went 'too far' and was tantamount to expropriation (i.e. regulatory or indirect expropriation). Compensation was therefore required, imposing a fiscal burden on the state.

Investment law literature has emphasized how decisions such as *Mahon* can shape the relationship between foreign investors and states. One is through the chilling of regulation.[44] Because of the indeterminacy of property and contracts rights, and due to vague treaty standards, arbitrators must decide if measures go 'too far' on a case-by-case basis. The scarcity of guidelines may create doubts among public authorities about whether or not a regulation is legal under investment treaties, chilling future regulation. Foreign investors can also take advantage of this uncertainty to criticize new initiatives, threatening to bring ISDS disputes against a state. Furthermore, investment treaties and awards can create moral

[42] Nicolás M. Perrone and David Schneiderman, 'International Economic Law's Wreckage: Depoliticization, Inequality, Precarity' in Emilios Christodoulidis, Ruth Dukes, and Marco Goldoni (eds.), *Research Handbook on Critical Legal Theory* (Edward Elgar Publishing 2019) 446–72, 446.

[43] *Pennsylvania Coal Co v. Mahon*, 260 US 393 (1922). See Carol M. Rose, 'Mahon Reconstructed: Why the Takings Issue is Still a Muddle' (1984) 57 Southern California Law Review 561–99.

[44] Kyla Tienhaara 'Regulatory Chill and the Threat of Arbitration: A View from Political Science' in Chester Brown and Kate Miles (eds.), *Evolution in Investment Treaty Law and Arbitration* (CUP 2011) 606–28.

hazard.[45] Foreign investors may only calculate for the costs and risks included in the legislation when investing, as they know that regulatory changes could breach their rights under investment treaties and be compensated. Strong foreign investor rights can thus lead to overinvestment, meaning inefficient projects, which undermines sustainable investment.

The consequences of investment treaties and ISDS are not limited to foreign investors and states. Mahon was also a property owner. Nuisance and health regulations are often justified to protect people like Mahon,[46] but such public measures may affect foreign investment, and investors can threaten to bring an ISDS case against the state. The government may choose to stand by the regulation, but if it loses the case every citizen will help pay the compensation through their taxes, and actors such as Mahon might see their rights unprotected in the future due to regulatory chill. Strong protection of foreign investor rights, in other words, often means less protection for other rights.[47]

Those whose rights may be impacted by a foreign investment project have rarely given their consent or received compensation.[48] In cases of general legislation or sectoral regulation, it may be argued that the issue was in the public domain and a democratic decision binds other owners. Yet such a decision should also respect other rights, which may require informing those affected in a timely way, procuring their consent, and offering compensation. The democratic justification, moreover, weakens when the government has granted specific commitments or representations. The legislature may not have played any role in the decision to do that, and that decision may also not be in the public domain. Lastly, the situation is even more problematic when those affected are politically weak, such as indigenous peoples, who have less or no political representation. Evidence suggests that weak actors are more vulnerable to public measures affecting their entitlements.[49]

Meanwhile, the social implications of investment treaties and ISDS can be broad and long-lasting. One reason for this is that sacrifice is an essential basis of social and community life; indeed, 'sacrifice makes collective democratic action possible'.[50] States take decisions that affect individuals both positively and negatively on an almost everyday basis, and a community may require help today but give support tomorrow. In the long run, the sacrifices people make and the benefits they obtain from the state and the community compensate each other through

[45] Bonnitcha (n. 27) 74, 317.

[46] Alexander and Peñalver (n. 5) 169

[47] David Kennedy, 'Some Caution about Property Rights as a Recipe for Economic Development' (2011) 1 Accounting, Economics, and Law (article 3), 31–2.

[48] As Waldron explains, a Kaldor–Hicks efficient outcome still implies an 'imposition' to the losing party. Jeremy Waldron, 'Nozick and Locke: Filling the Space of Rights' (2005) 22 Social Philosophy and Policy 81–110.

[49] William Fischel, *Regulatory Takings: Law, Economics, and Politics* (Harvard University Press 1995) 107.

[50] Danielle Allen, *Talking to Strangers: Anxieties of Citizenship since Brown v. Board of Education* (University of Chicago Press 2004) 29.

long-term reciprocity.[51] Only excessive burdens—irreducible individual losses—should therefore be compensated. The narrative around investment treaties and ISDS, however, often describes foreign investors as outsiders undermining a moral justification for their obligations to host country and community. If investment treaties and ISDS allow foreign investors to enjoy benefits without making sacrifices, it is because they are treated as actors 'interested only […] in what can be extracted from a given society'.[52]

Another reason is that large economic transformations require the destruction of some rights and the creation of others. Private, communal, and common property rights may pose obstacles to such transformations. In *Mahon*, the right to the house stood in the way not only of Pennsylvania Coal Company but also of the mining industry. Property scholarship illustrates how legislatures and adjudicators have favoured industrial, mining, rail, and, more recently, technology investors by facilitating the destruction of certain rights and urging the general population to catch up with the new technologies and business organizations.[53] States also need to adapt to these changes. Large economic transformations frequently require institutional restructuring. The importance given to attracting foreign investment in development policy since the 1990s has helped remodel states from within. As Saskia Sassen explains, it has impacted their political economies, resulting in less relevant legislatures, more influential finance ministries, and the creation of investment promotion agencies.[54]

People have diverse views about such transformations, but in most cases they are difficult to undo. As David Kennedy observes, 'property rights are less a legal "system" than a historical record of winners, losers and social accommodation'.[55] The transformation created by the colonial order is relevant for the analysis here. Colonialism simultaneously facilitated the clustering of industrial activity in the Global North and a deindustrialization and specialization on natural resources in the Global South, creating the 'Great Divergence'.[56] The South intended to regain control over its natural resources and change this international distribution of labour through decolonization. The many obstacles it has faced in doing so include

[51] Hanoch Dagan, 'Reimagining Takings Law' in Gregory S. Alexander and Eduardo M. Peñalver (eds.), *Property and Community* (OUP, 2010) 39–56, 46–50.

[52] Jeremy Waldron, *The Rule of Law and the Measure of Property* (CUP 2012) 105–6. Also, William Twining, *Globalisation and Legal Theory* (Butterworths 2000) 68.

[53] Morton J. Horwitz, *The Transformation of American Law, 1780-1860* (Harvard University Press 1977) 31–62; Stefano Rodotà, *El terrible derecho: estudios sobre la propiedad privada* (trans. Luis Diez-Picazo) (Civitas 1986) 145–62. More recently, Frank K. Upham, *The Great Property Fallacy: Theory, Reality, and Growth in Developing Countries* (CUP 2018) 12–33.

[54] Saskia Sassen, *Losing Control? Sovereignty in an Age of Globalization* (Columbia University Press 1996) 25. Also, John M. Stopford and Susan Strange with John S. Henley, *Rival States, Rival Firms: Competition For World Market Shares* (CUP 1991) 56.

[55] Kennedy (n. 47) 20.

[56] See Pim De Zwart, *Globalization and the Colonial Origins of the Great Divergence: Intercontinental Trade and living Standards in the Dutch East India Company's Commercial Empire, c. 1600-1800* (Brill 2016) 13–14.

foreign investor rights under international law, which, as Antony Anghie has observed, have contributed to hiding the imperial past.[57] As we will see in the next chapter, the norm entrepreneurs of the 1950s and 1960s had an interest in prolonging the colonial division of labour.

D. Foreign investor rights and states' right to regulate

The way ISDS tribunals imagine the relationship between foreign investors and host states is central to the resolution of disputes. Lawyers and arbitrators rarely discuss this imaginary directly, although it does define how they approach and resolve cases. Arbitrators may overlook the situations of people, like Mahon, but cannot ignore states and their actions. The heart of most ISDS cases involves public actions or omissions, and states are parties to these arbitrations, appoint an arbitrator, and provide their views on the facts and the law.

Since the first ISDS awards in the early 2000s, the debate over international investment law has focused on the relationship between foreign investors and host states. The public law approach portrays international investment law as a form of *global governance* that is crucial for that relationship.[58] Investment treaties and ISDS may impose limitations on states intending to regulate for the public interest, including non-discriminatory regulations. As seen earlier, this is true beyond the resolution of specific cases because an expansive interpretation of foreign investor rights can create regulatory chill and moral hazard. The public law approach examines these limitations by focusing on the tension between foreign investor rights and states' right to regulate. Some scholars have concentrated on how arbitrators could accommodate both sets of rights in concrete situations using tools such as balancing and proportionality, while several states have taken stock of the risks created by ISDS to states' right to regulate, introducing language in their investment treaties that explicitly recognize this right.[59]

The question is not as simple as a binary choice between states' right to regulate for the public interest and no regulation whatsoever. As noted in the introduction, our norm entrepreneurs were aware that states' right to regulate could not be completely annulled. Equally, ISDS practice has never suggested that states cannot regulate foreign investment. The first ISDS awards recognized that governments take measures that are 'an ordinary expression of the exercise of the state's police

[57] Antony Anghie, *Imperialism, Sovereignty and the Making of International law* (CUP 2005) 241. Also, Sundhya Pahuja, *Decolonising International Law: Development, Economic Growth and the Politics of Universality* (CUP 2011) 128.

[58] Gus Van Harten and Martin Loughlin, 'Investment Treaty Arbitration as a Species of Global Administrative Law' (2006) 17 European Journal of International Law 121–50, 145.

[59] See, e.g., Caroline Henckels, *Proportionality and Deference in Investor-State Arbitration* (CUP 2015) 42, 126–71.

power' and require no compensation.[60] Since the mid-2000s, arbitral decisions have also adjusted the interpretation of states' right to regulate, being 'reflexive'[61] to critique and receptive to the 'return'[62] of the state after the 2008 financial crisis. ISDS tribunals have never denied states' right to regulate and have remained open to recalibrating their interpretations.

The issue, then, concerns tensions within states' right to regulate and foreign investor rights. Investment law literature shows that the questions of whether international investment law allows or renders impossible state regulation and whether it is private or public do not go to the core of the matter. As Zachary Douglas, Alvarez, and Schill explain, this legal regime is either 'hybrid'[63] or 'transnational',[64] and comprises elements of public as much as private law. The disagreement has always been about how public and private law are conceived in investment treaties and ISDS, and the background ideas about law, economics, and politics that shape this conception.

This tension is not unique to international investment law. People have quite diverse views about the role of individuals and the state in society, and these are often expressed in opinions about property, contracts, and public law.[65] Such normative discrepancies are ubiquitous between and within most countries, despite considerable support for private property in capitalist societies. The fact that no legal system—including international investment law—has a clear formula to distinguish between reasonable and illegitimate uses of public authority is a reflection of this.[66]

For this reason, understanding how the norm entrepreneurs of the 1950s and 1960s and current ISDS tribunals imagine foreign investment relations requires an openness to these normative tensions. ISDS tribunals can be cognitively open to critique and concerns, but as David Schneiderman notes, they have remained normatively closed.[67] Also, it is important not to lose sight of the analytical and

[60] *TecMed v. Mexico* (ICSID Case No. ARB (AF)/00/2) Award, 29 May 2003, para. 115.

[61] David Schneiderman, 'Legitimacy and Reflexivity in International Investment Arbitration: A New Self-Restraint?' (2011) 2 Journal of International Dispute Settlement 471–95, 494

[62] José E. Alvarez, 'Why are we 'Re-calibrating' our Investment Treaties?' (2010) 4 World Arbitration and Mediation Review 143–61, 144.

[63] Douglas (n. 8) 153; José E. Alvarez, 'Is Investor-State Arbitration "Public"?' (2016) 7 Journal of International Dispute Settlement 534–76, 535.

[64] Stephan W. Schill and Kerem Gülay, 'Approaches to Foreign Direct Investment in Legal Research' in Markus Krajewski and T. Rhea Hoffmann (eds.), *Research Handbook on Foreign Direct Investment* (Edward Elgar Publishing 2019) 39–71. Also, Nicolás M. Perrone, 'International Investment Law as Transnational Law' in Peer Zumbansen (ed.), *Oxford Handbook of Transnational Law* (OUP forthcoming).

[65] See, e.g., Jedediah Purdy, *The Meaning of Property: Freedom, Community, and the Legal Imagination* (Yale University Press 2010) 4–5, 115–16; Roy Kreitner, *Calculating Promises: The Emergence of Modern American Contract Doctrine* (Stanford University Press 2006) 1, 232.

[66] Gregory Alexander, *The Global Debate over Constitutional Property: Lessons for American Takings Jurisprudence* (University of Chicago Press 2006) 57–62. In the case of international investment law, see Rudolf Dolzer and Christoph Schreuer, *Principles of International Investment Law* (OUP 2012) 101, 112.

[67] Schneiderman (n. 61) 494.

normative interdependencies between private and public authority. The public law approach looks at foreign investor rights and states' right to regulate as two opposing forces. The regulatory chill argument can thus be interpreted as if states always wanted to regulate in favour of the public interest, with investment treaties and ISDS undermining that. Yet foreign investors and states often cooperate before, during, and even after an investment to establish and continue the project. Claire Cutler refers to an 'alliance' between private and public authority for 'the expansion of capitalism through the further disembedding of international commerce from national, social and democratic controls'.[68] The following subsections provide an analytical and historical framework mapping various ways we can approach the relationship between foreign investors and host states, which is both cooperative and conflictive, and how these ways may visualize or hide certain issues relevant to international investment law.

1. A regulatory and a transactional model

The relations between foreign investors and states can be interpreted through a regulatory or a transactional model. Both recognize private and public authority, and both can take different intermediate forms. However, their imaginaries of private–public relations are markedly distinct.[69] A regulatory model describes the interaction between investors and states as relations of supremacy and subordination, while a transactional model is about promises between equals and coordination. In the regulatory model, foreign investors are rule-takers who accept the domestic jurisdiction when entering into the country. States have the authority to pass new rules affecting foreign investment, and investors are expected to accept and adapt to those rules. In this model, foreign investor rights are *general rights*.[70] There is no bargaining related to their scope and strength. These rights are creations of the state, and remain subject to legal changes except for the obligation to pay compensation in cases of direct expropriation or measures imposing an excessive burden.

The regulatory model is prevalent in most domestic legal systems and in public international law,[71] but some conceptions of property situate the relationship between individuals and states closer to a transactional model. Conceptions of

[68] Claire Cutler, 'Artifice, Ideology and Paradox: The Public/Private Distinction in International law' (1997) 4 Review of International Political Economy 261–85, 262.

[69] See, e.g., Peer Zumbansen, 'The Law of Society: Governance through Contract' (2007) 14 Indiana Journal of Global Legal Studies 191–233, 195, 206.

[70] Waldron distinguishes between general-right-based and special-right-based property, depending on whether or not their conception is tied to 'the occurrence of some contingent event or transaction': Jeremy Waldron, *The Right to Private Property* (Clarendon Press 1988) 116, 106–17.

[71] See Hersch Lauterpacht, *The Function of Law in the International Community* (OUP 2011 [1933]) 425; James Crawford, *Brownlie's Principles of Public International Law* (OUP 2012) 608–9.

property that focus on individual autonomy and calculability, and frequently describe the state as arbitrary or inefficient, are inclined to contractualize relations between private property owners and states. These include classical, neoliberal, and neo-institutionalist conceptions.[72] If relations between foreign investors and states are construed in transactional terms, the interpretation of rights responds to other principles. The rule is closer to *pacta sunt servanda*, and entitlements are negotiated or *special* rights.[73] They emerge from a special relationship between investor and state. In this model, foreign investors are both rule-makers and rule-takers, and states' regulatory space to pass new regulations is limited by their previous commitments. Interestingly, this resembles the way states govern their inter-state relations under international law. Due to the absence of a global sovereign, states relate to each through the *pacta sunt servanda* principle.[74]

Like property, contracts are conceived of in various ways. A chief distinction is whether the focus is on the transaction—that is, the will of the parties—or on notions of justice. Historically, the relevance of values is related to a pre-capitalist version of contracts, where actors were not equal and their status mattered in interpreting their relationship. This status view of contracts was superseded by the will theory, which portrays the two contracting parties as equal and concentrates on the transaction, disregarding the social and economic context.[75] As Morton Horwitz explains, the will theory was found to be more suitable to capitalism, where individuals are expected to be treated as equals despite their differing bargaining power.[76] During the 20th century, however, considerations other than the transaction gained weight in contract law and theory, either to adjust the parties' unequal bargaining power, increase their calculability, or both.[77]

2. From the postwar to the neoliberal consensus

The legal thinking of the post-World War II period opposed classical liberal property and the will theory of contracts.[78] Legal realists and institutional economists

[72] Locke, Robert Nozick, and Richard Epstein are examples of a contractarian account of the origin of property. Alexander and Peñalver (n. 5) 55. Neoliberals and neo-institutional authors favour strong and clear property rights as well as a shift towards contractual governance, see Kennedy (n. 47) 2–4; Zumbansen (n. 69) 193.

[73] Waldron (n. 70) 118.

[74] Lauterpacht (n. 71) 426–7.

[75] Henry Sumner Maine, *Ancient Law: Its Connection with the Early History of Society and Its Relation to Modern Ideas* (J.M. Dent & Sons Ltd. 1917 [1861]) 101.

[76] Horwitz (n. 53) 160, 185.

[77] See Zumbansen (n. 69) 215–16; Joseph William Singer, *No Freedom Without Regulation: The Hidden Lesson of the Subprime Crisis* (Yale University Press, 2015) 48.

[78] David Kennedy, 'The "Rule of Law," Political Choices, and Development Common Sense' in David M. Trubek and Alvaro Santos (eds.), *The New Law and Economic Development: A Critical Appraisal* (CUP 2006) 95–173, 104.

argued that private property is a creation of states, not a natural right, and it promotes the independence of owners as much as it coerces others. Joseph Singer concisely summarized this view: 'property is derived from sovereignty, but also creates sovereignty.'[79] Governments can thus do more than curb the costs and risks of some economic activities: they can reshape economic relations to achieve full employment or to improve the bargaining power of workers or other vulnerable actors. In the 1950s and 1960s, this instrumental interpretation of property and contracts enabled governments to create a large regulatory state and engage in some economic planning.[80]

This view also challenges a clear delimitation of private and public law, highlighting the interdependencies between private and public authority. Neither private nor public make much sense without reference to the other; they can be accommodated in ways that do not necessarily correspond to an essential quality or nature of either public or private law, but to their respective adjustment in a concrete context.[81] In the case of foreign investment relations, then, the issue is not only the relationship between foreign investor rights and states' right to regulate—or the interpretation of states' right to regulate—but also how we define the *inside* of foreign investor rights.[82] The private law aspects of international investment law can advance a progressive interpretation of property and contracts, accounting for ownership obligations or the large social effects of investment contracts and bargains. Put differently, there is a limit to what tools like balancing or proportionality can do to acknowledge states' right to regulate if ISDS tribunals promote a strong interpretation of foreign investor rights.

Further, the law can recognize and protect other individual or communal rights. In 1964, Charles Reich posited the existence of property rights over other forms of wealth, such as social benefits.[83] More relevant for my purposes here is Singer's analysis in his article 'The Reliance Interest in Property', which considers whether workers could have a right to continue operating a closed privatively owned factory because of the special relationship between capital and labour or due to the closure's social implications. Singer claims that the legal system requires the protection of the more vulnerable party to the relationship 'not because of reliance on specific promises, but because the parties have relied on each other generally and on the continuation of their relationship'.[84] A worldview that sees private property and contracts as serving not only the plans of the private owner (or their

[79] Joseph William Singer, 'Sovereignty and Property' (1991) 86 Northwestern University Law Review 1–56, 51.

[80] Kennedy (n. 78) 102, 106.

[81] See, e.g., Duncan Kennedy, 'The Political Stakes in "Merely Technical" Issues of Contract Law' (2001) 1 European Review of Private Law 7–28, 14–25.

[82] Singer (n. 37) 7.

[83] Charles A. Reich, 'The New Property' (1964) 73 Yale Law Journal 733–87.

[84] Joseph William Singer, 'The Reliance Interest in Property' (1988) 40 Stanford Law Review 611–751, 623.

calculability) but also the livelihood of vulnerable actors calls for the application of the 'counterprinciple of reliance'.[85]

In the next chapter, I delve into the critique that the norm entrepreneurs for international investment protection launched in the 1950s and 1960s against the post-World War II consensus. Significantly, they were not the only ones to attack it. Neoliberals were ardent detractors too. They argued that states' intervention affected economic freedom, because the economy was no longer the result of individual transactions—contracts entered into by autonomous individuals—but of economic planning and state intervention with private property and contract rules.[86] Market coordination depends on a classical interpretation of contracts, 'not merely in the sense that [people] agreed to be bound, but also in that they have agreed on the specific terms that bind them'.[87] They held that economies are complex systems and states lack sufficient information to engage in economic planning; state actions could only make an economy less calculable, reducing the scope for individual coordination. For neoliberals, the idea of economic sovereignty was in itself a misconception.[88] Friedrich Hayek, Wilhelm Röpke, and others, whom Quinn Slobodian groups within the Geneva School, believed that the role of states was limited to enforcing private property and contracts.[89]

Neoliberals and neo-institutional economists elaborated on the increasing role of contracts in social relations. For them, transactions are the central means to coordinate economic activities among an endless number of actors. Hayek wrote:

> The whole network of rights created by contracts is as important a part of our own protected sphere, as much the basis of our plans, as any property of our own.[90]

Similarly, Oliver Williamson referred to a 'world of contract' inhabited by 'the contractual man'.[91] This governance model requires high levels of calculability, which contracts can ensure by focusing on the singularity of the transaction while eliminating competing values or undefined responsibilities to others. Individuals should remain blind to the 'totality'.[92] Not even states should be exempted from this world of contract; they too should pursue most of their goals through market transactions.

[85] Ibid., 636.

[86] Quinn Slobodian, *Globalists: The End of Empire and the Birth of Neoliberalism* (Harvard University Press 2020) 28–9, 81.

[87] Kreitner (n. 65) 6.

[88] Michel Foucault, *The Birth of Biopolitics: Lectures at the Collège de France, 1978–1979* (Palgrave 2010) 283, 282–3; Slobodian (n. 86) 81, 224–51, 270.

[89] Slobodian (n. 86) 29.

[90] Friedrich A. Hayek, *The Constitution of Liberty* (University of Chicago Press 1978 [1960]) 141. Also, Wilhelm Röpke, *International Order and Economic Integration* (D. Reidel 1959) 79, 85.

[91] Oliver E. Williamson, *The Economic Institutions of Capitalism Firms, Markets, Relational Contracting* (Macmillan 1985) 30, 43.

[92] Foucault (n. 88) 279.

In the 1980s and 1990s, this way of thinking became the new global consensus, reshaping conceptions of private, public, and private–public relations.[93] Deeply influenced by this, business literature on foreign investment started portraying relations between foreign investors and states through contractual models, such as an 'obsolescing bargain' or a 'hold-up problem'.[94] Foreign investments thus came to be described as transactions; 'once the investor makes the investment and thereby places its capital under the sovereignty of the host state', these models underscore that 'its bargaining power diminishes, and the commitments received risk becoming obsolete in the eyes of the host government'.[95] In this account, state sovereignty is a source of 'political risk', which puts foreign investors in a weak position, affecting their calculability.[96]

Frequently, the obsolescing bargain and the hold-up problem are used to call attention to the risk of expropriation, but, as discussed above in Section A, the bargain also refers to the specific conditions of the investment project. These can include benefits, incentives, and concrete elements of the regulatory framework. As we will see, the norm entrepreneurs for international investment protection insisted on the essential nature of these conditions, asking states to be attentive to investors' regulatory demands. They were as concerned about expropriation—particularly incidents of regulatory takings—as about the need for securing and protecting regulatory givings.[97] By givings, I refer not only to incentives or benefits but also to changes in regulation that states make to attract foreign investment, and which are closely related to the expected profitability of a project.[98]

The interpretation of foreign investment relations implicit in the obsolescing bargain and hold-up models is not necessarily realistic. These models rely on the premise that the parties have a high level of information about the present and the future, as if states could know in advance all the potential benefits, costs, and risks associated with an investment project. As a result, when states intend to renegotiate or reconsider the bargain, these models assume that this change of attitude is arbitrary and unfair. The assumption is flawed, however, because circumstances do change and states cannot foresee how. Some of those who advocate this way of

[93] Kennedy (n. 78) 130, 128–37; Wendy Brown, *Undoing the Demos: Neoliberalism's Stealth Revolution* (Zone Books 2015) 22, 27.

[94] Vernon developed the obsolescing bargain model in 1971. Raymond Vernon, *Sovereignty at Bay: The Multinational Spread of U.S. Enterprises* (Longman 1971) 46–58. Despite the limitations of this model, as I explain below, it has remained popular as a frame to rationalize foreign investment relations. See, e.g., Srividya Jandhyala, Witold J. Henisz, and Edward D. Mansfield, 'Three Waves of BITs: The Global Diffusion of Foreign Investment Policy' (2011) 55 Journal of Conflict Resolution 1047–73, 1050, 1065.

[95] Jeswald W. Salacuse, 'The Emerging Global Regime for Investment' (2010) 51 Harvard International Law Journal 427–73, 451.

[96] Paul E. Comeaux and N. Stephen Kinsella, 'Reducing Political Risk in Developing Countries: Bilateral Treaties, Stabilization Clauses and MIGA and OPIC Investment Insurance' (1994) 15 New York Law School Journal of International and Comparative Law 1–48, 4.

[97] See Chapter 2, Section B.

[98] Abraham Bell and Gideon Parchomovsky, 'Givings' (2001) 111 Yale Law Journal 547–618, 563.

thinking, in fact, explicitly reject the idea that states could have such a high level of information when it comes to the economy.[99] From a development standpoint, moreover, the evidence shows that the contribution of foreign investment to sustainable development depends on the host state's active involvement; it is necessary to make adjustments throughout the life of an investment to maximize its public benefits.[100] This requires that the combination of rights in foreign investment projects remains somewhat dynamic and context-sensitive, as opposed to stable and fixed.[101]

In practice, most foreign investment projects do not occur under either a purely regulatory or a purely transactional model. The obsolescing bargain and hold-up problem models have been criticized precisely because foreign investors do not always enter into a transaction with states, and the transaction would be incomplete in any case: some foreign investors demand and obtain contractual commitments, while others invest under specific regulations or the general legislation.[102] Further, relations between foreign investors are more complex and dynamic than these models suggest. Empirical evidence shows that foreign investment relations are more cooperative than conflictual,[103] many bargains do not obsolesce,[104] and states sometimes lack relevant information or find themselves in a weak bargaining position.[105] This evidence is not directly related to whether or not these models influence ISDS practice, however. Images and imaginaries can be influential irrespective of their empirical accuracy.

[99] Neoliberals in particular rejected this possibility as states, otherwise, would be equipped to plan economic activity. See Slobodian (n. 86) 224–70.

[100] Dani Rodrik, 'Rethinking Growth Policies in the Developing World' The Luca d'Agliano Lecture for 2004, available at https://j.mp/2o5o9H1 (last visited 21 May 2020); Narcis Serra, Shari Spiegel, and Joseph E. Stiglitz, 'Introduction: From the Washington Consensus Towards a New Global Governance' in Narcis Serra and Joseph E. Stiglitz (eds.), *The Washington Consensus Reconsidered: Towards a New Global Governance* (OUP 2008) 3–13, 6.

[101] There are some limitations to this flexibility, however, as otherwise property and contracts would not perform other functions in society. See Thomas W. Merrill and Henry E. Smith, 'What Happened to Property in Law and Economics?' (2001) 111 Yale Law Journal 357–98, 360–83.

[102] Lorraine Eden, Stefanie Lenway, and Douglas A. Schuler, 'From the Obsolescing Bargain to the Political Bargaining Model' in Robert Grosse (ed.), *International Business and Government Relations in the 21st Century* (CUP 2005) 251–72, 255–6, 267–9.

[103] John M. Stopford, 'The Growing Interdependence between Transnational Corporations and Governments' (1994) 3 Transnational Corporations 53–76; Yadong Luo, 'Toward a Cooperative View of MNC–Host Government Relations: Building Blocks and Performance Implications' (2001) 32 Journal of International Business Studies 401–19.

[104] Rodolphe Desbordes and Julien Vauday, 'The Political Influence of Foreign Firms in Developing Countries' (2007) 19 Economics & Politics 421–51; Emma Aisbett and Carol McAusland, 'Firm Characteristics and Influence on Government Rule-Making: Theory and Evidence' (2013) 29 European Journal of Political Economy 214–35.

[105] Bruce McKern, 'Transnational Corporations and the Exploitation of Natural Resources' in UNCTAD, *Transnational Corporations and World Development* (Thomson Business Press 1996) 327–58, 345–50.

E. Distribution, recognition, and the embeddedness of foreign investor rights

Mapping the multiple social relations of foreign investment, in particular the various instances of struggle, is fundamental to understanding the legal imagination of the norm entrepreneurs for international investment protection. This imagination shapes those social relations, while new circumstances and disputes may pose challenges that require it to evolve and adapt. Conflicts relate to states' right to regulate, as just discussed, but may also concern silenced issues and actors made invisible. The next sections provide two additional categories to supplement and expand the analytical toolkit.

1. Distribution and recognition

The distinction between distributive and recognition claims, pioneered by Nancy Fraser and Axel Honneth, concerns two types of conflicts that frequently arise in foreign investment.[106] Distributive conflicts pertain to the allocation of the benefits, costs, and risks of a project. The law is closely associated with this allocation, as property, contracts, and public law affect not only the resolution of specific disputes but also shape the existing distribution of resources and power.[107] The allocation of the benefits arising from the extraction of natural resources depends on the ownership structure, and if this structure is left to party negotiation—between, say, the foreign investor and the host state—it will likely respond to their respective bargaining power. A core feature of distributive conflicts is that the benefits, costs, and risks of projects are, in principle, commensurable. Policymakers and arbitrators can balance them out in specific cases as much as in the ground rules. The winners can also, hypothetically, compensate the losers.

During the 1960s and 1970s, tensions between foreign investors and states essentially occurred over distribution.[108] Distributive conflicts had a case-by-case dimension—disputes over concession contracts and renegotiations—but also a structural dimension expressed in the struggle over the underlying ground rules. Global South countries advocated for a New International Economic Order (NIEO), which questioned existing economic relations between the North and the South, including foreign investment relations. The ISDS cases I will review in this book show that distributive concerns continue to play a major role in investment

[106] Nancy Fraser and Axel Honneth, *Redistribution or Recognition?: A Political-Philosophical Exchange* (Verso 2003). This section follows from Fraser, who argues that neither claims of distribution nor claims of recognition can be reduced to the other. Ibid., 3.

[107] Kennedy (n. 37) 328–30.

[108] Tagi Sagafi-nejad and John H. Dunning, *The UN and Transnational Corporations: From Code of Conduct to Global Compact* (Indiana University Press 2008) 51.

disputes, especially those involving costs and risks. At the same time, state attempts to redistribute benefits or change the underlying ground rules, common in the 1960s and 1970s, are now less so.

On the other hand, as I will discuss in Chapter 7, some recent ISDS cases relate to claims of recognition. As Fraser explains, these claims correspond to the emergence of a broader 'politics of recognition',[109] which in the context of foreign investment relations means tensions between investment projects and local forms of livelihood, culture, and tradition. Large projects may turn a self-dependent agricultural community into a group of atomized workers with no choice but to retrain and work in the new industry. The consequences related to these transformations are more difficult to balance or compensate.

Demands for recognition are not new in foreign investment relations. In the 1960s, the postcolonial movement put forward claims of cultural domination, pointing out that the domination over the Global South was not only a matter of economic structure but of cultural hierarchies.[110] Cultural differences were used to portray the South as 'inferior, excluded, wholly other or simply invisible'.[111] To some extent, the NIEO captured this recognition dimension, as Global South countries demanded a legal regime that recognized the harm foreign investors cause to people in host countries. However, national elites remained more interested in maximizing the development contribution of foreign investment, or, more crudely, in perpetuating their local dominance through alliances with foreign investors.[112] Today, states take issues of recognition more seriously than sixty years ago, but some national elites still support investment projects that serve their interests while adversely affecting local communities.[113]

In ISDS practice, local communities are the main source of recognition claims. Many investment projects affect their livelihood and values, either directly or indirectly, and they are better organized and have more awareness of their rights than in the 1960s and 1970s. Local communities mobilize to resist projects and put forward concrete legal demands both at the domestic and international level—sometimes before ISDS tribunals in the form of amicus curiae submissions. Crucially, investment disputes involving recognition claims are more difficult to resolve than those concerning distributive conflicts, as arbitrators cannot balance the benefits of mining with the loss of self-realization. These elements are incommensurable.[114]

[109] Fraser and Honneth (n. 106) 7.

[110] See, e.g., Franz Fanon, *A Dying Colonialism* (Haakon Chevalier, trans) (Grove Press 1965 [1959]); Franz Fanon, *The Wretched of the Earth* (C. Farrington, trans) (Grove Press 1968 [1961]).

[111] Fraser and Honneth (n. 106) 29.

[112] John Linarelli, Margot Salomon, and Muthucumaraswamy Sornarajah, *The Misery of International Law: Confrontations with Injustice in the Global Economy* (OUP 2018) 108.

[113] Balakrishnan Rajagopal, *International Law from Below: Development, Social Movements, and Third World Resistance* (CUP 2003) 1–2, 187, 293.

[114] Fraser and Honneth (n. 106) 33; Alexander et al. (n. 28) 743.

2. The embeddedness of foreign investor rights

Tensions between the global and local levels of foreign investment projects relate to what legal anthropologists describe as the *embeddedness* of property. Following Karl Polanyi, they explore how property relations reflect broader social considerations. People 'build their social identities through holding and using a variety of "things" in their environments'.[115] For many local communities, land remains embedded in cultural, social, and political relations; the latter shaping questions of distribution as much as recognition. Embedded rights are often opposed to a commodity conception of property, which removes resources from social relations, and introduces them into the universal logic of markets or the production process.[116] There they can be exchanged or reorganized irrespective of the community or its values.

Property law and theory have highlighted the tension between a commodity and a socially embedded view of property. Margaret Radin's notion of personal property focuses on individual autonomy and personhood. She contrasts this Hegelian conception of property, where the object has intrinsic value for the individual, with a fungible idea of property.[117] Similarly, progressive property scholars have emphasized that property rights cannot be interpreted outside the social context. Property expresses social practices and values. This socio-legal conception of property contrasts with liberal or utility-based conceptions, such as those of Locke, Bentham, or Ronald Coase, who defined property rights based on universal values that transcend a 'specific time and place'.[118] In these interpretations, the meaning of individual freedom is universal, and resources serve the same purposes regardless of location.[119]

Thinking about foreign investor rights as commodity or fungible rights, however, overlooks the organization of foreign investors and the social dimension of their activities. The advantage of using Polanyi's idea of embeddedness is that it allows us to resist the premise that foreign investment projects are not embedded in social relations.[120] International business scholars stress the importance of

[115] C. M. Hann, 'Introduction: The embeddedness of property' in C. M. Hann (ed.), *Property Relations: Renewing the Anthropological Tradition* (CUP 1998) 1–47, 3. Also, Franz von Benda-Beckmann, Keebet von Benda-Beckmann, and Melanie Wiber, 'The Properties of Property' in Franz von Benda-Beckmann, Keebet von Benda-Beckmann, and Melanie Wiber (eds.), *Changing Properties of Property* (Berghahn Books 2006) 1–39, 19–23.

[116] See, e.g., Lorenzo Cotula, 'The New Enclosures? Polanyi, International Investment Law and the Global Land Rush' (2013) 34 Third World Quarterly 1605–29, 1610, 1618.

[117] Margaret Jane Radin, 'Property and Personhood' (1982) 34 Stanford Law Review 957–1015, 994–6. Also, Gregory S. Alexander, *Commodity & Propriety: Competing Visions of Property in American Legal Thought, 1776-1970* (University of Chicago Press 1997) 3.

[118] Amnon Lehavi, 'The Global Law of The Land' (2010) 81 University of Colorado Law Review 425–71, 457.

[119] The follow-on from this premise would be that a global theory of law and property is possible. See Twining (n. 52) 67, 53.

[120] The commodity approach, as Singer notes, 'relativizes both property and the relation between the public and private spheres and situates them within a context of multiple, contested, overlapping

embeddedness, borrowing Polanyi's claim that in capitalist societies 'instead of economy being embedded in social relations, social relations are embedded in the economic system'.[121] But they also go beyond this structural interpretation of embeddedness to underscore 'its multidimensionality, dynamics and duality'.[122] This literature challenges the premise that foreign investor rights are unembedded or removed from a social context like a simple commodity.

Business scholars point to the multiple embeddedness of multinational corporations (MNCs) 'across heterogeneous contexts at two levels': internal embeddedness within the firm, and external embeddedness in the host country.[123] In the 1990s, foreign investment was expected to facilitate a cultural convergence around the world; some authors described MNCs as the pillars of an 'emerging global civilization'.[124] This convergence never occurred, however, and firms have developed strategies to deal with host countries' cultural and institutional complexities. MNCs are in a good position 'to tap into resources and capabilities from multiple local contexts and integrate and leverage them to create a range of competitive advantages'.[125] But they also need to make their global strategies work locally, taking into account that increased local embeddedness does not come free. Their objective is to make the most efficient use of locational advantages and the institutional framework at the lowest possible cost.

As Martin Heidenreich explains, the business studies analysis is still primarily economic and disregards sociological dimensions. Sociological work points us to the different levels of external and internal embeddedness of MNCs. Following Mark Granovetter, Heidenreich treats MNCs as being embedded in 'networks of interpersonal relations'—at the level of the global economy, the MNC itself, and the host country.[126] The world of global business is characterized by 'cross-border perceptions, common practices, benchmarks and relationships, common discourses and patterns of identification, cross-border conflicts and strategic games'.[127]

human relations': Singer (n. 37) 208. These authors also overlook the global economic context, see David Schneiderman, 'Constitutional Property Rights and Elision of the Transnational: Foucauldian Misgivings' (2015) 24 Social & Legal Studies 65–87, 66–7.

[121] Karl Polanyi, *The Great Transformation: The Political and Economic Origins of our Time* (Beacon Press 2001[1957]) 60.

[122] Martin Heidenreich, 'The Social Embeddedness of Multinational Companies: A Literature Review' (2012) 10 Socio-Economic Review 549–79, 572.

[123] Klaus E. Meyer, Ram Mudambi, and Rajneesh Narula 'Multinational Enterprises and Local Contexts: The Opportunities and Challenges of Multiple Embeddedness' (2011) 48 Journal of Management Studies 235–52, 235.

[124] In 1998–99, Howard V. Perlmutter, a pioneer in the study of MNCs, wrote four articles in the *Financial Times* on multinationals and the 'emerging global civilization'. See https://www.wharton.upenn.edu/wp-content/uploads/125anniversaryissue/perlmutter.html (last visited 22 May 2020).

[125] Meyer et al. (n. 123) 241.

[126] Heidenreich (n. 122) 553.

[127] Ibid., 571.

Individually, each MNC also constitutes a 'transnational space' shaped by 'global management, production, innovation, networking, benchmarking and accounting practices'.[128] Further, MNCs' relations with actors in host countries are primarily shaped by the objectives of facilitating their local operations and reducing uncertainties.[129] National elites who control the state apparatus are ideal candidates for this partnership. Foreign investors and national elites can struggle over the distribution of benefits, but likely share a long-term vision for the relevant economic sector. These two actors may belong to the same transnational capitalist class, or have similar political and economic views even if they occupy different places in the global hierarchy.[130]

Equally relevant is the fact that these networks of personal relations are dynamic. MNCs are powerful actors who can often decide how much to adapt to the demands of host states, national elites, and local communities. They are rule-makers as well as rule-takers, and can contest and negotiate the 'methods and degrees of local adaptations'.[131] MNCs thus often operate as 'bridging institutions' between the logics of the global economy, states, and local communities.[132] Their rights are embedded in a global understanding of economic activities, reflecting the common practices and perceptions of similar firms. At the same time, they also account for some particularities of the state and locality involved in each investment project. This level of local adaptation is variable, depending on the law, institutions, other firms, the national elite, and the foreign investors' ability to shape domestic rules and institutions.[133]

These insights from the international business literature also help refine the embeddedness of local communities. First, communities relate to foreign investors and the global economy. The main difference is that they are rarely rule-makers and are less likely to enjoy national elites' support. Local communities such as indigenous peoples and peasants have struggled and succeeded to obtain some legal recognition for their land and territorial rights. This domestic and international

[128] Ibid., 568.

[129] Ibid., 553, 556, 568–9.

[130] See Claire A. Cutler, *Private Power and Global Authority: Transnational Merchant Law in the Global Political Economy* (CUP 2003) 12, 181; Bhupinder Chimni, 'International Institutions Today: An Imperial Global State in the Making' (2004) 15 European Journal of International Law 1–37, 6.

[131] Mike Geppert and Christoph Dörrenbächer 'Politics and Power in the Multinational Corporation: An Introduction' in Mike Dörrenbächer and Mike Geppert (eds.), *Politics and Power in the Multinational Corporation: The Role of Institutions, Interests and Identities* (CUP) 3–38, 23.

[132] Tatiana Kostova and Kendall Roth 'Adoption of Organizational Practice by Subsidiaries of Multinational Corporations: Institutional and Relational Effects' (2002) 45 Academy of Management Journal 215–33, 216.

[133] As Boaventura de Sousa Santos explains, the global space reproduces existing asymmetries and power relations: Boaventura de Sousa Santos, *Toward a New Legal Common Sense: law, globalization, and emancipation* (CUP 2002) 179, 262.

recognition, however, remains quite weak when compared to investment treaties and ISDS.[134] Second, local communities are embedded in translocal networks where other communities struggle for recognition and other actors, such as non-governmental organizations (NGOs), may share their interests and values. Evidence shows that local resistance has been more successful when communities coordinate their actions and have transnational support.[135] But there are limitations for this strategy too. The environmental agenda of some NGOs, based on conservationism, can conflict with local livelihood or traditions.[136] Thus, while local communities can leverage the local embeddedness of their rights on translocal networks, their alliances may not be as strong and homogenous as those of foreign investors and national elites.

The interaction between the global, national, and local levels provides another entry point to understand conflict in foreign investment relations. Property can be embedded in social, political, and economic organizations that may or may not coincide with states. Foreign investor rights are never wholly embedded in the global economy, but investors aim to maintain their adaptation to the local level to a minimum. As I discuss in the following chapters, the norm entrepreneurs for international investment protection aimed to facilitate this process. The notions of private and public express the tension between foreign investor rights and states' right to regulate, but fail to distinguish this other level of struggle. Attending to the tension between the global and the local can fill in this gap, although balancing these conflicts may be a task more apt for political leaders than international arbitrators.

F. Protecting foreign investor rights through ISDS

Enforcing investment treaties requires arbitrators to interpret foreign investor rights, states' right to regulate, and the relationship between foreign investors, states, and, arguably, local communities. The legal text only provides a starting point.[137] Property is not self-defining, contracts are incomplete, and the contours of states' right to regulate are contentious. In most legal systems, moreover, property protection follows a two-level structure. The lower level consists of general legislation, sectoral regulation, specific commitments, and judicial

[134] See Lorenzo Cotula, *Human Rights, Natural Resource and Investment law in a Globalised world: Shades of Grey in the Shadow of the Law* (Routledge 2012) 128–35.

[135] David Schneiderman, *Resisting Economic Globalization: Critical Theory and International Investment Law* (Palgrave 2013) 103–12; Joanna L. Robinson, *Contested Water: The Struggle Against Water Privatization in the United States and Canada* (The MIT Press 2013) 109–78.

[136] See, e.g., Ben A. Minteer and Thaddeus R. Miller 'The New Conservation Debate: Ethical Foundations, Strategic Trade-offs, and Policy Opportunities' (2011) 144 Biological Conservation 945–47.

[137] Alexander (n. 66) 6–7, 57.

decisions interpreting these rights. The upper level comprises a constitutional property clause and the highest court, which interprets this vague clause and the rights involved in the dispute. The clause does not define the scope of rights, and often limits itself to preventing the state from expropriating or taking property without paying compensation. Most constitutions also grant procedural rights and incorporate due process requirements. As the previous sections suggest, there is a lot at stake in constitutional property disputes: these decisions resolve cases, but also shape and consolidate an economic, social, and political imaginary of society.

The international protection of foreign investor rights adds another layer to this institutional structure, contributing to the creation of 'a substantial body of property law at the international level'.[138] The idea of international property is a revolutionary deviation from basic principles of public and private international law. Traditionally, '[a] state enjoys an exclusive right to regulate matters of ownership of property of every kind which may be said to belong within its territory'.[139] Although some international treaties can create or shape the scope of certain rights, such as seabed mining or intellectual property rights, most relevant international property treaties only incorporate another level of protection consisting of different standards and a new adjudicator. International property cases operate, in this way, like constitutional property disputes. Owners can ask an international tribunal to decide whether a state's measure—administrative, legislative, or judicial—is consistent with the standards of protection included in the respective treaty or in customary international law. Like their domestic counterparts, international tribunals respect the eminent domain rule and only order monetary compensation. Restitution is uncommon in ISDS.[140]

The international protection of property and contracts opens up several institutional choices. Such protection may operate as a review of the state's measure, bypassing the domestic judiciary, or as a review of the final decision of the domestic judiciary. The rule on exhaustion of local remedies allows domestic courts to make difficult interpretative choices, involving questions of redistribution and recognition, although these decisions remain subject to the final say of an international tribunal. When that rule has been waived, however, the international tribunal makes the decisions rather than reviewing them. The international protection of property as a human right or under customary international law follows the exhaustion of local remedies rule. Exceptionally, ISDS does not.[141]

[138] John G. Sprankling, *The International Law of Property* (OUP 2014) 347.

[139] Charles C Hyde, *International Law Chiefly as Interpreted and Applied by the United States* (Fred B. Rothman & Co 1983[1947]), vol. 1, 650. Cited in ibid., 3.

[140] Dolzer and Schreuer (n. 66) 293–4.

[141] Matthew C. Porterfield, 'Exhaustion of Local Remedies in Investor-State Dispute Settlement: An Idea Whose Time Has Come?' (2015) 41 Yale Journal of International Law Online 1–12.

1. ISDS as a substitute for the domestic judiciary

Under most investment treaties, foreign investors do not need a final decision from the domestic judiciary—or even to initiate domestic proceedings—in order to launch an ISDS case. Strictly, then, these treaties do not provide an additional layer of protection but replace the domestic judiciary entirely.[142] This substitution poses some interpretative challenges. First, in the interpretation of domestic law, which likely defines some foreign investor rights. ISDS disputes inevitably touch on the scope and strength of these rights, and the ICSID Convention conflict of laws rule requires applying both domestic and international law. A lack of a domestic judicial decision begs the question of how to interpret domestic legislation. ISDS tribunals frequently appoint domestic law experts for the task. But this solution has limitations. One expert may be more convincing than another, yet the process is not equivalent to several lawyers and judges trained in that legal system discussing the issue. ISDS practitioners have highlighted this problem.[143]

A domestic judicial decision also provides insight into the social context, which international arbitrators would unlikely have otherwise. To illustrate this point, let's imagine one international tribunal reviewing the decision of the US Supreme Court in *Mahon* and another reviewing only the Kohler Act—the public measure that had affected investor rights. In the first case, the tribunal would review the reasoning of the US Supreme Court, including its assessment of the social context of the measure. This assessment would consider the relationship between private rights and public authority, the rights of other actors, and, possibly, the economic transformation associated with the mining industry—issues of distribution and recognition. The arbitrators may not share this reasoning, but they would still have a detailed overview of the social relations created by that investment project. In reviewing the Kohler Act directly, on the other hand, an international tribunal would likely lack the social dimensions of the case, which is not easy to gain for an international arbitral tribunal sitting in a different country, and whose jurisdiction is limited by the ISDS clause to the state and the foreign investor.

The entire substitution of the domestic judiciary does not provide foreign investors with a mechanism calibrated to amend unfair or arbitrary domestic decisions. If the goal of international investment protection were to mimic an *ideal* domestic court, free from political interference, the exhaustion of local remedies rule would play a central role: the domestic judicial decision would be the indispensable comparator for such a regime to operate correctly, and would be more appropriate than notions of comparative or global administrative law, which

[142] Tom Ginsburg, 'International Substitutes for Domestic Institutions: Bilateral Investment Treaties and Governance' (2005) 25 International Review of Law and Economics 107–23.

[143] Mélida Hodgson and Melissa Stewart, 'Experts in Investor-State Arbitration: The Tribunal as Gatekeeper' 9 (2018) Journal of International Dispute Settlement 453–63, 454–5, 461.

again would likely miss the local context. ISDS tribunals do something different. They provide their own interpretation of foreign investor rights and the relationship between foreign investors, states, and local communities. ISDS is a platform from which arbitrators can develop the law without the interference of states or doctrines based on domestic public law imperatives. The 'doctrine' in the awards therefore becomes the law of foreign investment relations.[144]

This analysis differs from the view of Aron Broches and Ibrahim Shihata, general counsels of the World Bank, who promoted the ICSID Convention for decades. They argued that this dispute settlement mechanism was intended to *depoliticize* foreign investment disputes, insulating such cases 'from the realm of politics and diplomacy'.[145] Without ISDS, the argument went, foreign investors would have to exhaust local remedies and seek the diplomatic protection of their home countries, which may or may not be provided. Broches and Shihata were right to an extent: the practice around state responsibility for injuries to aliens, which was significant in the 1920s and 1930s, has almost completely been replaced by ISDS and international arbitration.[146] The question of whether these arbitrations have reduced the role of diplomacy is still debated.[147]

However, depoliticization or insulation do not capture the situation appropriately. ISDS is political in multiple ways.[148] In this book, I am primarily interested in two of these ways. First, private standing in international litigation allows investors to bring cases that states would consider *politically* too 'hot'.[149] The political views of the norm entrepreneurs indicate that 'hot' disputes were to be expected, as these bankers, business leaders, and international lawyers imagined a legal regime capable of counterbalancing state economic intervention. Secondly, international arbitration is prone to privilege the global embeddedness of foreign investor rights over local imperatives. Judges may be libertarian, progressive, or conservative, but they are socially and culturally immersed in the host country. International arbitrators, on the other hand, constitute a transnational community, which is much

[144] Riles argues that property law knowledge comes from doctrine, from 'the artefact of the accumulation of individual cases', and not from relations of ownership and their meaning: Riles (n. 31) 782.

[145] World Bank Consultative Meeting of Legal Experts, Addis Ababa, December 16–20, 1963, Summary Record of Proceedings (per Broches, 16 December 1963) in ICSID, Convention on the Settlement of Investment Disputes between States and Nationals of other States, Documents concerning the origin and formulation of the convention, vol. II (World Bank 1968) 242; Ibrahim Shihata, 'Toward Greater Depoliticization of Investment Disputes: The Roles of ICSID and MIGA' (1986) 1 ICSID Review 1–25, 4.

[146] International commercial arbitration also plays a fundamental role. See International Chamber of Commerce, 'ICC Dispute Resolution 2018 Statistics' (2019) 9, available at https://nyiac.org/wp-content/uploads/2019/08/icc_disputeresolution2018statistics.pdf (last visited 20 November 2020).

[147] See Bonnitcha et al. (n. 18) 196.

[148] See the discussion in Martins Paparinskis, 'Limits of Depoliticisation in Contemporary Investor-State Arbitration' in James Crawford and Sarah Nouwen (eds.), *Select Proceedings of the European Society of International Law*, vol. 3 (Hart 2010) 271–82.

[149] Karen J. Alter, 'Private Litigants and the New International Courts' (2006) 39 Comparative Political Studies, 22–49, 24.

closer to the global economy;[150] some even sit on the board of directors of global banks,[151] which may affect how they interpret foreign investment relations, including the facts of a dispute.

2. Fact-finding and ISDS cases

Facts are fundamental for the resolution of a legal dispute. The parties argue about facts as much as about law. Defining the facts is also not that different from interpreting the law. Facts require interpretation, and there is never a complete account of a dispute. Adjudicators favour a certain understanding of the facts for similar reasons why they prefer a particular interpretation of the law: 'when people have different expectations they are apt to see the facts differently'.[152]

In property and contract disputes, the relevance of facts varies depending on the type of rights at stake. For standardized rights, the legislator includes as much information as possible in the legal text and institutions. Registration of land, the *numerus clausus* rule, and consumer contracts are legislative choices in favour of standardization. The situation is different in investment disputes, which involve sectoral regulations as well as negotiations and agreements. Repeatedly, ISDS tribunals have observed that facts are fundamental to resolving disputes.[153] This significance of facts opens up a space of arbitral subjectivity, allowing arbitrators to portray the relationship between foreign investors and states in different ways. Many ISDS tribunals, for instance, have depicted foreign investors as weak actors in foreign investment relations, as they do not participate in domestic politics and may not speak the language or understand the business culture.[154] The literature suggests that this assessment is inaccurate,[155] but this sort of narrative continues to

[150] Dezalay and Garth refer to international arbitrators as a transnational elite. See Yves Dezalay and Bryant G. Garth, *Dealing in Virtue: International Commercial arbitration and the Construction of a Transnational Legal Order* (University of Chicago Press 1996) 10, 144. In the Foreword, Pierre Bourdieu suggests that international arbitrators—and those who work closely to this field—represent the 'partisans' of the global, ibid., viii. Also, Sergio Puig, 'Social Capital in the Arbitration Market' (2014) 25 European Journal of International Law 387–424, 402.

[151] See Jarrod Hepburn, 'Argentina Re-opens Arbitrator Ethics Issues in Bid to Set-aside Water Concessions Award' IAReporter, 3 August 2015.

[152] C. B. Macpherson, 'The Meaning of Property' in C. B. Macpherson (ed.), *Property, Mainstream and Critical Positions* (University of Toronto Press 1978) 1–14, 1.

[153] *Joseph Charles Lemire v Ukraine* (ICSID Case No. ARB/06/18) Decision on Jurisdiction and Liability, 14 January 2010, para. 284; *Merrill & Ring Forestry v. Canada* (ICSID Case No. UNCT/07/1), Award, 31 March 2010, para. 210; *Spyridon Roussalis v. Romania* (ICSID Case No. ARB/06/1) Award, 7 December 2011, para. 318.

[154] *Azurix v. Argentina* (ICSID Case No. ARB/01/12) Award, 14 July 2006, paras. 310–11; Separate Opinion of Thomas Wälde in *International Thunderbird Gaming v. Mexico* (UNCITRAL—NAFTA) 1 December 2005, paras. 4, 12, 33, 57; *Joseph Charles Lemire v. Ukraine* (ICSID Case No. ARB/06/18) Award, 28 March 2011, para. 57.

[155] Bonnitcha et al. (n. 17) 150.

shape some awards.[156] Such an interpretation of these or other circumstances can suggest an *aura* of mistreatment of the foreign investor or a *sense* of legitimacy of the public regulation. In either case, storytelling plays a fundamental role.

There is an intimate connection between one's conception of property and contracts and one's approach to facts. ISDS tribunals can think about foreign investment as a relationship solely between investor and investment or investor and state, or they may also include the local community. Conceptions focused only on the owner and the thing or the transaction, discussed above, do not only disregard the social implications but silence the interconnectedness of the legal system and overlook how the law evolves out of 'conflicts involving real human emotions and desires'.[157] The fact that ISDS disputes are resolved through arbitration, which some scholars describe as a type of contract,[158] reifies the premise that foreign investment relations involve investors and states only.

The purpose of investment treaties and ISDS also matters for determining which facts are relevant. Facts are interpreted through the lens of purposes.[159] If the objective of these treaties was sustainable development, ISDS tribunals would be expected to discuss issues such as whether the investor paid attention to sustainable development goals defined by the international community and the host country. This would include looking into how the foreign investor adapted to the needs of the locality. The narrative of most ISDS awards is different, however, because the primary objective of the ISDS regime is aligned with the interests of foreign investors. Arbitrators focus on their calculability and the protection of their ability to rely on the conditions existent when the investment was made.

3. Acquired rights and legitimate expectations

While arbitrators rarely decide a case by explicitly focusing on the property–contract distinction, the character of foreign investor rights is significant in investment arbitration. Tribunals have distinguished between reforms to general laws, sectoral regulations, and changes affecting specific commitments or representations. The doctrines of acquired rights and legitimate expectations illustrate two ways in which ISDS arbitrators can protect the calculability of foreign investors—in

156 See, e.g., *Bilcon v. Canada* (Permanent Court of Arbitration (PCA) Case No. 2009-04) Award on Jurisdiction and Liability, 17 March 2015 (and the Dissenting Opinion of Donald McRae).

157 Gerald Korngold and Andrew Morriss, 'Introduction: The Story of Property Stories' in Gerald Korngold and Andrew Morriss (eds.), *Property Stories* (Foundation Press 2009) 1–8, 2. Also, Carol M. Rose, 'Property as Storytelling: Perspectives from Game Theory, Narrative Theory, Feminist Theory' (1990) 2 Yale Journal of Law & the Humanities 37–58.

158 Historically, the two dominant positions concerning the theoretical basis of arbitration are the business 'contractual' and the legalistic 'judgement' or jurisdictional theories. Gordon Battle, 'The Two Fundamental Concepts of Arbitration and Their Relation to Rules of Law' (1930) 16 Virginia Law Review 255–60, 255.

159 Kim Lane Scheppele, 'Facing Facts in Legal Interpretation' (1990) 30 Representations 42–77, 55.

this case, focusing on substance, not due process. Both acknowledge that states negotiate the conditions of a project with foreign investors, but they construe foreign investor rights differently. The doctrine of acquired rights allows adjudicators to distinguish between rights that have been vested on the investor and other simple uses of the resources that states can legitimately modify; only the annihilation of a vested right requires compensation.[160] International law recognizes the acquired rights doctrine, although there is also some disagreement on what exactly constitutes a vested or an acquired right.[161]

Broad generalizations are difficult, but the main features of acquired rights are their origin and specificity. Acquired rights emerge from the law and contracts. They are either legal creations or the result of the will of the state as expressed in a contract.[162] Laws and contracts, including their judicial interpretation, can vest rights on individuals but they have to be specific about the entitlement and the beneficiary. Crucially, it is agreed that facts or negotiations do not create vested or acquired rights. There cannot be acquired rights related to clientele, goodwill, a certain amount of profit or interest, general economic conditions, or freedom of trade or industry. These concepts are either too general or rarely based on the law or contracts.[163]

Numerous international courts have used the doctrine of acquired rights. In 1934, the Permanent Court of International Justice was asked to decide a diplomatic protection case brought by the United Kingdom, on behalf of Oscar Chinn, against Belgium. The court ruled that international law recognizes acquired rights as a general principle of law, but that in the case at hand 'anything in the nature of a genuine vested right' was affected.[164] In 1959 the first UN rapporteur on state responsibility, Francisco García Amador, elaborated further on the acquired rights doctrine:

> Paradoxical though it may be, international law has established the principle of respect of acquired rights without defining or systematically classifying the rights in question. This is to be explained in part by the fact that under international law private patrimonial rights, whatever their nature or the nationality of their possessor, are governed, in the absence of treaties or of certain contractual relations between States and specific aliens, by municipal legislation. Nevertheless,

[160] Daniel H. Cole and Peter Z. Grossman, 'The Meaning of Property Rights: Law Versus Economics?' (2002) 78 Land Economics 317–30, 322.

[161] Martins Paparinskis, *The International Minimum Standard and Fair and Equitable Treatment* (OUP 2013) 61–2, 73, 79.

[162] Pierre A. Lalive, 'The Doctrine of Acquired Rights' in International and Comparative Law Center, Southwester Legal Foundation, Rights and Duties of Private Investors Abroad (M. Bender 1965) 145–200, 150–3.

[163] Ibid., 187–9.

[164] *Oscar Chinn Case* (*Britain v. Belgium*) [1937] PCIJ Series A/B, No. 63 (12 December 1934), para. 99.

> certain questions raised by the nature and content of 'acquired rights' are undeniably international in character, and many of those questions seem to have been resolved in practice.[165]

During decolonization, the Global South strongly opposed the doctrine of acquired rights under international law. The main reason for this was that former colonial powers claimed their investors had acquired rights over natural resources in the newly independent countries based on the previous colonial legal system and concession contracts.[166]

In contrast to acquired rights, the doctrine of legitimate expectations aims to protect the ability of individuals to rely on the acts or conduct of other actors. Legitimate expectations emerge from relations as opposed to laws or contractual rights. The latter are still relevant, but they are events alongside other facts and circumstances in a *special* relationship such as a foreign investment.[167] These expectations are not vested by states or acquired by investors; they emerge when investors reasonably rely on state representations and inducements to make a decision. Unlike the acts that create acquired rights, these representations or inducements do not need to be legally binding.[168] Although the protection of legitimate expectations relates to the practice of promising, the object of protection is not the promise—the will or intention of the promisor—but the reliance of the promisee on the representations.[169]

The notion of reliance is relevant in both public and private law contexts. In private law, pre-contractual civil law liability and common law promissory estoppel are such examples; reliance is also related to good faith in contract law. In public law, it is the basis for estoppel and procedural and substantive legitimate expectations. Reliance is more accepted in private than public law, but in no case is it without controversy.

Reliance became popular in public law in the 1990s as the source of substantive legitimate expectations, doctrine which has been admitted in some legal systems but resisted in others.[170] Substantive expectations were criticized because 'the public law considerations that support the free exercise of the decision-maker's

[165] F. V. García Amador, 'Fourth Report on State Responsibility by Mr. F.V. Garcia-Amador, Special Rapporteur' [1959] Yearbook of the International Law Commission, vol. 2, A/CN.4/119 (United Nations 1959) 1–35, 9.

[166] Anghie (n. 57) 198, 213.

[167] The relationship may be special per se or may be special as a result of an act of inducement. See Teerawat Wongkaew, *Protection of Legitimate Expectations in Investment Treaty Arbitration* (CUP 2019) 126, 135, 176.

[168] Ibid., 215.

[169] Andrew Gold, 'A Property Theory of Contract' (2009) 103 Northwestern University Law Review 1–62, 19, 22.

[170] See Paul P. Craig, 'Substantive Legitimate Expectations in Domestic and Community law' (1996) 55 The Cambridge Law Journal 289–312; Trevor Zeyl, 'Charting the Wrong Course: The Doctrine of Legitimate Expectations in Investment Treaty Law' (2011) 49 Alberta Law Review 203–35, 20.

discretion are squeezed out and substantive protection is justified'.[171] Protecting substantive expectations could affect the ability of a government to implement measures for the public interest or reforms when democratic preferences change. *Ultra vires* representations or inducements, moreover, could disrupt the distribution of competences in a state, affecting the balance of power.[172]

In private law, some scholars and courts have also resisted the protection of legitimate expectations. In general, judges do not protect reliance when cases involve sophisticated parties, reasoning that these parties could have entered into an agreement or included the controversial point in a contract already entered into.[173] Protecting reliance implies intervening in a bargain between two autonomous parties. Randy Barnet observes that reliance refers to 'cases whose only common characteristic [is] the absence of a bargain'.[174] Through legal doctrines such as promissory estoppel and legitimate expectations, actors can create obligations without being aware of it. It is unsurprising, then, that libertarians such as Barnet reject reliance altogether because the principle of 'freedom of contract' includes 'freedom from contracts'.[175] As explained in Section D.2., progressive academics support the protection of reliance but only when the favoured party is the more vulnerable actor: the 'counterprinciple of reliance' can serve to adjust the parties' unequal bargaining power.

The status of reliance and legitimate expectations is likewise controversial in international law. A detailed analysis by Martins Paparinskis concludes that the primary sources of international law do not recognize legitimate expectations.[176] The decision of the International Court of Justice (ICJ) in *Obligation to Negotiate Access to the Pacific Ocean* case seems to confirm this position.[177] In ISDS practice, however, the protection of legitimate expectations is considered a core element of the FET and a part of the minimum standard of treatment under customary international law.[178] Although tribunals have not defined legitimate expectations consistently,[179] sometimes conflating them with contractual commitments, their protection has never been successfully challenged.[180] As Emmanuel Gaillard has

[171] Christopher Forsyth, 'Legitimate Expectations Revisited' (2011) 16 Judicial Review 429–39, 439.

[172] Paul Reynolds, 'Legitimate Expectations and the Protection of Trust in Public Officials' (2011) 2 Public Law 330–52, 340–1.

[173] Elise Bant and Michael Bryan, 'Fact, Future and Fiction: Risk and Reasonable Reliance in Estoppel' (2015) 35 Oxford Journal of Legal Studies 427–452, 445; Stephen A. Smith, *Contract Theory* (OUP 2004) 44.

[174] Randy E. Barnett, 'The Death of Reliance' (1996) 46 Journal of Legal Education 518–36, 524.

[175] Ibid., 528.

[176] Paparinskis (n. 161) 252–9.

[177] The ICJ noted that legitimate expectations are not a general principle of law, but it did not discuss the treatment of aliens under customary international law. *Obligation to Negotiate Access to the Pacific Ocean* (*Bolivia v. Chile*), Judgment, ICJ Reports 2018, 507, para. 162 (1 October 2018).

[178] *Glamis v. USA* (UNCITRAL—NAFTA) Award, 8 June 2009, paras. 621–2; *Gold Reserve v. Venezuela* (ICSID Case No. ARB(AF)/09/1), Award, 22 September 2014, paras. 575–6.

[179] Wongkaew (n. 167) 5-9.

[180] Only some dissenting opinions have concluded that investment treaties do not protect legitimate expectations. See Separate Opinion of Pedro Nikken in *Suez and others v. Argentina* (ICSID Case No.

observed, legitimate expectations operate as a kind of over-inclusive 'magic formula' that has replaced the notion of acquired rights in ISDS practice.[181]

There is, furthermore, some confusion in ISDS awards concerning the rationale for the protection of legitimate expectations. Although some arbitrators have justified it on the good faith principle or through the estoppel doctrine, most agree that the source of these expectations lies in the reliance of foreign investors.[182] In *Merrill v. Canada*, the arbitrators underscored that:

> Legitimate expectations are no doubt an important element of a business undertaking, but for such expectation to give rise to actionable rights requires there to have been some form of representation by the state and reliance by an investor on that representation in making a business decision.[183]

The tribunal in *Suez v. Argentina* elaborated on the rationale for the protection of legitimate expectations:

> When an investor undertakes an investment, a host government through its laws, regulations, declared policies, and statements creates in the investor certain expectations about the nature of the treatment that it may anticipate from the host State. The resulting reasonable and legitimate expectations are important factors that influence initial investment decisions and afterwards the manner in which the investment is to be managed. The theoretical basis of this approach no doubt is found in the work of the eminent scholar Max Weber, who advanced the idea that one of the main contributions of law to any social system is to make economic life more calculable and also argued that capitalism arose in Europe because European law demonstrated a high degree of 'calculability.'[184]

As a final point, substantive expectations should be distinguished from procedural expectations. Substantive expectations refer to situations in which an individual—such as a foreign investor—is entitled to expect that a particular benefit or situation will continue. In the case of procedural expectations, on the other hand, the individual is only entitled to a certain procedure—for example,

ARB/03/17) 30 July 2010, paras. 2–4, 12–25, 38–40; Concurring Opinion of Luis Herrera Marcano in *Total v. Argentina* (ICSID Case No. ARB/04/01) 12 December 2010, paras. 2–3; Separate Opinion of Georges Abi-Saab in *Micula v. Romania* (ICSID Case No. ARB/05/20) 5 December 2013, paras. 2–5.

[181] Emmanuelle Gaillard, 'Chronique des sentences arbitrales—Centre International pour le Règlement des Différends Relatifs aux Investissements (CIRDI)' (2008) 1 Journal du droit international 311–64, 332–4.

[182] Wongkaew (n. 167) 33–49.

[183] *Merrill & Ring Forestry v. Canada* (ICSID Case No. UNCT/07/1) Award, 31 March 2010, para. 150.

[184] *Suez and others v. Argentina* (ICSID Case No. ARB/03/17) Decision on Liability, 30 July 2010, para. 222.

that a particular public authority will review and carefully consider a situation. ISDS practice has focused primarily on substantive expectations. Procedural legitimate expectations have been recognized on a few occasions only,[185] but this may change in the future as ISDS practice appears to be making a pivotal shift in favour of due process and the procedural protection of foreign investor rights.

Conclusion

This chapter introduced the main characteristics of foreign investor rights, critically examined the purpose of investment treaties, and provided an analytical framework to visualize these rights as social relations. Foreign investor rights create multiple relations between foreign investor, state, and local communities, and these relations can lead to various sorts of conflicts. Importantly, these conflicts may concern not only states' right to regulate or distributive tensions but also recognition claims and the social embeddedness of rights.

The second part of the chapter examined how ISDS relates to foreign investor rights. It brought up the role of storytelling and introduced the acquired rights and the legitimate expectations doctrines as two alternatives to cater for the calculability of foreign investors. ISDS practice has embraced the latter. The next chapter examines the world-making project of the norm entrepreneurs for international investment protection, the role of foreign investor rights in that project, and the way in which they expected arbitrators to interpret those rights so as to ensure investors' calculability.

[185] *Invesmart v. Czech Republic* (UNCITRAL) Award, 26 June 2009, para. 351. The *Saluka* tribunal found that the investor had a procedural legitimate expectation when it concluded that it was 'entitled to expect that the host State takes seriously a proposal that has sufficient potential to solve the problem and deal with it in an objective, transparent, unbiased and even-handed way'. *Saluka v. Czech Republic* (UNCITRAL) Partial Award, 17 March 2006, para. 363.

2
The Norm Entrepreneurs of the 1950s and 1960s

In the post-World War II period, certain international bankers, lawyers, and business leaders decided it was time they rewrote the rules of the global economy. The nationalization of the Anglo-Iranian Oil Company in 1951 and of the Suez Canal in 1956, together with increasing state economic intervention all around the world, occasioned their call for action. The goal of this coalition was to enable and safeguard a world of free enterprise; protecting foreign private investment was then a top priority. This chapter examines who these norm entrepreneurs were, their networks, and how they captured the space of international investment law to advance their world-making project. These individuals and their professional associations imagined quite detailed institutions and content for this legal field. They discussed the character of foreign investor rights, indirect expropriation, fair and equitable treatment, the internationalization of contracts, reliance, the inadequacy of local remedies, and the key role of international arbitration. The views of the norm entrepreneurs were a reaction against Communism, decolonization, and state economic intervention in their own countries; at the same time, however, they insisted that their proposals responded to everyday problems and practical experience.

A. The norm entrepreneurs for international investment protection

In April 1959, hundreds of business leaders gathered at the International Chamber of Commerce in Washington, DC to hear Henry Luce, editor-in-chief of *Time* magazine, an active opponent of Roosevelt's New Deal, and one of the most influential men in the US of his day.[1] Luce talked about a world in which 'enlightened business' would shape global institutions.[2] The past belonged to politicians and lawyers, he said; now those in business must leave behind their interest in

[1] Alan Brinkley, *The Publisher: Henry Luce and his American century* (Knopf 2010) 7. Luce was convinced of the eventual failure of the New Deal, after which he predicted a very active role for business in government, ibid., 320.

[2] Henry Luce, 'Peace through Law' Speech before the International Chamber of Commerce, 1959 Washington Congress, in Society to Advance the Protection of Foreign Investments, Convention on Investments Abroad with Comments, Speeches and New Literature, Publication No. 3 (Bergisch Gladbach, J. Heider 1960) 36–40, 39 (hereinafter I refer to this volume as *Society to Advance the Protection of Foreign Investment*, Publication No. 3 (1960)).

Investment Treaties and the Legal Imagination. Nicolás M. Perrone, Oxford University Press (2021). © Nicolás M. Perrone.
DOI: 10.1093/oso/9780198862147.003.0003

'certain rules', which might advance their immediate goals, and favour 'universal rules' that would ensure a world of peace and economic prosperity.[3] They would not be alone in this difficult task—they would be joining 'the leading banker of the world', Hermann Abs, who had 'made a proposal of great interest and importance', his 'Magna Carta of international commerce'.[4] In a world shaped by 'enlightened business', investor rights had to be universal.

Ten years later, Abs was still thankful that Luce's endorsement had brought international attention to his Magna Carta.[5] He was aware that his initiative to protect foreign investment depended on the support of other 'enlightened' business leaders, with the social capital and political determination to influence governments and international organizations. Also, Abs himself could be a divisive figure. He had been accused of participating in the expropriation of Jewish property during the Third Reich, and had negotiated major debt relief for Germany after World War II—both actions of the kind that champions of the cause of private property would condemn.[6]

What the record shows is that Abs was a practical man who was deeply involved in the business world through his position at the Deutsche Bank. In the 1930s, he was director of many large firms, including MNCs such as IG Farben.[7] After the Rockefellers, the largest shareholder in Standard Oil of New Jersey was IG Farben (the two firms held reciprocal investments), which also had shared interests in the petrochemical sector with Du Pont and Royal Dutch Shell.[8] Later, after World War II, Abs was again appointed to the board of several corporations, such as Deutsche Shell, becoming concerned about the return of German assets seized during the war and the protection of foreign private investment. He knew that his role during the Third Reich could be an obstacle for his initiatives in these areas, and for this reason hired the services of a US public relations firm: the Chicago-based Julius Klein & Associates.[9]

Fortunately for Abs, he was not the first, nor the last, to promote foreign investor rights during the post-World War II decades—what I call the norm entrepreneurs for international investment protection. The International Chamber

[3] Ibid., 40.

[4] Ibid., 39, 38–40. This was not the only occasion in which Luce openly promoted Abs's Magna Carta and international arbitration. Henry R. Luce, 'The Way of the Law: The Road to the Mountain of Vision' (1959) 45 American Bar Association Journal 482–525, 524.

[5] Hermann J. Abs, *Die rechtliche Problematik privater Auslandsinvestitionen*. Vortrag gehalten vor der Juristischen Studiengesellschaft in Karlsruhe, am 16. Dezember 1968 (Müller 1969) 11.

[6] Quinn Slobodian, *Globalists: The End of Empire and the Birth of Neoliberalism* (Harvard University Press 2018) 139.

[7] Central Intelligence Agency, 'Abs, Hermann Josef' 1970 Current Biography (Disclosed under the Nazi War Crimes Disclosure Act), available at https://www.cia.gov/library/readingroom/docs/ABS%2C%20HERMANN%20J._0051.pdf (last visited 2 July 2020) 2–3.

[8] Mira Wilkins, *The History of Foreign Investment in the United States, 1914-1945* (Harvard University Press 2009) 406–13.

[9] Paul Manning, *Martin Bormann, Nazi in Exile* (Stuart 1981) 266–8.

of Commerce had discussed the idea of international investment protection in 1931, and made a concrete proposal for a Code on Fair Treatment for Foreign Investments in 1949.[10] In 1948, the International Law Association prepared the two Draft Statutes of the Arbitral Tribunal for Foreign Investment.[11] During the 1950s and 1960s, these and other projects for international investment protection were discussed by the International Chamber of Commerce, the International Law Association, the International Bar Association, L'Institut de Droit International, the Swiss Bankers Association, L'Institut International D'Etudes Bancaires, the European League for Economic Cooperation, the American Bar Association, the Council of European Industrial Federations, the American Law Institute, and the International Conference of Manufacturers.[12]

But the Abs–Shawcross draft—that is, the revised version of the 'Magna Carta'—stood out among the efforts of the norm entrepreneurs, and not because of its balanced approach. According to many scholars, it lacked realism and was over-protective. It was considered too friendly to investors and incapable of gathering support from the Global South.[13] The US was also hesitant, as the level of protection could violate its own domestic laws.[14] For the American Bar Association, however, the Abs–Shawcross draft was a relative success thanks to 'sponsorship by a private association of business and banking interests both [in the US] and abroad'.[15] Schwarzenberger observed that it was 'the most determined effort made by banking and oil interests in Western countries'.[16] The project was welcomed by the Rockefeller family[17] and the Bilderberg Group, to which Abs had

[10] Arthur S. Miller, 'Protection of Private Foreign Investment by Multilateral Convention' (1959) 53 American Journal of International Law 371–8, 372–3; International Chamber of Commerce, '1949 International Code of Fair Treatment for Foreign Investments' in UNCTAD, *International Investment Instruments: A Compendium*, vol. 3 (United Nations 1996) 273–8.

[11] International Law Association, 'Draft Statutes of the Arbitral Tribunal for Foreign Investment' in UNCTAD, *International Investment Instruments: A Compendium*, vol. 3 (United Nations 1996) 259–72.

[12] See, e.g., George W. Haight, 'Activities of the International Chamber of Commerce and other Business Groups' (1960) 54 Proceedings of the American Society of International Law at its Annual Meeting 200–5.

[13] Stanley D. Metzger, 'Multilateral Conventions for the Protection of Private Foreign Investment' (1960) 9 Journal of Public Law 133–46, 43–4; A. A. Fatouros, 'An International Code to Protect Private Investment-Proposals and Perspectives' (1961) 14 University of Toronto Law Journal 77–102, 92–9; Georg Schwarzenberger, *Foreign Investments and International Law* (Stevens & Sons 1969) 111, 134.

[14] See Loftus Becker, 'Just Compensation in Expropriation Cases: Decline and Partial Recovery' Speech before the American Society of International Law, 1958, in *Society to Advance the Protection of Foreign Investment*, Publication No. 3 (1960) 68–80, 76; American Bar Association, *The Protection of Private Property Invested Abroad. A Report by the Committee on International Trade and Investment. Section of International and Comparative Law* (1963) 82.

[15] American Bar Association (n. 14) 21.

[16] Georg Schwarzenberger, 'Decolonisation and the Protection of Foreign Investments' (1967) 20 Current Legal Problems 213–31, 221.

[17] Nelson A. Rockefeller, 'Why Not a Wider Consensus among Nations?' in James Daniel (ed.), *Private Investment: The Key to International Industrial Development: A Report of the San Francisco Conference, October 14–18, 1957* (McGraw Hill 1958) 78–80, 79. I have found no explicit evidence that David Rockefeller approved of Abs's initiative; however, the two were members of the Bilderberg Group, participated in similar forums, and David Rockefeller highlighted that host countries must adopt 'enlightened policies in order to make [foreign] investments possible and productive'. David Rockefeller,

been admitted right after he presented his Magna Carta in 1957.[18] Crucially, the initiative was coordinated by two organizations Abs created purely to promote and protect foreign investment: the Society to Advance the Protection of Foreign Investments (hereinafter the Cologne Society) and the International Association for the Promotion and Protection of Private Foreign Investments (hereinafter the Geneva Association).

Created in 1956 in Cologne, the Cologne Society included influential German business leaders and aimed to advance the protection of foreign investment as a means to promote free enterprise and world development. To mark the society's creation, Abs invited his friend Ludwig Erhard, then German minister of economics, to deliver an inaugural lecture. Erhard announced that the 'violation of private property [was] sneaking like poison in the Western world'.[19] The demands of the welfare state meant higher taxes and increasing chances of expropriation, which were 'dangerous for private property'.[20] In making these remarks, Erhard acknowledged Abs's pioneering work. Both men also highlighted the principal reasons for protecting foreign capital. They said that German capital could help other countries develop, as US capital had done for Germany through the Marshall Plan, but that German investors should only invest where property was sufficiently protected.

A year later, at the first International Industrial Development Conference, Abs presented his Magna Carta before hundreds of business leaders from non-Communist countries, including Eugene Black, president of the World Bank.[21] He declared that foreign investment could contribute to international development, benefiting the less developed regions, but that investors are 'legally and psychologically favourable to the security of their investments'. He then referred the audience to his proposal for a Magna Carta, which he introduced as 'an effective system of international protection of foreign rights'. He concluded by asking for the support of all like-minded investors.[22]

'The Aspirations of Mankind in a Troubled World' Address at the International Industrial Conference, San Francisco, 17 September 1965, 7.

[18] This small group of business and political leaders from Europe and the United States aims to promote free market and Western interests. Abs was not a member and did not participate in the meetings of the Bilderberg Group until the 1958 Buxton Conference. See J. H. Retinger, 'The Bilderberg Group' (1956), available at https://info.publicintelligence.net/bilderberg/BilderbergGroupRetinger.pdf (last visited 3 July 2020) 13–18; Bilderberg Meetings, 'Buxton Conference' 13–15 September 1958, available at https://info.publicintelligence.net/bilderberg/BilderbergConferenceReport1958.pdf (last visited 3 July 2020) 23.

[19] *Die Zeit*, 'Vermögensschutz' (5 April 1956) 9.

[20] Ibid.

[21] Edgar R. Baker, 'Preface' in James Daniel (ed.), *Private Investment: The Key to International Industrial Development: A Report of the San Francisco Conference, October 14-18, 1957* (McGraw Hill 1958) v.

[22] Hermann J. Abs, 'The Safety of Capital' in ibid., 69–77, 76–7.

Many bankers, lawyers, and business leaders were interested in the initiative.[23] In the same year, the Institut International D'Etudes Bancaires published Abs's proposal.[24] The president of the Institut, Louis Camu, wrote that '[e]conomic development is closely linked to honouring agreements'.[25] Because insecurity of capital was a primary obstacle for foreign investment, Camu welcomed initiatives such as the International Chamber of Commerce's 1949 Code on Fair Treatment for Foreign Investments and Abs's Magna Carta. In his view, Abs was appealing to bankers as the new world leaders, 'transferring to the economic plane the ethical principles underlying the Declaration of the Rights of Man'.[26]

In the wake of this interest, in 1958 Abs and influential business leaders and lawyers created the Geneva Association, which supplanted the Cologne Society on the international scene. This organization included representatives of 'banking, oil and other forms of primary production'[27] committed to 'increas[ing] the flow of private foreign investments in particular by means of the establishment of a satisfactory climate of security for such investments'.[28] In 1966, the president of the Geneva Association was Eberhard Reinhardt. He was chief general manager of Credit Suisse Bank, a former Swiss secretary of finance, and vice-president of the Swiss Bankers Association. The Directing Committee gathered the executives of the most prominent (largely Western) international banks, corporations, and law firms of the time, including Credit Suisse, Deutsche Bank, United States Steel, Banca Comerciale Italiana, Rio Tinto, Sullivan & Cromwell LLP, Banco Español de Crédito (Banesto), Standard Oil of New Jersey, Bank of Tokyo, Amsterdam-Rotterdam Bank (AMRO), Compagnie Française des Pétroles (Total), Royal Bank of Canada, Creditanstalt-Bankverein, Bank of New South Wales, British-American Tobacco, Banque de Paris et des Pays-Bas (Paribas), Royal Dutch Shell, Banque de Bruxelles, Davis Polk & Wardwell LLP, Privatbanken i København (Scandinavian Banking Partners), Nestlé, and Stockholms Enskilda Bank (SEB).[29]

Membership of the Geneva Association also included Hartley Shawcross, general counsel of Royal Dutch Shell, a member of the Executive Council of the International Law Association, and the former British prosecutor at the Nuremberg trials. Abs and Shawcross were old friends. Their relationship had started during the inter-war period and continued during and after World War II. Shawcross had 'many friendly conversations with Dr. Abs, who was under house arrest for a time in 1945', suspected of collaborating with the Nazi regime.[30] Under

[23] Fatouros (n. 13) 86.

[24] Hermann J. Abs, *Proposals for Improving the Protection of Private Foreign Investments* (Institut International D'Etudes Bancaires 1958) 26.

[25] Louis Camu, 'Preface' in ibid., 14. Camu was also a member of the Bilderberg Group.

[26] Ibid.

[27] Schwarzenberger (n. 13) 109.

[28] International Association for the Promotion and Protection of Private Foreign Investments, 'A.P.P.I.' (1966) 3.

[29] Ibid., 6–7.

[30] Manning (n. 9) 72.

the auspices of the Geneva Association, Shawcross and Abs worked together on the Abs–Shawcross draft, combining their model conventions and addressing some of the criticisms directed against Abs's Magna Carta. Shawcross explains in his memoirs that the Abs–Shawcross draft was produced jointly by Abs's team of bankers and businessmen and his team of international lawyers.[31] The group consisted of German, British, Swiss, and Dutch nationals,[32] and included Elihu Lauterpacht (son of Hersch Lauterpacht) who played a major role in preparing the draft—particularly the dispute settlement clause.[33]

Like Abs, Shawcross presented the proposal as a universal project that would benefit the whole world, especially the Global South.[34] This developmentalist leitmotiv concealed Abs's and Shawcross's own particular interests in the project. For Abs, these included the encouragement and protection of German foreign investments and the profitability of the banking industry. International flows of portfolio investment had dried up after the 1920s, and most movements of international capital between 1930 and 1950 consisted of foreign direct investment.[35] For Shawcross, the timing was ideal because he was then general counsel of an MNC dedicated to natural resources during a time of decolonization and Communist expansion.[36]

There is evidence that the Geneva Association carried out relevant activities until the 1970s. Germany submitted the Abs–Shawcross draft for the consideration of the Organisation for European Economic Cooperation—the predecessor of the Organisation for Economic Cooperation and Development (OECD), while Switzerland supported the initiative and proposed amendments. The Geneva Association had close connections in these countries: Abs was a personal friend of Erhard and an advisor to German President Konrad Adenauer, and the group was closely related to the Swiss government through Reinhardt. An internal report of 1965 further indicates that the Geneva Association contributed to the development and clarification of the ICSID Convention and promoted the Abs–Shawcross draft before the OECD.[37] The negotiation around this text led to the 1967 OECD

[31] Hartley Shawcross, *Life Sentence: The Memoirs of Hartley Shawcross* (Constable 1995) 307–8. Also, Fatouros (n. 13) 87–8.

[32] Society to Advance the Protection of Foreign Investments, 'Introduction' in *Society to Advance the Protection of Foreign Investment*, Publication No. 3 (1960) 5–6, 5.

[33] Yuliya Chernykh, 'The Gust of Wind: The Unknown Role of Sir Elihu Lauterpacht in the Drafting of the Abs-Shawcross Draft Convention' in Stephan W. Schill, Christian J. Tams, and Rainer Hofmann (eds.), *International Investment Law and History* (Edward Elgar Publishing 2018) 241–85, 242.

[34] Hartley Shawcross, 'The Promotion of International Investment' Speech before the Society to Advance the Protection of Foreign Investments, Cologne 1959, in *Society to Advance the Protection of Foreign Investment*, Publication No. 3 (1960) 46–60, 50–1.

[35] See George W. Ball, 'The Role of Lawyers in the International Investment Field' (1959–1960) 11 Virginia Law Weekly 1–9, 2.

[36] Schwarzenberger (n. 13) 161.

[37] International Association for the Promotion and Protection of Private Foreign Investments, 'Note: Reunion de l'APPI à Zurich,' Berne 15 November 1965 (Swiss Diplomatic Documents, dodis.ch/31990).

Draft Convention on the Protection of Foreign Property (hereinafter the 1967 OECD Draft).[38]

Abs and Shawcross also had influential friends at the World Bank. Abs was close to Black, the bank's president and himself a former banker at the Chase National Bank. In 1959 Black invited Abs—'in his personal capacity'—and two other senior bankers to participate in a key mission to India and Pakistan.[39] Internally, the three bankers were known as 'the Three Wise Men'.[40] In its review of Black's presidency, the World Bank refers to him as somebody well respected by the 'financial community and its leaders, the Rockefellers, Hermann Abs of Germany, and others'.[41] Shawcross also had relevant information about the plans for the ICSID Convention; one of his assistants, John Blair, was involved in formulating the 1961 draft, alongside Broches, the bank's general counsel. The elaboration of this draft, moreover, was sponsored by the American Bar Association—which had lobbied the Vice-President of the World Bank in the summer of 1960—and included the participation of other norm entrepreneurs, notably G. W. Haight, who also worked for Royal Dutch Shell and the International Chamber of Commerce.[42] The connection between the Abs–Shawcross draft, the OECD negotiations, and the ICSID Convention is highlighted by Schwarzenberger, who observed at the time that the World Bank 'took over' the topic after the resistance faced by the Abs–Shawcross draft at the OECD.[43]

The Geneva Association was involved in other activities to promote and protect foreign investment. It stimulated external relations with other 'enlightened business' organizations, such as the International Bar Association, the International Law Association, the International Chamber of Commerce, the Business and Industry Advisory Committee at the OECD, and the Progress Alliance (Organization of American States). Shawcross, for instance, participated in the 1960 Conference that the International Chamber of Commerce organized in Karachi to discuss its 1949 Code and the prospects of international investment protection. This conference recommended a review of the 1949 Code,[44] and

[38] Schwarzenberger (n. 13) 153. The OECD members never turned this text into an international treaty, although the negotiation process could count on some support in the early years, including that of the Council of Europe. See Council of Europe, 'Opinion on the OECD Draft Convention on the Protection of Foreign Property' (1964) 3 International Legal Materials 133–50.

[39] Walt Whitman Rostow, *Concept and Controversy: Sixty Years of Taking Ideas to Market* (University of Texas Press 2010) 241; Hermann J. Abs, Oliver Franks, and Allan Sproul, 'Bankers' Mission to India and Pakistan February-March, 1960: A Letter to Eugene R. Black, President, International Bank for Reconstruction and Development' (World Bank 1960).

[40] World Bank, *World Bank Group Archivists' Chronology 1944-2013* (World Bank 2014) 90–3.

[41] Jochen Kraske, *Bankers with a Mission: The Presidents of the World Bank, 1946-91* (World Bank 1996) 112.

[42] Clifford J. Hynning, 'The World Banks' Plan for the Settlement of International Investment Disputes' (1965) 51 American Bar Association Journal 558–63, 559; Taylor St John, *The Rise of Investor-State Arbitration: Politics, Law, and Unintended Consequences* (OUP 2018) 132.

[43] Schwarzenberger (n. 13) 138.

[44] Edwin I. Nwogugu, *The Legal Problems of Foreign Investment in Developing Countries* (Manchester University Press 1965) 144.

later the International Chamber of Commerce supported the negotiations of the Draft Convention on the Protection of Foreign Property at the OECD and of the ICSID Convention at the World Bank.[45] Meanwhile, Abs and other members of the Geneva association, such as Vice-Chairman of the Stockholms Enskilda Bank Markus Wallenberg, continued arguing for international investment protection, among others, at the next editions of the International Industrial Conference (the term development was dropped from the title), which were held in San Francisco every four years under the auspices of the US National Industrial Conference Board and the Stanford Research Institute.[46]

Further, Reinhardt's correspondence with members of the Swiss government confirm the role of the association in promoting investment treaties and resolving specific disputes.[47] Internal reports from 1972 and 1973 indicate that the Geneva Association monitored expropriations and nationalizations in the Global South, where it had employed reporters since 1961.[48] It also proposed the creation of an international risk insurance agency, sought to obtain observing status at UNCTAD, and organized annual meetings with influential speakers.[49] In 1972, for instance, the keynote was delivered by the president of the International Finance Corporation (World Bank Group).[50]

Like Erhard, the norm entrepreneurs for international investment protection favoured minimal state intervention in the economy. Yet they were not neoliberals, and it is unclear whether neoliberals influenced the norm entrepreneurs, or vice-versa. Most likely the influence was mutual. Slobodian notes that some neoliberals had 'adopted their global perspective from the ICC', which was their employer through the 1920s and early 1930s.[51] Indeed, the International Chamber of Commerce had been working on foreign investor rights as a special type of rights since the 1920s, and eminent neoliberals such as Röpke and Hayek continued discussing the topic for

[45] International Chamber of Commerce, 'Statements and resolutions of the ICC, 1963-1965. 20th Congress' (1965) 21–3, 96–7.

[46] Robert L. Baker (ed.), *Business Leadership in a Changing World; A Report of the International Industrial Conference in San Francisco, September 11–15, 1961* (McGraw Hill 1962) 154–61, 137–45.

[47] Eberhard Reinhardt, Letter to Prof. Dr F. Wahlen, Swiss Federal Council, Political Department, 23 January 1964 (Swiss Diplomatic Documents, dodis.ch/31989); F. Wahlen, Answer to Eberhard Reinhardt's letter dated 23 January, 28 January 1964 (Swiss Diplomatic Documents, dodis.ch/31413); Willy Spühler, Letter to Eberhard Reinhardt, 16 August 1967 (Swiss Diplomatic Documents, dodis.ch// 32862).

[48] International Association for the Promotion and Protection of Private Foreign Investments, 'Fourth half-yearly report on events affecting private foreign investment in some capital-receiving countries,' 35/72, August 1972; International Association for the Promotion and Protection of Private Foreign Investments, 'Fifth Biannual report on events affecting private foreign investment in some capital-receiving countries', 13/73, May 1973.

[49] International Association for the Promotion and Protection of Private Foreign Investments (n. 37).

[50] See William S. Gaud, 'Private Foreign Investment in the '70s' (1972) Annual Meeting of the Association Internationale pour la Promotion et la Protection des Investissements Privés en Territoires Étrangers, Munich, 31 October 1972 [Gaud William S.—Articles and Speeches (1969–1973)—Volume 02] [1651742] World Bank Group Archives, Washington, DC, United States, 83.

[51] Slobodian (n. 6) 128. When I refer to neoliberals, I include both neoliberals and ordoliberals.

decades.[52] It is unlikely that the norm entrepreneurs were unaware of this work, as the two groups had a special interest in how international law could contribute to reducing state intervention in the economy. However, there is no reference to neoliberals in the documents of the Cologne Society, the Geneva Association, or the other 'enlightened business' organizations that I reviewed for this book.

A difference between the intellectual work of neoliberals and the activities of the norm entrepreneurs is that the latter insisted on their practical approach to real problems demanding concrete solutions. Neoliberals frequently talk in terms of individual freedoms—such as freedom of movement, trade, and employment—whereas the norm entrepreneurs, as we will see next, were against state economic intervention but did not gloss over the fact that foreign investment was also a way of organizing the world economy. So while Hayek affirmed that 'liberty is not merely one particular value [. . .] it is the source and condition of most moral values', business leaders such as John D. Rockefeller recognized that the future was in the hands of corporations: 'Individualism is gone, never to return.'[53] Similarly, the norm entrepreneurs approached the law in practical terms. Abs made this explicit on several occasions. Discussing the return of seized German assets in 1955, he said that the protection of private property was not solely a legal or moral question but 'rather the expression of a firm belief based on experience that entrepreneurship and private initiative are the driving and fundamental elements of economic progress'.[54] Likewise, Luce described Abs's initiative as based on 'a practical banker's concern'—a banker who still speaks 'in terms of a Magna Carta'.[55]

The rest of the norm entrepreneurs followed this practical approach. The International Chamber of Commerce and the Geneva Association prepared ambitious drafts for multilateral conventions, but talked in technical terms and were ready to accept realistic solutions such as bilateral treaties.[56]

52 Ibid., 185, 285. The relationship between international investment law and neoliberal ideas is discussed in Ntina Tzouvala, 'The Ordo-Liberal Origins of Modern International Investment Law: Constructing Competition on a Global Scale' in John D. Haskell and Akbar Rasulov (eds.), *European Yearbook of International Economic Law. Special Issue: New Voices and New Perspectives in International Economic Law* (Springer 2019) 37–54; David Schneiderman, 'Constitutional Property Rights and Elision of the Transnational: Foucauldian Misgivings' (2015) 24 Social & Legal Studies 65–87.

53 Friedrich A. Hayek, *The Constitution of Liberty* (University of Chicago Press 1978) 6; Rockefeller quoted in Alan Trachtenberg, *The Incorporation of America: Culture and Society in the Gilded Age* (Hill and Wang 1982) 86.

54 Abs (n. 5) 9.

55 Luce (n. 2) 39.

56 United States Council of the International Chamber of Commerce, 'Intelligent International Investment' A Report of the Committee on Business Participation in Foreign Economic Development, April 1949, 9; James Greene, *The Search for Common Ground; A Survey of Efforts to Develop Codes of Behavior in International Investment.* A special report to the US Committee, Pacific Basin Council (The Conference Board 1971) 5. Also, Hermann J. Abs, 'Die Konjunktur bleibt ruhig' (1959) 32 Vortragsreihe des Deutschen Industrieinstituts 1–4, 3–4; *Die Zeit*, 'Eigentum ist auch bei uns nicht sicher' (13 July 1979) 18. In this 1979 interview, Abs highlighted the success of the bilateral approach to investment treaties despite the lack of multilateral support for his Magna Carta.

B. A world of law and prosperity

The members of this norm-entrepreneurial coalition were involved in a world-making project for the expansion of free enterprise at a global scale. For them, foreign investment was key for this objective. Shawcross observed that the promotion of foreign investment was the task of those who 'believe that the best hope for the future lies in the steady increase of international trade and commerce'.[57] Bankers and lawyers, Rhyne affirmed, 'should pool their resources to develop a mechanism to provide the universal security for private export capital which is requisite to a healthy system of world investment'.[58] The US branch of the International Chamber of Commerce was critical of US President Harry Truman's Four Point development project (1949), arguing that a programme based on foreign private investment required avoiding 'undue government supervision of private business'.[59] It was concerned that anti-trust laws, technology transfer requirements, and development aid would impose such interference, reducing foreign investment flows. Instead, the US should support

> a world experiment in which the American experiment can continue to exist, and that the core of this experiment is the achievement of the maximum freedom for the individual and that maximum freedom has a material basis.[60]

The norm entrepreneurs thought there was a close relationship between foreign investor rights and a world economy of free enterprise. They demanded universal rules appropriate for the new world economy, but conceded that the prospect of this economy depended on creating legal institutions capable of encouraging foreign investment. In introducing Abs's Magna Carta, the Cologne Society stated that 'the interlacing of economic interests builds up confidence among the peoples and perpetuates cooperation'.[61] Equally, Shawcross claimed that foreign investment could lead towards a 'real international society [...] based on our ideas [...] of democracy and individual liberty'.[62] The problem of development aid, Abs added, was not only that it was too little. The issue was that these flows of capital had neither the transformative power nor the capacity to 'secure western liberal philosophy'.[63]

[57] Shawcross (n. 34) 60.
[58] Charles S. Rhyne, 'World Law to Protect World Investment' Speech before the American Bankers Association, New York 1958, in *Society to Advance the Protection of Foreign Investment*, Publication No. 3 (1960) 61–7, 64.
[59] United States Council of the International Chamber of Commerce (n. 56) 5.
[60] Ibid., 3.
[61] Society to Advance the Protection of Foreign Investments, 'International Convention for the Mutual Protection of Private Property Rights in Foreign Countries: draft' (1957) 2.
[62] Shawcross (n. 34) 46.
[63] Abs (n. 22) 70.

A central objective of the norm entrepreneurs was convincing governments and international organizations that foreign investment had this transformative power. Abs claimed that firms invest 'as a result of a common philosophy of assisting other countries'[64] on a 'humanitarian ground'.[65] Similarly, the 1957–1959 Biennial Report of the International Chamber of Commerce notes that the expansion of foreign investment was a priority, 'especially in those less developed countries which have a crying need for capital to bring their resources into full play'.[66] Capital flows would play a 'pre-dominant role in developing the economies and increasing the standards of living everywhere'.[67] A 1958 International Bar Association resolution also embraces the contribution of foreign investment to economic development, contending that the best way to attract and preserve foreign investment was 'by respect of the rule of law'.[68]

These efforts were not in vain. In the 1963 Annual Address of the World Bank President, George Woods foregrounded the role of private enterprise and foreign investment. He said that development aid was 'never going to be more than marginal to the requirements of developing countries'.[69] The World Bank therefore had an obligation to 'unlock' foreign investment, and this required establishing a conciliation and arbitration centre.[70]

But for the norm entrepreneurs, unlocking foreign investment in practice required two things: in addition to the rule of law and arbitration, it was necessary to facilitate profitability. The promotion of foreign private investment depended on the prospect of economic returns. As Rhyne explained:

> The plan is admittedly not only designed to serve those peoples of other lands where present poverty and discontent creates one of the causes of war but our own self-interest, our own desire to increase world investment and trade, and to make a profit on that trade and investment.[71]

[64] Ibid., 76.
[65] Abs (n. 24) 24.
[66] International Chamber of Commerce, 'Biennial Report 1957/1958' in *Society to Advance the Protection of Foreign Investment*, Publication No. 3 (1960) 44–5, 44.
[67] Otto Wolff von Amerongen, 'Need for World Investment Charter' Speech before the International Chamber of Commerce, 1959 Washington Congress, in *Society to Advance the Protection of Foreign Investment*, Publication No. 3 (1960) 41–3, 43.
[68] International Bar Association, 'Cologne Conference Resolution 1958' in *Society to Advance the Protection of Foreign Investment*, Publication No. 3 (1960) 35, 35.
[69] George D. Woods, 'Annual Address by the President of the Bank and its affiliates,' 30 September 1963, 13. Three years earlier, Eugene Black had noted that 'No substitute can take the place of private enterprise and private capital [. . .] The World Bank will do on its power to cooperate with private investors': Eugene R. Black, 'The World Bank, An Appraisal of its Activities' (1959–1960) 11 Virginia Law Weekly 16–20, 20.
[70] Woods (n. 69) 14.
[71] Rhyne (n. 58) 62.

Luce and Shawcross asked 'enlightened business' for more than a profit-seeking attitude, but admitted that foreign investment would not go to less developed regions unless there was 'a reasonable prospect of economic return'.[72] The 1957–1959 Biennial Report of the International Chamber of Commerce concurred, adding that political risk was not the only problem: profitability is often lower in the less developed parts of the world, and there are not enough economic incentives, such as tax benefits, to make up for this disadvantage.[73] 'Ministers should see it that government departments are imbued with the spirit of cooperation and encouragement', it stated.[74]

Facilitating profitability required establishing game rules that guaranteed the stability of the regulatory givings. In 1958, some of the most prominent US international lawyers prepared a report related to this subject for the American Branch of the International Law Association (hereinafter the Hyde et al. report): James N. Hyde (chairperson), Richard R. Baxter, Dudley Bonsal, Kenneth S. Carlston, Milo G. Coerper, Martin Domke, Richard N. Gardner, G. W. Haight, Philip C. Jessup, Cecil G. Olmstead, George W. Ray, Edward D. Re, Stephen M. Schwebel, Otto C. Sommerich, and John R. Stevenson. They wrote of a need to create 'the bases for fair and continuing relationship between existing, as well as future, foreign private investment and the state which explicitly or implicitly invites its use, in combination with its own assets'.[75] These bases, essentially, were *pacta sunt servanda* and international law. The Cologne Society made the same point by referring to a 1959 speech by US President Dwight Eisenhower focused on the necessity of contracts for 'world progress', and the need for a 'universal' body of law 'adapted to the changing needs of today's world'. Eisenhower had observed that '[t]he sanctity of contracts has been the vehicle for more explosive and extensive economic change in the world than any other factor'.[76]

But translating this legal thinking into concrete principles and rules was not easy, and required creativity and careful drafting. Some of the norm entrepreneurs initially proposed quite drastic solutions. The Cologne Society introduced Abs's Magna Carta by noting not only that national treatment is ineffective for promoting foreign investment, but also that this objective 'makes it necessary to interfere in the national legal and economic orders of the nations concerned'.[77] The advantage would be that '[p]roperty protection would be uniform in many

[72] Shawcross (n. 34) 51; Luce (n. 2) 39.

[73] International Chamber of Commerce (n. 66) 44–5.

[74] International Chamber of Commerce, 'Attracting Foreign Investment' Statement adopted by the Executive Committee of the ICC, February 1959, 4.

[75] American Branch of the International Law Association, 'Response to the Questionnaire of the International Committee on Nationalization, 1958' in *Society to Advance the Protection of Foreign Investment*, Publication No. 3 (1960) 81–96, 82.

[76] Dwight D. Eisenhower, 'A World of Growth, a World of Law' Speech at Delhi University 1959, in *Society to Advance the Protection of Foreign Investment*, Publication No. 3 (1960) 31–2, 31.

[77] Society to Advance the Protection of Foreign Investments (n. 61) 27.

countries, so that a clear and legally equal situation for investments over extensive economic areas would be created'.[78] Not everybody agreed. Shawcross himself criticized Abs's Magna Carta and the 1949 International Chamber of Commerce code as demanding 'too much protection for the private investor'.[79] Still, he claimed that this had been addressed by the Abs–Shawcross draft. The position of the norm entrepreneurs was that this draft complied with 'the rules of international law' and did 'not violate the sovereignty of the governments'.[80]

For many states, including those in both the Global South and North, this was not obvious. A legal advisor of the US Department of State, Loftus Becker, expressed some concerns about the Abs–Shawcross draft. He said that Abs's Magna Carta had incorporated 'strong rules for property protection'[81] which most countries would find difficult to accept. While Becker conceded that the Abs–Shawcross draft was 'less ambitious', as it had removed pre-establishment obligations, it still went 'further than the United States would be prepared to go at this time'.[82] In his view, the proposed text could raise constitutional problems in his country and other Western countries that protect private property. Becker also thought improbable that Global South countries would support the text, as they would want to privilege their own laws and courts.[83]

C. Restoring the past through other means

The norm entrepreneurs were aware of the many obstacles their project faced. They competed with other worldviews, namely those of decolonization, Communism, and state economic intervention. For Abs, international investment protection was a means to combat 'excessive governmental influence' in the Global South and the Global North, ending the legal and economic legacy of World War II.[84] The norm entrepreneurs also knew that their project for world peace and prosperity implied considerable continuity—specifically, the continuation of imperial divisions of labour and economic categories through other means and actors. The world they proposed was to be organized by MNCs, not as agents of the former metropolises, but as the new masters themselves.

Decolonization and Communism were serious obstacles. Decolonial thinking portrayed foreign investment as a form of indirect control or 'neo-imperialism'.[85]

78 Ibid.
79 Shawcross (n. 34) 54, 54–5.
80 Society to Advance the Protection of Foreign Investments, Convention on Investments Abroad with Comments, Speeches and New Literature, Publication No. 3 (Bergisch Gladbach, J. Heider 1960) 5.
81 Becker (n. 14) 75.
82 Ibid.
83 Ibid., 78–9.
84 Abs (n. 24) 17, 17–18.
85 Schwarzenberger (n. 16) 214.

The Global South distrusted the former colonial powers, including 'the very capital that is so necessary for their economic development'.[86] At the same time, Global North countries were concerned about how they intervened in the South because they did not want those countries to react by joining ranks of the Communist bloc.[87] The US defended the importance and safety of foreign investment, but it also had other interests that were equal or higher priorities.[88]

This situation contributed to the erosion of customary international rules on the protection of private property.[89] In 1962, a US Court of Appeals referred to international law as a 'hazy concept' of 'nebulous nature'.[90] The norm entrepreneurs were particularly anxious about the increasing acceptance of the practice of partial compensation,[91] and the claim that decolonization authorized states to take measures that otherwise would have required compensation.[92] This claim built on arguments made before World War II by Fischer Williams, Hersch Lauterpacht, and Lassa Oppenheim in the context of the socialist revolutions in Europe.[93] These earlier scholars had claimed that non-discriminatory partial compensation was legal under international law. A more restrictive position would impose unacceptable limits on states' right to change their social and economic organization. In 1969, Abs noted with concern that two international lawyers, Hans Dölle and Konrad Zweigert, had applied the same argument for the case of decolonization. They wrote that 'economic de-colonisation is similar to socialist reforms in Western countries; they are legitimate programmes within the international laws on expropriation, especially when the implementation of these programmes is non-discriminatory'.[94]

This sort of interpretation posed a serious threat for the norm entrepreneurs. Abs responded intrepidly: 'We will go on losing until we restore international law and order and, in particular, the sanctity of private property and private contracts.'[95] Becker and German businessman Otto Wolff von Amerongen agreed. Speaking on behalf of the US government and the International Chamber of Commerce, they viewed the goal as taking 'things back to normal' and 're-establishing confidence'.[96] The Cologne Society similarly declared that Abs's Magna Carta was

[86] American Bar Association (n. 14) 6.

[87] Abs (n. 22) 73–4.

[88] Douglas Dillon, 'The Role of Private Capital in US Foreign Policy' (1959–1960) 11 Virginia Law Weekly 10–15, 14.

[89] American Bar Association (n. 14) 7–8.

[90] *Banco Nacional de Cuba v. Sabbatino*, 307 F 2d 845 (2d Cir. 1962), paras. 859, 860.

[91] Society to Advance the Protection of Foreign Investments (n. 61) 6–9.

[92] Ibid., 13; Becker (n. 14) 69–70.

[93] John Fischer Williams, 'International Law and the Property of Aliens,' (1928) 9 British Yearbook of International Law 1–30; Lassa Oppenheim and Hersch Lauterpacht, *International Law: A Treatise* (Longmans 1948) 317–18.

[94] Abs (n. 5) 8. Also, American Bar Association (n. 14) 75, referring to the position of a Bremen Court in a dispute concerning the expropriation of Dutch property in Indonesia.

[95] Abs (n. 22) 76.

[96] Becker (n. 14) 69; Wolff von Amerongen (n. 67) 43. Wolff von Amerongen was also a member of the Bilderberg Group.

> designed to resuscitate, on a reciprocal basis, the principle of inviolability of private property and other private rights, thus affording a material contribution to the reestablishment of international confidence in business relations, which will benefit the recipients and investors of capital alike.[97]

The economic corollary of taking 'things back to normal' was, of course, the continuation of imperial economic relations through other means. The norm entrepreneurs asked the Global South to focus on the present, not the past,[98] but their message was ambiguous at best. Shawcross insisted that foreign investment would help to combat poverty, but the immediate goal for him was not 'universal industrialisation'; for some time, less developed countries would have to continue depending on their natural resources.[99] Similarly, Abs criticized newly independent countries for wanting to immediately enjoy the level of prosperity 'the West needed centuries of gradual progress to achieve'.[100] Their dependence on natural resources would not be a problem, the Hyde et al. report chipped in, because Global South countries have resources 'far beyond the foreseeable requirements of the states in which they are found'.[101] The chairperson of Anglo-Australian MNC Rio Tinto, Val Duncan, added that this state of affairs suited the increasing demand of natural resources in the Global North.[102]

Decolonization was not the only concern of the norm entrepreneurs. They were also anxious about the attitude of some Western governments during and after World War II. Wolff von Amerongen was troubled by a 'growing feeling of uncertainty' created by deficits and excessive nationalism.[103] Likewise, Shawcross held negative views about attempts to create a 'state industry', which he thought was destined to fail in the South as much as in the West.[104] The attitudes of Western countries, Abs held, were 'responsible to a small degree for the younger nations' conduct'.[105] The Cologne Society wrote:

[97] Society to Advance the Protection of Foreign Investment (n. 61) 5.

[98] Abs (n. 24) 19–20.

[99] Shawcross (n. 34) 46. Also, Rhyne (n. 58) 62. As opposed to the World Bank, the norm entrepreneurs of the 1950s and 1960s did not recommend industrializing the Global South as rapidly as possible, see Woods (n. 69) 9.

[100] Abs (n. 24) 18. David Rockefeller held similar views concerning Latin America and foreign investment, recommending these countries focus on the agriculture sector, to which foreign investors could make a useful contribution. David Rockefeller, 'What Private Enterprise Means to Latin America' (1966) 44 Foreign Affairs 403–16, 403, 408, 412.

[101] American Branch of the International Law Association (n. 75) 81.

[102] Val Duncan, 'The International Company and Overseas Investment' in The Institute of Economic Affairs, 'Overseas Investment or Economic Nationalism?' (1967) Occasional paper No. 15, 18–25, 20.

[103] Wolff von Amerongen (n. 67) 41.

[104] Shawcross (n. 34) 49; Hartley Shawcross, 'Introductory Address' in The Institute of Economic Affairs, 'Overseas Investment or Economic Nationalism?' (1967) Occasional paper No. 15 9, 9.

[105] Abs (n. 24) 21.

> Western industrial countries have often set the development countries a bad example. It is accordingly essential that these latter countries should also again without restriction guarantee the protection of private property, rights and interests.[106]

The report illustrated this claim by pointing at the Egyptian measures against British, French, and Israeli property after the 1956 nationalization of the Suez Canal, which were modelled 'word for word' on the regulations of the British World War II Trading with the Enemy Act.[107]

Moreover, in development aid the norm entrepreneurs saw the seeds of state economic intervention on a world scale. They took every opportunity to insist that public aid would not bring world prosperity. In addition to the problem of raising enough funds, they considered aid to be too political, creating the risk of donor-state intervention in foreign investors and recipient countries.[108] Rhyne observed that 'the usual stimulus for this type of aid is political advantage' and it 'is seldom creative as a result'.[109] Foreign investors, on the other hand, would follow different incentives; Shawcross claimed that 'industrial enterprises are usually at the greatest pains to avoid any kind of political involvement', and that there had been no problems in the US, Canada, or Australia.[110]

To address decolonization and state economic intervention, the norm entrepreneurs proposed a partnership between foreign investors and local business. Foreign investment had to be about partnering up, creating a 'feeling of partner' so locals can 'take pride in their accomplishments'. This would be 'best for them' and 'certainly best for us'.[111] Equally, Abs said, the exclusion of locals favoured Eastern propaganda that 'Western capitalism pursues a policy of exploitation'. Mutual trust required admitting 'local capital into genuine partnership' and countries 'should receive a proper share of the proceeds of developing the resources of the soil'.[112]

This sense of partnership, however, is nowhere to be found in the provisions of Abs's Magna Carta or the Abs–Shawcross draft. Discussing the *quid pro quo* of the draft, Shawcross recognized that it contained no explicit obligations for foreign investors: 'the convention seeks protection from Acts of states not of individuals'.[113] But in his interpretation the Abs–Shawcross draft was not a one-sided deal, for host countries would 'receive more private investment and with the capital, the

106 Society to Advance the Protection of Foreign Investment (n. 61) 4.
107 Ibid., 10.
108 Abs (n. 22) 70; Wolff von Amerongen (n. 67) 41–3; Rockefeller (n. 100) 403, 408; Hartley Shawcross, 'A Warmer Welcome from the Developing Countries' in The Institute of Economic Affairs, 'Overseas Investment or Economic Nationalism?' (1967) Occasional paper No. 15, 26–9, 26.
109 Rhyne (n. 58) 63.
110 Shawcross (n. 34) 48.
111 Rhyne (n. 58) 63. Also, Camu (n. 25) 13.
112 Abs (n. 24) 21–2, 24.
113 Shawcross (n. 34) 56.

benefits of the technical and commercial skills that go with them'.[114] Further, if governments wanted to protect themselves, they could use investment contracts or, in the future, insert 'some obviously reciprocal provisions' in investment treaties.[115]

D. Making international foreign investor rights

The project of the norm entrepreneurs was not about the clarity and enforcement of property rights and contracts per se. This was not the issue; after all, there were property and contract rights in revolutionary Mexico.[116] The struggle was about which particular imagination of property and contracts would shape world economic relations in the following decades. In the words of Abs, it was about 'restor[ing] confidence in connection with the protection of private investment abroad'.[117] Legally, this task was multiple and of diverse complexity. Protecting against direct expropriation, including restoring the full compensation standard, raised fewer challenges than creating an imaginary of property and contracts that could markedly reduce state economic intervention.

States' practice between the 1920s and 1950s may have suggested the legality of partial compensation. The Cologne Society, nonetheless, was right to point out that international treaties and tribunals had never validated this practice.[118] The full compensation standard—the prompt, adequate, and effective formula—was supported by the former colonial powers and the US. On the other hand, there was never consensus on how to handle state economic interventions. Chandler Anderson, a founding member of the American Society of International Law, noted that this was 'a fundamentally different question'.[119] An International Chamber of Commerce report reiterates the difficulty of this problem, highlighting that expropriation is only the extreme case. Hard cases involve 'the equitable treatment and positive encouragement in the normal course of day-to-day administration'.[120]

The issue was made more complicated by the post-World War II consensus in law and policy, which conceived of property and contracts in terms of legal realism and the social function of property. Countries could enforce strong protection one day but were not bound to follow that conception in the future. Abs explained: 'If this state changes its corresponding constitutional norms, the foreign investor has

[114] Ibid.

[115] Ibid., 56–7.

[116] See Willem Assies and Emilio Duhau, 'Land Tenure and Tenure Regimes in Mexico: An Overview' in Janine M. Ubink, André J. Hoekema, and Willem J. Assies (eds.), *Legalising Land Rights. Local Practices, State Responses and Tenure Security in Africa, Asia and Latin America* (Leiden University Press 2009) 355–86.

[117] Abs (n. 24) 17.

[118] Society to Advance the Protection of Foreign Investment (n. 61) 11–13.

[119] Chandler P. Anderson, 'Basis of the Law against Confiscating Foreign-Owned Property' (1927) 21 American Journal of International Law 525–33, 525.

[120] International Chamber of Commerce (n. 74) 6. Also, Council of Europe (n. 38) 136–7.

no influence.'[121] This is why the norm entrepreneurs agreed that international law was the appropriate mechanism to protect foreign investors from state economic intervention and nationalism.[122] They believed that the flaw of domestic law is that states can change it unilaterally, and that this creates uncertainty, is bad for business, and affects foreign investment flows to the Global South.

But the international law solution required not only restoring but also *transforming* the discipline. In this respect, Shawcross and Abs were optimistic about the possibility of 'the conventional progress of international law', particularly by creating an international court or arbitration system to resolve foreign investor disputes.[123] International arbitration was fundamental to the plan, as the standards in international investment treaties, such as due process and fairness, are inherently vague and ambiguous. An American Bar Association report remarked that international arbitration was 'extremely important to the final determination of the value of the operational provisions, since there is considerable room for interpretation and construction.'[124]

The specific interpretation of the rules and principles that the norm entrepreneurs hoped to establish can be found in their discussions of Abs's Magna Carta, the Abs–Shawcross draft, and the 1962 and 1967 OECD Drafts. The next subsections examine their views on the definition of property, the general standard of protection, indirect expropriation, the standard of compensation, state undertakings and reliance, the internationalization of contracts, derogation, and the dispute settlement mechanism.

1. Definition of investment and general standard of protection

Like most constitutions, neither Abs's Magna Carta nor the Abs–Shawcross draft define private property, instead they provide a general standard of protection. In Abs's Magna Carta, this standard was to 'accord full protection to the property, rights and interests of the nationals of each of the other High Contracting Parties'.[125] The Cologne Society explained that this standard followed the language of certain friendship, commerce and navigation treaties which state that '[p]roperty of nationals and companies of one Party shall enjoy the fullest protection and security within the territories of the other Party'.[126] For others, however, this standard was overly rigid. Shawcross, admitting that it went too far, replaced

121 Abs (n. 5) 10.

122 Abs (n. 22) 76; Hartley Shawcross, 'Problems of Foreign Investment,' 102 Recueil des Cours (1961) 339–63, 342; American Branch of the International Law Association (n. 75) 83–5; Marcus Wallenberg, 'Evaluation of Structures in International Finance' in Baker (n. 46) 137–45, 142.

123 Shawcross (n. 34) 53. Also, Shawcross (n. 122) 339; Abs (n. 22) 75–6.

124 American Bar Association (n. 14) 56. A similar point is made by Schwarzenberger (n. 13) 116, 137.

125 Society to Advance the Protection of Foreign Investment (n. 61) 32, 43.

126 Ibid., 17, 43–4.

it in the Abs–Shawcross draft with the formula 'fair and equitable [and] the most constant protection and security'.[127]

Elihu Lauterpacht, who had participated in the elaboration of the Abs–Shawcross draft, was later asked by the Organisation for European Economic Cooperation to prepare a report for its member countries. In relation to the general standard of protection, he wrote that 'fair and equitable treatment' conformed 'in effect to the "minimum standard" which forms part of customary international law', and that the phrase 'protection and security' reflected an obligation to 'exercise due diligence' to protect foreign-owned property.[128]

Both treaty drafts include a broad definition of foreign investor rights: 'property, rights and interests'.[129] The Cologne Society stated that this definition followed existing practice in international law and, 'despite some deviations in the various law systems, is presumably more or less unequivocal'.[130] A conference held in 1929 'for the purpose of codifying the law pertaining to non-nationals' rights in business' had used the same formula.[131] The Cologne Society also said that hybrid and intangible property rights, such as licences, 'play a great part in international economic life' and 'must accordingly be included in the Convention'.[132] This definition 'is not limited to the matter of protecting foreign property against expropriation, but quite generally seeks to give protection to the activities of private investors'.[133] The 1967 OECD Draft uses the same terminology.

Other proposals at the time followed a similar approach when defining foreign investor rights. The International Law Association used the language of 'acquired rights' and 'undertakings'.[134] The Harvard Draft Convention included 'rights and interests in property', and the Draft Restatement of the American Law Institute refers to 'any interest in property if that interest has reasonably ascertainable value'.[135] The Hyde et al. report similarly stipulates that international protection should cover 'alien interests, legal or equitable, in property and contract'.[136] As we can see, the norm entrepreneurs preferred a flexible definition of foreign investor rights as opposed to a standardized or *numerus clausus* approach.

[127] Shawcross (n. 34) 54–5; Hermann J. Abs and Hartley Shawcross, 'The Proposed Convention to Protect Private Foreign Investment: Introduction' (1960) 9 Journal of Public Law 115–24, 116.

[128] Elihu Lauterpacht, 'Organisation for European Economic Co-operation. Summary of Mr Lauterpacht's Explanations' in *Society to Advance the Protection of Foreign Investments*, Publication No. 3 (1960) 19–28, 20. Also, OECD, 'OECD Draft Convention on the Protection of Foreign Property' (1968) 2 The International Lawyer 331–53, 333; American Bar Association (n. 14) 97–8.

[129] Abs and Shawcross (n. 127) 117.

[130] Society to Advance the Protection of Foreign Investment (n. 61) 48.

[131] Ibid., 23.

[132] Ibid., 49.

[133] The same rationale inspired the wording of the 1949 International Code of Fair Treatment for Foreign Investments, International Chamber of Commerce. Ibid., 24.

[134] International Law Association, 'Washington Congress Resolution 1959' in *Society to Advance the Protection of Foreign Investments*, Publication No. 3 (1960) 34, 34.

[135] American Bar Association (n. 14) 111–12.

[136] American Branch of the International Law Association (n. 75) 82.

For others, however, that definition was far from 'unequivocal' and implied the creation of new rights. Becker observed that the Abs–Shawcross draft only addressed this problem partially, by reducing 'the large body of new property rights'.[137] His concerns were reiterated by Elihu Lauterpacht, who concluded that this definition also comprises contractual rights: 'The word property is used in its largest sense. It includes but it is not limited to investments.'[138]

2. Indirect expropriation

The issue of indirect expropriation—measures 'to deprive [investors] indirectly of their property'[139]—was also controversial. For the norm entrepreneurs, however, it was crucial. They accepted that Western constitutions recognize policy powers, as governmental authority to impose taxes, fines, and restrictions in the public interest. Yet they also held that these measures 'often amount to concealed confiscation. For this reason, such measures must not be abused.'[140] Abs's Magna Carta regulates not only 'deprivation of property' but also 'restrictions of the business activity of foreign investors'.[141] These are cases 'where the confiscatory character of the measures objected to is not immediately evident'.[142] The Abs–Shawcross draft also covers cases of indirect expropriation. According to Shawcross, it should be limited to the 'minimum security which the international investor may reasonably require'.[143]

Other international lawyers were likewise concerned about indirect expropriation. Rhyne discussed the problem of 'concealed confiscations',[144] and Becker acknowledged that new challenges required lawyers' attention, particularly 'creeping confiscation' and other 'equally invidious techniques [...] whereby everything is taken except for the bare title'.[145] The Hyde et al. report stated that 'the opportunities of the state to regulate or abuse the rights of foreigners are manifold'.[146]

In his analysis of the Abs–Shawcross draft, Elihu Lauterpacht explained that the expropriation provision covers both direct and indirect expropriation. He recognized the increasing gravity of the latter, describing such cases as attempts to reduce foreign investors' benefits or to increase states' control of projects through, for example, 'excessive and arbitrary taxation', 'compulsory lending to the state',

137 Becker (n. 14) 75.
138 Lauterpacht (n. 128) 19–21.
139 Abs and Shawcross (n. 127) 116.
140 Society to Advance the Protection of Foreign Investment (n. 61) 12.
141 Ibid., 50.
142 Ibid., 43.
143 Shawcross (n. 34) 55.
144 Rhyne (n. 58) 65.
145 Becker (n. 14) 80–1.
146 American Branch of the International Law Association (n. 75) 83.

or 'prohibition of dismissal of personnel'.[147] An American Bar Association report drew similar conclusions, pointing out that some authors had suggested that the expropriation provision might prohibit measures constituting 'something less' than a direct expropriation.[148] Schwarzenberger was particularly concerned about the reference to due process, which he characterized as '"secret weapon" in reserve'.[149] This possibility was rejected by the commentary to the 1967 OECD Draft, however, which distinguished between 'wrongful interference', protected under the fair and equitable standard, and interference amounting to indirect expropriation.[150]

The norm entrepreneurs agreed that these disputes are hard cases, and could not be resolved in the abstract. For Elihu Lauterpacht and the American Bar Association, courts and tribunals must conduct a case-by-cases analysis, drawing the line according to 'the facts of each particular case'.[151] But how exactly they intended this case-by-case analysis to operate in practice is not simple to determine. During the 1950s and 1960s, no international arbitrations dealt with indirect expropriation, and their publications remain quite general on this point.

On several occasions, however, the Cologne Society, the Geneva Association, and other norm entrepreneurs focused on the *CADE* dispute to illustrate the problem of indirect expropriation.[152] A Swiss and Belgian investment had exclusive control over two power companies, CADE and CHADE, in Argentina; the dispute arose in 1957 when the Argentine government cancelled the licence to operate the project, which had last been extended in 1936. The effects were significant. For the Cologne Society, this constituted a 'flagrant' example of 'expropriation-like deprivation'.[153]

Notably, its analysis of the dispute omitted relevant circumstances. In 1932, the Argentine authorities had opened an investigation into CADE to determine if the foreign investor had arbitrarily raised tariffs. The inquiry showed several irregularities, but CADE was favoured with a new licence after bribing several Argentine officials, including a former president. CADE was also accused of contributing to the 1930 military coup against Argentina's democratically elected President Hipólito Yrigoyen. Two decades later, the Argentine government conducted a full investigation into these events, the Rodríguez Conde report, which led to the licence cancellation.[154] None of these allegations or the content of the Rodríguez Conde report

[147] Lauterpacht (n. 128) 22, 26–7.
[148] American Bar Association (n. 14) 71, 71–2.
[149] Ibid., 119.
[150] OECD (n. 128) 338.
[151] Lauterpacht (n. 128) 27; American Bar Association (n. 14) 72.
[152] Society to Advance the Protection of Foreign Investment (n. 61) 10; Rhyne (n. 58) 64; Reinhardt (n. 47).
[153] Society to Advance the Protection of Foreign Investment (n. 61) 10.
[154] Jorge Del Rio, *Política argentina y monopolios eléctricos* (Cátedra Lisandro de la Torre 1957); Jorge Del Rio, *Electricidad y liberación nacional. El caso S.E.G.B.A.* (Peña Lillo 1960). The key facts—including the payments of bribes—have been confirmed by the well-known Argentine historian Félix Luna in *Alvear: Las luchas populares en la década del* 30 (Schapire 1975) 196–222.

was mentioned by Abs, Rhyne, or Reinhardt when discussing the *CADE* dispute or making representations in favour of the Swiss and Belgian investors before the Swiss government.[155]

3. Standard of compensation

The norm entrepreneurs argued for restoring the full compensation standard. Abs's Magna Carta and the Abs–Shawcross draft include a formula similar to the Hull standard: prompt, adequate, and effective compensation.[156] For Abs, there was a contradiction between the desire to attract foreign private investment and the arguments in favour of partial compensation.[157] Western countries strongly supported this position. As legal advisor of the US State Department, Becker insisted that partial compensation equalled unjust enrichment—'a compromise with principle'.[158] The Hyde et al. report added that there was no reason why 'the foreign investor should bear the burden of a State's experimentation', particularly if that foreigner was not going to enjoy the alleged benefits of such a transformation.[159] European states were less consistent: they defended the full compensation rule in international investment law while still advocating for partial compensation in the European context.[160]

4. Protecting contract rights and investors' reliance

The telling of the *CADE* story illustrates a narrative that the norm entrepreneurs frequently employed to justify international investment protection. This narrative portrays foreign investors as actors who invest in good faith, and whose expectations are later disappointed by governments unwilling to keep their promises. Abs and others relied on a reasoning similar to the obsolescing bargain and the hold-up problem, albeit decades before these models were introduced by the academic literature. Following his practical business approach, Abs accused states of creating a good investment climate or granting specific benefits, and later changing their minds due to political pressures. He was concerned about states' 'ambivalent' policy and their ability to disappoint foreign investors without repercussions or

155 Reinhardt (n. 47).

156 Society to Advance the Protection of Foreign Investment (n. 61) 35–6; Abs and Shawcross (n. 127) 116.

157 Abs (n. 24) 19; Abs (n. 5) 7-8. Also American Bar Association (n. 14) 18.

158 Becker (n. 14) 79.

159 American Branch of the International Law Association (n. 75) 86.

160 Norman S. Marsh, 'A Note on the European Convention for the Protection of Human Rights and Fundamental Freedoms, 1950, in Relation to the Protection of Property' in Joseph G. Starke (ed.), *The Protection and Encouragement of Private Foreign Investment* (Butterworths 1966) 137–40, 139.

penalties. This dynamic, Abs found, worsened when states were in economic difficulties.[161] The International Chamber of Commerce echoed these points, insisting on the value of incentives and encouraging states to give the 'information required for a correct estimate of economic conditions [...] as well as their legal, political and administrative systems'.[162]

Unlike bankers and business leaders, international lawyers did not discuss foreign investment relations using this business language, preferring to stick to legal terminology. They translated the risk of 'ambivalent' state behaviour into the language of contracts and *pacta sunt servanda*.[163] The report Hyde et al. prepared for the American Branch of the International Law Association declared that no state has an obligation to accept foreign investment into the country: 'Yet, when it does, certain obligations come into being.'[164]

The Abs–Shawcross draft opened up a space for such a transactional model by introducing a provision on state undertakings. Abs's Magna Carta stresses the relevance of principles such as *venire contra factum proprium*,[165] but only incorporates a reference to state contracts or assurances in the provision concerning expropriation.[166] The Abs–Shawcross draft takes a different approach, stating that each party 'shall ensure at all times the observance of any undertakings which it may have given in relation to investments'.[167] In this respect, Schwarzenberger noted, 'the observance of any undertakings is probably the arch of [this treaty model]'.[168]

If Abs was an early proponent of the obsolescing bargain model, Shawcross advanced a way of thinking that resembles influential work in contemporary international investment law. He was convinced that domestic law was inadequate to enforce the principle of *pacta sunt servanda* in foreign investment relations; more was needed 'to give any real security'.[169] In international treaty law, a main principle is that states 'should carry out their specific engagements'.[170] The challenge was how to create a new category of undertakings, governed by international law and equal to international treaty obligations, which countries could not modify unilaterally. This same concern has inspired the academic work of Paulsson and other influential arbitrators in the 2000s, in discussing how states can make 'meaningful' promises.[171]

[161] Abs (n. 24) 19–20. Also Wallenberg (n. 122) 142.
[162] International Chamber of Commerce (n. 10) 277 (Article 12). Also, United States Council of the International Chamber of Commerce (n. 56) 6; International Chamber of Commerce (n. 74) 4–5.
[163] Shawcross (n. 34) 55; Shawcross (n. 122) 351.
[164] American Branch of the International Law Association (n. 75) 82.
[165] Society to Advance the Protection of Foreign Investment (n. 61) 54.
[166] Ibid., 55.
[167] Abs and Shawcross (n. 127) 116.
[168] Schwarzenberger (n. 13) 160, 116.
[169] Shawcross (n. 34) 53.
[170] Ibid., 55.
[171] See Jan Paulsson, 'The Power of States to Make Meaningful Promises to Foreigners' (2010) 1 Journal of International Dispute Settlement 341–52; Michael W. Reisman, '"Case Specific Mandates" versus "Systemic Implications": How Should Investment Tribunals Decide?' (2013) 29 Arbitration

Shawcross's particular interest in this question also reflected that of other lawyers representing MNCs in the natural resource business. Particularly, they were preoccupied with the fact that states could breach concession contracts, as occurred in the 1951 case of the Anglo-Iranian Oil Company.[172] In 1962, further, the UN General Assembly had passed the resolution on the Permanent Sovereignty over Natural Resources, clarifying that states have a right to expropriate under international law.[173] For the norm entrepreneurs, this resolution could be inconsistent with the commitment assumed by some Global South countries not to expropriate concessions for a certain number of years.[174] They did not oppose states' right to expropriate, but claimed that they could not expropriate a concession contract when they had provided a commitment against expropriation.[175]

This transactional model of foreign investment relations was further discussed by the Hyde et al. report, which stated that '[p]erformance is the universal interest' and a necessary requirement for the 'maximum flow of international capital and trade interest'.[176] These experts favoured '[t]he application to alien property interests of [the] axiom of the supremacy of international law', concluding that this principle and *pacta sunt servanda* 'embrace the field of treatment of property and contractual interests'.[177] Like the Abs–Shawcross draft, they defined undertakings broadly, noting that restrictions to state authority may be 'found in a treaty; may be expressed or implied by contract; in either case, international law requires they be respected'.[178]

This broad definition of undertakings connected the business concerns of Abs and others to the protection of foreign investors' reliance. Protection should extend to investors' reliance on 'policy statements; favorable legislation and regulation [. . .] and promises in the form of treaties, contractual arrangements and otherwise'.[179] In this regard, the Hyde et al. report asserted that

> If a state invites a foreign investment pursuant to the terms of a given law, its right unilaterally to alter the law, in derogation of investment made in reliance upon it, is open to question. Not only may the principles set above govern the question [i.e. the supremacy of international law], but the further principle of estoppel or preclusion may be applicable.[180]

International 131–52, 151; Jeswald W. Salacuse, 'The Emerging Global Regime for Investment' (2010) 51 Harvard International Law Journal 427–73.

[172] American Bar Association (n. 14) 85–9. See also Schwarzenberger (n. 13) 66–83, 161.
[173] Permanent Sovereignty over Natural Resources, UNGA Resolution 1803(xvii), 17th Session (14 December 1962).
[174] American Bar Association (n. 14) 87–9.
[175] Shawcross (n. 122) 352–3.
[176] American Branch of the International Law Association (n. 75) 91.
[177] Ibid., 87.
[178] Ibid., 91.
[179] American Bar Association (n. 14) 2.
[180] American Branch of the International Law Association (n. 75) 91, footnote 20.

When the meaning of undertakings was discussed by the Committee for Invisible Transactions at the Organisation of European Economic Cooperation, some member states objected to the protection of reliance, as this could 'be going too far'.[181] Elihu Lauterpacht's report not only reiterates that reliance was meant to be protected under the Abs–Shawcross draft, but also anticipates the interpretative and policy problems associated with the doctrine of legitimate expectations. For him, undertakings can be general or specific. Specific undertakings take 'the form of contract or a concession', while general undertakings mean 'a legislation, a license or otherwise' in which governments make a promise upon which foreign investors rely to invest.[182] Lauterpacht suggested that the drafters' intention was not to protect general undertakings, but that they were 'only concerned to protect a situation by which the state by its conduct gives rise to a legitimate expectation of the continuance of a particular state of affairs'.[183] The comments to the final version of the 1967 OECD Draft make a similar clarification concerning the protection of reliance and legitimate expectations.[184]

Yet, the protection of state undertakings and reliance remained controversial. Key issues included whether states through contracts or other undertakings could give up their sovereign right to expropriate or regulate property. An American Bar Association report examined these questions in the context of the 1962 OECD Draft (a preliminary version to the 1967 final draft), admitting that a transactional model puts foreign investors and states on a level playing field, whereby states could enter into transactions about their sovereign powers.[185] For some countries, such as the US, this was problematic for the right to eminent domain.[186] The authors of the Harvard Draft had similar concerns. They agreed that states can give up sovereign rights through treaties, but found it debatable whether contracts could have similar effects. Contracts require fewer formalities; bureaucrats or lower-ranked officials often sign investment contracts.[187] Richard R. Baxter, one of the authors of the Harvard Draft, reportedly noted that the discussion was being 'overcome by the fumes of petrol'.[188]

The American Bar Association report considered the implications of contractual commitments for the right to expropriate and for police powers in more detail. In the first case, the report observed that states, under domestic law, can rely on the 'overriding power of the government to take the contract', irrespective of its terms and conditions.[189] This was clear under US, British,

[181] Lauterpacht (n. 128) 26.
[182] Ibid., 25.
[183] Ibid., 26.
[184] OECD (n. 128) 336–7.
[185] American Bar Association (n. 14) 82.
[186] Ibid., 82–4.
[187] Discussed in ibid., 91.
[188] James E. O'Brien, 'James E. O'Brien: Odyssey of a Journeyman Lawyer' Interview by Carole Hicke in 1987–1990, Oral History Center, The Bancroft Library, University of California, Berkeley, 1991, 184.
[189] American Bar Association (n. 14), 82.

and French law. In Britain, 'the state […] cannot be prevented by contract from performing functions essential to its existence'.[190] But the same situation in international law 'appeared to require qualification'.[191] The report noted that these overriding powers do not exist under international law, and international tribunals should therefore enforce the commitment because of 'the reliance placed upon it by the alien'.[192] The American Bar Association admitted that domestic judges were unlikely to enforce it, but 'an independent tribunal outside the state would be expected to apply the contract in accordance with its terms'.[193]

The case of police powers was different. The report concluded that states cannot contract out their police powers to pass 'measures necessary to secure the health, safety, good order, comfort, or general welfare of the community'.[194] International law only prohibits arbitrary and discriminatory public measures. The report reasoned that these powers are 'essential to the existence of the state', and contracting them out would equal to 'transferring the state functions to a private entity'.[195] This would be 'tantamount to agreeing not to act as a state'.[196] Also, the report explained, states cannot have a real sense of the content of this obligation, as governments do not know what kind of regulation the future will demand.[197]

But this deferential position to police powers was debated at the time. In 1961, Robert Jennings wrote that it was unclear whether states could incur responsibility under international law for the use of police powers, particularly in concessions or economic development agreements.[198] Some of the norm entrepreneurs argued that this question should be answered affirmatively. Schwebel held that states are internationally responsible if they employ their governmental authority 'to undo the fundamental expectation on the basis of which parties characteristically contract'. This responsibility exists regardless of whether the measure promotes the national public welfare because a foreign investor is a 'sojourner in the community ruled by the State'.[199]

[190] Ibid., 83, 83–5.
[191] Ibid., 82.
[192] Ibid., 88.
[193] Ibid., 85.
[194] Ibid., 93.
[195] Ibid., 94.
[196] Ibid.
[197] Ibid.
[198] Robert Y. Jennings, 'State Contracts in International Law' (1961) 37 British Yearbook of International Law 156–82, 176–7. Another important international lawyer, F. A. Mann, agreed with the American Bar Association: F. A. Mann, 'State Contracts and State Responsibility' (1960) 54 American Journal of International Law 572–91, 576–7.
[199] Stephen M. Schwebel, 'On Whether the Breach by a State of a Contract with an Alien is a Breach of International Law' in Stephen M. Schwebel, *Justice in International Law: Selected Writings* (CUP 1994) 425–35, 435.

5. The internationalization of contracts

The norm entrepreneurs were in favour of internationalizing investment contracts. In the Abs–Shawcross draft, the issue is included in the provision on state undertakings, which would transform a concession agreement into an international law obligation, preventing states from unilaterally modifying a contract.[200] In the early and mid-20th century, the internationalization thesis was discussed by scholars and international courts and tribunals in relation to international loans and concession contracts. Although internationalization was controversial at first, it gained substantial support during the 1960s and 1970s.[201]

Shawcross did not ignore the fact that some international decisions had not favoured the internationalization thesis.[202] Yet he preferred to overlook the status of international law, focusing instead on the work of scholars such as Herman Mosler, Alfred Verdross, and Georg Dahm, who agreed with his views and proposed, on this specific point, the progressive evolution of international law. These authors argued that breaching an undertaking, when the foreign investor had acted upon it, would violate the *venire contra factum proprium* and good faith principles, meaning a violation of international law.[203] Similarly, the Hyde et al. report concluded that '[c]ontractual obligations are not less binding on states than treaties'.[204] Foreign investors are 'directly entitled to international rights', and a paradigmatic example of these 'international rights' are the contractual rights contained in investment contracts.[205]

6. Derogation

Abs's Magna Carta, the Abs–Shawcross draft, and the 1967 OECD Draft all have a derogation provision somewhat similar to that included in the investment treaties the US signed during the 1980s and 1990s. European states did not include such a

200 Abs and Shawcross (n. 127) 120–1; Lauterpacht (n. 128) 21.

201 Some of the lawyers involved in the coalition of norm entrepreneurs, such as Shawcross and Elihu Lauterpacht, had participated in important international arbitrations during the inter-war period. See Andrea Leiter-Bockley, *Making the World Safe for Investment: The Protection of Foreign Property 1922-1959* (2019) Doctoral thesis, University of Melbourne & University of Vienna, 108. Also, Muthucumaraswamy Sornarajah, *The International Law on Foreign Investment* (CUP 2017) 339–56.

202 *Payment of Various Serbian Loans Issued in France* (*France v. Serbia*) [1929] PCIJ, Series A, No. 20 (12 July 1929); *Payment in Gold of the Brazilian Federal Loans Contracted in France* (*France v. Brazil*) [1929] PCIJ Series A, No. 21 (12 July 1929); *Anglo-Iranian Oil Company case* (*United Kingdom v. Iran*) [1952] ICJ Rep 93 (22 July 1952). Shawcross provides his interpretation and critique of these decisions in Shawcross (n. 122) 352; Abs and Shawcross (n. 127) 120.

203 Shawcross (n. 34) 55. Verdross went as far as arguing that investment contracts are 'quasi-international agreements': Alfred Verdross, 'Quasi-International Agreements and International Economic Transactions' (1964) 18 Yearbook of World Affairs 230–47.

204 American Branch of the International Law Association (n. 75) 88.

205 Ibid.

provision in their treaties. For the norm entrepreneurs, the purpose of the provision was to authorize measures in violation of foreign investor rights during wartime. Abs's Magna Carta provided a very limited derogation clause, requesting states 'to act as trustees safeguarding the interests of the owners'.[206] The Abs–Shawcross draft expanded the scope of the exception, albeit marginally, to cover cases of 'public emergency which threaten its life'.[207] Elihu Lauterpacht's report discussed whether this provision could include other situations, such as a foreign exchange crisis. In his view, this was possible but only if it was an 'extremely serious one'. He also noted that the strict terminology in the provision could be interpreted as limiting other exceptions under general international law, such as force majeure.[208] The 1967 OECD Draft added the notion of 'essential security interests' to the provision. Again, the wording is quite narrow, requiring measures to 'be limited in extent and duration to those strictly required by the exigencies of the situation'.[209] Importantly, the American Bar Association report noted that this provision would not apply to police powers. Normal functions of government, such as taxation, are not exceptional.[210]

7. Enforcing audacious interpretations

For the norm entrepreneurs, a world of progress depended on establishing a world of law, in which states would respect foreign investor rights. They argued that foreign investors should have the privilege to enforce their rights directly through an international court or arbitration, while some accepted that this mechanism could be expanded to 'other human rights' in the future. This dispute settlement arrangement was included in both Abs's Magna Carta and in the Abs–Shawcross draft.[211] As stated earlier, this position was not original in the late 1950s. The International Chamber of Commerce had advocated for international investment protection in 1931 and 1949, and the International Law Association included ISDS in the two 1948 Draft Statutes of the Arbitral Tribunal for Foreign Investment.[212] Both drafts have a close resemblance to the ICSID Convention.

Some of the norm entrepreneurs were explicit about the paramount importance of ISDS. For the American Bar Association, it was imperative for two reasons. The first was to avoid the 'vagaries' of diplomatic protection.[213] Abs, Shawcross, and

206 Society to Advance the Protection of Foreign Investments (n. 61) 57, 56–8.
207 Abs and Shawcross (n. 127) 116–7.
208 Lauterpacht (n. 128) 28, 27–8.
209 OECD (n. 128) 342, 342–4.
210 American Bar Association (n. 14) 101–3.
211 Society to Advance the Protection of Foreign Investment (n. 61) 37–8 (ISDS was not made explicit but it can be inferred from the comments, 60-1); Abs and Shawcross (n. 127) 118.
212 International Law Association (n. 11).
213 American Bar Association (n. 14) 58.

others had reason to fear that Global North states would be reluctant to bring diplomatic protection cases against Global South countries, not only because of the perceived Communist threat but also because these disputes could involve economic measures similar to those implemented at home. The second reason was that the provisions in the draft treaties were vague and ambiguous; a direct remedy against treaty violations would allow 'the establishment of arbitral or judicial case law in order to clarify the rights of all parties concerned'.[214]

Moreover, the norm entrepreneurs shared the view that the exhaustion of the local remedies rule should not apply to foreign investment relations. This would mean a radical shift in international law, as Schwarzenberger recognized at the time.[215] The Hyde et al. report stated that foreign investors could be asked to exhaust local remedies, but that domestic courts were 'inconsistent and confused'.[216] It concluded that:

> These traditional patterns are not without merit [. . .] Yet, the expanding pace of world development, the rising level of international trade [. . .] and the multiplication of sovereignties [. . .] have led to a search for new procedures for the lawful disposition of disputes.[217]

In terms of the composition of these arbitral tribunals, Abs and Shawcross had differing views. For Abs, the 'special international court of arbitration' should be composed of 'outstanding economists and bank representatives'.[218] Shawcross, however, preferred a dispute settlement mechanism that respected the basic principles of legal adjudication. Arbitrators had to be 'completely impartial'. Significantly, both he and the American Bar Association were quite optimistic about the capacity of arbitrators to resolve these hard cases on a case-by-case basis. He wrote that 'properly qualified and impartial arbitrators, I think, would have little difficulty in arriving at just decisions'.[219]

The norm entrepreneurs knew that the prior consent of governments was a fundamental pillar of the arbitral dispute settlement mechanism. They were aware that the enforceability of foreign investor rights depended not on dreaming about international arbitration, but on convincing governments to subscribe to the idea.[220]

[214] Ibid., 58, 106–9. Also, Council of Europe (n. 38) 137.

[215] Schwarzenberger (n. 13) 117. Also, Lauterpacht (n. 128) 21; Aron Broches, 'Problems of Private Foreign Investment' Speech before the Third Annual Institute on Corporate Counsel, devoted to foreign Operations of American Enterprises, Fordham University School of Law, 8 December 1961 (Broches, M. Aron—Articles and Speeches (1951–1982)—vol. 1) (1651418) World Bank Group Archives, Washington, DC, United States, 5.

[216] American Branch of the International Law Association (n. 75) 93. Similarly, American Bar Association (n. 14) 110.

[217] American Branch of the International Law Association (n. 75) 93.

[218] Abs (n. 24) 30.

[219] Shawcross (n. 34) 59; American Bar Association (n. 14) 72, 103.

[220] Shawcross (n. 34) 59; American Bar Association (n. 14) 9.

In 1969, Abs was still concerned about this problem and critical of the ICSID Convention, which does not oblige states to submit disputes to international arbitration.[221] That same year, however, Italy and Chad signed the first investment treaty with an ISDS provision following the advice of ICSID Secretariat.[222]

Conclusion

The norm entrepreneurs of the late 1950s and 1960s contributed to international investment law in multiple ways. They made ambitious proposals, lobbied governments and international organizations, and, most momentously, crafted a legal imagination devoted to the international protection of foreign investment. They were aware that they sometimes acted in the domain of future law (*de lege ferenda*), but discussed and debated their proposals as if these views were to be implemented. The norm entrepreneurs in question did not care that some of the ideas were particularly controversial, such as a broad definition of foreign investor rights, indirect expropriation, internationalization of contracts, the protection of reliance, and ISDS. Thanks to their discussions and networking, the strategy would pay off in the long run, as their legal imagination gradually came to occupy the space of international investment law. In particular, the norm entrepreneurs were right about the pivotal role of international arbitration. Embedding foreign investor rights into their world-making project of free enterprise and a global economy was an audacious move, but one for which international arbitration would prove to be a fertile terrain. Some of the norm entrepreneurs, moreover, would become arbitrators themselves.[223]

[221] Abs (n. 5) 15.

[222] St John shows that the ICSID Secretariat actively promoted the inclusion of ISDS provisions in investment treaties. See St John (n. 42) 183.

[223] E.g., Stephen M. Schwebel.

3

Competing Imaginaries and the 1970s

The long 1970s was a difficult time for those promoting investment treaties and ISDS. OECD members had not adopted a multilateral convention and only a few countries signed bilateral investment treaties or joined ICSID. The Global South and the labour movement demanded new rules of the game, which they saw as reproducing colonial relations and as having no mechanism to discipline the activities of MNCs. The norm entrepreneurs' self-confidence was decreasing.[1] In this challenging context, the International Chamber of Commerce took the initiative and put forward a conception of foreign investor obligations consistent with investment treaties and ISDS. This move conceded little to the Global South or the labour movement: the best companions to strong foreign investor rights are weak or even *voluntary* foreign investor obligations. For a while, however, the outcome was uncertain, as different imaginations competed for the space of international investment law. This chapter examines some of these competitors, including the 1974 UN report on the impact of MNCs, the US position on the topic, and the 1974 UN Charter of Economic Rights and Duties of States. In addition to having historical interest, each of these alternatives provides us with an insightful benchmark to assess the implications of the legal imagination of the norm entrepreneurs of the 1950s and 1960s.

A. A business approach to balance: the International Chamber of Commerce and the OECD

The changing climate of the 1970s demanded a different approach to foreign investment relations. In 1972, the International Chamber of Commerce responded to criticisms from the labour movement and Global South countries by releasing the Guidelines for Foreign Investment (hereinafter ICC Guidelines).[2] This project was led by John Blair, an international relations advisor to Shell and former assistant of Shawcross, who had also been involved in drafting the ICSID Convention

[1] Georg Schwarzenberger, *Foreign Investments and International Law* (Stevens & Sons 1969) 168.

[2] Francesco Petrini, 'Capital Hits the Road: Regulating Multinational Corporations during the long 1970s' in Knud Andresen and Stefan Müller (eds.), *Contesting Deregulation: Debates, Practices and Developments in the West Since the 1970s* (Berghahn Books 2017) 185–98, 188.

Investment Treaties and the Legal Imagination. Nicolás M. Perrone, Oxford University Press (2021). © Nicolás M. Perrone.
DOI: 10.1093/oso/9780198862147.003.0004

in the early 1960s.[3] The ICC Guidelines provided practical recommendations to promote a 'better understanding' of the objectives of foreign investors, host states, and home states.[4] They were not intended to become an international convention or replace investment treaties[5]—the International Chamber of Commerce and those who promoted the ICC Guidelines, such as the president of Shell and the executive vice-president of Exxon, insisted that countries should still sign investment treaties and join the ICSID Convention.[6]

The ICC Guidelines highlighted the benefits but also noted some problems related to foreign investment. The introduction associated foreign capital with the 'integration of markets' and described it as 'the major external source of capital and technology' for the Global South.[7] It also acknowledged some host states' concerns, differences about the role of foreign investment in an economy, and the need for foreign investors to adapt to national development plans. It suggested that these concerns related to the idea that international economic interdependence 'may conflict with aspirations for national economic independence'.[8] The balance between global and local, overlooked by Western business leaders in the 1950s, was now part of the discussion. The guidelines underscored the need for 'mutual understanding' and 'mutual confidence' as prerequisites for a good investment climate.[9]

The ICC Guidelines differed significantly from both the 1949 ICC Code of Fair Treatment for Foreign Investments and the Abs–Shawcross draft. They incorporated standards of behaviour applicable to foreign investors, host states, and home states. Their structure recognized that the success of foreign investment projects requires cooperation between all three actors to protect both investor and state rights. They required each to consider the expectations of the others concerning: (i) investment policies; (ii) ownership and management; (iii) finance; (iv) fiscal policies; (v) legal framework; (vi) labour policies; (vii) technology; and (viii) commercial policies. Yet, the content and language of these sections—the provisions on

[3] Blair was the chairperson of the working group that prepared the ICC Guidelines. F. M. Black, 'Memorandum: Roundtable of Private Foreign Investment in Latin America' OECD FMB/878, 27 February 1973 (Edwin Martin Personal Papers, The John F. Kennedy Library, Box 37).

[4] International Chamber of Commerce, '1972 Guidelines for International Investment' in UNCTAD, *International Investment Instruments: A Compendium*, vol. 3 (United Nations 1996) 279–91, 280 (hereinafter ICC Guidelines). The idea of voluntary codes for business was not new. At the request of the US President's International Development Advisory Board (also known as the Rockefeller Committee), the International Chamber of Commerce worked on several documents between 1952 and 1954. However, interest in these codes waned until the 1970s. James Greene, *The Search for Common Ground: A Survey of Efforts to Develop Codes of Behavior in International Investment*. A special report to the U.S. Committee, Pacific Basin Council (The Conference Board 1971) 9–11.

[5] The ICC Guidelines recommended states to enter into investment treaties and join the ICSID Convention. ICC Guidelines, 281.

[6] UN Department of Economic and Social Affairs, *Summary of the Hearings Before the Group of Eminent Persons to Study the Impact of Multinational Corporations on Development and International Relations*, ST/ESA/15 (United Nations 1974) 38, 414–15.

[7] ICC Guidelines, 279.

[8] Ibid.

[9] Ibid., 280.

foreign investor obligations and the rights of the states—were considerably vaguer than those on foreign investor rights.

The International Chamber of Commerce wanted to turn the guidelines into a new standard for foreign investment relations. It submitted the document to the OECD, asking for comments and support. Unlike the UN or the European Economic Community, the OECD was considered the right organization for 'finding a common approach and reaching balanced conclusions, considering not only malpractices but also benefits conferred by MNCs'.[10] The OECD, particularly its Development Assistance Committee, produced several reports and gathered experts' reactions. It is worth noting here that the OECD had also shifted its position since the 1967 OECD Draft. It had acknowledged that the draft 'may have been somewhat misunderstood by developing countries'.[11] The OECD now believed that a fair balance between rights and obligations was necessary. What remained a matter of discussion, however, was whether or not to supplement the 1967 OECD Draft 'by a series of general principles constituting a balanced statement of the rights and responsibilities of the parties concerned'.[12]

Despite trying to strike a balance, the ICC Guidelines failed to convince most non-business actors. The report prepared by the secretariat of the OECD Development Assistance Committee (hereinafter the Secretariat Report) notes that while the guidelines did recognize some states' concerns, they made several controversial statements, proposals, and omissions. They did not discuss the renegotiation of investment contracts, which 'was widely recognised' in the early 1970s, and encouraged countries to sign investment treaties and accept international arbitration although many Global South countries were opposed to these initiatives.[13] Their notion of foreign investors' obligations was vague, the Secretariat Report finds, and they neglected to acknowledge that foreign investors were treated better than domestic investors in most parts of the Global South. The report also notes that it was 'not certain to what extent [the standards of protection] represents general principles of law […]. The problem was to obtain agreement on what is "fair and equitable treatment" or "just compensation" '.[14] An Annex and other memos

[10] Memo of the Business and Industry Advisory Committee to the OECD. Cited in Francesco Petrini, 'Who'll Stop the Runaway Shop? The Battle to Regulate Multinationals' Activities Inside the EEC at the Dawn of Globalization' paper presented at EUSA Twelfth Biennial International Conference, Boston. 2011, 11.

[11] OECD Development Assistance Committee, 'Review of OECD/DAC Activities in the Field of Private Investment' Background document for the UN Panel Meeting in Amsterdam on Foreign Private Investment and the Development Process, 7 February 1969 (Edwin Martin Personal Papers, The John F. Kennedy Library, Box 37).

[12] Ibid.

[13] Secretariat of the OECD Development Assistance Committee, 'Comments on the ICC Guidelines for International Investment' DAC(73)19, 22 March 1973 (Edwin Martin Personal Papers, The John F. Kennedy Library, Box 37) 3.

[14] Ibid., 5.

similarly observe that the ICC Guidelines resembled a business proposal, did not express a fair balance, and missed 'the political dimension' of foreign investment.[15]

The OECD Business and Industry Advisory Committee (BIAC) strongly disagreed with the Secretariat Report. It responded that the guidelines had 'no relevance to countries which want to reduce or eliminate foreign investment in their territories'.[16] It insisted that renegotiation was a matter of dispute, and pointed out that forty-two Global South countries had ratified bilateral investment treaties while another twenty-two had signed or were negotiating them. BIAC also said that most states accept international arbitration, Latin America being one of a few exceptions.[17] Its comments suggested more consensus than the Secretariat Report acknowledged for investment treaties and international arbitration.

Evidence from the time, however, indicates that BIAC was wrong about this consensus. In the *Barcelona Traction* case, the ICJ noted that despite the expansion of the multinational activities of corporations, 'the evolution of law has not gone further and that no generally accepted rules in the matter [i.e. foreign investment] have crystallized on the international plane'.[18] Also, Poulsen shows that European countries had problems convincing Global South countries to sign investment treaties.[19] Indeed, in a 1979 interview Abs himself recognized that his Magna Carta had the support of neither the OECD nor the Global South.[20]

The ICC Guidelines did not end the deadlock between North and South. In 1972, the US newspaper *International Herald Tribune* referred to them as a 'catalogue of pious wishes'.[21] Discussions at the Roundtable on Private Foreign Investment in Latin America, where the guidelines were reviewed in February 1973, show that they failed to create a sense of mutual confidence or understanding in this region. Stating that the guidelines were 'not intended to deal with economic development, but with investments',[22] John Blair defended ISDS and noted some willingness to compromise on a regional arbitration centre. Latin American countries disagreed. They demanded the right to unilaterally determine the terms and conditions of

[15] Ibid., Annex. Also, M. André Vincent, 'Memorandum: International Chamber of Commerce Guidelines for International Investment' DAC/FPD(72)791, 27 December 1972 (Edwin Martin Personal Papers, The John F. Kennedy Library, Box 37); A. Vincent, 'Memorandum: International Chamber of Commerce: Guidelines for International Investment' OECD AV-1446, 4 January 1973 (Edwin Martin Personal Papers, The John F. Kennedy Library, Box 37).

[16] Business and Industry Advisory Committee, 'Observations on the Note by the Secretariat of the OECD Development Assistance Committee Related to the International Chamber of Commerce Guidelines for International Investment' Meeting on 25 June 1973 (Edwin Martin Personal Papers, The John F. Kennedy Library, Box 37) 1.

[17] Ibid., 2–4.

[18] *Barcelona Traction, Light and Power Company* (*Belgium v. Spain*) [1970] Judgment, ICJ Rep 3, para. 89 (5 February 1970).

[19] Lauge N. Skovgaard Poulsen, *Bounded Rationality and Economic Diplomacy: The Politics of Investment Treaties in Developing Countries* (CUP 2015) 69.

[20] *Die Zeit*, 'Eigentum ist auch bei uns nicht sicher' (13 July 1979) 18.

[21] Cited in M. André Vincent (n. 15) 2.

[22] Black (n. 3) 2.

foreign investment and 'summarily dismissed' the idea of a regional arbitration centre.[23]

Lack of support for the ICC Guidelines did not end the discussions about MNCs at the OECD. In 1975, this organization created a Committee on International Investment and Multinational Enterprises to carry out a programme dedicated to MNCs.[24] After some negotiations, this programme focused on standards of behaviour, the principle of national treatment, and incentives and disincentives, leaving other controversial issues off the agenda—notably foreign investors' property and contractual rights. In a context of disagreement, even among OECD members, this was the preferred strategy to promote a good investment climate while balancing relations between foreign investors and states.[25]

A significant outcome of these negotiations was the 1976 OECD Guidelines for Multinational Enterprises (hereinafter the OECD Guidelines), the roots of which lie in the ICC Guidelines.[26] These guidelines included no standards of foreign investment protection, only voluntary recommendations from governments to firms on responsible business conduct. The OECD Guidelines are still relevant for analysing foreign investor rights for two reasons. First, capital-exporting countries relied on them to legitimize MNCs, as well as to balance their rights with national goals. Second, the guidelines drew a line concerning the issue of international obligations on MNCs, an idea that Global North countries and most MNCs continue to reject.[27] The OECD guidelines thus constituted a 'bargaining platform' for OECD countries in other negotiations,[28] to which I turn next.

B. Embedded liberalism and foreign investment: the United Nations and the Group of Eminent Persons

The mutual confidence rhetoric of the ICC and OECD Guidelines contrasted with actual growing tensions in foreign investment relations. The conflicts affected foreign investors and states alike. The 1970s witnessed a record number of expropriations, including nationalizations in Gulf States and Chile, intensifying debate over standards of compensation. Governments also had serious problems with foreign

[23] Ibid., 2, 4.

[24] Roger Blanpain, *The OECD Guidelines for Multinational Enterprises and Labour Relations, 1976-1979: Experience and Review* (Springer 1979) 31.

[25] Ibid., 33, 48; Karl P. Sauvant, 'The Negotiations of the United Nations Code of Conduct on Transnational Corporations: Experience and Lessons Learned' (2015) 16 Journal of World Investment & Trade 11–87, 13 22.

[26] James K. Rowe, 'Corporate Social Responsibility as Business Strategy' in Ronnie D. Lipschutz with James K. Rowe (eds.), *Globalization, Governmentality and Global Politics: Regulation for the Rest of us?* (Routledge 2005) 122–60, 158.

[27] Jean-Michel Marcoux, *International Investment Law and Globalization: Foreign Investment, Responsibilities and Intergovernmental Organizations* (Routledge 2018) 71–4, 90.

[28] Blanpain (n. 24) 127; Sauvant (n. 25) 31.

investors. Global South leaders accused MNCs of unacceptable forms of political machinations,[29] while opposition was increasing in the North too. In 1967, Jean Jacques Servan-Schreiber discussed the expansion of US MNCs in his book *The American Challenge*, sparking anxiety in France and Europe.[30] A year later, Noam Chomsky opined that 'the rise of supranational corporations poses new dangers for human freedom', in response to which Detlev Vagts affirmed that this was because of their 'peculiar effectiveness', that is, their capacity to remove 'decisionmaking power far from the reach of people intimately affected by it'.[31]

In this context, in 1972 the United Nations established a Group of Eminent Persons to report on MNCs' impact on development and international relations.[32] This group consisted of 10 members from capital-exporting countries and another 10 from capital-importing and Eastern countries. Unlike the Abs–Shawcross draft and the ICC Guidelines this was not solely a business initiative, yet the balance was still not ideal: the group included academics, government officials, and businesspeople, but excluded the international labour movement. The group's mission was to discuss the challenges posed by foreign private investment and make proposals to improve its governance.[33] In the background was not only the work of the International Chamber of Commerce and the OECD, but also calls to regulate MNCs and create a general agreement on foreign investment akin to the General Agreement on Tariffs and Trade (GATT).[34] These aimed to bring 'embedded liberalism'[35] into international investment law.

The Report of the Group of Eminent Persons (hereinafter the UN Report), released in 1974, provided a detailed and comprehensive analysis of foreign investment and MNCs. Covering economic, political, social, and cultural aspects, it probed the complex role and implications of foreign investment not only for home states, host states, and foreign investors but also for labour and consumers. The broad scope of debate spanned domestic employment, social and cultural values,

[29] Tagi Sagafi-nejad and John Dunning, *The UN and Transnational Corporations: From Code of Conduct to Global Compact* (Indiana University Press 2008) 41–54.

[30] Jean Jacques Servan-Schreiber, *The American Challenge* (Penguin Books, 1969 [1967]).

[31] Detlev F. Vagts, 'The Multinational Enterprise: A New Challenge for Transnational Law' (1970) 83 Harvard Law Review 739–92, 739, 791.

[32] Sagafi-nejad and Dunning (n. 29) 55–9. The question of foreign investment regulation and the role of international law was previously discussed at UNCTAD, and eventually taken to the UN Economic and Social Council. See Sundhya Pahuja and Anna Saunders, 'Rival Worlds and the place of the Corporation in International Law' in Jochen von Bernstorff, Philipp Dann (eds), *The Battle for International Law in the Decolonization Era* (OUP 2018) 141-67, 162.

[33] UN Department of Economic and Social Affairs, *The Impact of Multinational Corporations on Development and on International Relations*, ST/ESA/15 (United Nations 1974) 19–22.

[34] Ibid., 9; Also, Paul M. Goldberg and Charles P. Kindleberger, 'Toward a GATT for Investment: A Proposal for Supervision of the International Corporation' (1970) 2 Law and Policy in International Business 295–325.

[35] According to Ruggie, the essence of the 'embedded liberalism compromise' was that 'multilateralism would be predicated upon domestic interventionism'. John Gerald Ruggie, 'International Regimes, Transactions, and Change: Embedded Liberalism in the Postwar Economic Order' (1982) 36 International Organization 379–415, 393.

the bargaining power of states and labour unions vis-à-vis MNCs, the quality of products, expropriation, and 'unclear and frequently changing government policies'.[36] While it acknowledged that many states and the United Nations saw a fundamental role for foreign investment in the development process, it also found that 'widespread concern and anxiety' suggested that 'the present modus vivendi should be reviewed at the international level'.[37] The report concluded that foreign investment can promote development but that it was imperative to 'safeguard the legitimate interests of all the parties involved [including workers and consumers]'.[38]

The UN Report dedicated a full section, 'World Perspective', to tensions between the global, national and local levels. Economic goals were important, the report maintained, but overstating them could lead to the deterioration of 'man's habitat, both physical and spiritual [... and] the individual is being increasingly manipulated by forces over which he has little control or influence'.[39] The report explained that these forces resulted from the transnational features of MNCs, which caused tensions with sovereign states and some local actors. Corporate planning mechanisms situated in a few industrialized countries focused on global markets to make crucial decisions about 'the allocation of resources, with respect to what, how, and for whom to produce'.[40] The report was thus not optimistic about promoting partnership between foreign investors and local business, as this sort of local participation 'may confer some benefits on a small elite group of nationals' but not resolve the main problems.[41]

None of these conclusions implied that foreign investment could not contribute to development. The UN Report claimed that for most people in the Global South the issue was attaining a basic level of subsistence, and that foreign investment could help. The problem was that the firms were 'not *per se* geared to the goals of development' (emphasis in original).[42] Foreign investment may increase inequality between and within countries, amplifying the differences between those countries and peoples not integrated into the global economy. The report disapproved of critics of developmental aid, concluding that aid should be raised while countries reform their trade and investment laws and increase efforts to deal with inequality.[43]

The UN Report thus held that states should be protagonists of foreign investment relations: governments must formulate clear development strategies and steer foreign investment according to their national policies. It discussed certain measures for ensuring that foreign investors would adapt to local needs and objectives. First,

[36] UN Department of Economic and Social Affairs (n. 33) 26, 25–6.
[37] Ibid., 25.
[38] Ibid., 27.
[39] Ibid., 28.
[40] Ibid., 30.
[41] Ibid., 61.
[42] Ibid., 28.
[43] Ibid., 29.

developing countries needed 'to develop the capacity to monitor the pattern of the distribution of benefits between themselves and the multinational corporations'.[44] This required increasing host states' ability to bargain with and regulate foreign investment. Second, as the contribution of foreign investment to development is not straightforward, national planning should be prioritized over regulatory givings.[45] Third, because foreign investment impacts social institutions and cultural values as much as the economy, Global North and Global South countries needed 'to be certain of the degree to which they wish to rely on foreign enterprises for their growth and prosperity'.[46]

This view of foreign investment relations, quite apart from that of the norm entrepreneurs of the 1950s and 1960s, led the UN Report to approach the topic of protection in a different manner. The discussion of treatment, ownership, and control followed the 'needs and aspirations' of host states and populations,[47] recognizing that the respect of local preferences requires more than vague corporate obligations. The UN Report favoured a legal imagination whereby the primary expectation would be that foreign investors adapt and contribute to host states' plans. It criticized the political intrusions of MNCs, observing that this kind of interference 'can take less direct and obvious forms'.[48] Arguing that foreign investors should be encouraged to identify with the interests of host countries, it asked investors not to

> lose sight of the fact that domestic policies for social and structural change which appear onerous to them may well be in their interest in the longer term, as well as that of host and home countries.[49]

At the same time, the UN Report was not indifferent to the concerns of foreign investors. It stated that the essential counterpart to the principle of adaptation was that host states should treat foreign investors in a fair, non-discriminatory manner. Evidence, it said, suggested that the relationship between foreign investors and host states deteriorated when host states' policies lacked clarity or regulatory givings proved unsustainable.[50] Pinpointing the central issue as the question of how to address changes in circumstances and policies, the report underscored the necessity of a mechanism to 'keep under review the policies and performance of the MNCs'.[51]

[44] Ibid., 32.
[45] Ibid., 33.
[46] Ibid., 36.
[47] Ibid., 59.
[48] Ibid., 45.
[49] Ibid., 46.
[50] Ibid., 40, 143.
[51] Ibid., 39, 55.

Further, the UN Report suggested some compromises. In relation to the standard of compensation, it emphasized the consensus over the sovereign right to expropriate and the obligation to pay fair compensation. Denial or reduction of compensation should not be entirely excluded, the report conceded, but it should be subject to a legal proceeding according to the due process. In principle, such proceedings should be governed by the laws and courts of host states, although countries may choose to submit a dispute to international arbitration—to ICSID, for example.[52] In other areas compromise turned out to be impossible: the UN Report overlooked tensions between foreign investor rights and states' right to regulate, and omitted discussion of indirect expropriation, the internationalization of contracts, and legitimate expectations. The UN experts were well aware of these issues, as their individual comments show, but decided to leave them out of the report due to the lack of consensus.[53]

The twenty Eminent Persons did agree on the importance of 'the rules of the game' for foreign investment relations. Their report noted that the world economy and the international division of labour were closely related to the rules applicable to foreign investment. Ultimately, then, the debate about these rules would be about which world economy, whose decisions, and whose interests. The approach favoured by the report was 'conscious planning, both public and private', although it admitted that this would require mechanisms to balance global and local interests.[54] It contended that 'many of the measures that we think necessary will be ineffective and frustrated unless they are accompanied by action at the international level which promotes co-operation and harmonization'.[55] It therefore proposed a programme of action that, in the long term, should conclude with a GATT-like international treaty for foreign investment.

In the meantime, the UN Report recommended the creation of a commission on MNCs, a research centre, and the elaboration of a non-compulsory code of conduct addressed to both governments and foreign investors. It also highlighted the need for increasing efforts to gather information on MNCs and assess relations between foreign private investment and technology, employment and labour, consumer protection, competition, transfer pricing, and taxation. These recommendations led to the creation of the short-lived United Nations Centre on Transnational Corporations (1975–1992) and informed the negotiation of a Code of Conduct for states and MNCs.[56]

Despite being under negotiation for almost two decades, the Code of Conduct was eventually abandoned in the early 1990s. States managed to agree on some guidelines for foreign investors—such as that their activities should adhere to

52 Ibid., 47–8.
53 Ibid., 104–6, 109, 135, 143, 146.
54 Ibid., 43, 42–3.
55 Ibid., 51.
56 Sagafi-nejad and Dunning (n. 29) 89; Sauvant (n. 25) 13.

national economic goals and development objectives—but consensus on foreign investor rights was much more difficult. As Karl Sauvant explains, the negotiations were marked by a lack of agreement over the balance between rights and obligations.[57] Global South countries demanded international obligations for foreign investors, while capital-exporting countries only accepted voluntary guidelines following the standard set by the 1976 OECD Guidelines. Moreover, the South opposed the strong standards of protection demanded by the OECD countries. In more than fifteen years of negotiation, no agreement was reached on the meaning of the FET standard or the dispute settlement mechanism.[58]

C. The United States' approach to balance: discussions before the US Senate

Public opinion was turning against MNCs, not only in host but also in home states. In the US, the country's MNCs were considered responsible for the international deficit, the export of jobs and technology, and for political interventions in other states—the International Telephone and Telegraph were involved in the 1973 military coup in Chile, for example.[59] These concerns led to a special inquiry on MNCs within the US Senate's Committees on Finance and Foreign Relations, which generated several reports and hearings between 1973 and 1976.[60]

The US Senate invited submissions from labour unions, corporations, and the US Department of Commerce. Labour unions complained that MNCs were increasing their imports from US subsidiaries abroad, and exporting jobs to countries with lower working conditions.[61] The firms participating disagreed, pointing to the significance of their multinational operations for both their competitiveness and for US 'economic supremacy'.[62] The MNCs observed that the world economy was undergoing structural changes, and they had no option but to adapt accordingly; European and Japanese firms had triggered international competition, posing new challenges for US multinationals.[63] Moreover, MNCs involved in the natural resource sector insisted on the special character of their business: 'a narrow spirit of isolationism seems signally inappropriate in view of the relative scarcity of most mineral resources, their geographic distribution, and the fact that world

[57] Ibid., 47–8.
[58] Ibid., 50.
[59] Harvey D. Shapiro, 'Multinationals' *New York Times*, 18 March 1973.
[60] US Senate, *Multinational Corporations and United States Foreign Policy. Hearings before the Subcommittee on Multinational Corporations of the Committee on Foreign Relations*. Ninety-third Congress, part I (US Govt Print Off, 1973–1976) 1–3.
[61] US Senate, *Multinational Corporations a Compendium of Papers Submitted to the Subcommittee on International Trade of the Committee on Finance of the United States* (US Govt Print Off, 1973) 1–3, 59–84.
[62] Ibid., 9, 350.
[63] Ibid., 5–6, 11, 15, 219.

demand for them is drastically increasing'.[64] Their operations were crucial if the US were to guarantee inflows of strategic natural resources.

The US Department of Commerce acknowledged the growing tensions between MNCs and states, observing that MNCs' supranational point of view had led to frictions with special interest groups and host governments; MNCs had a 'common world strategy' and managed it through 'a common nerve center based on a flow of common information'.[65] While creating a new 'world economic and political community', foreign investors were disrupting 'old cultural patterns and antiquated economic practices'.[66] In the 1970s, all this was becoming a source of political problems, as the world experienced rising 'economic nationalism' and governments aimed to 'retrieve the levers of economic control and to reassert political sovereignty'.[67] For the US Department of Commerce, the solution was to strike a balance between 'the degree of freedom' of MNCs and 'divergent national interests'.[68] In addition to 'setting conventions of conduct and for settling investment disputes', this objective required implementing 'requisite arrangements for balancing national and corporate objectives'.[69]

US foreign policy on MNCs followed some of these conclusions in the mid-1970s. In 1975, US Secretary of State Henry Kissinger affirmed that the US was willing to agree on 'basic principles' for MNCs.[70] He later spoke to the UN General Assembly about a necessity to 'articulate standards of conduct for both enterprises and government' that 'reflect the interests of all parties concerned'; otherwise, the new rules 'would exacerbate rather than moderate the frictions which have damaged the environment for international investment'.[71]

For the Global South the implications of this policy shift were not evident, for the US still favoured strong foreign investment protection and voluntary guidelines for foreign investors. The natural resource sector also remained a concern, because, following the opinion of US MNCs, the US Department of Commerce now distinguished between foreign investments pursuing new markets or lower labour conditions and those seeking resources: 'Certain industries are by nature international and their motives for investing abroad are clear. These include the extractive and plantation industries.'[72]

64 Ibid., 7, 253.
65 Ibid., 42.
66 Ibid., 42, 52.
67 Ibid., 43.
68 Ibid., 42.
69 Ibid., 54.
70 Cited in Sauvant (n. 25) 44.
71 Ibid.
72 US Senate (n. 61) 47.

D. The Global South and economic sovereignty: the Charter of Economic Rights and Duties of States

In the 1970s, emboldened by the decolonization process and significant diplomatic victories, the Global South put forward its own vision of foreign investment relations. Foreign investors' flows of capital were a central preoccupation of the NIEO: they were seen as necessary for development but were also a source of conflict and political interference.[73] To tackle this, the NIEO articulated a desire to change the rules of international law to promote and protect economic sovereignty.

The foundations of the NIEO were laid by Algerian President Houari Boumédiène during his 1974 speech before the UN General Assembly. He said the NIEO was focused on 'the allocation of world resources' as a means to realize 'a profound reorganization of economic relations between rich and poor countries'.[74] The United Nations had the duty to provide 'all the operational aid with regard to operating and marketing that [the Global South] might need'.[75] Global South countries were interested in controlling their natural resource sector, as stated in the 1962 UN General Assembly Resolution on the Permanent Sovereignty over Natural Resources, but the NIEO would go further, envisioning new rules for 'all spheres of economic activities'.[76]

The NIEO programme for foreign investment was enshrined in the 1974 UN Charter of Economic Rights and Duties of States (CERDS), the first draft of which was inspired by the 1917 Mexican Constitution.[77] It was the opposite of the Abs–Shawcross draft, with the exception that both documents expressed a world-making project through the language of law and rights. Mexican Ambassador to the UN Jorge Castañeda, elected head of the Working Group tasked with the draft, said that the CERDS aimed 'not only to codify the rules already embodied in international law, but to make progress [. . .], to establish new rules to meet the current and future needs of international society'. He aspired to create 'an objective and universal order' that could guarantee 'peace and stability' taking seriously 'the most vulnerable sector of the international economy'.[78]

[73] See Houari Boumédiène, 'Declaration and Programme of Action on the Establishment of a New International Economic Order' UN General Assembly Official Record, 6th Special Sess, prov verbatim rec A/PV.2208 (10 April 1974); Declaration and Programme on the Establishment of a New International Economic Order, UN General Assembly Resolution 3201/2, 6th Special Sess, A/RES/3201-2(S-VI) (1 May 1974).

[74] Boumédiène (n. 73) 3.

[75] Ibid., 7; Declaration and Programme on the Establishment of a New International Economic Order (n. 73) 8.

[76] Ibid., 3.

[77] Lawrence Whitehead, 'La política económica del sexenio de Echeverría: ¿qué salió mal y por qué?' (1980) 20 Foro internacional 484–513, 495–6.

[78] UNGA Official Records, 29th Sess, A/C.2/SR.1638 (25 November 1974) 385.

The CERDS protects a broadly defined set of rights of states and peoples. It protects the economic rights of all countries, particularly developing ones, as in their right to the 'full permanent sovereignty [. . .] over all [their] wealth, natural resources and economic activities'.[79] It also aims to ensure 'the full respect of the rights of all peoples', including their 'equal rights and self-determination'.[80] Every state has the right to choose 'its economic system [. . .] in accordance with the will of its people'.[81]

Negotiating the CERDS at the United Nations was a difficult process. The issue of state undertakings, which caused major differences between the Global South and Global North, became a 'chief stumbling-block'.[82] Capital-exporting countries claimed that the legal bond between company and state is 'a bond of international law', and that if a country 'accepted foreign capital under certain conditions and concluded an agreement', that agreement should be fulfilled in good faith.[83] The UN Group of 77—most Global South countries—did not challenge the binding nature of such contracts, but insisted that they were governed by host-state laws. This caused a huge disagreement. Another significant difference concerned a minimum international standard. The CERDS did not include one, clarifying that '[n]o State shall be compelled to grant preferential treatment to foreign investment'.[84] This was one of the main reasons why the US, the UK, Belgium, Denmark, Germany, and Luxembourg voted against the charter.[85]

Neither was there consensus on expropriation. States agreed on the obligation to pay compensation, but not on the applicable law and standard. The Group of 77 argued that applying international law to the relations between foreign investors and states would, unacceptably, 'place States on an equal legal and political footing with foreign corporations'.[86] As for the standard of compensation, the Group of 77 promoted 'appropriate [compensation] provided that all relevant circumstances call for it', whereas capital-exporting countries favoured a 'just compensation' standard in 'light of all relevant circumstances'.[87] Remarkably, the issue of indirect expropriation was not discussed.

The CERDS ultimately reflected the position of the Group of 77, which outnumbered capital-exporting countries at the UN General Assembly. Some

[79] Charter of Economic Rights and Duties of States, UNGA Resolution 3281(xxix), 29th Sess (12 December 1974) 52 (Article 2).

[80] Ibid., 51 (Chapter I).

[81] Ibid., 52 (Article 1)

[82] UNGA Official Records (n. 78) 383.

[83] Ibid.

[84] Charter of Economic Rights and Duties of States (n. 79) 52 (Article 2).

[85] G. W. Haight, 'The New International Economic Order and the Charter of Economic Rights and Duties of States' (1975) 9 International Lawyer 591–604, 603.

[86] Emilio Óscar Rabasa Mishkin, Speech of the Mexican Ambassador before the General Assembly of the United Nations, UNGA Official Records, 29th Sess, A/PV.2315 (12 December 1974) 1378.

[87] Haight (n. 85) 602.

capital-importing countries, however, later clarified that they remained committed to the fundamental principles of international law. These included states that had accepted the application of international law and the inclusion of international arbitration in their concession contracts, such as Singapore, Thailand, Malaysia, Kuwait, and Iran.[88]

Predictably, the CERDS was strongly opposed by the norm entrepreneurs. The US Council of the International Chamber of Commerce opined that it was 'the cutting edge of a threat to the well-being and even the existence of foreign-owned private enterprise and to the security of foreign investment in many countries'.[89] Former legal advisor to the US State Department (and future ISDS arbitrator) Charles Brower, noted that some elements of the CERDS implied an 'utter rejection of international law',[90] while G. W. Haight described the initiative as 'radical' and 'aggressive'.[91] Haight's position was not surprising; in the 1950s and 1960s, he had actively promoted international arbitration and investment protection as general counsel of the US affiliate of Shell and head of the US Section of the International Chamber of Commerce.[92]

Conclusion

Although neither the CERDS nor the UN Report were ever implemented, they remain useful to understand the full implications of the legal imagination enshrined in investment treaties and ISDS. The work of the Group of Eminent Persons reminds us that distribution, recognition, and embeddedness are closely related. Further, the CERDS points us towards the situation of local communities and their rights in foreign investment relations. Lastly, the report of the US Department of Commerce highlights that each type of foreign investment can be subject to a different embeddedness. Natural resources may be seen as a truly global sector, while production be regarded as a group of economic activities that should be governed

[88] Ibid., 602–3.

[89] US Council of the International Chamber of Commerce, 'A New Challenge to Private Enterprise' (1975) 1. Cited in Gillian White, 'A New International Economic Order?' (1976) 16 Virginia Journal of International Law 323–45, 323.

[90] Charles N. Brower and John B. Tepe, 'The Charter of Economic Rights and Duties of States: A Reflection or Rejection of International Law?' (1975) International Lawyer 295–318, 305. Forty years later, Brower maintained the same view, contending that the denunciation of the ICSID Convention and the critical review or termination of investment treaties in the late 2000s created the risk of a 'NEO-NIEO'. Notably, like the norm entrepreneurs of the 1950s and 1960s, he suggested that the Global North was becoming a negative influence on the South. Charles N. Brower and Sarah Melikian. '"We Have Met The Enemy And He Is US!" Is the Industrialized North "Going South" on Investor–State Arbitration?' (2015) Arbitration International 19–26.

[91] Haight (n. 85) 591–2.

[92] See Chapter 2, Sections A, C, and D and Thomas Hale, *Between Interests and Law: The Politics of Transnational Commercial Disputes* (CUP 2015) 217.

according to embedded liberalism. The future trajectory of international investment law was not evident in the long 1970s, as the views of the norm entrepreneurs and the OECD were challenged by the Global South and the labour movement. As we will see next, however, the norm entrepreneurs maintained the control of the field in the long run.

4

The Rise of Investment Treaties and ISDS in the 1990s and Since

By the early 1980s, many countries had not signed investment treaties or joined the ICSID Convention. Neither was there any ISDS practice. This situation would change quickly, however, as the views of the norm entrepreneurs of the 1950s and 1960s became part of the global consensus on development thinking. In the 1990s, the work of the World Bank and UNCTAD was quite consistent with the norm entrepreneurs' world-making project, for they championed the transformative force of foreign investment as a means to catch up with the global economy. These international organizations also put themselves at the forefront of efforts to promote investment treaties and ISDS, a task for which they had the support of organizations such as the American Bar Association, a strong advocate of international investment protection since the 1950s. The investment treaty network rapidly expanded, most states joined ICSID, and the first ISDS cases emerged.

Finding fertile terrain for itself, the legal imagination of the norm entrepreneurs developed and consolidated. This evolution was aided by a series of non-ISDS awards rendered during the 1970s and 1980s, which provided sources for ISDS awards as well as an opportunity to train a generation of US and European investment lawyers and arbitrators for ISDS: when such cases began in the late 1990s, international arbitrators were ready for the job. Some acted as pioneers of a new legal field, while others wrote in celebration of the fact that the proposals of the 1960s had now become *the law*—much to the chagrin of some states. Crucially, they also resolved the disputes in the background of the legal imagination.

A. The Washington Consensus and the role of UNCTAD and the World Bank

In the 1980s, the sort of economic intervention that the norm entrepreneurs opposed came under attack more generally. The election of President Ronald Reagan in the US in 1981 and Prime Minister Margaret Thatcher in Britain in 1979 marked a significant change in economic thinking.[1] Both implemented neoliberal

[1] Jamie Peck, *Constructions of Neoliberal Reason* (OUP 2010) 2–16.

Investment Treaties and the Legal Imagination. Nicolás M. Perrone, Oxford University Press (2021). © Nicolás M. Perrone.
DOI: 10.1093/oso/9780198862147.003.0005

programmes, trusting the private sector with vital public functions and services. It was a time of privatizations, market liberalization, and private–public partnerships.[2] A similar transformation was occurring in the Global South. Under World Bank sponsorship, some governments in Africa implemented structural adjustment programmes that included privatizing state enterprises and utilities.[3] Everywhere governments were relinquishing authority over the economy. They created and enforced market institutions, essentially private property and contracts, choosing to pursue public interests through the market or adopting market principles.[4] In the Global South, these economic policies became known as the Washington Consensus on development thinking because they were promoted by Washington, DC-based institutions.

Within a few years the Communist bloc collapsed, emerging economies abandoned import-substitution policies, and most countries adopted an economic model in which foreign private investment was to pursue the transformative role that the norm entrepreneurs had envisioned. The 1970s had been dominated by a consensus on the need to balance global and local dimensions of foreign investment; while significant differences between the Global North and the Global South existed, so did agreement on the need to make foreign investment serve divergent national interests. This quest for balance was practically absent in policy discourse of the 1990s. The change was profound and fast. Foreign investors were suddenly perceived as 'catalytic agents in the development' of the South[5] and 'major organisers of economic activity', bringing into host countries technology and organization skills.[6] As the 1999 World Investment Report observed: 'Twenty years ago or so, many governments saw TNCs as part of the "development problem". Now, they are part of the "solution."'[7]

This new consensus was followed by international initiatives to promote and protect these flows of capital. Unlike in the post-World War II decades, however, professional associations of bankers, lawyers, and business leaders were not at the forefront of the efforts; it was mainly the World Bank, UNCTAD, and Global North governments, with the support of organizations such as the American Bar Association.[8] The World Bank and UNCTAD recommended that countries sign

[2] Ibid.; Faranak Miraftab, 'Public-Private Partnerships: The Trojan Horse of Neoliberal Development?' (2004) 24 Journal of Planning Education and Research 89–101, 91.

[3] Francis Owusu, 'Pragmatism and the Gradual Shift from Dependency to Neoliberalism: The World Bank, African Leaders and Development Policy in Africa' (2003) 31 World development 1655–72.

[4] Wendy Brown, *Undoing the Demos: Neoliberalism's Stealth Revolution* (Zone Books 2015) 22–7.

[5] UNCTAD, *World Investment Report 1991: The Triad in Foreign Direct Investment* (United Nations 1991) 90.

[6] UNCTAD, *World Investment Report 1994: Transnational Corporations, Employment and the Workplace* (United Nations 1994) 163, 163–7.

[7] UNCTAD, *World Investment Report 1999: Foreign Direct Investment and the Challenge of Development* (United Nations 1999) 152.

[8] Lauge N. Skovgaard Poulsen, *Bounded Rationality and Economic Diplomacy: The Politics of Investment Treaties in Developing Countries* (CUP 2015) 71–99.

investment treaties based on their potential to facilitate foreign investment, signal a good investment climate to markets, and lock in domestic reforms.[9] These reforms were significant in some countries, as governments entirely overhauled foreign investment regulations; they opened their economies to foreign capital, but also implemented quite favourable regulatory regimes. This period was marked by generous regulatory givings to attract foreign investment. Sauvant notes that 'during the heyday of liberalization in the 1990s, some 95% of all (1,641) national FDI policy changes were in the direction of making the investment climate more welcoming for foreign investors'.[10]

The World Bank and UNCTAD did a good job. Over 1,500 international investment treaties were concluded in the 1990s—four per day between 1994 and 1996.[11] This represented a sharp increase in the stock and geographical reach of treaties: with the exception of Brazil, the Latin American countries now signed and ratified agreements. Many authors consider the Abs–Shawcross draft a key antecedent of these investment treaties, and indeed the similarities are remarkable. They include provisions on direct and indirect expropriation, the full compensation rule, the FET standard, state undertakings, and ISDS.[12] While the treaties signed during the 1950s and 1960s had no ISDS provision, investment treaty practice had evolved to incorporate it in the late 1960s thanks to the efforts of the ICSID Secretariat and the support of the norm entrepreneurs.[13]

The next subsections turn to how UNCTAD and the World Bank approached foreign investment and the relationship between these capital flows and development. The analysis also looks at the two institutions' views on international investment law, which focused mainly on foreign investor rights, investment treaties, and ISDS. A balanced international investment regime was not a priority on either of their agendas. The issue of foreign investment obligations had been taken over by MNCs themselves and other United Nations agencies. Many MNCs had created their own voluntary codes of conduct, and in 2000 the United Nations launched its Global Compact to convince MNCs to commit to observing basic human rights principles and complying with international labour and environmental standards on a voluntary basis.[14] This approach clearly aligned with the

[9] Ibid., 73–4, 82, 86, 91, 94.

[10] Karl P. Sauvant, 'The Negotiations of the United Nations Code of Conduct on Transnational Corporations: Experience and Lessons Learned' (2015) 16 Journal of World Investment & Trade 11–87, 61–2.

[11] UNCTAD, *World Investment Report 2013: Global Value Chains—Investment and Trade for Development* (United Nations 2013) 102.

[12] Rudolph Dolzer and Christoph Schreuer, *Principles of International Investment Law* (OUP 2012) 8–9; Andrew Newcombe and Lluís Paradell, *Law and Practice of Investment Treaties: Standards of Treatment* (Kluwer Law International 2009) 21–2; Chin Leng Lim, Jean Ho and Martins Paparinskis, *International Investment Law and Arbitration: Commentary, Awards and other Materials* (CUP 2018) 25.

[13] See Chapter 2, Sections A and D.7.

[14] Olivier De Schutter, 'The Challenge of Imposing Human Rights Norms on Corporate Actors' in Olivier De Schutter (ed.), *Transnational Corporations and Human Rights* (Hart 2006) 1–40, 1–17.

views of the International Chamber of Commerce and firms such as Royal Dutch Shell.[15]

1. UNCTAD

After the failure of the UN Code of Conduct for MNCs, and the shutdown of the United Nations Centre on Transnational Corporations in 1992, UNCTAD became the main UN agency on foreign investment and the World Investment Report would be one of its flagship publications. In the 1990s, these reports contended that MNCs could contribute to 'the establishment of a market economy' by disseminating private forms of ownership and entrepreneurship.[16] Foreign investment and privatizations had the power to transform the economic culture, but this required states to 'make their investment climate congenial to transnational corporations'.[17] Governments had to 'catch up with the market', adapting their policies to regional and world scales.[18] States needed to restructure 'according to modern organizational and management practices' so as to create a 'national enabling framework'.[19] In this respect, the World Investment Reports discussed three generations of measures. The first consisted of measures to liberalize, facilitate, and protect foreign investment. The second comprised policies 'actively seek[ing]' foreign investment and 'marketing […] countries',[20] including replacing red tape with a red carpet through the creation of investment promotion agencies. Once this economic, political, and social transformation was complete, states should focus on a third generation of measures aimed at 'target[ing] foreign investors according to the country's development priorities'.[21]

This development strategy constituted a paradigm shift, the World Investment Reports proclaimed: a shift from control to inducement of foreign investment.[22] If foreign investors were supposed to adjust to host-state development plans in the 1960s and 1970s, governments in the 1990s were expected to entice MNCs. The reports expected states to 'match' corporate needs with state locational assets 'as opposed [to] unilaterally seeking to impose [public] objectives on [MNCs]'.[23]

[15] Ibid., 32. Jean-Michel Marcoux, *International Investment Law and Globalization: Foreign Investment, Responsibilities and Intergovernmental Organizations* (Routledge 2018) 71–75.

[16] UNCTAD (n. 6) 104–5, 111. For an analysis of UNCTAD's World Investment Reports, see Nicolás M. Perrone, 'UNCTAD's World Investment Reports 1991–2015: 25 Years of Narratives Justifying and Balancing Foreign Investor Rights' (2018) 19 Journal of World Investment & Trade 7–40.

[17] UNCTAD (n. 5) 90.

[18] UNCTAD, *World Investment Report 1996: Investment, Trade and International Policy Agreements* (United Nations 1996) 129.

[19] UNCTAD, *World Investment Report 1993: Transnational Corporations and Integrated International Production* (United Nations 1993) 216.

[20] UNCTAD, *World Investment Report 2001: Promoting Linkages* (United Nations 2001) 123–4.

[21] Ibid.

[22] UNCTAD (n. 18) 191.

[23] UNCTAD (n. 7) 154–6.

This new policy approach shaped the imaginary of foreign investment relations. The 1990s World Investment Reports described each foreign investment project as the result of a transaction—a deal or bargain—in which MNCs offer a bundle of assets, such as technology, and host countries offer a package of location-specific assets.[24] The reports acknowledged that incentives and benefits might be needed in the case of Global South countries, due to increasing competition for foreign investment and their lack of trustworthy institutions. The general applicable framework sometimes needed to be 'augmented' or even 'overshadowed' by contractual provisions.[25]

Further, the 1990s World Investment Reports cautioned states against politically motivated regulation. They promoted market supervision, such as competition laws, but not regulation aimed at curbing costs and risks associated with foreign investment.[26] They opposed politics and the rule of power, favouring instead efficiency and rule of law as the two main criteria for public regulation. Politics was seen as focusing on short-term costs at the expense of long-term benefits. Global South countries were advised to 'minimize' interventions when uncertain or lacking administrative capabilities.[27]

In this context of reform and transformation, investment treaties and ISDS played a central role for UNCTAD. They clarified the rights and obligations of the parties involved in foreign investment relations, establishing 'a degree of stability, transparency and predictability'.[28] Investment treaties had effects on three different levels. First, they locked in reforms, helping states resist the temptation of short-term politics. Second, they served as a framework for domestic policy-making by prescribing 'the conduct that [was] expected' from states[29]—conduct that was more than 'mere equality of treatment'.[30] Third, investment treaties gave a positive signal to markets.

The World Investment Reports did not discuss the content of investment treaties in detail, but UNCTAD delved into their provisions in its 'Series on Issues in International Investment Agreements', also known as the 'Pink Series'. Coinciding with the increase in ISDS cases, the initiative covered various issues, including the controversial expropriation and FET provisions. Its publication on expropriation, published in 2000, focused on the debate between the Global South and Global North in the 1970s, recognizing the growing relevance of indirect expropriation. It stated that investment treaties resolve the issue of the standard of compensation in favour of full compensation, but admitted that the provisions do not provide

[24] UNCTAD, *World Investment Report 1992: Transnational corporations as engines of growth* (United Nations 1992) 4–5, 190–2, 295–7.
[25] UNCTAD (n. 7) 177, 324–8.
[26] UNCTAD (n. 24) 225–6.
[27] UNCTAD (n. 7) 174–6, 261, 316–8, 325.
[28] UNCTAD (n. 18) 194.
[29] Ibid., 189.
[30] Ibid., 183.

sufficient criteria to distinguish expropriations from 'tolerable' regulations.[31] Reductions on the profitability or value of an investment, for instance, could be considered a variable indicating an indirect expropriation. Interestingly, the publication linked the controversy over indirect expropriation to 'constitutional debates within domestic legal systems'.[32] It found, in this respect, that '[t]he extent to which States will accept that regulatory measures could be covered by a takings provision remains uncertain'.[33]

The 1999 publication on FET described that standard as inherently vague with implications that 'are not always easy to anticipate'.[34] Among other factors, this uncertainty emerged from the lack of consensus over whether the provision was an autonomous standard or a reflection of customary international law.[35] The publication suggested that states still introduced it in their treaties 'in the hope that this will enhance their reputation as countries hospitable to foreign capital'.[36] The FET standard signalled to the international community 'that investment within its jurisdiction will be subject to treatment compatible with some of the main expectations of foreign investors'.[37]

From the mid-2000s, UNCTAD became less optimistic about investment treaties. The 2003 World Investment Report noted that such treaties had been criticized for 'imposing too much control over the sovereign discretion to limit the enjoyment of private property in the public interest'.[38] The notion of indirect expropriation was problematic, the report stated, given 'the ever increasing and changing conception of property rights and, in particular, of the social function of property'.[39] After the 2008 economic crisis, the World Investment Reports further focused attention on the tension between investment treaties and states' right to regulate. The 2008 report found that 'there is some concern that improved protection and certainty for foreign investors has come at the price of too much of a reduction in the government's regulatory flexibility'.[40] This problem, however, raised 'difficult legal questions about the borderline between permitted regulatory activities of the State and illegal interference with investor rights'.[41] Striking a balance

[31] UNCTAD, *Taking of Property. UNCTAD Series on Issues in International Investment Agreements* (United Nations 2000) 6, 11–12.
[32] Ibid.
[33] Ibid., 24.
[34] UNCTAD, *Fair and Equitable Treatment. UNCTAD Series on Issues in International Investment Agreements* (United Nations 1999) 57, 5–6, 11, 62.
[35] Ibid., 37.
[36] Ibid., 5.
[37] Ibid., 3.
[38] UNCTAD, *World Investment Report 2003: FDI Policies for Development: National and International Perspectives* (United Nations 2003) 112–13.
[39] Ibid., 111.
[40] UNCTAD, *World Investment Report 2008: Transnational Corporations, and the Infrastructure Challenge* (United Nations 2008) 168.
[41] UNCTAD, *World Investment Report 2015: Reforming International Investment Governance* (United Nations 2015) 124. Also, *UNCTAD, Investment Policy Framework for Sustainable Development* (United Nations 2012).

between foreign investor rights and states' right to regulate became a major policy challenge.

2. The World Bank

The World Bank has contributed to the promotion and protection of foreign investment since its creation. Its 1985 World Development Report insisted on the central role of international capital for development, particularly in the aftermath of the financial turbulences of late 1970s and early 1980s. That report gave an account of the World Bank's activities in this area, including the creation of ICSID, the Multilateral Investment Guarantee Agency, and the International Finance Corporation.[42] The latter assisted states in revising foreign investment laws, privatizing state-owned corporations, and discouraging performance requirements or other restrictive measures.

For the 1985 World Development Report, a principal obstacle to foreign investment inflows, albeit not the only one, was 'political risk—the threat of expropriation, blocked currency, war, revolution, or insurrection'.[43] This risk also included other actions that may 'undermine the value of property rights'.[44] The 2005 World Development Report added that '[f]oreign investors are often particularly vulnerable',[45] because politicians may find it attractive to target foreigners, domestic courts may be reluctant to rule against the host government, and large natural resource and infrastructure projects—especially in sensitive sectors—may be exposed to government efforts to unilaterally renegotiate terms. To address this, the World Bank advised that countries sign investment treaties, join ICSID, and consider investment guarantee schemes.[46]

The 2005 report also described some of the trade-offs involved in these treaties. It argued that an effective system of international dispute settlement, such as ICSID, should not be measured by 'the number of cases heard, but in the incentives it creates for the parties to adhere to their commitments'.[47] The World Bank believed that improving the 'credibility of government commitments can be especially important for countries with domestic institutions at an early stage of development'.[48] At the same time, it warned that investment treaties may 'enhance policy credibility' but at the cost of less flexibility. Similarly, entering into investment

[42] World Bank, *World Development Report 1985: International Capital and Economic Development* (World Bank 1985) 132–3.
[43] Ibid., 131
[44] World Bank, *World Development Report 2005: A Better Investment Climate for Everyone* (World Bank 2005) 94.
[45] Ibid., 92.
[46] Ibid., 175–80.
[47] Ibid., 179.
[48] Ibid., 184.

treaties may signal a commitment to global standards to markets; however, these standards may be 'less customized to local circumstances'.[49]

World Bank general counsels Broches and Shihata were convinced of the advantages of investment treaties as 'an incentive for investors to assume long-term commitments'.[50] As Poulsen observes, the ICSID position was that 'if [developing countries] wanted to convince foreign investors to commit for the long term, it would be prudent to adopt investment treaties as part of their governing apparatus'.[51] The legal views of the World Bank and ICSID are found in the 1992 World Bank Report and Guidelines on the Treatment of Foreign Direct Investment (hereinafter the World Bank Guidelines) and in the handbook for investment treaty negotiators, published in 1995 under the title *Bilateral Investment Treaties*. In the preface, Shihata wrote that the book 'presents all the elements of modern BITs and explains what the main problems are'.[52]

The World Bank Guidelines hoped to improve the investment climate and facilitate investment flows, with the stated aim of bringing substantial benefits to the world economy and 'developing' countries.[53] The report accompanying the guidelines acknowledged the existence of rules on international investment but questioned their suitability to promote foreign investment; thus the World Bank was 'progressively developing rather than merely codifying applicable rules in the field'.[54] The goal was to ensure that foreign investment flows were 'governed only by economic considerations' and not 'hampered by avoidable non-commercial factors'.[55]

The scope of application of the World Bank Guidelines is broad, with ISDS as the preferred dispute settlement mechanism. The guidelines apply to bona fide foreign private investments with the only exception of portfolio investment. The lack of foreign investor obligations—such as those included in the UN Code of Conduct—was justified because the World Bank Guidelines only apply to investors acting 'in good faith and in full conformity with the laws and regulations of the host State'.[56] Recognizing that foreign investors and states may sometimes fail to amicably resolve disputes through negotiations, the report suggested that in such cases international arbitration (ISDS) would be the ideal way to resolution.[57]

[49] Ibid., 175–6.

[50] Aron Broches, *Selected Essays: World Bank, ICSID and other Subjects of Public and Private International Law* (Martinus Nijhoff Publishers 1995) 263. Also, Ibrahim Shihata, 'Factors Influencing the Flow of Foreign Investment and the Relevance of a Multilateral Investment Guarantee Scheme' (1987) 21 The International Lawyer 671–94, 685–6.

[51] Poulsen (n. 8) 74.

[52] Rudolf Dolzer and Margrete Stevens, *Bilateral Investment Treaties* (Martinus Nijhoff Publishers 1995) vi.

[53] World Bank, *Legal Framework for the Treatment of Foreign Investment, Volume II: Guidelines* (World Bank 1992) 3.

[54] Ibid., 6.

[55] Ibid., 13.

[56] Ibid., 9–10.

[57] Ibid., 30.

The substantive standards of protection included in the World Bank Guidelines are similar to those in investment treaties, except for more detailed rules on investment contracts and compensation standards. The FET provision responded to a perceived need for an objective standard of treatment under international law, in addition to national treatment, but the report accompanying the guidelines neither defined nor explained this standard.[58] In relation to expropriation, the report clarified that indirect expropriations are 'measures, such as excessive and repetitive tax or regulatory measures, that have a de facto confiscatory effect [. . .] depriving the investor in fact from his ownership, control or substantial benefits over his enterprise'.[59] Notably, the World Bank recognized that states might only pay partial compensation in cases of 'large scale social reforms following the most exceptional circumstances', although these circumstances 'rarely occur and [. . .] may be expected to become more uncommon in future'.[60]

The guidelines hold that states can expropriate contracts and that the unilateral alteration of contracts can violate international law. The report further explained that sovereign acts affecting investment contracts are governed by international law—by the same expropriation standards—whereas contractual measures remain subject to the applicable law to the contract.[61]

Bilateral Investment Treaties was sponsored by ICSID and authored by Rudolph Dolzer and Margrete Stevens, an influential investment scholar and an active figure in the development of ICSID respectively. Like the World Bank Guidelines, Dolzer and Stevens did not shed much light on the meaning of the FET provision. They wrote that this 'basic' standard was 'detached from host state's domestic laws' but there was 'no general agreement on the precise meaning of the phrase'.[62] Crucially, they asserted that a reason for its indeterminacy lay in its unsettled relationship with the minimum standard of treatment under international law. They noted that while some authors claimed that the FET standard was 'tantamount' to the minimum standard, others argued that it was an 'independent, self-contained' concept that went 'far beyond the minimum standard'.[63] Dolzer and Stevens supported the second thesis.

The discussion of indirect expropriation, on the contrary, was quite detailed. International investment treaties were said to cover direct expropriations, nationalizations, and indirect and creeping expropriations, 'and accord to them all the same legal treatment', including the need to pay prompt, adequate, and effective compensation.[64] Dolzer and Stevens recognized that determining what constitutes

58 Ibid., 20.
59 Ibid., 24.
60 Ibid., 28–9.
61 Ibid., 29.
62 Dolzer and Stevens (n. 52) 58.
63 Ibid., 59–60.
64 Ibid., 99.

an indirect expropriation was of relevance to both investors and host states: the interpretation of this provision would affect foreign investors' economic returns as much as states' right to regulate 'the rights and obligations of owners'.[65] Yet they admitted that there was no clear definition of indirect expropriation, and a wide variety of state measures may constitute it. Tribunals often decided 'on the basis of its attending circumstances'. Thus Dolzer and Stevens argued that the effects of a measure on foreign investors' rights was a particularly relevant circumstance. They claimed that if the effects were similar to those in an 'outright expropriation', states must pay compensation.[66]

Dolzer and Stevens also looked at state obligations or undertakings with regard to foreign investors, a provision also known as the umbrella clause. They explained that it sought 'to ensure that each Party to the treaty will respect specific undertakings towards nationals of the other Party'.[67] Its importance lay in the disagreement about whether any interference—caused by a simple breach of contract or by administrative or legislative acts—could constitute a violation of international law.[68] The reference to undertakings or obligations here is vague, without any discussion of whether this provision could serve to protect and enforce foreign investors' reliance.

B. Antecedents in investment (non-ISDS) arbitration

The policy developments of the 1990s occurred in the background of significant arbitral developments in international investment law. These arbitrations concerned disputes over oil concessions after decolonization, US citizens' claims against Iran following the 1979 Islamic Revolution, and the consequences of the 1997–98 Asian financial crisis in Indonesia. Although these cases were not based on investment treaties, they represented decisive stepping-stones in the development of the field, influencing ISDS practice considerably. These arbitrations were also formative for a generation of US and European lawyers and arbitrators who later acted in ISDS cases.

After decolonization, several disputes arose between foreign investors and oil-producing countries involving concession contracts and their status under international law. The *Anglo-Iranian* case was one of the first and most relevant. The UK argued before the ICJ that the concession contract between the Anglo-Iranian Company and Iran had a double character—on the one hand it was a contract between the firm and Iran, and on the other a treaty between Britain and Iran.[69] The

[65] Ibid.
[66] Ibid., 100.
[67] Ibid., 81.
[68] Ibid., 82.
[69] *Anglo-Iranian Oil Company case* (*United Kingdom v. Iran*) [1952] ICJ Rep 93 (22 July 1952).

court rejected that argument and dismissed the case in 1952, but this did not end the discussion. In his dissent, Judge Levi Carneiro exposed concerns similar to those of the norm entrepreneurs:

> When there are so many countries in need of foreign capital for the development of their economy, it would not only be unjust, it would be a grave mistake to expose such capital, without restrictions or guarantee, to the hazards of the legislation of countries in which such capital has been invested.[70]

Debate over the internationalization of contracts continued for decades. Despite the ICJ's decision, many international lawyers argued that concession contracts constituted quasi-international treaties, or that international law applied to them, so as to prevent unilateral state action.[71] The work of these scholars contributed to the progressive development of international law, as arbitral awards gradually came to accept the internationalization of concession contracts.[72]

This thesis consolidated and crystallized in René-Jean Dupuy's 1977 award in *Texaco v Libya*.[73] As Anghie and Sornarajah have explained, that award did not constitute an abrupt shift in the interpretation of concession contracts.[74] It was audacious in its connection of the internationalization of investment contracts with economic development,[75] but it ultimately represented the 'culmination of a series of legal developments which focused on identifying the unique character of these contracts and then formulating the principles of law which applied to their operation'.[76] The most fundamental of these principles was found to be the strict observation of *pacta sunt servanda*, even if the original circumstances have changed. In *Revere Cooper v. OPIC*, a 1978 award later referenced in ISDS practice, the arbitrators explained that *pacta sunt servanda* was indispensable for foreign investors'

[70] Ibid., Dissenting Opinion of Judge Levi Carneiro, 151. Cited in Hermann J. Abs, *Die rechtliche Problematik privater Auslandsinvestitionen*. Vortrag gehalten vor der Juristischen Studiengesellschaft in Karlsruhe, am 16. Dezember 1968 (Müller 1969) 6.

[71] Ivar Alvik, *Contracting With Sovereignty: State Contracts and International Arbitration* (Hart 2011) 62–8. In addition to important international lawyers, such as Alfred Verdross and Arnold McNair, those who promoted this thesis included George Ray and Lowell Wadmond, counsels of Arabian American Oil Company in the *Aramco* case. See Mohamed Bin Abdul Latif and Bin Mohamed Almulhim, *Middle East Oil: A Redistribution of Values Arising from the Oil Industry* (University Press of America 2009) 94, 96, 101.

[72] See, e.g., the *Aramco Arbitration* (1963 [1958]) 27 International Law Reports 117; *Sapphire v. NIOC* (1963) 35 International Law Reports 136.

[73] *Texaco Overseas Petroleum Company v. Libya* (1979 [1977]) Yearbook of Commercial Arbitration 177.

[74] See Muthucumaraswamy Sornarajah, *The International Law on Foreign Investment* (CUP 2017) 339–49; Antony Anghie, *Imperialism, Sovereignty and the Making of International Law* (CUP 2005) 223–35.

[75] See Julien Cantegreil, 'The Audacity of the Texaco/Calasiatic Award: René-Jean Dupuy and the Internationalization of Foreign Investment Law' (2011) 22 European Journal of International Law 441–58, 445.

[76] Anghie (n. 74) 226. Also, see Jean Ho, *State Responsibility for Breaches of Investment Contracts* (CUP 2018).

calculability. Regardless of domestic law, international investors require states to respect 'the undertakings and assurances given in good faith to such aliens as an inducement to their making the investment'.[77] Otherwise, there is 'no way in which rational decisions can be made'.[78]

The decisions of the Iran-US Claims Tribunal made another significant contribution to international investment law.[79] These awards created a 'significant body of precedent' on controversial issues, including the internationalization of contracts and indirect expropriation.[80] Many of the disputes between US investors and Iran after the Islamic Revolution involved allegations of indirect expropriation, in some cases due to the managers and supervisors that Iran appointed in foreign-owned firms. These disputes led to awards later cited in ISDS practice. In *Tippetts v. TAMS-AFFA Consulting Engineers of Iran* (1984), the arbitrators concluded that the public measure constituted a taking of property not because of the appointments *per se*, but as a result of the actions taken by the appointed manager. They reasoned that '[a] deprivation or taking of property may occur under international law through interference by a state in the use of that property or with the enjoyment of its benefits, even where legal title to the property is not affected'.[81]

Even if the awards of the Iran-US Claims Tribunal also concluded that the normal exercise of police powers does not create a right to compensation, only one case was dismissed on these grounds: *Too v. Greater Modesto Insurance Associates* (1989).[82] The arbitrators acting in these cases were unconvinced that compensation could be waived when the measures were motivated by worthy economic or social objectives.[83]

The Iran-US Claims Tribunal contributed to the development of international investment law in other far-reaching ways. These awards marked a clear breakthrough from the NIEO. One arbitrator observed that the tribunals had 'been less affected by the "New International Economic Order" and collectivist economic theories than [many] would have been predicted in the 1970s'.[84] Further, a generation of US and European investment lawyers who started their careers in the Iran-US Claims Tribunal later worked on many ISDS cases.[85]

[77] *Revere Copper v. Overseas Private Investment Corporation* (AAA Case No. 1610013776) Award, 24 August 1978, para. 37

[78] Ibid., para. 115.

[79] See *Merrill & Ring Forestry v. Canada* (ICSID Case No. UNCT/07/1) Award, 31 March 2010, para. 207.

[80] George H. Aldrich, 'What Constitutes a Compensable Taking of Property? The Decisions of the Iran-United States Claims Tribunal' (1994) 88 American Journal of International Law 585–610, 586.

[81] *Tippetts and others v. TAMS-AFFA Consulting Engineers of Iran*, 6 Iran-US Cl Trib Rep, 219, paras. 225–6.

[82] Aldrich (n. 80) 605.

[83] Ibid., 590, 605.

[84] Ibid., 590.

[85] One of the most notable cases is that of Charles Brower, who actively opposed the NIEO in the 1970s. He was 'one of the few and one of the leading voices to respond to investment arbitration's critics by insisting that the system is not unbalanced and needs no revision'. Pierre-Marie Dupuy and Julie Maupin, 'Of Wit, Wisdom, and Balance in International Law. Reflections on the Tokyo Resolution

Lastly, among other antecedents, it is worth mentioning the arbitrations related to the Indonesian crisis of the late 1990s. Although probably less influential than the cases mentioned above, these awards anticipated the reasoning and tone of certain influential ISDS awards. The Indonesian crisis brought about complex legal questions concerning the treatment of foreign investment, which Louis Wells and Rafiq Ahmed discussed in their 2007 book *Property Rights and National Sovereignty*. Wells and Ahmed criticized arbitrators for privileging 'a rigid view of contract and other property rights',[86] which could lead to moral hazard and regulatory chill.[87] But some arbitrators went further than that, to discuss, in passing, policy options for 'modern Indonesian society'. In *Himpurna California Energy Ltd (Bermuda) v. Indonesia* (1999), the tribunal said that:

> Given the important place Indonesia occupies in the world stage, the relative deficiencies of the country's legal framework stand in stark and unfortunate contrast—as though an eagle had to live with the wings of a sparrow. This Arbitral Tribunal has of course no mandate to prescribe policy. On the other hand, it is essential, for the reasoning of this Award to be understood, that the Arbitral Tribunal note the opaque and fragmented normative environment of the Parties' contractual relationship.[88]

C. ISDS and the progressive development of international investment law

The ratification of thousands of investment treaties in the 1990s was followed by a string of ISDS cases starting at the decade's end. For the first time, arbitrators had to interpret these treaties and their provisions on indirect expropriation or FET, discussing where to draw the line between a treaty violation and a legitimate public regulation. The following sections look at the reasoning and *obiter dicta* of these ISDS awards, as well as interviews and the academic work of arbitrators. In deciding these disputes, as I show next, arbitrators embraced the legal imagination of the norm entrepreneurs.

of the Institut de Droit International' in David Caron, Stephan W. Schill, Abby Cohen Smutny, and Epaminontas E. Triantafilou (eds.), *Practising Virtue: Inside International Arbitration* (OUP 2016) 706–21, 708.

[86] Louis T. Wells and Rafiq Ahmed, *Making Foreign Investment Safe: Property Rights and National Sovereignty* (OUP 2007) 285.

[87] Ibid., 287, 290.

[88] *Himpurna California Energy Ltd. v PT. (Persero) Perusahaan Listruik Negara (Indonesia)* (UNCITRAL Ad Hoc) Award, 4 May 1999, para. 70.

1. Arbitrators as law creators and storytellers

The provisions of investment treaties, and the consent of the parties to ISDS, indicate that the role of arbitrators is to resolve controversies between foreign investors and states according to the applicable treaty and the arbitration rules.[89] Arbitrators often highlight this limited mandate when states rely on contract or domestic law obligations to bring a counterclaim, or when civil society or local communities want to participate in an ISDS case.[90] These foreign investor obligations or the participation of local communities are outside the jurisdiction of the tribunal because they are beyond the consent of the parties. Arbitrators' attitude is different when it comes to the law applicable to the dispute. In most legal systems, judges describe their role as objective interpretation of the facts and the legal text; they resist the label of law creators, as this could undermine their authority or create personal anxiety.[91] Some investment arbitrators, Todd Tucker explains in his book, feel similarly—they 'apply the law; that is it'. They find their job 'boring and clerical', admitting that fact-finding grants arbitrators some more—albeit still limited—discretion.[92]

Notably, however, the majority of arbitrators regard the job as requiring contributions to the progressive development of the law. Tucker notes that most of the arbitrators he interviewed were in the creative middle. They believe that resolving ISDS cases requires 'creating the law as you go along'. Some even see the job as that of a 'pioneer' involved in a 'revolution in the legal system'.[93] Overall, arbitrators recognize that ISDS awards have developed 'a more international body of law with respect to investment'.[94] At the same time, these individuals have a different approach to creativity when exercised by academic arbitrators. Law firms do not want to appoint academics as arbitrators, they explain, because academics will be 'thoughtful and creative and come up with something new and unexpected'.[95] This

[89] *UPS v. Canada* (ICSID Case No. UNCT/02/1) Decision of the Tribunal on Petitions for Intervention and Participation as Amici Curiae, 17 October 2001, paras. 39–43. In *Glamis v. USA*, the arbitrators highlighted their 'case-specific mandate' while noting also that they would decide the case taking into account 'the context within which it operates'. *Glamis v. USA* (NAFTA—UNCITRAL) Award, 8 June 2009, paras. 1, 7. Also, Moshe Hirsch, 'Investment Tribunals and Human Rights Treaties: A Sociological Perspective' in Freya Baetens (ed.), *Investment Law within International Law: Integrationist Perspectives* (CUP 2013) 85–105, 99.

[90] *Urbaser v. Argentina* (ICSID Case No. ARB/07/26) Award, 8 December 2016, para. 1206; *Burlington v. Republic of Ecuador* (ICSID Case No. ARB/08/5) Decision on Ecuador's Counterclaims, 7 February 2017 (Burlington expressly consented to the jurisdiction of the tribunal in this case). ISDS practice concerning *amicus curiae* participation is inconsistent. See Chapter 7, Section B.

[91] Duncan Kennedy, *A Critique of Adjudication [fin de siècle]* (Harvard University Press 1997) 55, 61, 191–4.

[92] Todd N. Tucker, *Judge Knot: Politics and Development in International Investment Law* (Anthem Press 2018) 126–7.

[93] Ibid., 128.

[94] Ibid., 79.

[95] Ibid., 131.

suggests that although there is significant judicial creativity going on in ISDS, some actors have expectations about the sort of creativity that is and is not acceptable.

Arbitrators who praise judicial creativity show a similar approach to fact-finding. Some of those interviewed by Tucker affirm that the interpretation of facts explains the outcome of most ISDS cases. Arbitrators follow their 'conviction' or 'gut feeling'.[96] They 'go by the facts of the case […]. So that then from that, you bridge it to fair and equitable treatment'.[97]

Many awards and academic articles confirm the views expressed in Tucker's interviews. Paulsson asserts that 'it is pointless to resist the observation that precedents generate norms of international law'.[98] Gabrielle Kaufmann-Kohler adds that 'the less developed the body of rules is, the more important the role of the dispute resolver will be with respect to the creation of rules'.[99] Arbitrators are not obliged to follow earlier decisions, but they acknowledge that previous awards may provide a 'useful light' or constitute a jurisprudence constante.[100] In key areas of international investment law, such as legitimate expectations, awards constitute the primary source of law, while the reasoning shows that arbitrators follow a case-by-case approach and pay significant attention to facts.[101] The case-by-case approach also dominates decisions on indirect expropriation claims.[102]

This situation is prone to creating tension between the legislator, namely states, and arbitrators. The distinction between creating and interpreting law is 'a legal fiction', as Campbell McLachlan has written, but one that is crucial for international law in order to maintain the idea that states control law's development.[103] This delicate balance contrasts with the attitude of those ISDS tribunals that have shown less restraint when resolving disputes than domestic or other international adjudicators.[104] The latter also face problems of indeterminacy, and inevitably make law,

[96] Ibid., 129.

[97] Ibid.

[98] Jan Paulsson, 'International Arbitration and the Generation of Legal Norms: Treaty Arbitration and International Law' in Albert Jan van den Berg (ed.), *International Arbitration 2006: Back to Basics?* (Kluwer Law International 2007) 879–89, 881.

[99] Gabrielle Kaufmann-Kohler, 'Arbitral Precedent: Dream, Necessity or Excuse?: The 2006 Freshfields Lecture' (2007) 23 Arbitration International 357–78, 375.

[100] *UP and CD Holding Internationale v. Hungary* (ICSID Case No. ARB/13/35) Award, 9 October 2018, para. 289; *Burlington v. Republic of Ecuador* (ICSID Case No. ARB/08/5) Decision on Liability, 14 December 2012, para. 187.

[101] *Spyridon Roussalis v. Romania* (ICSID Case No. ARB/06/1) Award, 7 December 2011, para. 318; *Joseph Charles Lemire v. Ukraine* (ICSID Case No. ARB/06/18) Decision on Jurisdiction and Liability, 14 January 2010, para. 284. Also, Martins Paparinskis, *The International Minimum Standard and Fair and Equitable Treatment* (OUP 2013) 252–6.

[102] *Generation Ukraine v. Ukraine* (ICSID Case No. ARB/00/9) Award, 16 September 2003, para. 20.29.

[103] Campbell McLachlan, 'Investment Treaties and General International Law' (2008) 57 International and Comparative Law Quarterly 361–401, 392. Also, Anthea Roberts, 'Power and Persuasion in Investment Treaty Interpretation: The Dual Role of States' (2010) 104 American Journal of International Law 179–225, 184, 189.

[104] Gus Van Harten, *Sovereign Choices and Sovereign Constraints: Judicial Restraint in Investment Treaty Arbitration* (OUP 2013) 158.

but, unlike investment arbitrators, are inclined to downplay the legislative dimension of their job.[105]

2. Modernity and good governance in ISDS practice

The first ISDS cases were resolved in the 1990s and early 2000s, in the background of the Washington Consensus and the ratification of thousands of investment treaties. Some of those awards show a blend of legal creativity and opinions expressed, in passing, about foreign investment relations and what the investor community expected from states. A frequent arbitrator interviewed by Tucker notes that 'in the beginning arbitrators were too enthusiastic about this. Oh look at what we can say!'[106]

The first ever investment treaty dispute was *AAPL v. Sri Lanka*, awarded in 1990. This tribunal had to decide whether Sri Lanka was responsible for the destruction of a shrimp farm in the eastern region of the country, which was affected by the ongoing civil war. That conflict lasted for twenty-six years and caused the deaths of between 40,000 and 100,000 people.[107] The arbitrators held that Sri Lanka had to pay compensation despite the war, arguing that it had fallen below what was expected from a 'modern state'.[108] They observed that international law had evolved from an 'old "subjective" criteria' to an '"objective" standard of vigilance', which did not take into account 'the relatively limited possibilities of local authorities in a given context'. The arbitrators focused on 'what should be legitimately expected to be secured for foreign investors by a reasonably well organized modern State'.[109]

The level of protection required by investment treaties in the context of internal armed conflicts was debated again in an ISDS case against Zaire.[110] The tribunal in *AMT v. Zaire* discussed the state's responsibility for the destruction and looting of a factory by members of its army. Zaire argued that domestic and foreign business alike were not compensated for the violent events that occurred there in the early 1990s.[111] In 1997, however, the arbitrators decided that Zaire was obliged to 'take all necessary measures to ensure the full enjoyment of protection and security of

[105] Kennedy (n. 91) 55; Farewell Speech of Seung Wha Chang at the WTO Dispute Settlement Body, 26 September 2016, available at https://www.wto.org/english/news_e/news16_e/changfarwellspeech_e.pdf (last visited 29 September 2020); Farewell Speech of Peter Van den Bossche at the WTO Dispute Settlement Body, 28 May 2019, available at https://www.wto.org/english/tratop_e/dispu_e/farwellspeech_peter_van_den_bossche_e.htm (last visited 29 September 2020).

[106] Tucker (n. 92) 58.

[107] Krista Mahr, 'Sri Lanka to Start Tally of Civil-War Dead' *Time Magazine*, 28 November 2013.

[108] *AAPL v. Sri Lanka* (ICSID Case No. ARB/87/3) Award, 27 June 1990, para. 77.

[109] Ibid.

[110] More than 200 people were killed in this conflict. Bill Berkeley, 'Zaire: An African Horror Story' *The Atlantic*, August 1993.

[111] *AMT v. Zaire* (ICSID Case No. ARB/93/1) Award, 21 February 1997, paras. 3.12, 6.10.

its investments'. To escape liability, they said, Zaire 'must show that it has taken all measure of precaution to protect the investment'.[112]

On the other hand, arbitrators were more deferent when states were trying to catch up with the market. *Genin v. Estonia* is a case in point. This dispute concerned the cancellation of an operating licence by the Central Bank of Estonia. Despite some irregularities, the arbitrators dismissed the claim in 2001, reasoning that Estonia should be judged by a different standard as it had recently embarked on a complex 'political and economic transition'.[113] They also added, however, that '[i]t is to be hoped […] that Bank of Estonia will exercise its regulatory and supervisory functions with greater caution regarding procedure in the future.'[114]

ISDS tribunals also praised states for moving in the *right direction* and creating a hospitable climate for foreign investment. The *Fedax v. Venezuela* case involved certain promissory notes issued by Venezuela and acquired through endorsement by Fedax. In 1998, the arbitrators noted, to their 'satisfaction', that this ISDS case was the first involving a 'prominent member of the Latin American region, a fact which in itself illustrates well the evolution that the legal treatment of foreign investments has had in this region as elsewhere in the world'.[115] Venezuela's behaviour, they felt, was 'fully consistent with its good standing in the international financial community'.[116] The arbitrators also commended the 'prominent Venezuelan lawyers' who were the counsels for claimant and respondent.[117]

As UNCTAD anticipated, some states criticized the interpretation of investment treaties. The tribunal in *Pope and Talbot v. Canada* was asked to review the implementation of an agreement on softwood lumber which Canada had concluded with the US. Canada claimed that non-discriminatory regulations are beyond the reach of the rules regarding expropriation, and that the minimum standard of treatment only protects investors against egregious conduct. In two awards, rendered in 2000 and 2001, the arbitrators disagreed. They reasoned that such 'a blanket exception for regulatory measures would create a gaping loophole in international protections against expropriation'.[118] Similarly, the tribunal explained that Canada's interpretation of the minimum standard of treatment undermined NAFTA's objective to create a 'hospitable climate that would insulate [foreign investors] from political risks or incidents of unfair treatment'. It was 'doubtful' that the NAFTA parties wanted to present potential investors with protection 'against anything but

[112] Ibid., para. 6.05.
[113] *Genin v. Estonia* (ICSID Case No. ARB/99/2) Award, 25 June 2001, para. 370.
[114] Ibid., 372.
[115] *Fedax v. Venezuela* (ICSID Case No. ARB/96/3) Award, 9 March 1998, para. 36.
[116] Ibid.
[117] Ibid.
[118] *Pope & Talbot v. Canada* (UNCITRAL—NAFTA) Interim Award, 26 June 2000, para. 99. Other tribunals have underscored the same point, see *TecMed v. Mexico* (ICSID Case No. ARB (AF)/00/2) Award, 29 May 2003, para. 121. *Bilcon v. Canada* (PCA Case No. 2009-04) Award on Jurisdiction and Liability, 17 March 2015, para. 597.

egregiously unfair conduct'.[119] In view of the facts, the arbitrators concluded that Canada had failed to abide by the minimum standard, observing that '[w]hile administration, like legislation, can be likened to sausage making, this episode goes well beyond the glitches and innocent mistakes that may typify the process'.[120]

The NAFTA parties struck back. Mexico, the US, and Canada issued a binding interpretation of NAFTA Article 1105, clarifying that this provision only requires the minimum standard under customary international law. Canada further argued that the standard should be interpreted according to the decision in *Neer v. Mexico* of the 1920s.[121] Again, the tribunal disagreed, saying in a 2002 award that Canada's views 'were perhaps shaped by its erroneous belief' that the law had remained static for more than eighty years.[122] International investment law had evolved since the 1920s, the FET standard was now a central provision of international investment treaties, and countries had signed more than 1,800 treaties, the arbitrators noted. They pointed at the significance of the 1967 OECD Draft in this evolution, which marked a shift in favour of 'an independent consideration of how host countries should treat foreign owned property'.[123] Notions such as due process denote 'more rigorous standards for evaluating what governments do to people and companies'.[124] Most subsequent ISDS tribunals have agreed with this assessment of international investment law's evolution, observing that 'reality' had changed.[125]

At this juncture, around the early 2000s, arbitrators engaged in a 'fierce competition [. . .] to author a pithy single-paragraph proclamation' of the FET standard.[126] This standard became the platform from where arbitrators could provide their imaginary of foreign investment relations. The tribunal in *CME v. the Czech Republic* held in 2000 that the FET standard is 'at the heart of investment treaties' because it 'may prohibit actions—including State administrative actions—that would otherwise be legal under both domestic and international law'.[127]

The most influential tribunals interpreted the FET standard using the language and rhetoric of good governance. The *Metalclad v. Mexico* tribunal is a notable example.[128] This dispute was about potential disagreements between the

[119] *Pope & Talbot v. Canada* (UNCITRAL—NAFTA) Award on the Merits of Phase 2, 10 April 2001, para. 116.

[120] Ibid., para. 181.

[121] *Pope & Talbot v. Canada* (UNCITRAL—NAFTA) Award on Damages, 31 May 2002, para. 46.

[122] Ibid., para. 62.

[123] Ibid., para. 60.

[124] Ibid., para. 64.

[125] *Merrill & Ring Forestry v. Canada* (ICSID Case No. UNCT/07/1) Award, 31 March 2010, para. 210. See also Dolzer and Schreuer (n. 12) 139–41.

[126] Zachary Douglas, 'Nothing if not Critical for Investment Treaty Arbitration: Occidental, Eureko and Methanex' (2006) 22 Arbitration International 27–52, 27.

[127] *CME v. the Czech Republic* (UNCITRAL) Partial Award, 13 September 2001, para. 156.

[128] *Metalclad v. Mexico* (ICSID Case No. ARB(AF)/97/1) Award, 30 August 2000. It remains debatable whether this was the first award to conflate foreign investor rights and good governance. In *Saag Papier*, the arbitrators had emphasized that the investor 'could not be expected to know what Poland's own government authorities at a higher level apparently ignored'. *Saar Papier v. Poland* (UNCITRAL) Award, 16 October 1995, para. 93(b). For an analysis of the good governance narrative in ISDS, see

different levels of governments—a recurrent risk for foreign investors—and how to distribute the costs and risks of inconsistencies in federal and democratic states. According to the award, rendered in 2000, the principle of transparency required that 'all relevant legal requirements for the purpose of initiating, completing and successfully operating investments made, or intended to be made […] should be capable of being readily known to all affected investors'.[129] Mexico did not to live up to this expectation, failing 'to ensure a transparent and predictable framework for Metalclad's business planning and investment'.[130] This finding on transparency was later annulled by a Court of British Columbia, but the reasoning has remained influential in ISDS practice.[131]

For some time, the winner of the competition to define the FET standard was the tribunal in *TecMed v. Mexico*, which rendered its award in 2003. These arbitrators focused on an interpretation appropriate 'to the modern eye'.[132] They relied on the principle of good faith to conclude that Mexico was required to treat TecMed according to the 'basic expectations that were taken into account by the foreign investor to make the investment'. The tribunal reasoned that 'the foreign investor expects the host State to act in a consistent manner, free from ambiguity and totally transparently […] so that it may know beforehand any and all rules and regulations that will govern its investments'.[133] Zachary Douglas described this standard as 'perfect public regulation in a perfect world'.[134] Unsurprisingly, Mexico failed to abide by it.

In 2006, arbitrator Thomas Wälde discussed the doctrinal and policy bases of this good governance programme in his separate opinion in *Thunderbird v. Mexico*. He reasoned that foreign investors are exposed to political and regulatory risks—they are in a 'situation of relative weakness'—and therefore 'the risk of ambiguity of a governmental assurance is allocated rather to the government than to a foreign investor'. Foreign investors 'need to rely on […] government's regulatory and administrative messages'.[135] Interestingly, Wälde made this argument in a dispute in which the investor had misled the Mexican authorities to obtain a licence. The two other arbitrators did not object to the doctrine of legitimate expectations, but

Mavluda Sattorova, *The Impact of Investment Treaty Law on Host States: Enabling Good Governance?* (Bloomsbury Publishing 2018).

[129] *Metalclad v. Mexico* (ICSID Case No. ARB(AF)/97/1) Award, 30 August 2000, para. 76.
[130] Ibid., para. 99.
[131] See Dolzer and Schreuer (n. 12) 150. These authors claim that the decision of the Court of British Columbia was 'incorrect'.
[132] *TecMed v. Mexico* (ICSID Case No. ARB (AF)/00/2) Award, 29 May 2003, para. 153 (citing *Mondev v. USA* (ICSID Case No. ARB(AF)/99/2) Award October 11 2002, para. 116).
[133] Ibid., para. 154.
[134] Douglas (n. 126) 28.
[135] Separate Opinion of Thomas Wälde in *International Thunderbird Gaming v. Mexico* (UNCITRAL—NAFTA) 1 December 2005, paras. 4–5.

rejected Wälde's view because Thunderbird could not have legitimate expectations based on this type of behaviour.[136]

The *TecMed* programme for good governance influenced other awards. In *Occidental v. Ecuador 1*, decided in 2004, the tribunal was asked to decide on certain tax measures affecting an oil investment. Examining the antecedents of *Metalclad* and *TecMed*, the arbitrators concluded that the 'stability of the legal and business framework is [. . .] an essential element of fair and equitable treatment'.[137] The arbitrators in *MTD v. Chile*, awarded that same year, also relied on the *TecMed* award to decide on a dispute concerning inconsistent state conduct. They concluded that investment treaties prescribe a 'proactive' attitude as opposed to a 'passive behavior of the State or avoidance of prejudicial conduct to the investors'.[138] Chile's conduct did not meet this standard, although the investor was also responsible due to lack of oversight and due diligence.

In the course of the annulment proceedings of the *MTD* award, Chile criticized the *TecMed* position on good governance. Citing the expert opinions of two influential arbitrators, Arthur Watts and Jan Paulsson, it argued that the *TecMed* programme 'is extreme and does not reflect international law'.[139] In its 2007 decision, the annulment committee was sympathetic to this criticism, but did not annul the award because of the foreign investor's legitimate expectations. It observed that 'legitimate expectations generated as a result of the investor's dealings with the competent authorities of the host State may be relevant to the application of the guarantees contained in an investment treaty'.[140]

Tucker's interviews confirm the views expressed in these awards. Arbitrators criticize the postcolonial attitude of some states and the capacity of domestic courts to resolve foreign investment disputes. One arbitrator argues that people should 'bypass their traditions and sort of handicaps what [they] inherited' and that colonialism 'was a phase in history' that should not be taken 'as an evil thing'.[141] For Francisco Orrego Vicuña, a late ISDS arbitrator, '[t]he significant participation of individuals and corporations in the global society creates a need for them to have access to dispute settlement, which thus far has been only a limited feature of the inter-state system'.[142] Another arbitrator notes that domestic courts are 'embedded in the culture of the local host country, they cannot be neutral [. . .] local judges have denser social ties and more localized information, and this fuels bias'.[143] This

136 *International Thunderbird Gaming v. Mexico* (UNCITRAL—NAFTA) Award, 26 January 2006, paras. 166–7, 196.

137 *Occidental v. Ecuador 1* (LCIA Case No. UN3467) Award, 1 July 2004, para. 183.

138 *MTD v. Chile* (ICSID Case No. ARB/01/7) Award, 25 May 2004, para. 113.

139 *MTD v. Chile* (ICSID Case No. ARB/01/7) Annulment decision, 21 March 2007, para. 66.

140 Ibid., para. 69.

141 Tucker (n. 92) 80.

142 Francisco Orrego Vicuña, *International Dispute Settlement in an Evolving Global Society: Constitutionalization, Accessibility, Privatization* (CUP 2004) 29.

143 Tucker (n. 92) 81.

includes all judges, whether Norwegian, French, US, or from elsewhere. The advantage of international arbitrators is that they have no interest in the broader effects of a case in the host country, and understand what is going on 'in the outside world'.[144]

Tucker's interviews also show that arbitrators hold positions on development matters that coincide with the Washington Consensus.[145] One describes ISDS tribunals as 'a good government operation' for which 'little countries should be grateful. We are to teach them how to govern themselves'.[146] Arbitrators also have negative views of state officials, whom they sometimes describe as 'greedy' or 'corrupt'.[147] Of all the governmental agencies, they find that the best-informed ones are those ministries and departments that negotiate international economic treaties and deal with disputes. But these agencies, they also claim, had little or no idea of what they were doing when negotiating treaties.[148]

3. Procedural protection and legitimate expectations

The good governance approach of *Metalclad* and *TecMed* was broadly criticized elsewhere. Several arbitrators took issue with it in academic articles, expert opinions, and awards.[149] For many scholars it embodied an illegitimate encroachment of democracy and sovereignty,[150] or it needed to be adjusted to accommodate the 'return'[151] of the state after the 2007–2008 economic crisis. Subsequent ISDS awards took on board some of this criticism, highlighting the need to *balance* foreign investor rights and states' right to regulate. These tribunals not only recognized the importance of public regulation, but also reiterated that laws are expected to change. 'Economic and legal life is by nature evolutionary', it was conceded.[152] But foreign investors, arbitrators also insisted, are entitled to expect that regulatory changes follow due process and respect their legitimate expectations; governments' actions need to be reasonable and proportionate.

Several awards reflect this recalibrated position. Two influential cases are *Waste Management v. Mexico 2*, awarded in 2004, and *Saluka v. the Czech Republic*,

[144] Ibid., 81.
[145] Ibid., 94.
[146] Ibid., 79.
[147] Ibid., 70.
[148] Ibid., 77, 131.
[149] See, e.g., Douglas (n. 126) 51; *El Paso v. Argentina* (ICSID Case No. ARB/03/15) Award, 31 October 2011, paras. 344, 368.
[150] See David Schneiderman, *Constitutionalizing Economic Globalization. Investment Rules and Democracy's Promise* (CUP 2008) 2–4.
[151] José E. Alvarez, 'Why are we "Re-calibrating" our Investment Treaties?' (2010) 4 World Arbitration and Mediation Review 143–61, 144.
[152] *El Paso v. Argentina* (ICSID Case No. ARB/03/15) Award, 31 October 2011, para. 352; *Eli Lilly v. Canada* (UNCITRAL, ICSID Case No. UNCT/14/2) Award, 16 March 2017, para. 310.

decided in 2006. After examining several NAFTA antecedents, the arbitrators in *Waste Management 2* concluded that:

> the minimum standard of treatment of fair and equitable treatment is infringed [. . .] if the conduct is arbitrary, grossly unfair, unjust or idiosyncratic, is discriminatory and exposes the claimant to sectional or racial prejudice, or involves a lack of due process leading to an outcome which offends judicial propriety—as might be the case with a manifest failure of natural justice in judicial proceedings or a complete lack of transparency and candour in an administrative process. In applying this standard it is relevant that the treatment is in breach of representations made by the host State which were reasonably relied on by the claimant.[153]

The notions of grossly unfair or unjust are quite the opposite of perfect public regulation, and would seem to grant states a wider margin of deference when regulating. Similarly, the complete lack of transparency test contrasts with total transparency. The *Waste Management 2* award can thus be interpreted as a significant shift in favour of proceduralism. Yet there is a proviso: this interpretation echoes *TecMed* on one key aspect. The application of the minimum standard (or FET) depends on the existence of 'representations made by the host State which were reasonably relied on by the claimant'. In this respect, when it comes to the protection of foreign investors' legitimate expectations, the *Waste Management 2* award is not markedly different from the decision in *TecMed*. [154]

The *Saluka v. the Czech Republic* tribunal also contradicted the *TecMed* programme for good governance, arguing that '[n]o investor may reasonably expect that the circumstances prevailing at the time the investment is made remain totally unchanged'.[155] States do not have to compensate for implementing bona fide regulation that is reasonable, non-discriminatory, consistent, transparent, and even-handed, it said, yet resolving ISDS cases requires weighing 'the Claimant's legitimate and reasonable expectations [...] and the Respondent's legitimate regulatory interests'.[156] As in *Waste Management 2*, the arbitrators reconciled proceduralism with the protection of foreign investors' legitimate expectations. The investment decision, including the laws at the moment of investment as well as any legitimate expectations, constituted a key *benchmark* for the *Saluka* tribunal.[157]

These two awards illustrate the shift to proceduralism in ISDS practice, as limited by the legitimate expectations proviso. Arbitrators have maintained that

[153] *Waste Management v. Mexico 2* (ICSID Case No. ARB(AF)/00/3) Award, 30 April 2004, para. 98.

[154] International investment law is not the only area of international economic law that has shifted towards proceduralism. In international trade law, however, the notion of expectations has been completely abandoned. See Andrew Lang, *World Trade Law After Neoliberalism: Re-imagining the Global Economic Order* (OUP 2011) 255–71.

[155] *Saluka v. the Czech Republic* (UNCITRAL) Partial Award, 17 March 2006, para. 305.

[156] Ibid., para. 306.

[157] Ibid., para. 301.

the protection of foreign investors' legitimate expectations is a 'central' dimension of FET and the minimum standard of treatment.[158] In hundreds of cases, only a few dissenting opinions have criticized the protection of these expectations.[159] Tribunals have only narrowed down these expectations, clarifying that what matters are the views of objective investors, whereas subjective expectations are not protected, and explaining that the representations need to be somewhat specific. (The award in *Glamis v. USA* went exceptionally further by restricting these expectations to 'quasi-contractual' assurances.[160]) This support for protecting investors' reliance on state representations or assurances is not surprising. For influential academics and arbitrators, investment treaties are all about *pacta sunt servanda*, and host states' promises or ability to provide meaningful legislative guarantees to investors.[161] Tucker finds that arbitrators 'are likely to encourage states' governments to behave less like states (with attributes such as democracy, federalism, and political bargaining) and more like a contractual counterparty'.[162]

Of course, the costs and risks for states and local communities do not emerge from foreign investors' legitimate expectations alone. In the late 1960s, in relation to the 1967 OECD Draft, Schwarzenberger had already warned that ensuring investors receive due process was a '"secret weapon" in reserve'.[163] If arbitrators are optimistic about the shift to proportionality and proceduralism in order to strike the right balance, tribunals still apply these standards to the facts of a dispute on a case-by-case basis, and can come down on the side of investors in three main ways.

First, interpretative techniques designed to weigh foreign investors' rights and states' right to regulate against each other, such as balancing or proportionality, depend on the definition of the rights and the purpose of the legal regime.[164] Strong definitions of foreign investor rights naturally make it more difficult for states to pass balancing or proportionality tests.[165] In ISDS practice, the violation

[158] *Oxus Gold v. Uzbekistan* (UNCITRAL) Award, 17 December 2015, para. 313; *Gold Reserve v. Venezuela* (ICSID Case No. ARB(AF)/09/1) Award, 22 September 2014, paras. 575–6; *Glamis Gold v. USA* (UNCITRAL—NAFTA) Award, 8 June 2009, paras. 621–2.

[159] Separate Opinion of Pedro Nikken in *Suez and others v. Argentina* (ICSID Case No. ARB/03/17) 30 July 2010; Concurring Opinion of Luis Herrera Marcano in *Total v. Argentina* (ICSID Case No. ARB/04/01) 12 December 2010; Separate Opinion of Georges Abi-Saab in *Micula v. Romania* (ICSID Case No. ARB/05/20) 5 December 2013.

[160] *Glamis v. United States* (UNCITRAL—NAFTA) Award, 8 June 2009, para. 766.

[161] See, e.g., Jan Paulsson, 'The Power of States to Make Meaningful Promises to Foreigners' (2010) 1 Journal of International Dispute Settlement 341–52.

[162] Tucker (n. 92) 93.

[163] Georg Schwarzenberger, *Foreign Investments and International Law* (Stevens & Sons 1969) 119.

[164] Gregory Alexander, *The Global Debate over Constitutional Property: Lessons for American Takings Jurisprudence* (University of Chicago Press 2006) 207–08, 214–18; David Schneiderman, 'Judging in Secular Times: Max Weber and the Rise of Proportionality' (2013) 63 Supreme Court Law Review 557–77, 558–60.

[165] *TecMed v. Mexico* (ICSID Case No. ARB (AF)/00/2) Award, 29 May 2003, paras. 122, 133. Also, Erlend Leonhardsen, 'Looking for Legitimacy: Exploring Proportionality Analysis in Investment Treaty Arbitration' (2012) 3 Journal of International Dispute Settlement 95–136, 121, 134–5.

of foreign investors' expectations has led to awards against states in most instances, although arbitrators insist these expectations should be balanced against states' right to regulate. In other cases, tribunals have discussed the notion of a reasonable rate of return, balancing the remaining profitability of the investment project—as opposed to foreign investor rights—against states' right to regulate.[166]

Secondly, tribunals may conflate substantive and procedural protection, reasoning that states must 'respect the legitimate expectations insofar as the investor should be treated with an appropriate degree of due process'.[167] Arbitrators may criticize the notion of stability and predictability, but still conclude that states should ensure foreign investors a 'climate of cooperation in support of investor activities'. According to the *Urbaser v. Argentina* award, rendered in 2016, '[i]nvestors must have trust in the host State's best efforts to sustain their operation on this State's territory.'[168] Arbitrators, for instance, may find that investment treaties do not require 'full disclosure',[169] as the *Metalclad* and *TecMed* tribunals suggested, but do bind states to inform investors 'reasonably soon' or in a 'timely manner' of any measure that may affect their interests.[170]

Thirdly, deciding on the reasonableness of a measure depends on how arbitrators assess the public 'rational decision-making process': tribunals have underscored that states need 'good reasons' for change.[171] According to ISDS practice, arbitrators assess public measures focusing on existing scientific and technical evidence.[172] States may manage to justify local demands on scientific or technical grounds, and recent tribunals have accepted that political and technical reasons may coincide.[173] Yet this sort of justification may not always be possible, and will be more difficult for Global South states, and even more so for local communities.[174] Relying on technical and scientific evidence may serve to justify measures

[166] I discuss these two scenarios in Chapter 6, Sections A.1 and B.1.

[167] *Franck Charles Arif v. Moldova* (ICSID Case No. ARB/11/23) Award, 8 April 2013, para. 537. Legal systems recognize substantive and procedural expectations, but draw the line between these two categories in different ways. See Paparinskis (n. 101) 256.

[168] *Urbaser v. Argentina* (ICSID Case No. ARB/07/26) Award, 8 December 2016, para. 628.

[169] *Micula v. Romania* (ICSID Case No. ARB/05/20) Award, 11 December 2013, para. 533.

[170] Ibid., paras. 869, 870.

[171] *LG&E v. Argentina* (ICSID Case No. ARB/02/1) Decision on Liability, 3 October 2006, para. 158; *Continental v. Argentina* (ICSID Case No. ARB/03/9) Award, 5 September 2008, para. 254.

[172] Jürgen Kurtz, *The WTO and International Investment Law: Converging Systems* (CUP 2016) 153–67.

[173] *Urbaser v. Argentina* (ICSID Case No. ARB/07/26) Award, 8 December 2016, paras. 881, 945; *Impreglio v. Argentina* (ICSID Case No. ARB/07/17) Award, 21 June 2011; *AES v. Hungary* (ICSID Case No. ARB/07/22) Award, 23 September 2010, para. 10.3.23.

[174] Evidence indicates that influential Global North countries have a better chance of convincing ISDS tribunals of their cases. Malcolm Langford and Daniel Behn, 'Managing Backlash: The Evolving Investment Treaty Arbitrator?' (2018) 29 European Journal of International Law 551–80, 579. The difficulties faced by local communities to document and prove the environmental and health costs of an investment project are illustrated by the Cerro Matoso case in Colombia. Interview with leaders of the Zenú Community, Bogotá, 1 August 2018; Alvaro J. Idrovo, 'Cerro Matoso Mine, Chemical Mixtures, and Environmental Justice in Colombia' (2018) 391 *The Lancet* 2320.

to curb costs and risks, mainly when these are acknowledged by global standards, but may create problems for attempts to modify ground rules or address claims of recognition. The idea of a technical and scientific approach to public regulation is consistent with the embeddedness of foreign investor rights. It facilitates the emergence of a global view of which reasons are good reasons (and which are not) while disciplining public measures aimed at protecting local goals and values or experimenting with alternative policy models.

This preference for global knowledge and institutions is an underlying principle of ISDS practice. Tucker's interviews indicate that arbitrators value the existence of 'independent determinations'. By 'independent', however, they actually mean knowledge or consensus coming from the global terrain, as the issue in actual cases often hinges on whether there 'was enough evidence around the world that countries were getting rid of this'.[175] States that act without having this sort of evidence either go too fast or are politically motivated, focusing on short term costs instead of long term benefits. In this sense, Van Harten's finding that ISDS arbitrators show less judicial restraint than judges when dealing with non-discriminatory measures is not surprising.[176] ISDS asks for more than a domestic judiciary—or at least for something else—to decide that a measure falls within states' police powers and does not require compensation.

Equally important, the preference for technical and scientific evidence corresponds to the purpose of investment treaties as seen from the perspective of foreign investors—that is, to maximize their calculability. Business historians highlight multiple 'organized efforts' to 'overcome' uncertainty: 'situations in which risk cannot be calculated'.[177] At the time of investing, foreign investors can calculate the costs and risks associated with a project or at least foresee potential public measures in light of the existing regulatory framework and the state of scientific evidence. Measures that are reasonable within this context can be internalized as part of the business risk without disrupting calculability. As Philip Scranton and Patrick Fridenson observe, investors have 'reliable knowledge' over these questions.[178] For arbitrators, the situation is different when it comes to local goals and values. They find that investors have to live with the fact that projects may become non-viable for technical reasons, and that circumstances may vary and call for adjustments, but they can reasonably assume that states have already sorted out the politics of the investment. A scientific and technical assessment may change, as a result of new evidence, but local goals and values should not.

[175] Tucker (n. 92) 74–5.
[176] Van Harten (n. 104) 9–18, 157–64.
[177] Philip Scranton and Patrick Fridenson, *Reimagining Business History* (John Hopkins University Press 2013) 114.
[178] Ibid.

Conclusion

In the 1990s, international organizations such as the World Bank and UNCTAD suggested and promoted policies closely associated with the world-making project of the norm entrepreneurs of the 1950s and 1960s, including investment treaties and ISDS. Later, when the first ISDS cases hit states, arbitrators decided these disputes following a reasoning remarkably similar to the legal imagination of the norm entrepreneurs: foreign investor rights are globally embedded, ISDS is an antidote to localism, and legitimate expectations must be protected. The main difference is that these expectations are protected under FET instead of the provision on undertakings (known today as the umbrella clause).

Not content with resolving disputes, moreover, the first ISDS tribunals also took the opportunity to talk about modernity and good governance in ways that resembled the norm entrepreneurs' project. These enthusiastic arbitrators went too far, according to their moderate colleagues; indeed, it could even be argued that they surpassed the position of the norm entrepreneurs. In the 1950s and 1960s, the lawyers involved in that coalition were conscious of the legal and policy limitations of encroaching states' right to regulate. Like today's more moderate ISDS arbitrators, the norm entrepreneurs emphasized the value of facts and case-by-case analyses for resolving investment disputes, even if they did not fully anticipate the shift to proportionality and proceduralism. The next chapters simultaneously zoom in to examine investment disputes and ISDS cases since the turn of the millennium more closely, and zoom out to bring the socio-political context and impact into view.

5
ISDS in Action

The legal imagination framing ISDS practice is closely related to how arbitrators connect storytelling with the interpretation of investment treaties and other relevant laws. This chapter examines several influential awards, placing the facts of each dispute within the broader social and political context of the investment, the conflict, and the economic sector. The analysis aims to bring attention to how arbitrators think of foreign investment relations, and the extent to which they focus on, or silence, issues of distribution, recognition, and embeddedness. The cases are discussed chronologically in order to identify what has changed—and what has not—in arbitrators' reasoning.

The chapter begins with the *Santa Elena v. Costa Rica* case, awarded in 2000, examining how arbitrators dealt with a highly political dispute, and what happened to the case after *depoliticization*. The next two cases are *Metalclad v. Mexico* and *TecMed v. Mexico*, which concern regulatory capture, givings, and a controversial development model which the local community strongly opposed and resisted. These awards generated intense criticism of investment treaties and ISDS, and civil society began paying attention to a string of disputes involving environmental protection, namely *SD Myers v. Canada*, *Methanex v. USA*, *Glamis v. USA*, and *Chemtura v. Canada*. These awards illustrate the shift to proceduralism as well as the limits of this approach to judicial review. The discussion continues with the 1 billion USD decision in *Occidental v. Ecuador 2*, in which the arbitrators reviewed the actions taken by Ecuador to safeguard its natural resources. The last two cases are *Philip Morris v. Uruguay* and *Eli Lilly v. Canada*, awarded in 2016 and 2017 respectively, which relate to intellectual property rights and public health.

A. *Santa Elena v. Costa Rica*: the politics of investment disputes

In 1978 the government of Costa Rica decided to expropriate various estates in order to expand the Santa Rosa and Guanacaste National Parks, which lie close to the border with Nicaragua. These expropriations were part of a national policy of environmental conservationism that would turn Costa Rica into a celebrated ecotourism destination by the 1990s.[1] Among the areas expropriated in 1978 was

[1] Sterling Evans, *The Green Republic: A Conservation History of Costa Rica* (University of Texas Press 2010) 215–44.

Investment Treaties and the Legal Imagination. Nicolás M. Perrone, Oxford University Press (2021). © Nicolás M. Perrone.
DOI: 10.1093/oso/9780198862147.003.0006

the Santa Elena estate owned by US businessman Joseph Hamilton, who planned to build a tourist resort there. Recognizing the expropriatory character of the measure, Costa Rica followed the domestic legal procedure and offered Hamilton compensation. This was consistent with international law. The point of contestation between the government and Hamilton was the amount of compensation; Hamilton requested three times what Costa Rica had offered. The Costa Rican authorities tried but failed to negotiate a deal with the owner.[2]

The dispute dragged on for over two decades. The 1980s were difficult times for Central America: El Salvador and Nicaragua were immersed in civil wars, while the US was directing guerrilla insurgencies in both countries. They were difficult for the Santa Elena estate too, as the site turned out to be a strategic location for covert US operations in support of right-wing groups in Nicaragua. The US Central Intelligence Agency built an airport in the estate, and recruited a former marine to negotiate the purchase of the property from Hamilton, who had himself been a pilot during World War II.[3] Meanwhile, the US government put increasing diplomatic pressure on Costa Rica to desist from the expropriation. US Senator Jesse Helms insisted that the estate be permanently returned to Hamilton and authored the Helms Amendment, whereby the US Government could not approve development aid to countries that had expropriated property of US citizens. In 1995, the US used this amendment to put a loan for Costa Rica at the Inter-American Development Bank on hold.[4]

This pressure led Costa Rica to accept the jurisdiction of an arbitral tribunal, under the auspices of ICSID, to decide the amount of compensation. This occurred in March 1995, just after the US blocked the loan. Costa Rica had only ratified the ICSID Convention in 1993, and its explicit consent was necessary to start the proceedings as it had no investment treaty with the US. Roberto Echandi explains that the ratification of ICSID was 'the best way' out of this dispute for Costa Rica, rather than facing 'formal and informal diplomatic pressure from Washington'.[5] It remains unclear, however, why Costa Rica did not submit the claim to arbitration earlier; through the years Costa Rica suffered US pressure from different

[2] Álvaro Francisco Umaña Quesada, *El Aeropuerto de Santa Elena: la historia política del Parque Nacional de Guanacaste* (Fundación CRUSA 2016) 36–7, 41–2, 133–4. Umaña Quesada was President Arias' Minister of Environment (between May 1986 and May 1990). Also, Giannina Segnini, 'Fijan pago por Santa Elena' La Nación, 18 February 2000, available at http://www.nacion.com/ln_ee/2000/febrero/18/pais1.html (last visited 25 May 2020).

[3] Lee H. Hamilton and Daniel K. Inouye, *Report of the Congressional Committees Investigating the Iran/Contra Affair* (US House of Representatives Select Committee to Investigate Covert Arms Transactions with Iran, US Senate Select Committee on Secret Military Assistance to Iran and the Nicaraguan Opposition 1987) 61–2; Umaña Quesada (n. 2) 7, 45, 55, 78.

[4] Umaña Quesada (n. 2) 136.

[5] Andrea K. Bjorklund, 'Improving the International Investment Law and Policy System. Report of the Rapporteur. Second Columbia International Investment Conference: What's Next in International Investment Law and Policy?' in José E. Alvarez, Karl P. Sauvant with Kamil Ahmed and Gabriela Vizcaino (eds.), *The Evolving International Investment Regime* (OUP) 213–46, 226 (Roberto Echandi remarks).

motives: first, to use Santa Elena as a clandestine airport, and later to pay Hamilton a higher sum as compensation. Also, Costa Rica never signed an investment treaty with the United States, and only in 2009—more than a decade later—it ratified the Dominican Republic–Central America Free Trade Agreement, which includes an investment chapter.

The only legal issue placed before the arbitral tribunal was that of determining the amount of compensation. Because Costa Rica and the US had no treaty, the arbitrators first had to decide which law was applicable to the question. They favoured the application of Costa Rican law while noting that, in case of any inconsistency, 'international law must prevail'.[6] If not, they reasoned, the purpose of the ICSID Convention would be frustrated. A significant consequence of this decision was that the environmental purpose of the expropriation was made irrelevant: following the 1984 *Tippetts* award (by the Iran-US Claims Tribunal), the arbitrators embraced the sole effects doctrine and concluded that Costa Rica's obligation to protect this unique ecological site was not relevant to determine the compensation. An expropriatory measure requires the payment of a full compensation, the arbitrators observed, 'no matter how laudable and beneficial to society as a whole'. This required looking at the 'highest and best use' of the property; in this case, a 'resort and tourism-related development'.[7]

Another controversial factor in calculating the compensation was the date of the expropriation. The issue required the tribunal to discuss the notion of indirect expropriation, although the existence of the taking was not debated by Costa Rica. The arbitrators reasoned that an indirect expropriation takes place when the measures 'deprived the owner of his rights or has made those rights practically useless'. Determining when this occurs, they added, is 'a matter of fact [. . .] to assess in the light of the circumstances of the case'.[8]

After passing through the prism of international arbitration under the ICSID rules, the complexity of the Santa Elena dispute faded away. For the arbitrators, the case was about a failed 'tourism-related development'. Focusing only on the effects of the measure on the foreign investor allowed the tribunal to disregard Costa Rica's conservation policy, which was a success, and brought economic benefits to investors and the state alike. Neither did the arbitrators discuss the geopolitics that turned the Santa Elena estate into a clandestine airport, dragging Costa Rica into a military intervention against Nicaragua. This is unsurprising given that the purpose of ICSID was precisely to 'depoliticize' disputes.

[6] *Santa Elena v. Costa Rica* (ICSID Case No. ARB/96/1) Award, 17 February 2000, para. 64.

[7] Ibid., paras. 72, 70, 45. Other ISDS tribunals and influential scholars have followed the sole effects doctrine. See *Azurix v. Argentina* (ICSID Case No. ARB/01/12) Award, 14 July 2006, paras. 309–11; Rudolf Dolzer, 'Indirect Expropriations: New Developments' (2002) 11 New York University Environmental Law Journal 64–93, 86.

[8] *Santa Elena v. Costa Rica* (ICSID Case No. ARB/96/1) Award, 17 February 2000, para. 78.

B. The *Metalclad* and *TecMed* disputes: the costs and risks of economic development

Maquiladoras have been a pillar of Mexican industrial policy for several decades. In 1965, after the US unilaterally broke an agreement on reception of workers—the so-called Bracero Programme, through which Mexican citizens were admitted for seasonal agricultural work in the US—the Mexican government decided to industrialize the border zone and promote the assembly and processing of products for export. This industry was tied to the ups and downs of the US economy until NAFTA, which came into force in 1994, consolidated and expanded the maquiladora complex in the north of Mexico.[9] This boom had mixed results. Maquiladoras generated several socio-economic and environmental challenges, all exacerbated by the asymmetries between Mexico and the US. One of these was the disposal of the hazardous waste that maquiladoras produced.[10]

Waste was a problem from the beginning of the maquiladoras policy, for Mexico lacked the infrastructure to recycle and process multiple types and large amounts of waste. In 1983, Mexico and the US signed the La Paz Agreement, whereby maquiladoras were required to export hazardous waste back to the country from which it had been imported—generally the US. Mexico also prohibited the import of hazardous waste for final disposal. In the early 1990s Mexico improved its environmental standards, but the enforcement of the regulation remained deficient. Evidence shows that there was little interest in enforcement, especially during the country's 1994 economic crisis.[11] This was a generalized problem in the Global South, Wälde explained in 1992, recommending that states such as Mexico should promote third-party or self-enforcement mechanisms based on independent audits, community participation, and litigation.[12]

During this period, Metalclad and TecMed invested in the Mexican hazardous waste management sector. These business projects were promising under NAFTA, as Mexico's dependence on maquiladoras was on the rise. At the same time, the sector was dominated by lack of transparency, corporate influence in setting standards, illegal import of hazardous waste from the US, water pollution, and transportation spills. Increasing local awareness about these problems fuelled demands for measures and regulations to deal with the costs and risks of the hazardous waste

[9] Cyrus Reed, Marisa Jacott, and Alejandro Villamar, 'Hazardous Waste Management in the United States-Mexico Border States: More Questions than Answers' Texas Center for Policy Studies, Austin Texas (2000), available at http://www.texascenter.org/publications/haz2000.pdf (last visited 25 May 2020) 5, 9.

[10] Ibid. Also, Gary Clyde Hufbauer and Jeffrey J. Schott, *NAFTA Revisited: Achievements and Challenges* (Peterson Institute 2005) 153.

[11] Reed et al. (n. 9) 9–12, 16, 21, 35. Also, Jennifer Clapp, 'Seeping through the Regulatory Cracks' (2002) 22 SAIS Review 141–55, 147, 149.

[12] Thomas Wälde, 'Environmental Policies towards Mining in Developing Countries' (1992) 10 Journal of Energy & Natural Resources Law 327–57, 347–9.

industry.[13] The federal and regional governments were caught in a difficult position. They wanted to promote economic growth by facilitating the necessary infrastructure for maquiladoras, but quickly found that most people perceived them as socially and environmentally unsustainable.

The US firm Metalclad entered into the Mexican waste disposal sector in 1991. It initially encountered difficulties in funding its projects in Santa María del Río, Veracruz, and Tamaulipas. But its owner, Grant Kessler, carried on with his plans and embarked on a more ambitious project in 1993: the building and operation of a hazardous waste disposal site in La Pedrera, a valley in the municipality of Guadalcázar, in San Luis de Potosí state. For this Kessler found an ally in the newly elected governor of San Luis de Potosí, who was interested in industrial promotion and looking to expand the capacity to treat hazardous waste. The regional environmental agency was less optimistic about the project's feasibility from the start, however, and warned Metalclad about the site's problems, which partly resulted from the previous activities of the Mexican firm Coterin.[14] In his case study, Bejarano González suggests that Metalclad ignored this warning and acquired Coterin because of its strategic location and federal licences. Metalclad was confident that these licences, federal and regional political backing, US diplomatic support, the promise to clean up the pollution left by Coterin, and having a former federal servant on its roster would enable the construction and operation of its landfill.[15] To a large extent, this calculation was correct. Metalclad had obtained assurances that 'all necessary permits for the landfill had been issued with the exception of the federal permit for operation of the landfill', which the investor obtained a few months later.[16]

What Metalclad had overlooked was the local context. For the local community, La Pedrera was a time bomb even before the firm's arrival. The municipality of Guadalcázar swiftly requested information from the regional and federal governments, and found out that Metalclad had acquired Coterin to build a hazardous waste disposal site without an appropriate environmental impact assessment.[17] This sparked local mobilization and opposition. Joining forces with regional groups and organizations like Greenpeace, the municipality and community managed to halt and eventually block the project. In addition to starting administrative proceedings due to the lack of environmental assessment studies, the Guadalcázar municipality never issued the construction permit. The local resistance led the

[13] Reed et al. (n. 9) 37, 41–5, 61; Héctor F. Duarte Tagles, 'CYTRAR: Detrás de los Residuos Peligrosos en Sonora' (2003) 13 Acta Universitaria (2003) 14–21, 16.

[14] Fernando Bejarano González, 'El conflicto del basurero tóxico de Metalclad en Guadalcázar, San Luis Potosí' in Laura Carlsen, Timothy A. Wise, and Hilda Salazar (eds.), *Enfrentando la globalización: respuestas sociales a la integración económica de México* (Porrúa 2003) 27–54, 32–3.

[15] Ibid., 33–5. Also, Reed et al. (n. 9) 45.

[16] *Metalclad v. Mexico* (ICSID Case No. ARB(AF)/97/1) Award, 30 August 2000, para. 33.

[17] Bejarano González (n. 14) 36.

San Luis de Potosí governor to change his mind about the project and declare La Pedrera a national park for the protection of a rare cactus.[18]

This decision ended Metalclad's project in Guadalcázar, but not the story. Metalclad launched an ISDS case under NAFTA Chapter 11 claiming that Mexico had treated Metalclad unfairly and indirectly expropriated the project. At the centre of the dispute was the question of whether the federal authorities had given Metalclad explicit or implicit representations that a municipal permit was not necessary to build the landfill. Metalclad claimed that Mexican laws were unclear on this, and that the federal authorities had confirmed that a municipal permit was not necessary. For the investor, ultimately, the creation of a national park amounted to an indirect expropriation.

The *Metalclad* tribunal discussed whether Mexico lived up to the objectives of NAFTA, namely 'transparency and the substantial increase in investment opportunities in the territories of the Parties'. The arbitrators decided that 'Metalclad was led to believe, and did believe, that the federal and state permits allowed for the construction and operation of the landfill'.[19] The rules were unclear and Mexico had granted representations that it later ignored by asking the investor to obtain a municipal construction permit, which was eventually denied. Even if Metalclad was required to obtain such a permit under Mexican law, the arbitrators stated, its denial was 'improper'. The municipality took this decision based on 'environmental impact considerations' and the 'opposition of the local population', rather than on the site's 'physical construction'.[20] Further, the decision was made at a meeting of the municipal town council to which Metalclad was not invited and had no opportunity to appear at.[21] For the arbitrators, in sum, Mexico was inconsistent and did not behave in a just and fair manner. It failed to satisfy what foreign investors should expect in terms of transparency and predictability. In case of doubt or confusion, the arbitrators noted, Mexico was required to 'ensure that the correct position is promptly determined and clearly stated'.[22]

Turning to the allegation of indirect expropriation, the tribunal embraced the sole effects doctrine, focusing only on the consequences the measures had on Metalclad. It argued that an indirect expropriation consists of a 'covert or incidental' interference that 'has the effect of depriving the owner, in whole or in significant part, of the use or reasonably-to-be-expected economic benefit of property even if not necessarily to the obvious benefit of the host State'.[23] The arbitrators concluded that the measures taken by the federal, regional, and municipal

[18] Ibid., 36–42.
[19] *Metalclad v. Mexico* (ICSID Case No. ARB(AF)/97/1) Award, 30 August 2000, paras. 70, 85.
[20] Ibid., paras. 86, 92.
[21] Ibid., para. 91.
[22] Ibid., para. 76.
[23] Ibid., para. 103.

governments—particularly their creation of the national park—had characteristics constituting an indirect expropriation.

The *TecMed v. Mexico* dispute resembles the *Metalclad* case in several ways. In 1996, Spanish investor TecMed bought a hazardous waste disposal facility built by US firm Ford in 1986. Originally constructed to process regular waste, the site was later acquired by the state of Hermosillo and converted into a hazardous waste disposal facility operated under a permit with no expiry date. Subsequent regulatory changes, however, required TecMed to renew this permit on a yearly basis.[24] For two years TecMed operated the landfill without incident, securing renewal, but in 1998 evidence of problems emerged, including an open toxic dump and the disposal of waste meant to be returned to the US. TecMed was also fined for exceeding the levels of waste it could treat on the site.[25]

These events led to local mobilization demanding the closure of the facility. Local community groups in Hermosillo complained that the landfill was becoming a national dumping site, opposed TecMed's expansion plans, demanded its relocation to at least 25km from the centre of any major city (as per new legislation), and pointed at evidence that it was receiving biological-infectious waste. This type of waste was outside TecMed's permit.[26] Although community groups obtained an order preventing the import of waste from outside the region, this was inadequately enforced. In response, around 300 people organized to block the entrance to the landfill. Activists also secured 30,000 signatures opposing the project. The community obtained a commitment from the newly elected municipal president to negotiate the site's relocation, but this plan ultimately failed. Opposition to the landfill grew at both municipal and regional levels, and Mexico's environmental authority decided not to renew the permit due to the misconduct attributed to TecMed.[27]

Disappointed, TecMed launched an ISDS arbitration under the Mexico–Spain bilateral investment treaty, claiming that the non-renewal constituted an indirect expropriation and a violation of FET. TecMed had bought the landfill in order to operate the hazardous waste disposal site and, without the permit, that investment had lost most of its economic value. A central question was whether the denial of the permit was a legitimate regulatory measure or the result of an arbitrary or discriminatory act.

The arbitrators sided with TecMed. They found that the permit denial had effects equivalent to an expropriation, radically depriving TecMed of 'the economical use and enjoyment of its investments'. The benefits to society did not affect

[24] Duarte Tagles (n. 13) 16–17.

[25] Ibid., 17–18; Reed et al. (n. 9) 43–5.

[26] David Schneiderman, *Resisting Economic Globalization: Critical Theory and International Investment Law* (Palgrave 2013) 121–2.

[27] Duarte Tagles (n. 13) 18–19. *TecMed v. Mexico* (ICSID Case No. ARB (AF)/00/2) Award, 29 May 2003, paras. 107–12.

this finding, the tribunal reasoned, citing the *Santa Elena* award. Neither did '[t]he government's intention', which 'is less important than the effects of the measures' on an investor.[28] The tribunal acknowledged, however, that not every regulation affecting a foreign investor requires compensation, and that in addition to the effects of a measure on the investor, tribunals must assess its reasonableness and proportionality.[29] In this case, such an analysis did not change the arbitrators' preliminary conclusion. For them, the Mexican authorities responded to a social protest rather than to environmental or public health risks. TecMed's misconduct had been appropriately addressed through the fine. Popular opposition to renewing the permit, instead of justifying the measure, was found to be evidence of Mexico's arbitrary behaviour. Only in 'a serious emergency situation, social crisis or public unrest', would the arbitrators have been prepared to count civil pressure as a legitimate justification for a measure.[30]

The tribunal expanded its reasoning in two directions. First, it observed that foreigners should bear a lower burden of public measures advancing social welfare. The reason was that a foreign investor has 'a reduced or nil participation in the taking of the decisions that affect it'.[31] The arbitrators arrived at this conclusion by relying on jurisprudence of the European Court of Human Rights (*James v. United Kingdom*), but the rationale for applying that precedent to the *TecMed* case was not discussed in detail. The case was quite different from the European Court precedent; for example, TecMed itself had created the costs and risks that sparked the local mobilization, and there was evidence of regulatory capture in the sector. Secondly, the tribunal found Mexico's actions to be short of what foreign investors are entitled to expect according to a 'modern eye'. The authorities were not 'explicit, transparent and clear' and gave no 'signs' warning the investor 'to adopt a behavior to prevent the non-renewal of the permit'. TecMed was entitled to expect that the authorities would only consider environmental—not social—costs or risks when renewing the permit.[32]

The arbitrators in *Metalclad* and *TecMed* concentrated on the perspective of the foreign investor, portraying foreign investment relations in a transactional manner and requiring states to behave as perfect and transparent regulators. At the same time, they provided no discussion of the complexity of the conflict or the economic sector. They silenced the social and environmental context of Mexico and the people living close to the border with the US. This context included the government's support for maquiladoras, regulatory capture, increasing need for industrial waste disposal capacity, incipient environmental regulation, lack of enforcement, and the local disposal of waste that should have been re-exported to the

[28] Ibid., paras. 115–16.
[29] Ibid., paras. 121–2.
[30] Ibid., paras. 124, 126–7, 133.
[31] Ibid., para. 122.
[32] Ibid., paras. 152, 161–2, 164–6.

US. In Guadalcázar, Hermosillo, and other parts of Mexico, hazardous waste disposal sites were imposed on local communities, who were never informed, never consented, and did not enjoy the benefits of these activities.[33] This lack of transparency and regulatory enforcement, however, was not pertinent for the arbitrators.

Local opposition was treated as relevant in both awards, but only as a sign of Mexico's arbitrary conduct. In *Metalclad*, the arbitrators were troubled by the inconsistent behaviour of the various levels of government. Not only did they say different things, but they also changed their minds about the project, apparently due to local opposition. What the tribunal downplayed is that the representations of the federal government were arguably *ultra vires*, and could not bind a different level of government against the distribution of powers defined in the Mexican Constitution. The arbitrators in *TecMed* found local mobilization and resistance to be evidence of arbitrary conduct. The problem concerning the enforceability of other regulatory responses, on the other hand, was not significantly discussed. As opposed to *Metalclad*, this award examined the proportionality of the measure Mexico had taken, but did so just to confirm that the effects of the measure on the foreign investor were significant.[34]

C. The *SD Myers*, *Methanex*, *Glamis*, and *Chemtura* disputes: environmental regulation, business, and activism

After the demise of the NIEO in the 1980s, the most influential critique against investment treaties was that ISDS could undermine environmental regulation. This argument was articulated by NGOs and think tanks based in the Global North, and in 1998 it was vital in blocking the negotiations for a Multilateral Investment Agreement at the OECD. During the negotiations, the *Ethyl v. Canada* case had caused concerns among environmentalists, although that dispute was settled.[35] In the early 2000s, however, the awards in *Metalclad* and *TecMed* confirmed their fears. These groups claimed that the legal doctrines developed by these ISDS tribunals not only imposed heavy financial burdens on the state, but could also chill regulation needed to protect the environment.[36]

[33] Bejarano González (n. 14) 51, 54; Reed et al. (n. 9) 69–70. After 2003, Mexico implemented the right to know and other information mechanisms and regulations, the efficacy of which remain unclear. See Marisa Jacott, Cyrus Reed, and Mark Winfield. 'The Generation and Management of Hazardous Wastes and Transboundary Hazardous Waste Shipments between Mexico, Canada and the United States Since NAFTA: A 2004 Update' (2004) Texas Center for Policy Studies, 1, 40, available at http://www.texascenter.org/publications/hazwaste04.pdf (last visited 2 July 2020).

[34] Erlend Leonhardsen, 'Looking for Legitimacy: Exploring Proportionality Analysis in Investment Treaty Arbitration' (2012) 3 Journal of International Dispute Settlement 95–136, 124.

[35] Konrad von Moltke, *An International Investment Regime?: Issues of Sustainability* (IISD 2000) iii, 19, 31; UNCTAD, *World Investment Report 1998: Trends and Determinants* (United Nations 1998) 60–1.

[36] IISD and The Royal Institute of International Affairs, 'Investment, Doha and the WTO: Background Paper to the Chatham House Meeting convened by RIIA and IISD Trade and Sustainable Development

The tensions between international investment protection and environmental measures arose against a background of broader cracks within the dominant regulatory approach and an emerging critique of globalization. Although the Washington Consensus discouraged government regulation of economic activities, a global agreement was emerging that, at least in some circumstances, states had to curb the costs and risks of business. In areas such as environmental regulation, the discussion shifted from whether to regulate or not to how states should regulate. The World Bank, UNCTAD, and the WTO now supported the need for environmental regulation, but still warned about the importance of due process and a science-based regulatory process.[37]

With this environmental concern in mind, civil society attention focused on a series of ISDS disputes against Canada and the US under NAFTA. Unlike Mexico, these two states had a longer history of environmental regulation, more administrative capacity, and a higher level of economic and institutional development. For these reasons, in the early days of NAFTA these states were not expected to face ISDS cases. This expectation turned out to be quite wrong. Global North and Global South countries alike can 'abuse' their regulatory powers, as the norm entrepreneurs had insisted decades ago, and the environmental lobby is stronger in the Global North, where governments could cave in to their demands and impose new standards on foreign investors. Wälde, writing in 2001, claimed that environmental concerns ranked high on the 'economic policy agenda of governments, financial institutions, and business leaders', but that they were 'being used as a Trojan horse by statist/bureaucrats, protectionists, environmentalists and others who oppose continuing trade and investment liberalisation and the role of global markets'.[38] For the ISDS tribunals in charge of resolving these disputes, the question was how to draw a line between acceptable regulation and Wälde's 'Trojan horses'.

The first of these cases was *SD Myers v. Canada*, awarded in 2002. Like Mexico, Canada's ability to deal with hazardous waste had some limitations, and NAFTA created business opportunities for US investors.[39] One of these related to the safe disposal of polychlorinated biphenyl (PCB). SD Myers, having capacity to process

Priorities Post-Doha' London, 7–8 April 2003, available at https://www.iisd.org/sites/default/files/publications/investment_riia_iisd.pdf (last visited 25 May 2020) 1, 9–10, 12, 15.

[37] See Håkan Nordström and Scott Vaughan, 'Trade and the Environment' (1999) WTO Special Studies No. 4, available at https://www.econstor.eu/bitstream/10419/107057/1/wto-special-study_4_e.pdf (last visited 25 May 2020); Per G. Fredriksson (ed.), 'Trade, Global Policy, and the Environment' (1999) World Bank discussion paper No. 402, available at http://documents.worldbank.org/curated/en/581201468277743126/pdf/multi-page.pdf (last visited 25 May 2020).

[38] Thomas Wälde and Abba Kolo, 'Environmental Regulation, Investment Protection and "Regulatory Taking" in International Law' (2001) 50 International & Comparative Law Quarterly 811–48, 811–2.

[39] In the first years of NAFTA, Canada's situation was somewhat similar to that of Mexico concerning capacity to manage and dispose of hazardous waste. See Daniel Faber, *Capitalizing on Environmental Injustice: The Polluter-Industrial Complex in the Age of Globalization* (Rowman & Littlefield Publishers 2008) 200–2.

it in the US, intended to import and treat Canadian PCB. The regulatory environment was not favourable, however. The US had imposed an import ban on PCB in the 1980s, and the Basel Convention on the Control of Transboundary Movements of Hazardous Wastes and their Disposal (hereinafter the Basel Convention) had been negotiated and adopted in 1989. The Convention entered into force in Canada in late 1992, and was signed but never ratified by the US. SD Myers was still optimistic in 1993, and established an office in Canada to solicit customers while it 'invested/lobbied heavily to get the border opened'.[40] These efforts paid off in 1995, when the US Environmental Protection Agency authorized the import of Canadian PCB. But SD Myers' prospects only rose briefly, for Canada introduced a prohibition on PCB exports that lasted until February 1997, and a few months later a US court permanently prohibited the import of PCB.[41]

SD Myers filed an ISDS case under NAFTA Chapter 11, arguing that the eighteen-month prohibition to export PCB was discriminatory and had indirectly expropriated the investment. The claim hinged on Canada's alleged protectionist intentions and the regulatory nature of the measure. Canada disagreed, countering that the ban was implemented for environmental reasons. Further, it pointed out that the Basel Convention required it to not export hazardous waste to non-member states and to instead generate domestic capacity to deal with PCB.

The tribunal recognized the environmental goals and Canada's obligations under the Basel Convention, but was not convinced that Canada implemented the ban for these reasons. They agreed with the investor that Canada had protectionist motivations and there was 'no legitimate environmental reason' for the ban. They accepted the view of those opposing the ban in Canada, who believed that 'PCBs destroyed in either country is positive for the environment', observing that the minister of the environment had insisted several times that PCB waste should be treated 'in Canada by Canadians'.[42] The tribunal also noted that a state 'can achieve its chosen level of environmental protection through a variety of equally effective and reasonable means'.[43] In this case less restrictive measures, such as a subsidy, could have promoted Canadian domestic capacity without affecting the rights of the foreign investor under NAFTA. Interestingly, in the damages phase, Canada argued—and the tribunal was sympathetic to this—that not closing the border could have attracted the ire of environmentalist groups, who could have resorted to mobilization and litigation to stop PCB exports.[44]

On the other hand, the tribunal rejected the indirect expropriation claim, and elaborated on some salient aspects of this standard of treatment. It noted 'that,

[40] *SD Myers v. Canada* (UNCITRAL—NAFTA) Partial Award, 13 November 2000, paras. 179, 105–14.
[41] Ibid., paras. 127–8.
[42] Ibid., para. 195 (also, paras. 177, 183, 185).
[43] Ibid., para. 221.
[44] *SD Myers v. Canada* (UNCITRAL—NAFTA) Second Partial Award, 21 October 2002, para. 270.

in legal theory, rights other than property rights may be "expropriated" and that international law makes it appropriate for tribunals to examine the purpose and effect of governmental measures'.[45] A fundamental criterion to draw the line between expropriation and legitimate regulations, the arbitrators reasoned, is the level of interference: 'Expropriations tend to involve the deprivation of ownership rights; regulations a lesser interference'.[46] Subsequent tribunals have agreed that the threshold for what is 'tantamount' or 'equivalent to' a direct expropriation is particularly high. This criterion has become a key factor in distinguishing legitimate regulation from expropriation.[47]

Civil society actors were also involved in a dispute between Canadian firm Methanex and the US. The *Methanex v. USA* case, awarded in 2005, is notable for being the first time an ISDS tribunal accepted an amicus curiae submission, where civil society organizations requested that arbitrators properly debate the environmental dimension of the case, particularly after the *Metalclad* award.[48]

Methanex marketed an oxygenate for blending with petrol, MTBE, which was immersed in controversy in the US over its health and environmental effects. In 1997, the state of California passed a law requesting the University of California to conduct a study on it. The results led first to the use of warning labels, and eventually the state of California prohibited MTBE due to its environmental and health risks. Methanex then initiated an ISDS dispute, arguing that California's conduct was discriminatory, arbitrary, and constituted indirect expropriation. A major aspect of its case was the claim that the Californian governor and US competitors had conspired to drive the Canadian firm out of the market. As SD Myers, Methanex argued that the real motives for the regulation were not environmental but protectionist. Methanex's lawyer started the case by acknowledging the delicate context: the foreign investor recognized 'that this case presents some thorny political issues', but it 'would like the case to be decided on its merits alone'.[49]

In examining Methanex's claim, the arbitrators conceded that foreign investment projects consist of a complexity of rights, focusing on the distinction between legitimate regulation and indirect expropriation. They said that investment

[45] *SD Myers v. Canada* (UNCITRAL—NAFTA) Partial Award, 13 November 2000, para. 281.

[46] Ibid., para. 282.

[47] See *National Grid v. Argentina* (UNCITRAL) Award, 3 November 2008, para. 149. At the same time, many of these tribunals have concluded that states are still liable for the violation of the FET standard. See Michael W. Reisman and Rocio Digón, 'Eclipse of Expropriation?' in Arthur Rovine (ed.), *Contemporary Issues in International Arbitration and Mediation, The Fordham Papers* (Martinus Nijhoff Publishers 2009) 27–46, 34–45.

[48] Howard Mann, 'The Final Decision in Methanex v. United States: Some New Wine in Some New Bottles' (2005) International Institute for Sustainable Development, available at https://www.iisd.org/sites/default/files/publications/commentary_methanex.pdf (last visited 25 May 2020) 11–12.

[49] Mark Drajem and Christopher Donville, 'Methanex Says California Additive Ban Illegal under NAFTA Rules' (2004) Institute for Agriculture and Trade Policy, 7 June 2004, available at https://www.iatp.org/news/methanex-says-california-additive-ban-illegal-under-nafta-rules (last visited 25 May 2020).

disputes are about a contemporary conception of property, related to 'a process that is wealth producing', but doubted that this case amounted to a deprivation of ownership as goodwill and market share are not themselves protected.[50] The tribunal also expounded on the premise that regulations rarely constitute indirect expropriations, explaining that 'as a matter of general international law, a non-discriminatory regulation for a public purpose which is enacted in accordance with due process [. . .] is not deemed expropriatory and compensable unless specific commitments had been given'.[51]

Moving to the core of Methanex's allegations, the arbitrators were satisfied with the process and regulatory basis of the measures implemented by California. They found no evidence of the conspiracy alleged by Methanex, and were convinced instead that the University of California study reflected 'a serious, objective and scientific approach to a complex problem'. The report had identified significant risks associated with MTBE, including the fact 'that MTBE contaminated groundwater was difficult and expensive to clean up'.[52] The tribunal also found that Methanex 'did not enter the United States market because of special representations', and was involved in a highly regulated industry in a region—the US and California—'operating under the vigilant eyes' of multiple actors concerned with health and the environment.[53]

Another ISDS dispute on the radar of environmental organizations was *Glamis v. USA*, awarded in 2009, in which a Canadian company objected to the imposition of new legal requirements to operate a mining project. Like *Methanex*, the dispute attracted a lot of attention and amicus curiae submissions from environmental groups. The case also concerned several Native American groups whose land and sacred sites were at risk; they submitted their own amicus brief to the tribunal. The arbitrators accepted these presentations, but ruled that they could resolve the case without addressing them.

The controversy about this mining enterprise, known as the Imperial project, had lasted decades. Glamis had started buying interests in mining claims at Imperial Valley, California, in 1987, with the intention of applying for a mining permit under the 1872 US Mining Law. Within a few years, the Imperial project consisted of '187 mining claims and 277 millsites on a total of almost 1,500 acres (almost 650 hectares)'.[54] Glamis planned to develop an open-pit cyanide heap-leach gold mine—a mining method that is costly for the environment and highly intensive in water. This would also have affected areas sacred to the Quechan

[50] *Methanex v. USA* (UNCITRAL—NAFTA) Final Award of the Tribunal on Jurisdiction and Merits, 3 August 2005, Part IV, Chapter D, para. 17.

[51] Ibid., Part IV, Chapter D, para. 7.

[52] Ibid., Part III, Chapter A, paras. 101–2.

[53] Ibid., Part IV, Chapter D, paras. 9–10.

[54] OXFAM, 'Glamis Gold: A Case Study of Investing in Destruction' (2003) Briefing paper, 2, available at https://www.oxfamamerica.org/explore/research-publications/investing-in-destruction-glamis-gold/ (last visited 11 June 2020).

Indian Nation. After a six-year review, the US Department of the Interior under the Clinton Administration rejected the project due to its high environmental and social costs. In November 2001, however, the Bush Administration reversed the permit denial, without public input or consultations with the indigenous peoples. In response, the state of California implemented new legislation requiring backfilling open pits and recontouring the landscape once mining operations were completed. This regulation applied to all new open pit mines, not just to the Imperial project.[55]

Glamis then filed an ISDS case, alleging that the measures taken by the federal and state governments violated the minimum standard of treatment under NAFTA and were tantamount to expropriation. It argued that the new requirements rendered the Imperial project uneconomical. The arbitrators observed that what distinguishes a regulation from an indirect expropriation is the intensity of interference in the foreign investment and the legitimacy of the regulation.[56] To determine the level of interference, they focused on the economic value of the project, as opposed to ownership rights, concluding that the profitability of the Imperial project was reduced but not entirely annihilated. For this reason, the tribunal concluded that there was no indirect expropriation, avoiding more contentious issues such as the legitimacy of the measure or whether compensation was still required despite the benefits to society.[57]

Later, the *Glamis* tribunal turned to reviewing the regulatory process under the minimum standard of treatment (NAFTA Article 1105), and defined this standard in quite a narrow manner compared to other cases. The arbitrators added that when reviewing state measures the international standard is objective, and does not change depending on the level of development or capacity of the respondent state.[58] Concretely, the standard to review the regulatory process was whether there was 'reasonable evidence' to take the various measures. The tribunal found the US had lived up to this standard, and no measure was manifestly arbitrary.[59] It also agreed with the US 'that governments must compromise between the interests of competing parties'.[60] It was satisfied that the measures had balanced the interests of multiple actors. As in the *Methanex* award, lastly, the arbitrators said that the situation would have been different had the US granted Glamis a quasi-contractual commitment to induce the investment, which would have given rise to investment-backed expectations.[61]

[55] Ibid., 2–4; *Glamis v. USA* (UNCITRAL—NAFTA) Award, 8 June 2009, paras. 152–3, 159.
[56] Ibid., paras. 356–7.
[57] Ibid., paras. 358, 366, 536.
[58] Ibid., paras. 601–22.
[59] Ibid., para. 786.
[60] Ibid., para. 804.
[61] Ibid., para. 813.

The last ISDS case of this saga was *Chemtura v. Canada*, awarded in 2010. This dispute revolved around a regulatory review and eventual phase-out of a fungicide (lindane) that the US investor used in canola production. John Vijgen et al. observe that the 'application of lindane and technical HCH during the last 5 decades has resulted in environmental contamination with global dimension'.[62]

Lindane had been marketed in Canada since 1938, but several countries had progressively limited its use from the 1970s due to health and environmental concerns, including the US. This restriction was internationally recognized in the Aarhus Protocol on Persistent Organic Pollutants, adopted by Canada in 1998, while the Stockholm Convention on Persistent Organic Pollutants included lindane as a designated substance for elimination in 2009. The US announced that it would not allow US farmers to use lindane-treated canola seeds after June 1998. These moves led Canada to carry out a special review on the use of lindane, which concluded that it created significant health risks and recommended a phase-out 'by suspension of registrations or voluntary discontinuation'.[63]

Chemtura responded by filing an ISDS case under NAFTA's Chapter 11 claiming that Canada had acted unfairly and in bad faith. It argued that these measures were motivated by trade concerns, and that the review process was unreasonably long and biased. The arbitrators assessed these claims against the minimum standard of treatment (NAFTA Article 1105), observing that this standard had evolved over time due to, among other factors, the impact of investment treaties.[64] The analysis still required a margin of deference as 'certain agencies manage highly-specialized domains involving scientific and public policy determinations'. Also, the foreign investor was 'a sophisticated registrant experienced in a highly-regulated industry'.[65]

Ultimately, the tribunal disagreed with Chemtura. It held that the objective of ISDS review was not to assess 'the correctness or adequacy' of the measures but only the reasonableness of the scientific evidence.[66] Canada's measures were motivated by environmental concerns and international obligations under the Aarhus protocol, it reasoned, not by trade considerations. Further, the arbitrators did not find the delays unreasonable; the standard was whether the review process was 'unfairly delayed', which required considering Chemtura's conduct as well as acknowledging that 'the operation of complex administrations is not always optimal in practice'.[67] As a final point, the tribunal held that this was not a case of substantial

[62] John Vijgen, Li Fan Yi, Martin Forter, Rup Lal, and Roland Weber, 'The Legacy of Lindane and Technical HCH Production' (2006) 68 Organohalog Comp 899–904, 899.

[63] *Chemtura v. Canada* (UNCITRAL—NAFTA) Award, 2 August 2010, paras. 30, 131–6.

[64] Ibid., para. 121. The tribunal also noted that it 'ought to follow solutions established in a series of consistent cases, comparable to the case at hand, but subject of course to the specifics of a given treaty and of the circumstances of the actual case'. Ibid, para. 109.

[65] Ibid., paras. 123, 149.

[66] Ibid., paras. 153, 138–53.

[67] Ibid., paras. 211, 215

deprivation of ownership, and that Canada's actions were a valid exercise of its police powers according to international law.[68]

Taken together, the awards in *SD Myers*, *Methanex*, *Glamis*, and *Chemtura* shifted attention from the effects on foreign investors to the state regulatory process. The tribunals described legitimate regulations as non-discriminatory measures implemented according to the due process. In practice, however, the main criterion to distinguish an expropriation from a legitimate regulation continues to be the extent of the effects. The four awards agreed that regulations rarely create effects equivalent to an expropriation, but *Methanex* remains one of the few cases in which a tribunal decided that a regulation that entirely annihilated a foreign investment did not require compensation. The *Chemtura* tribunal, in contrast, noted that the sale of lindane products 'were a relatively small part of the overall sales of Chemtura Canada at all relevant times'.[69]

These tribunals also reviewed the measures under the minimum standard of treatment (NAFTA Article 1105), highlighting that customary international law had evolved since the 1930s because of the lapse of time, economic changes, and the thousands of investment treaties. The only exception was perhaps the *Glamis* award. Compared to *Metalclad* or *TecMed*, the four awards showed a deferential approach to states' right to regulate, noting that arbitral review should take into account the industry and the state of science.[70] *Methanex*, *Glamis*, and *Chemtura* indicate that regulations are legitimate as long as states provide sufficient scientific or technical evidence, although *Methanex* suggests that tribunals may look into the correctness of the evidence as well.[71] *SD Myers* and particularly *Chemtura* also point at the significance of international standards to justify public measures. Regulating in accordance with these standards appears the safest way to avoid investment treaty liability.

All four awards portrayed the relationship between foreign investors and states as essentially regulatory. Foreign investors cannot expect that regulation will not change or that the regulatory process will be perfect; it is rather a mechanism to balance competing interests. But arbitrators recognize that the situation is different if states grant specific commitments or representations. According to these awards, the regulatory model represents the default lens through which to interpret foreign investment relations, but it also takes less than a contract for arbitrators to shift to a transactional model.

Overall, the *SD Myers*, *Methanex*, *Glamis*, and *Chemtura* awards are not inconsistent with a global embeddedness of foreign investor rights. Protecting the environment is not controversial; as Wälde admitted, the issue is how we conceive the

[68] Ibid., paras. 259–67.
[69] Ibid., para. 263.
[70] Jürgen Kurtz, *The WTO and International Investment Law: Converging Systems* (CUP 2016) 157–67.
[71] The position in *Methanex* implies a stricter review of the public measure. See ibid., 165.

relationship between the environment and the economy. The legal doctrine in these awards provides significant protection against Wälde's 'Trojan horses' by balancing opposing interests against scientific knowledge or standards, which are likely to have been produced in international organizations or some few Global North countries. This would create problems for states willing to reform the ground rules, which requires reshaping social relations (not balancing existing rights and obligations), or protecting interests that cannot be justified through science or have weak international recognition, to which I turn next.

D. *Oxy v. Ecuador 2*: states' right to protect their rights

Global South countries have less bargaining power and technical capacity to negotiate and regulate foreign investment than Global North countries. They also face more significant social and economic challenges. Economists are not entirely sure about what works and does not work to promote sustainable development, and an increasing consensus favours economic experimentation.[72] In practice, a large part of the Global South depends on its natural resources to promote economic growth and create jobs, but often lacks the capital, know-how, or technology to use these resources efficiently. These countries arguably need foreign capital either in the form of private investment, international loans, or developmental aid, each requiring different levels of state involvement. Either way, governments always need to remain vigilant. In the case of foreign private investment, they need to make sure that projects will turn mineral, oil, and large-scale agriculture not only into economic returns but also into sustainable development.[73]

The norm entrepreneurs promoted investment treaties as a means to promote foreign investment, particularly in the natural resource sector. Abs, Shawcross, and others even advised Global South countries to postpone their industrial ambitions. Current evidence indicates they were right about the relationship between these treaties and foreign investment in natural resources; studies generally show mixed, inconclusive results on the relationship between investment treaties and

[72] Experimental approaches to development have become central to development economics. See Yana van der Meulen Rodgers, Anthony Bebbington, Catherine Boone, Jampel Dell'Angelo, Jean-Philippe Platteau, and Arun Agrawal, 'Experimental Approaches in Development and Poverty Alleviation' (2020) 127 World Development 1–6. Also, Dani Rodrik, 'The New Development Economics: We Shall Experiment, but How Shall We Learn?' in Jessica Cohen and William Easterly (eds.), *What Works in Development?: Thinking Big and Thinking Small* (Brookings Institution Press 2010) 24–47.

[73] UNCTAD has highlighted the important role of states in maximizing the benefits of foreign investment. See Nicolás M. Perrone, 'UNCTAD's World Investment Reports 1991–2015: 25 Years of Narratives Justifying and Balancing Foreign Investor Rights' (2018) 19 Journal of World Investment & Trade 7–40, 13, 16, 23, 25. Also, Daniel Shapiro, Bersant Hobdari, and Chang Hoon Oh, 'Natural Resources, Multinational Enterprises and Sustainable Development' (2018) 53 Journal of World Business 1–14, 3–4.

foreign investment flows, but suggest that treaties do encourage foreign investment in natural resources.[74] The norm entrepreneurs remained largely silent, however, about how Global South governments could maximize the benefits and minimize the costs and risks of these projects within the institutional structure of investment treaties and ISDS. The Abs–Shawcross draft includes no mechanism for ensuring that investment projects contribute to sustainable development, and the norm entrepreneurs objected to the creation of foreign investor obligations under international law. Further, investment treaties have made things worse by prohibiting performance requirements and including stringent rules on transfer of funds.[75] For the Global South, the resulting situation poses several questions on the consistency of investment treaties with the international law principle that natural resources should be exploited 'in the interest of their national development and of the well-being of the people'.[76]

States have established various mechanisms to ensure that investment projects in the natural resource sector are carried out in the national interest. In many countries, for instance, regulations require legislative approval for investment contracts or prohibit foreign investors from transferring any interest in a project without governmental agreement.[77] In Ecuador, the latter was both a legal and a contractual obligation when the conflict with the US oil company Occidental started in the mid-2000s. According to the Hydrocarbons Law and the Participation Contract between Ecuador and Occidental, the transfer of any interest in the concession had to be previously authorized by the government, otherwise the contract could be terminated (*caducidad*). Occidental accepted this obligation when investing in Ecuador, but still transferred an operational interest to a Canadian investor without the approval of the Ecuadorian government. It had suggested the possibility of a transfer to the government, but only asked for formal approval four years later.[78]

This breach of contract occurred in the context of a previous ISDS case between Occidental and Ecuador and the efforts of the Ecuadorian government to renegotiate the terms of oil concessions with all the major players. The decision

[74] Liesbeth Colen and Andrea Guariso, 'What Type of FDI is Attracted by BITs' in Olivier De Schutter, Johan Swinnen, and Jan Wouters (eds.), *Foreign Direct Investment and Human Development: The Law and Economics of International Investment Agreements* (Routledge 2013) 138–56; Matthias Busse, Jens Königer, and Peter Nunnenkamp 'FDI Promotion through Bilateral Investment Treaties: More Than a BIT?' (2010) 146 Review of World Economics 147–77.

[75] The Abs–Shawcross draft did not contain rules on transfer of funds or performance requirements. Although the OECD considered transfer of funds relevant, Article 4 of the 1967 OECD Draft only contains a recommendation concerning the freedom of transfer. OECD, 'OECD Draft Convention on the Protection of Foreign Property' (1968) 2 The International Lawyer 331–53, 341.

[76] Permanent Sovereignty over Natural Resources, UNGA Resolution 1803(xvii), 17th Session, (14 December 1962). The rule of permanent sovereignty of natural resources is part of customary international law. See *Armed Activities on the Territory of the Congo (Congo v. Uganda)* [2005] Judgment, ICJ Rep 168, para. 244 (19 December 2005).

[77] See, e.g., Peter D. Cameron and Michael C. Stanley, *Oil, Gas, and Mining: A Sourcebook for Understanding the Extractive Industries* (World Bank 2017) 47, 77, 79–80, 85.

[78] *Occidental v. Ecuador 2* (ICSID Case No. ARB/06/11) Award, 5 October 2012, paras. 119, 158–60.

in *Occidental 1* was controversial. The arbitrators interpreted FET as a quasi-stabilization clause, and also concluded that the oil and flower sector were alike for the purposes of the national treatment standard.[79] Also, Occidental's breach was contemporary to Ecuadorian efforts to renegotiate contractual conditions so to redistribute the benefits of the oil sector. The government aimed to capture some of the benefits of huge price increases. The oil price was 32 USD a barrel when Occidental and Ecuador signed the contract (May 1999), but it was up to 91 USD when Ecuador enacted a windfall tax (Law 42) in April 2006.[80] Ecuador had first invited large foreign investors to renegotiate their contracts, but encountered fierce opposition from US and French companies. While Spanish, Brazilian, and Chinese investors accepted the new conditions, US and French investors launched ISDS cases.[81]

The situation for Occidental was different because, after examining its contractual breach for eighteen months, Ecuador decided to terminate its Participation Contract. The contract and the sectoral regulation characterized the unauthorized transfer of an interest as a fundamental breach, allowing Ecuador to terminate the agreement (*caducidad*). Occidental challenged this outcome, nonetheless, involving the US government and filing an ISDS case.

In *Occidental v. Ecuador 2*, the arbitrators focused on the effects and legitimacy of the termination. They had no doubt that the *caducidad* had effects equivalent to expropriation; the question was whether it was proportionate in the circumstances.[82] The arbitrators reasoned that this was not a contractual dispute, and that the *caducidad* of the contract was rather the outcome of Ecuador's exercise of sovereign authority over natural resources. It was necessary then to review the measure according to public law principles, including the proportionality between the sanction and the harm created by a private actor.[83] The arbitrators examined the balance between costs and risks, and the negative effects imposed on Occidental. A severe penalty such as the termination of the investment agreement,

[79] This stabilization approach was explicitly criticized in *EDF v. Romania* (ICSID Case No. ARB/05/13) Award, 8 October 2009, para. 218. Also, Christoph Schreuer, 'Fair and Equitable Treatment in Arbitral Practice' (2005) 6 Journal of World Investment & Trade 357–86, 374. Further, Diebold suggests that this tribunal transformed the national treatment provision into a 'non-restriction' obligation. Nicolas F. Diebold, *Non-Discrimination in International Trade in Services: 'Likeness' in WTO/GATS* (CUP 2010) 160.

[80] Oil prices according to https://www.macrotrends.net/1369/crude-oil-price-history-chart (last visited 11 June 2020).

[81] US Embassy in Quito, 'Oil Companies Considering Options under Ecuador's 99% Revenue Sharing Decree' 25 October 2007, available at https://wikileaks.org/plusd/cables/07QUITO2373_a.html; US Embassy in Quito, 'GOE Negotiating Oil Contracts—Again: Firms Agree to Use Services Model' 19 August 2008, available at https://wikileaks.org/plusd/cables/08QUITO764_a.html; US Embassy in Quito, 'Spanish Repsol Agrees to New Oil Contract with GOE; U.S. Partner Murphy Resists' 13 November 2008, available at https://wikileaks.org/plusd/cables/08QUITO1058_a.html (last visited 26 May 2020).

[82] *Occidental v. Ecuador 2* (ICSID Case No. ARB/06/11) Award, 5 October 2012, para. 455.

[83] Ibid., paras. 416–18.

they observed, would only be justified in the case of a serious harm and a flagrant breach. In very exceptional circumstances, states may impose a severe penalty for deterrence purposes. Otherwise, such a measure would be disproportionate. For the tribunal, the text of the Ecuadorian Hydrocarbons Law and the Participation Contract were secondary to the reasoning. The main obligation under Ecuadorian constitutional law and international law was for the state to act proportionately.[84]

The tribunal was not convinced that Occidental inflicted a serious harm, nor that Ecuador behaved proportionately. It concluded that Ecuador suffered either no or minor harm. The arbitrators noted that the 'integrity of Ecuador's hydrocarbons regulatory regime' was relevant, but the main issue was whether Ecuador suffered an economic harm, namely a reduction of the stream of public income generated by the oil sector.[85] In the case, Occidental's transfer of interest did not affect this stream of income and, in fact, it implied more foreign capital for Ecuador. Further, the tribunal decided that the termination of the contract was also disproportionate for deterrence purposes. Ecuador had other options, such as imposing a transfer fee.[86] The arbitrators opined that the bad relationship between the parties, resulting from the *Occidental 1* award, was instead a key motivation for the termination.[87] This did not imply that Occidental was entirely innocent; breaching the law and the contract was not a good thing, the arbitrators admitted, and Occidental had 'arrogated' some public authority. For this reason, they applied a 25% discount to the compensation.[88]

This outcome hinged on the tribunal's decision to place an otherwise contractual dispute within a regulatory model. It would have been more difficult to make this reasoning in a contractual context, particularly in the case of a sophisticated actor such as Occidental. The interpretative move effectively deprived Ecuador of the ability to enforce the bargain (*de facto* 'revising and rewriting the contract'[89]). Interestingly, when moving to discuss the consistency of Law 42 with the investment treaty, the majority of the tribunal shifted back to a transactional view of the relationship. These arbitrators decided that this law constituted a breach of the Participation Contract, and was not a matter of taxation, regulation, or Ecuador's sovereign authority.[90]

[84] Ibid., paras. 422–7.
[85] Ibid., paras. 449–50.
[86] Ibid., para. 434.
[87] Ibid., paras. 442–3.
[88] Ibid., paras. 448, 687. The dissenting arbitrator, Brigitte Stern, suggested a 50% discount.
[89] In a different ISDS case, Georges Abi-Saab observed that if the rights are created by contract, the contract governs the scope and strength of the right. To assert otherwise, he concluded, would 'amount to revising and rewriting the contract'. Dissenting Opinion of Georges Abi-Saab in *ConocoPhillips Petrozuata v. Venezuela* (ICSID Case No. ARB/07/30) Decision on Jurisdiction and Merits, 19 February 2015), para. 29.
[90] *Occidental v. Ecuador 2* (ICSID Case No. ARB/06/11) Award, 5 October 2012, paras. 515–36. Subsequent tribunals resolved this issue differently. See *Perenco v. Ecuador* (ICSID Case No. ARB/08/6) Decision on Remaining Issues of Jurisdiction and on Liability, 12 September 2014; *Burlington*

Another relevant aspect of the decision refers to the conduct of Occidental. In this regard, the problem was not only that the investor acted in breach of the Participation Contract. Occidental did not have a constructive approach to the renegotiations, like other US investors, and also sought the support of the US government to resolve the dispute in yet another breach of the contract. In 2012, the ISDS tribunal rejected this claim due to the lack of proof.[91] Cables from the US Embassy in Ecuador, now unofficially public, show that Occidental had effectively requested US diplomatic support and the embassy was involved in the dispute.[92]

Occidental 2 is not an outlier case. Other arbitral awards have produced similar conclusions concerning the relationship between foreign investor rights and mechanisms to ensure the public benefit of investment projects. The importance of legislative approval for contracts was overlooked in *Bankswitch Ghana Ltd v. Ghana*, a contractual arbitration awarded in 2014. The arbitrators relied on typical ISDS language to hold that a contract governed solely by Ghanaian law still had to respect some international law principles, including the doctrine of estoppel. Ghana was precluded from relying on a lack of parliamentary approval to annul the contract because government officials had represented to the foreign investor that the contract was valid.[93] Likewise in *Arif v. Moldova*, awarded in 2013, the tribunal confirmed that foreign investors can have legitimate expectations based on state acts subsequently declared in violation of domestic laws by the competent courts. In this case, Arif's concessions were found to be in breach of Moldovan competition laws. The arbitrators concluded that the judicial decisions were legitimate and consistent with the investment treaty, but Moldova was still required to respect Arif's reasonable expectations.[94]

The reasoning in these awards undermined mechanisms that states had put in place to ensure that investment projects contributed to sustainable development. Arbitrators minimized contractual and legal breaches, overlooking the importance of these mechanisms for states and their populations. They also balanced aspects of the disputes that were essentially different. The sovereignty of Ecuador, in this case, the integrity of its legal system, is not commensurable to oil revenues or inflows of capital. To be relevant, the comparison would have required taking into account the bargaining power of Ecuador, the foreign investor, and the home state.

v. Ecuador (ICSID Case No. ARB/08/5) Decision on Liability, 14 December 2012; *Murphy Exploration v. Ecuador* (PCA Case No. 2012-16) Award, 10 February 2017.

[91] *Occidental v. Ecuador 2* (ICSID Case No. ARB/06/11) Award, 5 October 2012, para. 860.

[92] US Embassy in Quito, 'Progress on Occidental case' 27 August 2004, available at http://wikileaks.org/plusd/cables/04QUITO2380_a.html (last visited 26 May 2020).

[93] *Bankswitch v. Ghana* (PCA Case No. 2011-10) Award, 11 April 2014, paras. 11.65–70.

[94] *Franck Charles Arif v. Moldova* (ICSID Case No. ARB/11/23) Award, 8 April 2013, paras. 538–9.

E. *Philip Morris v. Uruguay* and *Eli Lilly v. Canada*: intellectual property rights and public health

Intellectual property rights are a singular case in international investment law for two reasons. First, they are especially vital for foreign investors whose projects depend on states recognizing and protecting patents, trademarks, and copyright; investors may lose more than the actual value of a particular project if governments intervene in their intellectual property rights.[95] Second, international law contains rules on the scope of intellectual property rights. Unlike for most other economic rights, from land titles to concession contracts, WTO member states agreed on common standards for intellectual property rights in the 1995 Agreement on Trade-Related Aspects of Intellectual Property Rights (TRIPs). Some FTAs also contain TRIPs-plus rules. This level of global convergence is unique; a similar phenomenon in the natural resources or infrastructure sectors would be unthinkable.[96]

The strong protection of intellectual property under international law does not mean there is no controversy over these rights—quite the contrary. TRIPs was possible thanks to pharmaceutical and technology firms lobbying the US to insist on the inclusion of these rights in the WTO. Their case for special protection rested on utilitarian assumptions, as it would enable investors to calculate their potential returns and thus encourage innovation and knowledge creation.[97] Even in the best possible scenario, however, this protection comes with a cost. Patents and copyright grant monopolies over the use of new technology, increasing the price of medicines or software. This can make medicines unaffordable for millions of people.[98] For Global South countries, moreover, the high cost of technology makes development policies more expensive.[99] The problem could be addressed through technology transfer mechanisms, but the norm entrepreneurs have opposed this strategy since the post-World War II period. Discussing the programme to implement Truman's Four Point project, the International Chamber of Commerce argued that '[i]ndustrial technology cannot be transmitted by [development

[95] Richard Baldwin, *The Great Convergence: Information Technology and the New Globalization* (Harvard University Press 2016) 105, 237–8.

[96] The other cases of internationally defined rights or a high level of convergence involve resources that are outside the jurisdiction of specific states, and are difficult to extract, such as resources located in outer space or the sea bed. See John G. Sprankling, *The International Law of Property* (OUP 2014) 100–10, 116–98.

[97] Peter Drahos and John Braithwaite, 'Intellectual Property, Corporate Strategy, Globalisation: TRIPS in Context' (2001) 20 Wisconsin International Law Journal 451–80, 465; Peter Drahos and John Braithwaite, *Information Feudalism: Who Owns the Knowledge Economy?* (Earthscan 2002) 13–17.

[98] Carlos M. Correa, 'Public Health and Intellectual Property Rights' (2002) 2 Global Social Policy 261–78.

[99] Ha-Joon Chang, 'Intellectual Property Rights and Economic Development: Historical Lessons and Emerging Issues' (2001) 2 Journal of Human Development 287–309.

missions], either because it is not communicable at all or because a mission cannot give away something it does not possess.'[100]

Together, international intellectual property rules and investment treaties grant foreign investors an exceptionally high level of protection. Domestic rules must be consistent with TRIPs and any TRIPs-plus rules, and states can bring disputes against each other before the WTO or the dispute settlement mechanism of the FTA in cases of inconsistency. Further, foreign investors can file ISDS cases arguing that states' measures violate an investment treaty. As in any other case, arbitrators have to interpret foreign investor rights and states' right to regulate. The main difference, however, is that the scope of foreign investor rights is determined not only by domestic law, but also by the international rules contained in the TRIPs or applicable FTA. Domestic law still matters, but international law has harmonized significant aspects and created an expectation of convergence that is embedded in the global economy of 'Big Pharma' and 'Big Tech'. This expectation makes it likely that tribunals will rely on global and comparative benchmarks when discussing intellectual property rights, although this does not necessarily mean they will decide cases against states. It only suggests that global rationales will prevail over local considerations.[101] Two ISDS disputes illustrate these points.

The first is *Philip Morris v. Uruguay*, one of the highest-profile ISDS cases in history. The dispute arose when Uruguay took two measures that affected Philip Morris's trademarks: it stipulated an increase of health warnings on cigarette packaging from 50% to 80% of surface area, and a single presentation policy whereby tobacco producers could only market one variant of cigarette per brand family. Philip Morris filed an ISDS case under the Switzerland–Uruguayan investment treaty, arguing that the measures constituted indirect expropriation and violated other treaty standards.

The significance of this arbitration exceeded the particular dispute and investment. Philip Morris's ISDS case against Uruguay, awarded in 2016, represented a momentous episode in the 'Tobacco War' and thus raised alarms among civil society and the international organizations involved in this conflict, particularly the World Health Organization (WHO).[102] The Framework Convention on Tobacco Control, which includes recommendations on packaging and labelling of tobacco products, was the first treaty negotiated under the auspices of this international

[100] United States Council of the International Chamber of Commerce, 'Intelligent International Investment' A Report of the Committee on Business Participation in Foreign Economic Development, April 1949, 16.

[101] Similarly, Katharina Pistor, *The Code of Capital: How the Law Creates Wealth and Inequality* (Princeton University Press 2019) 142–3. For an argument that ISDS tribunals have interpreted intellectual property rights appropriately, see Julian Arato, 'The Private Law Critique of International Investment Law' (2019) 113 American Journal of International Law 1, 5, 44–9.

[102] See Sergio Puig, 'Tobacco Litigation in International Courts' (2016) 57 Harvard International Law Journal 383–432, 431–2; Eric Crosbie, Particia Sosa, and Stanton A. Glantz, 'Defending Strong Tobacco Packaging and Labelling Regulations in Uruguay: Transnational Tobacco Control Network Versus Philip Morris International' (2018) 27 Tobacco Control 185–94.

organization, entering into force in 2005. The arbitrators in the Uruguay case indicated the significance of the dispute when observing, in passing, that the parties together had spent more on the case than 'the base amount of damages claimed by the Claimants'.[103]

One of Uruguay's central arguments against Philip Morris was that the investor did not have a right to use its trademarks free from regulation, and therefore the public measures could not be expropriatory. According to Uruguay's laws, trademarks only grant a right to exclude others. The arbitrators conceded that 'to work out the legal scope of the property right, it is necessary to refer back to the *sui generis* industrial property regime in Uruguay'.[104] But they added that this analysis had to be supplemented by looking into any relevant international treaty ratified by Uruguay, namely the TRIPs Agreement, the Paris Convention, and the MERCOSUR Protocol.[105] The tribunal maintained that the issue was whether Philip Morris had an 'absolute' or 'exclusive right to use'. In this respect, it agreed with Uruguay that neither domestic laws nor the relevant treaties granted Philip Morris an absolute right. The investor only had a right 'to use the trademark in commerce, subject to the state's regulatory power'.[106] Further, it could not have failed to notice the tendency for 'progressively more stringent regulation of the sale and use of tobacco products'.[107] As in the awards analysed above involving environmental regulations, the arbitrators admitted that the situation would have been different had Uruguay given specific commitments to Philip Morris.[108]

Having defined the scope of Philip Morris's rights, the tribunal discussed the effects of the measure and the police powers doctrine, that is, states' right to regulate. It observed that ISDS practice had approached the first question inconsistently. While some tribunals assessed the impact of a measure looking at the specific business, it decided that the impact of the measures should be determined based on the 'investment as a whole'.[109] This question is paramount in regulatory takings, as the chances of finding an expropriation increase substantially when adjudicators concentrate on the effects caused by the measure on discrete parts of the business.[110] Focusing on Philip Morris's investment 'as a whole', as opposed to each of the foreign investor's brands, the tribunal concluded that the measures did not

[103] *Philip Morris v. Uruguay* (ICSID Case No. ARB/10/7) Award, 8 July 2016, para. 538.
[104] Ibid., para. 266.
[105] Ibid., paras. 258–65.
[106] Ibid., paras. 267, 271.
[107] Ibid., para. 430.
[108] Ibid., para. 377.
[109] For the *Philip Morris* tribunal, this issue 'largely depends on the facts of the individual case'. Ibid., para. 280.
[110] In comparative constitutional property scholarship, this issue is known as the problem of the denominator. See Santiago Montt, *State Liability in Investment Treaty Arbitration: Global Constitutional and Administrative Law in the BIT Generation* (Hart 2009) 177–91.

deprive Philip Morris of its business, which had in fact become more profitable since 2011.[111]

The arbitrators also stressed the importance of states' right to regulate, in line with the awards in *Methanex* and *Chemtura*. States' action in exercise of regulatory powers do not constitute indirect expropriation, they observed, if it is 'taken bona fide for the purpose of protecting the public welfare', and is 'non-discriminatory and proportionate'.[112] The measures taken by Uruguay satisfied these requirements. There was a proportionate relationship between the means and the ends. The tribunal found that unlike in the *Methanex* case, which involved the prohibition of a substance, the measure taken by Uruguay did not annihilate Philip Morris's business.[113] Further, the arbitrators held that Uruguay's behaviour was reasonable under the FET standard. Uruguay followed the WHO Framework Convention on Tobacco Control and the recommendations of the WHO and the Pan-American Health Organizations. They also said that Uruguay's actions were consistent with court decisions in the US, where Philip Morris was found to have misrepresented health risks associated with tobacco consumption.[114]

Interestingly, however, the analysis of the tribunal was less deferential to Uruguay when the government departed from international organizations' advice. It reached different opinions concerning the single presentation policy, which was not explicitly recommended by the WHO or the Pan-American organization. Although the majority validated the measure, the arbitrator appointed by Philip Morris insisted that this policy was introduced in violation of treaty standards, with no support 'in the extensive literature on anti-smoking regulations' and no appropriate 'study and deliberations'.[115]

Another significant ISDS intellectual property case is *Eli Lilly v. Canada*. For the firms collectively known as Big Pharma, TRIPs had been a key victory but not the end of their struggle for stronger intellectual property rights. They have continued promoting stronger rights, lobbying for the inclusion of TRIPs-plus commitments in FTAs. The battle for protection, moreover, means Big Pharma frequently goes to court and arbitration when, like Big Tobacco, it tries to either expand or resist encroachments on its rights.[116] The *Eli Lilly* case is an example of this sort of litigation. Eli Lilly complained that Canadian courts had affected a 'dramatic change' in patent law between 2002 and 2008, leading to the invalidation of two patents by

[111] *Philip Morris v. Uruguay* (ICSID Case No. ARB/10/7) Award, 8 July 2016, paras. 283–6.
[112] Ibid., para. 305.
[113] Ibid., paras. 306–7.
[114] Ibid., paras. 392–420.
[115] Concurring and Dissenting Opinion of Gary Born in *Philip Morris v. Uruguay* (ICSID Case No. ARB/10/7) 8 July 2016, para. 174.
[116] See Susan K. Sell, 'TRIPS was Never Enough: Vertical Forum Shifting, FTAs, ACTA, and TPP' (2010) 18 Journal of Intellectual Property Law 447–78; James Love, 'Access to Medicine and Compliance with the WTO TRIPS Accord: Models for State Practice in Developing Countries' in Peter Drahos and Ruth Mayne (eds.), *Global Intellectual Property Rights: Knowledge, Access and Development* (Palgrave 2002) 74–89, 78.

the Supreme Court.[117] It argued that this change constituted indirect expropriation and a violation of other NAFTA standards.

The *Eli Lilly* award discussed two fundamental questions. One was whether judicial decisions can amount to an indirect expropriation or constitute a violation of other treaty standards. The alternative is that judicial decisions can only constitute a denial of justice. Most ISDS awards support the first hypothesis, which the tribunal ratified in this case. These arbitrators reasoned that the conduct expected by foreign investors refers to the behaviour of the judiciary as much as of the executive or the legislative. The judiciary can also take property or violate the due process.[118]

The other issue was the possibility of implementing regulatory changes through judicial interpretation of laws and regulations. Eli Lilly argued that the allegedly new doctrine constituted a 'dramatic change' of Canada's intellectual property legislation, violating its rights under NAFTA. This doctrine aimed to ensure the utility of the invention, requiring applicants to identify a promise of utility and provide evidence related to a sound prediction of utility. It also prohibited the presentation of post-filing proof to show utility. For the arbitrators, the judiciary in common law jurisdictions has a role in developing the law. The 'evolution of the law through court decisions is natural, and departures from precedent are to be expected'. They noted, however, that 'dramatic changes' may exceed this 'natural' evolution and can violate foreign investor rights. The issue, then, was whether Eli Lilly was right when describing the changes as 'dramatic'.[119]

The arbitrators demurred. They observed that some elements of the controversial legal doctrine had developed over six years, and Eli Lilly itself had an application denied for not showing a sound prediction of utility in 2003.[120] More contentious was the prohibition to submit post-filing evidence, which the arbitrators accepted was 'unexpected'. But the reversal of a lower court decision, the tribunal noted, was normal in a tiered judicial system. The Supreme Court decision constituted a 'progressive development' of Canadian law and an 'incremental and evolutionary' change.[121] Further, the arbitrators added that Canadian courts applied regular interpretive principles and that '[s]ome level of unpredictability is present in the application of all law'.[122]

The tribunal supported these conclusions by contrasting Canadian law, and the controversial judicial decisions, with global standards and comparative law. Eli Lilly argued that other laws could be relevant to assess the significance of the changes effectuated in Canada, namely the laws of the other NAFTA states (Mexico

[117] *Eli Lilly v. Canada*, (UNCITRAL—ICSID Case No. UNCT/14/2) Award, 16 March 2017, paras. 5–6.

[118] Ibid., paras. 218–26.

[119] Ibid., paras. 310, 309–11.

[120] Ibid., para. 345.

[121] Ibid., paras. 337, 349–50.

[122] Ibid., para. 421.

and the US) as well as the discussions at the WTO and the World Intellectual Property Organization. The arbitrators heard expert evidence on the interpretation and application of the utility requirement in the US and Mexico, although they were ultimately unconvinced that other domestic legal systems could be of any help in resolving the case. They paid more attention to global standards and 'the 2014 and 2015 editions of the Special 301 Report of the USTR'. In these reports, the US had noted 'serious concerns about the lack of clarity and the impact of the heightened utility requirements for patents that Canadian courts have applied recently'.[123] These elements would have been relevant to the case, the arbitrators explained, had other countries, such as Mexico, voiced similar concerns against Canadian law. Lastly, like other tribunals, the arbitrators noted that the outcome would have been different had Canada granted a legitimate expectation over the rules applicable to Eli Lilly's patents.[124]

These two awards show how arbitrators have reviewed measures aimed at curbing the costs and risks of investment projects in recent years. There is no doubt that tobacco is a health risk or that intellectual property protection is socially costly. It is reasonable, then, that states want to balance benefits, costs, and risks. In this regard, the final outcomes in *Philip Morris* and *Eli Lilly* can be interpreted as validating states' right to regulate. At the same time, the arbitrators' reasoning revealed a preference for the global embeddedness of foreign investor rights. As in the environmental disputes, these tribunals appeared reluctant to justify public measures or legal changes that divert from global standards. The further states move from what is within the global space of possibility, for example in tobacco control or intellectual property regulation, the higher the chances a measure may violate foreign investor rights. In questions related to intellectual property, moreover, the risks are much higher because foreign investors can not only sue states directly under ISDS, but can also convince other states to initiate disputes before the WTO.

Conclusion

The investment disputes reviewed in this chapter represent relatively contrasting periods of ISDS practice. They show how arbitrators moved away from the sole effects doctrine in cases of indirect expropriation, embracing proportionality and proceduralism to review state measures. The more recent awards focus on how states implemented the measures in question, recognizing the legitimacy of

[123] Ibid., paras. 378, 377–8.

[124] The tribunal did not affirm that legitimate expectations are protected under NAFTA Article 1105, but still considered the factual basis presented by Eli Lilly, particularly Canada's actions under NAFTA Chapter 17 and the Patent Cooperation Treaty. Ibid., paras. 380–5 (footnote 515).

general, non-discriminatory regulation that complies with due process requirements. This interpretation of states' right to regulate corresponds to a regulatory model of foreign investment relations. The shift to proceduralism, however, obscures substantial continuities in the dominant imaginary of foreign investment relations. Facts continue to be framed in a narrow manner, whereby relevant circumstances for the state and the local community are silenced or may even signal arbitrary measures. These include issues of geopolitics, regulatory capture, local opposition, or national policies to organize the economy and promote sustainable development. A procedural stance may facilitate regulation to curb costs and risks associated with investment projects, but the weight given to scientific evidence and global standards in identifying what counts as costs or risks—and how they can be reasonably addressed—reifies the global embeddedness of foreign investor rights. Arbitrators stress that regulations need to be consistent with the global terrain of law and knowledge.

In this way, as the norm entrepreneurs of the late 1950s and 1960s expected, ISDS continues to operate as an antidote to public measures that escape the calculability of foreign investors. States may therefore have problems in redistributing benefits, or responding to claims of recognition. Next we will see how these problems increase if arbitrators find that states did grant representations or specific commitments.

6
Givings and ISDS

Foreign investment is associated with efficiency, economic growth, and jobs. Investors emphasize the benefits of potential projects, but also ask for regulatory givings to ensure economic returns and minimize their exposure to host-country risks. At times, international organizations have likewise highlighted both the benefits of foreign investment and the need for incentives to attract new projects. If states were to implement these business-friendly regulations, investors might then come in, but many would count on investment treaties and ISDS to interpret and enforce sectoral regulation, representations, or specific commitments. Disputes related to the 2001 Argentine crisis and the Spanish solar energy industry show that in these circumstances, when controversies lead to ISDS cases, arbitrators often put foreign investment relations within a transactional model, making regulatory reforms more difficult if projects fail, local expectations are disappointed, or circumstances drastically change.

A. Argentina—privatization and economic crisis

In Argentina, the 1990s wave of privatizations contained the promise of a modern state and efficient public utilities. Domingo Cavallo, then economic minister, affirmed that the new policy was 'conceived as a drastic change in the role of government'.[1] Argentina was following the advice of the World Bank's International Finance Corporation, which observed '[t]hat privatization can deliver a wide range of material economic benefits'. This 'is now a view so widely held that it scarcely needs elaboration'.[2] The benefits included a lower financial burden for the state, efficient public utilities for the population, and business opportunities for foreign investors. Privatizations in Argentina entailed a change in strategy for organizing public utilities, such as water, sanitation, and electricity, but more fundamentally they constituted essential steps in a major economic transformation, whereby the principles of solidarity and collective spaces were replaced by the dogma of self-preservation.[3]

[1] Domingo F. Cavallo, 'Lessons from Argentina's privatization experience' (1997) 50 Journal of International Affairs 459–74, 459.
[2] David J. Donaldson and Dileep M. Wagle, *Privatization: Principles and Practice* (International Finance Corporation—World Bank 1995) 7.
[3] Jamie Peck, *Constructions of Neoliberal Reason* (OUP 2010) 22.

Investment Treaties and the Legal Imagination. Nicolás M. Perrone, Oxford University Press (2021). © Nicolás M. Perrone.
DOI: 10.1093/oso/9780198862147.003.0007

Argentina's privatizations also put international organizations and foreign investors in a privileged position, reshaping the country's political economy.[4] The World Bank advised the Argentine government on how to privatize and regulate public utilities, and public officials organized several roadshows in key financial centres, attracting the attention of numerous foreign investors interested in the prospect of substantial economic returns. Starting in the early 1990s, the bank and foreign investors became significant players in Argentine politics, with a particular interest in maintaining the policies that made privatizations possible and profitable. In 1996, the World Bank praised Argentina for successfully implementing a quick, large-scale privatization process.[5]

By the turn of the century, however, the appraisal was not so positive. In 1999, the United Nations mentioned some advantageous aspects of the Argentine experience but, as opposed to the World Bank a few years before, it was critical of its speed and scale. For the UN Department of Social and Economic Affairs, Argentina did not have enough regulatory capacity to deal with the emerging challenges related to 'technological, political and social changes'.[6]

An implosion of the policies that had facilitated foreign investment in the utilities sector, particularly the scrapping of the 1991 Convertibility Law in 2001, created a backlash against privatizations and a revision of the 1990s legacy. Foreign investment in water, sanitation, telecoms, and electricity had been facilitated through a battery of incentives and regulatory givings; these incentives were originally tied to investment commitments, but many investors reduced these commitments thanks to renegotiations. Argentina had established a system of 'quasi-rents' through special regulatory regimes consisting of laws, decrees, bidding rules, and concession contracts.[7] Foreign investors seized most of the gains, 'exercising monopolistic power'.[8] What the World Bank and Cavallo had defended as a 'simple'[9] and 'minimal'[10] regulatory system was, events proved, too favourable to foreign investors.

US-dollar denominated tariffs and the Convertibility Law illustrate the problems of the Argentine framework. Foreign investors benefited from US-dollar denominated tariffs, guaranteed by sectoral and general rules, but also enjoyed an

[4] See Leopoldo Rodríguez-Boetsch, 'Public Service Privatisation and Crisis in Argentina' (2005) 15 Development in Practice 302–15, 303, 306, 314; Hulya Dagdeviren, 'Political Economy of Contractual Disputes in Private Water and Sanitation: Lessons from Argentina' (2011) 82 Annals of Public and Cooperative Economics 25–44, 35; James Haselip, Isaac Dyner, and Judith Cherni, 'Electricity Market Reform in Argentina: Assessing the Impact for the Poor in Buenos Aires' (2005) 13 Utilities Policy (2005) 1–14, 9.

[5] Hafeez Shaikh and Manuel Angel Abdala, *Argentina Privatization Program: A Review of Five Cases* (World Bank 1996) 1.

[6] UN Department of Economic and Social Affairs, *Privatization in Latin America in the early 1990s*, ST/ESA/PAD/SER.E/17 (United Nations 1999) 23, 18, 31–2.

[7] Werner Baer and Gabriel Montes-Rojas, 'From Privatization to Re-nationalization: What Went Wrong with Privatizations in Argentina?' (2008) 36 Oxford Development Studies 323–37, 326, 326–8.

[8] Rodríguez-Boetsch (n. 4) 313–4; Haselip et al. (n. 4) 9.

[9] Shaikh and Abdala (n. 5) 5, 116.

[10] Cavallo (n. 1) 474.

exception to the general legislation: price indexation was prohibited in Argentina under the Convertibility Law, but public utilities were entitled to index their tariffs according to inflation in the US. Werner Baer and Gabriel Montes-Rojas explain that '[t]he legal interpretation of this "exception" was that the Convertibility Law referred to indexation only in local currency, as no mention to other currencies was in the Law'.[11] In other words, foreign investors had the best of both worlds.

Under this framework foreign investors made high economic returns in Argentina: 'The general consensus in the post-devaluation governments was that tariffs had been set too high and that profits were excessive in the 1990s.'[12] Between 1993 and 2001, the regulatory arrangements allowed investors in the water and sanitation sector to obtain a 20% average annual rate of return, a much higher rate than that of the US (between 6 and 12.5%), the UK (between 6 and 7%), and France (6%). The flip side of these high returns was not always a more efficient service and more investments. While some services improved, such as telecommunications and electricity, others, such as water, sanitation, and transport, deteriorated.[13]

Several studies have concluded that the favourable arrangements for most privatized firms in Argentina was the result of regulatory capture, lobbying, and a political economy in which the World Bank and foreign investors defended privatizations and their high economic returns.[14] Argentina privatized most state-owned firms in just three years, creating a regulatory regime shaped by foreign investors, international organizations, and national elites. In the 1990s, the government adopted a minimal regulatory approach whereby regulation was 'removed from the political process'.[15] This favoured foreign investment's profitability and, while it may have worked out for the government for some years by reducing the fiscal burden, it was detrimental to most of the population—particularly the poorest.

The World Bank review illustrates this tension between the state and the rest of the population. It states that '[t]he Argentine government was a clear winner'. Privatizations gave a strong signal to markets, attracted foreign investment, and reduced the sovereign debt. But for the population the situation was more complicated: 'The impact of privatisations on consumers depend[ed] upon several factors.'[16] In the water and sanitation sector, as Hulya Dagdeviren explains, civil society had no participation in the privatizations and its preferences were not taken into account. When the privatizations were realized and when renegotiations occurred, the social context was neglected.[17] James Haselip et al. make similar claims

[11] Baer and Montes-Rojas (n. 7) 327 (footnote 7).
[12] Ibid., 328, 335; Haselip et al. (n. 4) 5, 12.
[13] Baer and Montes-Rojas (n. 7) 331-3.
[14] Ibid., 327, 333-5; Rodríguez-Boetsch (n. 4) 307, 313.
[15] Cavallo (n. 1) 474.
[16] Shaikh and Abdala (n. 5) 12, 13.
[17] Dagdeviren (n. 4) 29–31, 36.

about electricity. People's views were ignored, and energy prices rose considerably for the smallest residential consumers.[18] According to Baer and Montes-Rojas, privatization in Argentina could be described as a process of 'original capital accumulation', rewarding only the national elite and foreign investors.[19]

The 2001 economic crisis in Argentina abruptly put an end to high economic returns for foreign investors in the utilities sector. In light of the crisis, the government abandoned the US-dollar currency peg and tariffs were reduced to a third of the pre-crisis level. In 2002, most foreign investors in telecoms, water, sanitation, and electricity therefore saw negative profits. These firms were not the main losers, however. Unemployment hit 21.5%, and employed Argentines suffered the pesification of their salaries and savings. The promises made a decade before were gone with the wind. Locals could not do much about this, except emigrate or sue the government before domestic courts, but foreign investors could leverage diplomatic and economic pressure to obtain compensation for their losses, as well as sue Argentina using investment treaties and ISDS.

The situation was not free of paradoxes. One concerned the role of the World Bank: in the 1990s it had promoted and praised the privatizations for which the ensuing regulatory framework was in part responsible; ten years later, ICSID served as the forum for resolving many of the disputes between foreign investors and Argentina. Another paradox was that those investors who sued Argentina essentially took issue with the scrapping of the Convertibility Law, although they had relied on an exception to that law to index tariffs according to US inflation during the previous years. In other words, they contrived to be exempt from the general rules of the game both before and after the crisis.

Not all foreign investors continued their ISDS cases against Argentina; the government reached settlements with many. Interestingly, those that accepted the government's offer and dropped their cases were the most efficient, including the telecommunication companies. Those that did not accept, on the other hand, had either been criticized for bad service, such as the water and sanitation companies, or were no longer interested in Argentina because the golden days of high profitability were not going to be re-established.[20]

1. Energy disputes

The first foreign investors to sue Argentina were involved in the energy sector. Unlike water and sanitation, there is less controversy over the relative success of these privatizations. Energy companies' quality of service improved and average

18 Haselip et al. (n. 4) 12.
19 Baer and Montes-Rojas (n. 7) 326.
20 Ibid., 330; Rodríguez-Boetsch (n. 4) 314.

prices decreased, even though residential consumers faced significant tariff hikes during the 1990s. Haselip argues that the economic crisis increased the distributive tension between foreign investors and consumers, and the solution could only come from a 'protracted political process'.[21] After the Convertibility Law was discarded, energy companies put pressure on the government to raise tariffs by initiating ISDS cases, lobbying home states, and through 'veiled threats and actual interruptions of services'.[22] But the severity of the crisis meant that Argentina could not accept these demands, and offered instead to renegotiate contracts. Many foreign investors chose to push forward with ISDS, asking tribunals to issue awards on the merits of the disputes.

These cases were decided against Argentina. Tribunals dismissed claims of indirect expropriation, as the investors were still in control of their investments and could manage as well as sell the project at will. Yet they decided that Argentina had breached investors' legitimate expectations or dramatically changed the regulations. The government had granted representations over the regulatory framework to induce them to invest, and the measures to deal with the economic crisis frustrated these expectations or substantially changed the existing framework.

The first award was issued in *CMS v. Argentina* (2005), in which the arbitrators ordered Argentina to pay compensation for violating the FET standard and not observing the obligations entered into with regard to the investment. They found both international and domestic law to be relevant in deciding the dispute.[23] The tribunal decided that the special regulatory framework and licence included an entitlement to calculate the tariff in US dollars and adjust this amount pursuant to the US consumer price index. This right was not explicitly included in the licence, but the arbitrators reasoned that a different interpretation 'would be entirely contradictory to the intent of the contemporaneous privatization program and the interest in attracting foreign investment'.[24]

This conclusion was mainly based on the facts surrounding the investment projects. The arbitrators stated that 'in the context of the privatization it was abundantly clear', '[d]eclarations by public officials repeatedly confirmed', 'it was precisely because the right to tariff calculations in dollars [. . .] that the privatization program was as successful', and '[n]umerous bilateral investment treaties were also entered into at the time to provide additional guarantees under international law'.[25] The tribunal also rejected the idea that CMS's rights could be limited according to the '[t]he theory of "imprévision"' because the most appropriate interpretation of this

[21] James Haselip, 'Renegotiating Electricity Contracts after an Economic Crisis and Currency Devaluation: The Case of Argentina' (2005) 18 Electricity Journal 78–88, 78.

[22] Rodríguez-Boetsch (n. 4) 314.

[23] *CMS v. Argentina* (ICSID Case No. ARB/01/8) Award, 12 May 2005, paras. 115–18.

[24] Ibid., para. 163.

[25] Ibid., paras. 134, 137.

theory was not that elaborated by Argentine judges but that of the French Conseil d'État.[26]

The legal source of the entitlement to enjoy US-dollar denominated tariffs was not specified by the tribunal. Later, however, the Annulment Committee explained that 'legitimate expectations might arise by reason of a course of dealing between the investor and the host State'. It also clarified that 'these are not, as such, legal obligations, though they may be relevant to the application of the fair and equitable treatment clause contained in the BIT'.[27]

The remaining question was whether the change in methodology for calculating the tariffs amounted to a violation of this standard of treatment. From a literal reading of the preamble, the arbitrators concluded that FET requires states to maintain a 'stable legal and business environment'.[28] Argentina had failed to abide by this standard. It had 'entirely transform[ed] and alter[ed] the legal and business environment under which the investment was decided and made'. The tribunal noted that 'the legal framework and its various components were crucial for the investment decision'.[29] Decisively, it also reasoned that 'the rights of consumers and users' enshrined in the Argentine Constitution should be interpreted as 'as future aspirations rather than enforceable rights similar to fundamental constitutional rights'.[30]

The reasoning in the *LG&E v. Argentina* award (2006) was quite similar. These arbitrators also noted that both Argentine and international law applied to the dispute, although they said preference should be given to the latter due to the international nature of the dispute.[31] They affirmed that Argentina had an obligation to maintain 'a stable and predictable business environment' and protect foreign investors' legitimate expectations, although they acknowledged that 'business risk or industry's regular patterns' should also be taken into account.[32] The tribunal concluded that LG&E 'had relied upon' specific expectations that Argentina created among investors, and that '[t]he abrogation of these specific guarantees violates the stability and predictability underlying the standard of fair and equitable treatment'.[33] These expectations emerged from the conditions that the state offered when the investment was made. The facts of the dispute therefore showed that Argentina had 'acted unfairly and inequitably'.[34]

[26] Ibid., paras 222–6.
[27] *CMS v. Argentina* (ICSID Case No. ARB/01/8) Annulment Decision, 25 September 2007, para. 89.
[28] *CMS v. Argentina* (ICSID Case No. ARB/01/8) Award, 12 May 2005, para. 274.
[29] Ibid., para. 275.
[30] Ibid., para. 204.
[31] *LG&E v. Argentina* (ICSID Case No. ARB/02/1) Decision on Liability, 3 October 2006, paras. 93, 98–9.
[32] Ibid., paras. 130–1.
[33] Ibid., para. 133.
[34] Ibid., paras. 134–5.

These arbitrators further examined the relationship between foreign investors' expectations and the social and economic circumstances, including the rights of consumers. Argentina argued that without the modification of the tariff system 'many customers could not have had access to the gas service'.[35] While the tribunal recognized the difficult economic situation of the crisis, it reasoned that 'Argentina went too far by completely dismantling the very legal framework constructed to attract investors'.[36]

The *Sempra v. Argentina* tribunal (2007) also concluded that Argentina had violated the FET standard. It observed that the privatization memorandum was clear about the US-dollar denominated tariffs and the option of adjusting the amount according to the US consumer price index. If this was not the case, and an error had occurred, Argentina was 'duty-bound to issue a clarification to avoid the engendering of a false legitimate expectation'. No clarification was issued, however, and the arbitrators concluded that Sempra 'had a right to enjoy [the US-dollar denominated tariffs] under both the regulatory framework and the license'.[37] Further, they noted that Argentina had other participatory mechanisms to address the interests of the consumers, but the government preferred instead to act unilaterally. The abrogation of Sempra's rights substantially changed the legal and business framework under which 'the investment was decided and implemented. Where there was business certainty and stability, there is now the opposite.'[38]

The award in *Total v. Argentina* (2010) relied on a different reasoning to decide, again, that Argentina had violated the FET standard. As the previous tribunals, these arbitrators delved into the facts of the dispute, finding that Total was in a different situation than those investors who participated in the early 1990s bidding process and could thus rely on those specific rules. That was not the case for Total, and this tribunal noted, in passing, neither was it the case for CMS, LG&E, or Sempra.[39] The tribunal also rejected the position that FET provides investors with an entitlement to a stable legal regime, explaining that the legal issue instead is whether the foreign investor had legitimate expectations that the state later frustrated through the measures in question.[40] Further, they attested that a breach of legitimate expectations does not lead automatically to a violation of the treaty. The tribunal rejected this sole effects interpretation, holding that a 'host State's right to

[35] Ibid., para. 153.
[36] Ibid., para. 139.
[37] *Sempra v. Argentina* (ICSID Case No. ARB/02/16) Award, 28 September 2007, para. 113.
[38] Ibid., 303.
[39] *Total v. Argentina* (ICSID Case No. ARB/04/01) Decision on Liability, 27 December 2010, para. 179.
[40] Ibid., paras. 116–19. The dissenting arbitrator concluded instead that investment treaties do not protect legitimate expectations. Concurring Opinion of Luis Herrera Marcano, 12 December 2010, paras. 2–3.

regulate domestic matters in the public interest has to be taken into consideration as well'.[41]

For the *Total* tribunal, legitimate expectations could emerge from various sources. They could originate in a specific legal obligation on which 'the investor is therefore entitled to rely as a matter of law'. Equally, they could arise from representations 'specifically addressed to a particular investor' on which 'the investor relied in making investments'.[42] These representations could be either explicit or implicit but, crucially, must have been aimed at soliciting or inducing the investor to make the investment. The tribunal recognized that specific regulatory frameworks that were forward-looking could give rise to some expectations. The case of Total was different, however, as Argentina had already suspended the indexing of tariffs when this firm invested. A reasonable investor would have taken this situation into account when making the decision to invest.[43]

Nonetheless, the arbitrators reasoned that Total was still entitled to make 'reasonable profit' defined according to 'criteria of economic rationality, public interest [...], reasonableness and proportionality'.[44] An additional element that supported this conclusion, the tribunal said, was that Total had an acquired right to a price determination process under Argentine law. After the height of the crisis, Argentina was mandated to update the tariffs according to these criteria, but it did not comply. The arbitrators did not elaborate further on what would have been a proportionate tariff update that ensured both a reasonable return for the investor and affordable tariffs for consumers. Argentine law required a participatory process that would not make performance excessively onerous for the investor, but the arbitrators might have had something else in mind after observing that '[i]n the case of a "normal" devaluation of the peso, the de-dollarization of the gas tariffs would not have been economically justified nor socially necessary'.[45]

In *El Paso v. Argentina* (2011), the tribunal followed a similar line of argument. It criticized previous awards that granted foreign investors a right to legal stability and good governance or imposed on states a proactive attitude towards foreign investment. For these arbitrators, the issue instead was whether El Paso had a legitimate expectation to US-dollar denominated tariffs. They said that such expectations depend on the context—and that the central feature is not so much whether the commitment is 'legally binding'. The interpreter has to determine whether there

[41] *Total v. Argentina* (ICSID Case No. ARB/04/01) Decision on Liability, 27 December 2010, para. 123.

[42] Ibid., paras. 117, 119–20.

[43] Ibid., paras. 156–8

[44] Ibid., paras. 333–4.

[45] Ibid., paras. 334–5, 160–1. De-dollarizing the economy, however, was precisely what Argentina should have done earlier to avoid the severe economic crisis. See Miguel Kiguel, 'Argentina's 2001 Economic and Financial Crisis: Lessons for Europe' in (2011) Beyond Macroeconomic Policy Coordination Discussions in the G-20, 7–9, 7, available at https://www.brookings.edu/wp-content/uploads/2016/06/11_think_tank_20.pdf (last visited 4 June 2020).

was a 'specific commitment directly made to the investor, on which the latter has relied'.[46] The tribunal held that expectations are legitimate when states are specific about the addressee and the object and purpose of the commitment. The arbitrators did not go into the details, however, observing only that foreign investors' legitimate expectations can exist in 'a contract or in a letter of intent, or even through a specific promise in a person-to-person business meeting'. Following the award in *Continental v. Argentina* (2008), they also accepted that general legislative statements may 'engender reduced expectations'.[47]

For the arbitrators, El Paso had no legitimate expectations but was still entitled to some compensation for 'a total alteration of the entire legal setup for foreign investments'.[48] Neither roadshows, presidential declarations, or general legislation were specific enough to create legitimate expectations. The foreign investor, then, was not entitled to earn US-dollar denominated tariffs. However, the arbitrators reasoned, the specification in dollars (instead of pesos) of key elements of the energy framework was intentional and crucial for foreign investors. El Paso had to be prepared for 'reasonable changes', but could also expect that the main features of the regime would not be altered. The arbitrators concluded that while each individual reform in this case did not constitute a violation of the investment treaty, together their cumulative effects amounted to a creeping violation of the FET standard.[49]

As the cases above show, protecting foreign investors' legitimate expectations—about either specific or general features of the regulatory regime—has significant implications for states as well as populations. The issue in these awards was not whether the foreign investors had acquired a legally binding commitment to earn US-dollar denominated tariffs. Instead, the reasoning contrasted the facts of each case with an imaginary of foreign investment relations in which the key question was whether Argentina had given either explicit or implicit representations, and if the foreign investor had relied on these representations to make the investment. This imaginary provided no space for the protracted political process necessary to adjust for the distributive consequences of the Argentine crisis, or for considering the competing expectations or rights of the Argentine population. Arbitrators interpreted strong entitlements from Argentina's representations, which they noted were not legally binding, but reduced the consumer rights in the Argentine Constitution to mere 'aspirations'. The awards in *Total* and *El Paso* took a more demanding approach to determining legitimate expectations, and criticized previous decisions, but they still followed similar reasoning to focus on Total's reasonable

[46] *El Paso v. Argentina* (ICSID Case No. ARB/03/15) Award, 31 October 2011, paras. 376, 342–8, 356–76.
[47] Ibid., paras. 376–9.
[48] Ibid., para. 517.
[49] Ibid., paras. 400, 510–19.

rate of return and on El Paso's expectations of the regulatory regime's central features.

2. Water disputes

The ISDS cases in the water sector concerned service quality, investment targets, and tariff calculation both before and after the 2001 economic crisis. Problems with these privatizations started during the late 1990s, and further deteriorated with the crisis. Dagdeviren argues that a frequent issue was that foreign investors offered either high concession fees or significant investment targets, and asked Argentina for a renegotiation soon after receiving the concession. The government attempted to address these problems, but in most cases the deals proved unsustainable. Public officials preferred to lower investment targets and delay tariff increases.[50]

Postponing investments, however, resulted in bad quality of service, and ultimately did not resolve the persistent pressures for a tariff raise, particularly after the 2001 crisis. The population resisted these increases to the extent of not paying outstanding bills, citing unsatisfactory water quality, financial constraints, or both. The ISDS cases of *Vivendi v. Argentina* (Aguas del Aconquija), *Azurix v. Argentina* (Azurix Buenos Aires), and *Suez and others v. Argentina* (Aguas Provinciales de Santa Fe) illustrate the problems created by water service privatizations and how arbitrators resolved these disputes.

The case of *Vivendi* (Aguas del Aconquija) predates the 2001 crisis. In 1996, the provincial government initiated a renegotiation process with the foreign investor which was rejected by the legislature of Tucumán. The World Bank, which had an interest in protecting the reputation of its privatization policies, intervened to finalize the process, although the legislature of Tucumán remained reluctant to approve the new deal.[51] The situation failed to improve, however, and some months later provincial authorities unilaterally modified the terms of the concession, warned the population against the quality of the water, encouraged consumers not to pay their bills, and undermined or rejected Vivendi's proposals to save the project. The foreign investor initiated an ISDS case that, after the annulment of the first award, resulted in a decision (2007) against Argentina for indirect expropriation. The tribunal concluded that the province of Tucumán mounted a politically motivated and illegitimate campaign against the investor, forcing it to rescind the contract.[52]

In the case of *Azurix*, the dispute began in 2001 after the foreign investor requested the renegotiation of the concession. This investor had offered a 'concession

[50] Dagdeviren (n. 4) 26–30.
[51] Ibid., 35.
[52] *Vivendi v. Argentina* (ICSID Case No. ARB/97/3) Award, 20 August 2007, paras. 7.4.22-44.

fee, at least, six times greater than that of the next bidder'.[53] Azurix first asked for a change in the estimation of unmetered tariffs, which was mentioned by the privatization commission but rejected by the regulator because of previous tariff increases and the opposition of the population. While these discussions continued, the regulator noted that certain investments were delayed and the quality of water had deteriorated markedly. An algae outbreak was responsible for the water 'appearing cloudy and hazy and with earth-musty taste and odor'.[54] Public authorities blamed Azurix for this, suggesting that people should not pay their water bills in such circumstances. Azurix rejected this accusation and the non-payment proposal. It argued that the Province of Buenos Aires was responsible for the algae outbreak as necessary improvements in a water reservoir had not been carried out. The firm also claimed that the public authorities had incited public panic, explaining that 'although the Bahía Blanca network water is not drinkable from a physical/chemical standpoint, no microbial contamination that could cause infectious diseases was detected'.[55]

In light of these difficulties, Azurix filed for bankruptcy and sued Argentina for violating the US–Argentina investment treaty. The arbitrators were sympathetic to the claim (award of 2006). They relied on the sole effects interpretation of indirect expropriation, observing that the issue is not whether the measure is legitimate or serves a public interest, but 'whether it should give rise to a compensation claim'.[56] Also, the tribunal noted that FET requires states to protect foreign investors' legitimate expectations. This standard presupposes 'a favorable disposition towards foreign investment, in fact, a pro-active behavior of the State to encourage and protect it'.[57] Argentina did not commit an expropriation, but failed to behave according to the FET standard. Foreign investors, the arbitrators reasoned, have no role in domestic politics and should therefore carry a lower burden of measures promoting the public interest. They accepted Azurix's interpretation of the concession agreement only partially, but concluded that 'the tariff regime was politicized because of concerns with forthcoming elections or because the Concession was awarded by the previous government'.[58]

Although the *Suez* dispute started after 2001, the problems for Aguas Provinciales de Santa Fe dated from some years before the crisis. One contentious issue referred to several investments that Suez promised but did not carry out as a result of renegotiations that took place in 1997. Another problem related to the payment difficulties of low-income groups, which led to another reduction of Suez's investment obligations in 2000. In both cases the foreign investor was also

[53] Dagdeviren (n. 4) 30, 39.
[54] *Azurix v. Argentina* (ICSID Case No. ARB/01/12) Award, 14 July 2006, para. 124.
[55] Ibid., paras. 124, 124–5.
[56] Ibid., para. 310.
[57] Ibid., para. 372.
[58] Ibid., para. 375.

granted a tariff increase, of 14% and 10% respectively. Later, the regulator decided that tariffs could not be increased to compensate for the 2001 economic crisis and the end of the Convertibility Law. Argentina contended that freezing the tariffs was necessary to buffer the financial impact on citizens and guarantee an essential service and a human right. But this, according to Suez, would lead the firm to bankruptcy as the company was indebted in US dollars. The situation eventually led to the termination of the concession and bankruptcy of the company.[59]

The tribunal decided that Argentina did not commit an expropriation, but was liable for a violation of FET, specifically for disappointing the foreign investor's legitimate expectations (award of 2010). The majority professed that legitimate expectations are a key element of the FET standard.[60] In this case, the foreign investors had a legitimate expectation to have the tariffs adjusted after the 2001 crisis, an expectation which emerged from both the sectoral regulations and the bidding rules and contractual framework. Argentina had induced the foreign investors through representations and the 'investors, deriving their expectations from the laws and regulations adopted by the host country, acted in reliance upon those laws and regulations and changed their economic position as a result'.[61] The majority also condemned Argentina for trying to force the investors into a renegotiation that would have changed the concession's original equation.[62]

Moreover, the arbitrators rejected Argentina's contention that the conduct imposed by the FET standard was inconsistent with its human rights obligations. Argentina was subject to two international obligations, namely to respect foreign investor rights as per the applicable investment treaties and to protect the human right to water. These obligations were 'not inconsistent, contradictory, or mutually exclusive'. The majority of the tribunal observed that inconsistency would have existed only if breaching foreign investor rights was the 'only way' to protect the human right to water, but Argentina had alternatives—such as implementing a social tariff.[63]

Argentina is not the only country to face ISDS cases resulting from water and sanitation privatization. Two other high-profile disputes involved Bolivia and Tanzania; they also concerned issues around tariff increases and public service mismanagement. *Aguas del Tunari v. Bolivia* was never decided due to transnational pressure against the investor, while the arbitrators in *Biwater v. Tanzania* concluded—as in the *Azurix* award—that the contract termination was tainted

[59] Dagdeviren (n. 4) 40.

[60] *Suez and others v. Argentina* (ICSID Case No. ARB/03/17) Decision on Liability, 30 July 2010, paras. 203–5. The dissenting arbitrator concluded instead that investment treaties do not protect legitimate expectations. Separate Opinion of Pedro Nikken, 30 July 2010, paras. 2–4, 12–25, 38–40.

[61] *Suez and others v. Argentina* (ICSID Case No. ARB/03/17) Decision on Liability, 30 July 2010, paras. 207, 207–12.

[62] Ibid., paras. 217–18.

[63] Ibid., paras. 240, 238–40.

by political motivations and in breach of the investment treaty.[64] None of these tribunals, however, were entirely clear about what these investors were entitled to expect after the privatization had clearly failed. Implicitly, they seemed to suggest that public officials should have told the population to stay calm and continue paying their bills, while the foreign investor and the state worked out a solution. In the meantime, the human right to water of millions of people could be at risk. Unsurprisingly, international organizations are no longer so enthusiastic about water and sanitation privatization.[65]

3. Emergency and state of necessity

In every ISDS case related to the 2001 economic crisis, Argentina pleaded the defence of necessity. Its argument was that the severity of the crisis constituted a state of necessity, which precluded the wrongfulness of its behaviour either under the US–Argentina investment treaty (Article XI), when this treaty was applicable, or under customary international law (Article 25 of the Draft Articles on Responsibility of States for Internationally Wrongful Acts). For Argentina, the measures adopted were necessary for maintaining public order and safeguarding essential interests. The ISDS tribunals recognized the gravity of the crisis, but arrived at differing conclusions about the defence of necessity. They had different views about whether the situation compromised public order or the existence of the state, as well as significant disagreements on whether Argentina had contributed to the crisis and on the existence of alternative measures that were less harmful to foreign investors.[66]

Most of the awards concluded that Argentina could not rely on the necessity defence. Arbitrators pointed out that the crisis in Argentina was the result of internal and external factors, and that multiple governments had contributed to it by running large fiscal deficits and taking other controversial measures. They also argued that the termination of the US-dollar denominated tariffs (and the indexation of those tariffs according to the US consumer price index) was not the only

[64] *Biwater v. Tanzania* (ICSID Case No. ARB/05/22) Award, 24 July 2008, paras. 610, 615, 698; David Schneiderman, *Resisting Economic Globalization: Critical Theory and International Investment Law* (Palgrave 2013) 63–70, 93–112.

[65] Karen Bakker, *Privatizing Water: Governance Failure and the World's Urban Water Crisis* (Cornell University Press 2010) 92–104; Peter T. Robbins, 'Transnational Corporations and the Discourse of Water Privatization' (2003) 15 Journal of International Development 1073–82.

[66] Several scholars have analysed this question. See, e.g., Jürgen Kurtz, 'Adjudging the Exceptional at International Investment Law: Security, Public Order and Financial Crisis' (2010) 59 International & Comparative Law Quarterly 325–71; Diane A. Desierto, 'Necessity and Supplementary Means of Interpretation for Non-Precluded Measures in Bilateral Investment Treaties' (2009) University of Pennsylvania Journal of International Law 31 (2009) 827–934; José E. Alvarez and Tegan Brink, 'Revisiting the Necessity Defense: Continental Casualty v. Argentina' in Karl P. Sauvant (ed.), *Yearbook on International Investment Law & Policy 2010-2011* (OUP 2012) 319–62.

way to address the crisis. Argentina could have implemented less harmful solutions for the foreign investors. In many ways, this strict interpretation is similar to that intended by the authors of the Abs–Shawcross draft and the OECD 1967 Draft. Derogation was to be interpreted narrowly and limited to very specific cases, particularly war or other forms of military conflict. In the realm of the economy, according to the reasoning in *CMS*, *Total*, or *El Paso*,[67] it is unlikely that states can rely on the state of necessity because governments contribute—directly, indirectly, or tacitly—to economic crises, and alternative measures always exist, particularly if tribunals assume, like the *Suez* arbitrators, that the protection of foreign investors and human rights are rarely inconsistent with each other.

Aside from the dissent in *El Paso*, the two exceptions are the awards in *LG&E* and *Continental*. These arbitrators did not deny that Argentina had taken problematic economic measures, but they noted that the international community, including the International Monetary Fund, considered them to be sound policy at the time.[68] The question, therefore, was whether it was possible to reproach Argentina for taking those measures. The *Continental* tribunal also interpreted that the necessity requirement is not equal to 'indispensable'. Argentina had 'no choice but to act'. These arbitrators relied on WTO law, concretely GATT Article XX, to conclude that the issue was whether there were less inconsistent measures the state 'could reasonably be expected to employ'.[69] After analysing several alternatives, it decided that the measures taken by Argentina were necessary. This position was criticized, however, as GATT Article XX applies to the normal exercise of regulatory powers.[70] In a way, this award subverted the principle that derogation—as envisaged by the norm entrepreneurs—does not refer to normal policy measures.

B. Spain—green business and economic crisis

The problems with some privatizations, in sectors such as water and sanitation, did not undermine public officials' confidence in private actors taking up critical tasks for social wellbeing. In the late 1990s, the idea that market incentives and appropriate regulation could facilitate a transition from fossil fuel to renewable energy had many supporters in Europe. The European Union passed rules on

[67] *CMS v. Argentina* (ICSID Case No. ARB/01/8) Award, 12 May 2005, paras. 324–31; *Total v. Argentina* (ICSID Case No. ARB/04/01) Decision on Liability, 27 December 2010, paras. 345, 484; *El Paso v. Argentina* (ICSID Case No. ARB/03/15) Award, 31 October 2011, paras. 615–24, 656–65; *Suez and others v. Argentina* (ICSID Case No. ARB/03/17) Decision on Liability, 30 July 2010, paras. 236–42.

[68] *Continental v. Argentina* (ICSID Case No. ARB/03/9) Award, 5 September 2008, paras. 179–80, 179–97; Dissenting Opinion of Brigitte Stern in *El Paso v. Argentina* (ICSID Case No. ARB/03/15) Award, 31 October 2011, paras. 666–70. The award in LG&E similarly noted that Argentina had 'no choice but to act', and that the state had not contributed to the situation. *LG&E v. Argentina* (ICSID Case No. ARB/02/1) Decision on Liability, 3 October 2006, paras. 240, 257.

[69] *Continental v. Argentina* (ICSID Case No. ARB/03/9) Award, 5 September 2008, para. 195.

[70] See Alvarez and Brink (n. 66) 347–53, 355; Desierto (n. 66) 931–4.

subsidies in the green energy sector, and several countries implemented green energy programmes.[71] In the wake of the 2007–2008 financial crisis, other actors also described the green energy sector as a great investment opportunity. Key international institutions pointed out that renewable energies could allow countries to move out of the recession while paving the way for a new energy era. The United Nations promoted a 'Global Green New Deal',[72] while global banks observed that 'the colour of stimulus [had gone] green'.[73]

But for investors, particularly foreign investors, committing large sums of money to renewable energies was not an easy decision. Because economic returns were uncertain, they expected governments to give first 'a clear long-term international signal'.[74] The OECD and UNCTAD stated that increasing investment in the green energy sector required that governments deal with entry barriers and long-term uncertainties. The OECD specified that 'investors need a clear and credible price signal now to make the appropriate investment decisions for a greener future'.[75] UNCTAD made the same point in its 2010 World Investment Report, which was dedicated to foreign investment in the low carbon economy: 'more than in any other sector, investors in renewable energy [...] build their business cases on incentives, government promises of support and specific regulatory frameworks (e.g. market creating climate change regulations)'.[76] Further, this UN agency suggested that investment treaties might have a particular relevance for attracting low-carbon foreign investment: '[t]o the extent that IIAs can strengthen investors' confidence regarding the continuity and enforceability of such enabling frameworks or promises of support, they can positively impact firm's investment-decisions'.[77]

Many countries followed this policy advice. European states, Spain in particular, implemented a feed-in tariffs (FITs) mechanism—'commonly defined as state-backed incentives to invest in the generation of electricity from renewable

[71] Tomi Huhtanen, 'Europe and Green Growth: The Key to Recovery?' in Robert Schuman Foundation (ed.), *State of the Union 2010: Schuman Report on Europe* (Springer 2010) 91–8; Béatrice Cointe and Alain Nadaï, *Feed-in Tariffs in the European Union: Renewable Energy Policy, the Internal Electricity Market and Economic Expertise* (Palgrave 2018) 25–86.

[72] UN Environment Programme, 'Global Green New Deal: Policy brief' March 2009, available at https://www.greengrowthknowledge.org/resource/global-green-new-deal-policy-brief (last visited 17 June 2020).

[73] HSBC, 'A Climate for Recovery: The Colour of Stimulus Goes Green' 25 February 2009, available at https://www.globaldashboard.org/wp-content/uploads/2009/HSBC_Green_New_Deal.pdf (last visited 4 June 2019).

[74] OECD, 'Green Growth: Overcoming the Crisis and Beyond' (OECD 2009) 7. Similarly, the President of the World Business Council for Sustainable Development noted that 'business needs clear signals from governments as to where we are headed'. Björn Stigson, 'Moving ahead on Climate' in UN Environment Programme, *Climate Action: Getting Greener, Getting Slimmer, and Going Digital* (UN 2008) 17–19, 18.

[75] OECD (n. 74) 9.

[76] UNCTAD, *World Investment Report 2010: Investing in a Low-Carbon Economy* (United Nations 2010) 136.

[77] Ibid.

sources'.[78] This mechanism ensures investors a predictable return on investment by combining three elements: i) a commitment to purchase the energy; ii) a fixed price for green energy; and iii) a fixed period over which said price is guaranteed. Compared with other mechanisms, such as quotas, a salient feature of FITs is a commitment to buy the entire production of green energy with no limitation. While FITs provide a greater incentive to invest, including for small players, quotas 'are supposedly less subjected to the fluctuations of politics and to risks of regulatory capture'.[79]

Designing FITs is not simple. This is due, among other reasons, to the risk of regulatory capture and lack of information. Much of the information governments require to design this incentive is in the hands of investors, whose goal is to maximize their profitability, not the public interest.[80] Lobbying is also common: associations of renewable energy producers, including solar energy producers, are active lobbyists. A study by Steffen Jenner et al. finds that the existence of a solar energy association increases the probability that states adopt incentives.[81] Investors in renewables have interests that may clash with other energy producers, such as fossil fuel companies, with strong lobbying power. But while fossil fuel companies are politically and economically more powerful, renewable energy investors enjoy more credibility and are perceived more positively.[82]

In addition to this asymmetry of information and the chances of regulatory capture, governments need to take into account other elements which are difficult if not impossible to calculate in the long term. These include the evolution of energy prices, the fiscal burden, technological changes, and negative and positive externalities. Béatrice Cointe and Alain Nadaï explain that the problem is not static but dynamic; FITs can be in force for up to twenty or thirty years. These regulatory givings do not remove uncertainty but rather transfer the risks to the public.[83] An unexpected change in the circumstances existing at the time of implementing FITs can negatively affect the public budget and electricity bills or other social goals such as health or education.

[78] Cointe and Nadaï (n. 71) 4. In the 2000s, the business sector widely favoured the use of FITs. Miguel Mendonça, *Feed-in Tariffs: Accelerating the Deployment of Renewable Energy* (Earthscan 2007) xiv.

[79] Cointe and Nadaï (n. 71) 51, 49–51. Also, Mendonça (n. 78) xvi.

[80] Cointe and Nadaï (n. 71) 72–3, 79, 97.

[81] Steffen Jenner, Gabriel Chan, Rolf Frankenberger, and Mathias Gabel, 'What Drives States to Support Renewable Energy?' (2012) 33 Energy Journal 1–12, 11. Also, David Jacobs, *Renewable Energy Policy Convergence in the EU: The Evolution of Feed-in Tariffs in Germany, Spain and France* (Ashgate 2012) 127, 155. Jacobs concludes that 'regulatory competition in the case of feed-in tariffs has often led to improved framework conditions for renewable power producers, because such producers have been able to threaten to move their activities to other countries'. Ibid., 239.

[82] Hendrik Steringa, 'Energy Companies Divided over Renewable Energy in Brussels' Energy Post, 22 October 2015, available at https://energypost.eu/energy-companies-divided-renewable-energy-lobby-brussels/ (last visited 4 June 2020).

[83] Cointe and Nadaï (n. 71) 93–4, 96, 98–101.

For Spain, the 2007–2008 crisis was one of several unexpected factors that made the FITs regime unsustainable. In 2007, the country attracted more domestic and foreign investment than it expected (overflows) due to the high guaranteed returns in a context of crisis and certain technological changes that facilitated renewable energy projects. Further, the positive externalities were lower than originally thought. The sector did not create many jobs and most inputs were imported from China.[84] When the economic crisis hit the public finances, the increasing fiscal burden became intolerable for Spain and raising electricity tariffs was not an option—unemployment reached more than 17% in early 2009. As Cointe and Nadaï explain, FITs were not criticized for being 'insufficiently market-based, too dependent on arbitrary political decisions, or incompatible with competition law. New issues and expectations came into focus, such as industrial effects, employment, social cost, or the specificities of national political and economic contexts.'[85]

In this context, Spain decided to review, adjust, and finally considerably reduce the 2007 FITs regime. In 2010, it made three major changes. It limited the availability of the regime to thirty years, introduced a cap on the electricity that producers could sell enjoying the FIT price, and asked for new technological requirements to benefit from the regime. In 2012, Spain also decided to implement a 7% tax on electricity production. These measures, however, were not enough in the dramatic economic context. Spanish unemployment soared to 24.19% by early 2012 and 26.94% a year after. Spain made some additional changes to the FITs regime, such as reducing the availability of the regime to twenty-five years, but in 2013 the government considered the fiscal burden to be unsustainable and terminated the FITs regime, replacing it with a less onerous system for the state.[86]

These changes affected the foreign investors who had entered into the Spanish solar energy market enticed by the generous givings. These investors relied on the strong signal given by Spain's enactment of a favourable FITs mechanism, which was advertised in several roadshows under the slogan 'the sun can be yours'.[87] At a time when economic prospects looked uncertain, this investment opportunity promised significant economic returns with limited risks; in fact, the Spanish government was assuming the main risks. For many of these investors, the measures taken by Spain between 2010 and 2014 violated their rights under investment treaties, particularly the Energy Charter Treaty (ECT). While no tribunal has found an indirect expropriation so far, several have decided that Spain violated foreign investors' legitimate expectations. Notably, these disputes are being resolved

[84] At first the Spanish solar industry was regarded as a success, Mendonça (n. 78) xv, but the situation deteriorated after the financial crisis. Cointe and Nadaï (n. 71) 91, 95.

[85] Cointe and Nadaï (n. 71) 95.

[86] The string of measures adopted by Spain are detailed in *Novenergia II v. Spain* (SCC Case No. 2015/063) Award, 15 February 2018, paras. 139, 78–152.

[87] Ibid., para. 598.

just as an 'investment-centred conception' of FITs is being replaced by mechanisms to 'manage multiple political and economic uncertainties'.[88]

1. Solar energy disputes

The first case resolved was *Charanne v. Spain* (2016). This dispute only involved the measures taken in 2010, which reduced profitability but did not terminate the original Spanish FIT regime. The arbitrators rejected the view that the ECT incorporates an obligation of legal stability. They instead held that states can implement reasonable measures as long as they do not frustrate foreign investors' legitimate expectations, which could derive either from specific commitments or 'rules that are not specifically addressed […] but which are put in place with a specific aim to induce foreign investments and on which the foreign investor relied in making his investment'.[89] This legal test requires assessing the facts from the perspective of an objective investor at the moment the investment was made, recognizing that states are entitled to maintain a 'reasonable degree of regulatory flexibility to respond to changing circumstances in the public interest'.[90] The majority decided that Charanne had no legitimate expectations, as Spain never promised that the regulatory framework would remain unaltered, and the changes it implemented were 'adopted on the basis of objective criteria and cannot be considered irrational or arbitrary'.[91]

The second award was rendered in *Isolux v. Spain* (2016). This foreign investor challenged all the measures Spain had taken, including the termination of the FIT regime. The situation of Isolux was special, however, because it invested in 2013, when Spain had already implemented several changes the to the FIT regime and the economic crisis was severe. For the tribunal, the legal issue was whether Isolux could legitimately rely on a regime that had already been modified and the sustainability of which was uncertain. The arbitrators stated that foreign investors must carry out some 'due diligence' before establishing a project. This due diligence need not be extensive and exhaustive but 'it can be presumed that [the investor has] knowledge of the important decisions of the supreme judicial authority with respect to the investment's regulatory framework'.[92] In this light, the expectations

[88] Cointe and Nadaï (n. 71) 96.

[89] *Charanne v. Spain* (SCC Case No. V062/2012) Award, 21 January 2016, paras. 489, 485–9.

[90] Ibid., para. 500 (The arbitrators relied on *Electrabel v. Hungary* (ICSID Case No. ARB/07/19) Decision on Jurisdiction, Applicable Law and Liability, 30 November 2012, para. 7.77).

[91] Ibid., para. 534. The dissenting arbitrator said that Charanne had a legitimate expectation, and Spain was mandated to take this expectation into account when implementing new regulation, which Spain did not do. Dissenting Opinion of Guido Santiago Tawil, 21 December 2015, paras. 5–12.

[92] *Isolux v. Spain* (SCC Case V2013/153) Award, 17 July 2016, paras. 794, 781–93 (Translation from the Spanish by Damien Charlotin, 'In now-public Isolux v. Spain award, measures that later breached investor protections in Eiser case were not deemed to breach Isolux's legitimate expectations' IAReporter, 29 June 2017).

claimed by Isolux were not legitimate, and Spain's measures to protect energy consumers were deemed reasonable.[93]

After these two cases, a string of disputes concerning projects established around 2007 were resolved. These investors challenged all the measures Spain had taken, including the termination of the original FIT regime. In the first of these cases, *Eiser v. Spain* (2017), the arbitrators dismissed the claim that FET constitutes a guarantee to a stable legal regime—foreign investors should expect some changes. However, they argued that the situation is different when the state implements 'fundamental changes' and foreign investors had relied on that regime to make the investment. These investors have a legitimate expectation that the regime would not be 'radically altered'. Eiser was entitled to expect that the state would respect 'the fundamental characteristics' of the regime.[94] The tribunal noted that this was especially so in a sector where large upfront investments are required before starting production. Predictable prices were a central element of the business plan. The replacement of the FIT regime, the arbitrators concluded, 'deprived Claimants of essentially all of the value of their investment'.[95] Importantly, they remarked that they did not question the necessity of Spanish measures but the state 'had to act in a way that respected the obligations it assumed under the ECT'.[96]

The *Eiser* award did not specify whether the radical changes implemented by Spain would still constitute a breach of FET if an investment project remained profitable. This point was discussed by the tribunal in *Novenergia v. Spain* (2018), which said that FET does not guarantee legal stability and 'allows for a balancing exercise'. It observed that any regulatory change should occur within the boundaries of an 'acceptable range of legislative and regulatory behaviour'.[97] To define these boundaries, the arbitrators focused on foreign investors' legitimate expectations, which 'arise naturally from undertakings and assurances', possibly in the form of laws and regulations. Representations can be either explicit or implicit, and state intention is irrelevant. But foreign investors' reliance on these assurances must be reasonable.[98]

For these arbitrators, Novenergia could reasonably expect some stability, as most firms in the renewables sector did. The FIT regime was 'very favourable' and Spanish officers and marketing materials stressed these advantages, including the regime's stability. All this looked like 'a bait rather than a deterrent'.[99] The limited due diligence, which Spain criticized as insufficient, was enough for the tribunal because the regime 'was so adamantly clear that its understanding by common

93 Ibid., paras. 808–15, 823, 851.
94 *Eiser v. Spain* (ICSID Case No. ARB/13/36) Award, 4 May 2017, paras. 363, 382–3.
95 Ibid., para. 418.
96 Ibid., para. 371.
97 *Novenergia II v. Spain* (SCC Case No. 2015/063) Award, 15 February 2018, paras. 657, 655.
98 Ibid., para. 650.
99 Ibid., paras. 665, 674.

readers did not require a particularly sophisticated analysis'.[100] The arbitrators thus concluded that the first changes to the FIT regime were not outside of the acceptable range of reforms in light of foreign investors' legitimate expectations. But, as decided in *Eiser*, the 'radical and unexpected' termination of the FIT regime did amount to the frustration of Novenergia's expectations.[101]

A central difference between these two cases concerns the profitability of Novenergia, which was still an alleged post-tax return of 6.6%. For the arbitrators, however, this did not preclude Spain's liability. They reasoned that the FET standard does not have a radical deprivation threshold, unlike expropriation, and it requires instead balancing Novenergia's legitimate expectations and Spain's right to regulate. Spain had a right to regulate, but not an 'unfettered' right. The issue was not profitability but the radical change of 'the *essential characteristics* of the legal regime relied upon by investors in making long-term investments'.[102]

Subsequent awards have clarified other issues concerning the solar energy litigation against Spain. In *Greentech v. Spain* (2018), the arbitrators reasoned that foreign investors may have expectations about specific features of a regulatory regime or that the ECT otherwise grants them a reduced expectation that the regulatory framework would not be 'fundamentally and abruptly changed'.[103] In *Antin v. Spain* (2018), the arbitrators further discussed the issue of specificity, saying that expectations can emerge from 'certain features of a regulation aimed at encouraging investments in a specific sector'. For this tribunal the stability of the regulatory regime was 'the *leitmotiv* of Spain's acts at the time of the Claimants' investment'.[104] The question, then, was whether the new regime based on a 'reasonable return' frustrated the original legitimate expectations. The *Antin* tribunal concluded that this was the case, due to the lack of certitude about the calculation and adjustment of the economic returns.

Altogether, the resolution of these ISDS disputes against Spain has hinged on two issues: whether foreign investors have a legitimate expectation (and the necessary level of due diligence) and how arbitrators balance these expectations against states' right to regulate.[105] Tribunals have accepted that states can implement regulatory changes, but maintain that these changes need to be reviewed in light of legitimate expectations, particularly in a sector in which economic viability depends on incentives. It is noteworthy that when arbitrators have found that the foreign investor had a legitimate expectation, as in the cases related to the 2001 Argentine crisis, they rarely conclude later that the public measure was justified under a

[100] Ibid., para. 679.
[101] Ibid., paras. 695, 692–5.
[102] Ibid., paras. 688, 694.
[103] *Greentech v.* Spain (SCC Case No. 2015/150) Award, 14 November 2018, para. 365.
[104] *Antin v. Spain* (ICSID Case No. ARB/13/31) Award, 15 June 2018, paras. 538, 548, 562–3, 568.
[105] The *Masdar* tribunal referred that there are 'two schools of thought' on these issues. See *Masdar v. Spain* (ICSID Case No. ARB/14/1) Award, 16 May 2018, para. 490.

balancing or proportionality analysis. A violation of legitimate expectations seems to operate, in practice, depending on the effects on the foreign investor—that is, a sole effect test.[106]

Regulatory givings and incentives are a common feature in ISDS cases. In addition to Spain, solar energy litigation has been raised against other European countries, such as Italy and the Czech Republic. Another notable ISDS case related to the termination of an incentive regime is *Micula v. Romania* (2013). This case is remarkable because the termination of the incentives in question was necessary for Romania to join the European Union, a measure that—other things being equal—most investors would perceive as a positive signal. The tribunal decided in favour of the investor, however, reasoning that '[t]o obtain that investment, [Romania] offered certain tax benefits for a certain amount of time'.[107] This offer took the shape of 'explicit or implicit' representations, and Micula reasonably relied on it to make the investment according to both Romanian law and the EU accession process. Whether the state wanted to commit itself was irrelevant, the arbitrators explained, adding that these representations shifted the risk of regulatory change.[108] Like the tribunals in the Spanish cases, they also highlighted that the state's right to regulate was not affected; new regulations just needed to be both reasonable and consistent with foreign investors' legitimate expectations.

Conclusion

The ISDS awards emerging from the crises in Argentina and the Spanish solar energy industry illustrate some evolution in ISDS practice. Tribunals demanded from investors more specific representations and due diligence to protect their expectations, while indicating that these expectations needed to be balanced against states' right to regulate. The changes are marginal, however, compared to the impact of foreign investors' legitimate expectations in states' authority to deal with unforeseen circumstances. The awards discussed above show how arbitrators unplug foreign investment relations from domestic public law imperatives, and interpret those relations through the lens of a transactional model whereby states must treat foreign investors according to their expectations despite the local context. The situation can be severe, including high unemployment and people's inability to pay for basic public services. Storytelling supports this unplugging: in explaining their decisions, tribunals overlook the role of foreign investors and international organizations in defining the regulatory givings offered in the first place, and minimize the fact that states offered them with their own expectations in mind.

[106] I am grateful to David Schneiderman for raising this point.

[107] *Micula v. Romania* (ICSID Case No. ARB/05/20) Award, 11 December 2013, para. 686.

[108] Ibid., paras. 669, 665–9.

This interpretation is quite favourable to a global embeddedness of foreign investor rights. Investment projects begin with roadshows in the big financial centres and sometimes finish at ISDS, quite often, in Washington, DC. Foreign investors are systematically treated as outsiders. The awards discussed in this chapter silence local needs and make it difficult for states to address pressing demands for redistribution, let alone recognize that public services might relate to a society's values and aspirations. Only marginal changes with limited effects are permitted. States are implicitly blamed for economic crises, for not foreseeing all circumstances, and for accepting the foreign investors' demands and international organizations' policy advice. As we will see next, states are also the only actors to blame when local communities oppose and resist a project, leaving the government with no option but cancellation.

7
Local Communities and ISDS

Foreign investors and states frequently cooperate to facilitate investment projects in the natural resource sector. National elites tend to be involved in these cases, acting like *partners* to the foreign investors, because they often benefit economically from the projects and have an interest in the continuation of extractivism. Meanwhile, local communities are in a weak position, with limited or no public support and few legal options. They may still resist a project, sometimes forcing the state to cancel it, yet cancellation may only be a pyrrhic victory. Foreign investors may rely on investment treaties and ISDS to interpret and enforce the political signals and givings granted by the host state. The cases analysed below show how ISDS tribunals silence investor misconduct and the context of extractivist projects while making local communities invisible.

A. Foreign investment relations and local communities

In most investment projects, foreign investors and host states are not alone. The site of an investment can rarely be described as abandoned or uninhabited. People may have lived in the area for generations, sometimes since before the creation of the relevant nation-state. These local communities may share a common cultural and ethnic identity, as in the case of indigenous peoples, or may only be united by the investment's proximity and impact. In either case, the legal, economic, and business literature on foreign investment frequently overlooks the situation of local communities when talking about foreign investment. These disciplines focus on the bargaining dynamics, rights, and obligations of foreign investors and states at the expense of any discussion of local communities.[1] As such, the investment site is treated as a sort of *terra nullius*, whereby those who live there are not considered relevant to the establishment and operation of the investment project. This sort of reasoning is not new in international law. Under the logic of European colonialism, the notion of *terra nullius* was employed to describe land that could be acquired

[1] See Nicolás M. Perrone, 'Making Local Communities Visible: A Way to Prevent the Potentially Tragic Consequences of Foreign Investment?' in Alvaro Santos, Chantal Thomas, David Trubek (eds.) in *World Trade and Investment Law Reimagined A Progressive Agenda for an Inclusive Globalization* (Anthem Press 2019) 171–82, 173–4.

Investment Treaties and the Legal Imagination. Nicolás M. Perrone, Oxford University Press (2021). © Nicolás M. Perrone.
DOI: 10.1093/oso/9780198862147.003.0008

through discovery not because it was uninhabited, but because 'uncivilized' peoples did not count for the law.[2]

The invisibility of local communities in foreign investment relations hinges on the premise that states represent local interests in dealing with foreign investors. This is based on two controversial assumptions. One is that democratic governments are capable of representing non-state actors, who are impacted by foreign investment projects. Democratic mechanisms of representation are under crisis, however, and people distrust governments.[3] In the US, for instance, median income voters have 'a minuscule, near zero, statistically nonsignificant impact upon public policy' while 'the economic elites and organized groups representing business interests have substantial independent impacts on US government policy'.[4] Distrust is stronger among those who have not benefited from the economic globalization,[5] while some local communities blame states as the primary agent responsible for violations of their human rights.[6] The second assumption is the conflation of state and local interests: in international law, the tendency has been to focus on the state as the main and dominant actor.[7] But this premise is generally flawed, as it overlooks conflicts of interest and problems of representation. It is unlikely that every actor shares the same interests around a large foreign investment project in a host state. It is certainly not the case in international trade, where economists distinguish between the interests of exporters, importers, and consumers.[8]

While most states actively solicit foreign investment to promote economic growth, foreign investors and national elites sometimes seize most of the benefits,

[2] Andrew Fitzmaurice, *Sovereignty, Property and Empire, 1500–2000* (CUP 2014). Also, Antony Anghie, *Imperialism, Sovereignty and the Making of International Law* (CUP 2005) 103–4; Lindsay G. Robertson, *Conquest by Law: How the Discovery of America Dispossessed Indigenous Peoples of their Lands* (OUP 2005) 4, 72.

[3] Pierre Rosanvallon, *La contre-démocratie: la politique à l'âge de la défiance* (Groupe Seuil 2006) 10; Wolfgang Merkel, 'Is There a Crisis of Democracy?' (2014) 1 Democratic Theory 11–25, 24.

[4] Martin Gilens and Benjamin I. Page, 'Testing Theories of American politics: Elites, Interest Groups, and Average Citizens' (2014) 12 Perspectives on Politics 564–81, 575, 565.

[5] Richard Wike, Katie Simmons, Bruce Stokes, and Janell Fetterolf, 'Globally, Broad Support for Representative and Direct Democracy: But many also endorse nondemocratic alternatives' October 2017, Pew Research Center, 13–19.

[6] This view was unanimously expressed by five different local communities in focal group meetings held in Colombia (Bogotá, 1 and 2 August 2018). Experts from Costa Rica, Brazil, and Chile—interviewed between 2017 and 2019—noted that local communities in their countries also distrust governments, particularly national and mining authorities.

[7] Balakrishnan Rajagopal, *International Law from Below: Development, Social Movements, and Third World Resistance* (CUP 2003) 1–2, 187, 293. Some Global South countries oppose the recognition of any special status for local communities. Benedict Kingsbury, '"Indigenous Peoples" in International Law: A Constructivist Approach to the Asian Controversy' (1998) 92 American Journal of International Law 414–57, 415–16.

[8] In some parts of the Global South, the free trade debate historically finds pro-free trade groups, often associated with the extractive/export sector and transnational elites, set against those promoting nascent economic sectors or industrialization policies. See Peter B. Evans, *Embedded Autonomy: States and Industrial Transformation* (Princeton University Press 2012) 37, 62–3; C. Fred Bergsten, 'Globalizing Free Trade' (1996) 75 Foreign Affairs 105–20, 111, 113.

particularly in the case of extractive projects. Governments are under pressure to attract foreign investment to foster growth, create jobs, and join global value chains. In some parts of the Global South, this investment imperative takes a specific extractivist form, as states' main locational advantages for firms are in the natural resource sector. But locational advantages may not be enough to attract foreign investment. Potential investors ask for regulatory givings and economic freedom, and do not always react positively to measures that promote political freedom.[9] Quan Li and Adam Resnick show that democracy can hurt a country's attractiveness for certain foreign investment projects. Although democracy would likely support domestic institutions that serve to protect private property, stronger national elites may provide more givings while offering a buffer against distributive and recognition local demands.[10] This type of alliance often means local communities suffer most of the costs and risks of a project without necessarily enjoying the benefits.

The situation of the Andes region in Latin America, an area rich in natural resources, illustrates this dynamic. Foreign investors in the region have had a cosy relationship with autocrats. States, national elites, and foreign investors have forged alliances that have not only facilitated investment projects but also silenced and displaced local communities.[11] From a structural standpoint, these relations correspond to processes of 'accumulation by dispossession'[12] or 'coloniality',[13] whereby elites embrace the extractivist model of economic development left behind by the colonial legacy. National elites can challenge this model, as was the case in the NIEO, but Latin America has witnessed a new wave of extractivism in recent decades. The rules governing the extraction and production of natural resources are at the centre of this process, and they are controlled by elites, some state agencies, and investors.[14] Public policy on mining, Luis Vittor observes, imposes these activities on local communities, without much regard for their rights and land.[15]

[9] Aparna Mathur and Kartikeya Singh, 'Foreign Direct Investment, Corruption and Democracy' (2013) 45 Applied Economics 991–1002, 992, 1001.

[10] Quan Li and Adam Resnick, 'Reversal of Fortunes: Democratic Institutions and Foreign Direct Investment Inflows to Developing Countries' (2003) 57 International organization 175–211, 176–7, 202–3. The essence of these findings were reconfirmed by Li in a subsequent paper. Quan Li, 'Outlier, Measurement, and the Democracy-FDI Controversy' (2009) 4 Quarterly Journal of Political Science 167–81.

[11] Guillermo A. O'Donnell, *Bureaucratic Authoritarianism: Argentina, 1966-1973, in Comparative Perspective* (University of California Press 1988) 11–12. More recently, Anthony Bebbington, 'Extractive industries, socio-environmental conflicts and political economic transformations in Andean America' in Anthony Bebbington (ed.), *Social Conflict, Economic Development and Extractive Industry: Evidence from South America* (Routledge 2012) 3-26, 8-9.

[12] David Harvey, *The New Imperialism* (OUP 2003) 137.

[13] Aníbal Quijano, 'Coloniality of Power, Eurocentrism, and Latin America,' (2000) 1 Nepantla: Views from South 533–80.

[14] Pablo Andrade A., 'The Government of Nature: Post-Neoliberal Environmental Governance in Bolivia and Ecuador' in Fabio De Castro, Barbara Hogenboom, and Michiel Baud (eds.), *Environmental Governance in Latin America* (Palgrave 2016) 113–36, 117.

[15] Luis Vittor, 'Las consultas vecinales sobre la minería: experiencias y desafíos' in Raphael Hoetmer, Miguel Castro, Mar Daza, José De Echave C., and Clara Ruiz (eds.), *Minería y movimientos sociales en el*

Recent scholarship has focused on the practical dimensions of the alliances between foreign investors and national elites. Roger Merino shows that national elites support extractive projects 'through their everyday practices and imaginaries'.[16] Their efforts translate into flexible regulation, incentives, and a lax approach to granting mining titles, licences, and monitoring projects. Many of these groups also support free trade and minimum restrictions on the movement of capital. Further, national elites may work together with international organizations, lawyers, and MNCs when regulating a sector. The World Bank contributed to promoting the mining sector in Latin America and the Andes region; for instance, the mining code of Colombia was drafted by a large Colombian law firm and influenced by foreign mining corporations and the World Bank.[17] More recently, it is true, legislation in the Andes region has incorporated the language of participation and the environment. Yet Merino and Areli Valencia conclude that the extractivist imperative still prevails. '[D]iscourses about "sustainable mining" are designed to "conceal harm and neutralize critique"', while environmental law enforcement is deficient, local participation becomes formal paperwork, and the state remains absent only performing a light touch review function.[18] As Merino claims, the extractive state is a 'cynical' one.[19]

The situation is not markedly different in countries in which the elite underwent changes in the 2000s. Social unrest led to significant reforms in Bolivia and Ecuador, and the election of new governments which were expected to recognize social struggles and the environmental problems related to extractivism.[20] This did not happen, however, or at least the recognition of these problems did not satisfy local expectations. On the one hand, the Bolivian and Ecuadorian executives did put pressure on investors to renegotiate contracts, arguing that previous administrations had entered into bad deals; this triggered some ISDS litigation. On the other hand, neither government attempted to resolve the conundrum posed by extractivism. Constitutional reforms in these countries envisioned a different balance between the extraction of natural resources and local communities. Yet

Perú Instrumentos y propuestas para la defensa de la vida, el agua y los territorios (CooperAcción 2013) 503–11, 504.

[16] Roger Merino, 'The Cynical State: Forging Extractivism, Neoliberalism and Development in Governmental Spaces' (2020) 41 Third World Quarterly 58–76, 72.

[17] Ximena Sierra Camargo, *Derecho, Desarrollo y Extractivismo: La disputa por el oro en Colombia en un contexto de colonialidad global* (2018) Doctoral thesis, Universidad del Rosario (Colombia) 267. Also, Peter Van der Veen, Felix Remy, John P. Williams, *A Mining Strategy for Latin America and the Caribbean: Estrategia minera para América Latina y El Caribe* (World Bank 1997).

[18] Areli Valencia, *Human Rights Trade-Offs in Times of Economic Growth: The Long-Term Capability Impacts of Extractive-Led Development* (Palgrave 2016) 10. Also, Merino (n. 16) 58.

[19] Ibid. Also, Roger Merino, 'Re-politicizing Participation or Reframing Environmental Governance? Beyond Indigenous' Prior Consultation and Citizen Participation' (2018) 111 World Development 75–83, 76–7.

[20] Andrade A. (n. 14) 123–4.

extractivism remained fundamental to the political plans of the new progressive elites, including for their redistributive goals.[21]

Local communities are at the losing end of extractivism. Indigenous peoples have opposed this economic model since colonial times, and other groups have joined this resistance more recently as large-scale extractivism has proved unsettling in environmental, social, and economic terms. Politically, local communities are weaker than national elites and foreign investors: their primary means of resistance is social mobilization. In recent years their strategies have become more sophisticated, however. Many groups have implemented a translocal approach, coordinating their actions with civil society in the Global North. Evidence suggests that translocal mobilization increases their chances of success, particularly by making the conflict visible through the national and international media. In ISDS practice, translocal mobilization was important for the discontinuance of two important cases: *Aguas del Tunari v. Bolivia* in January 2006 and *Foresti v. South Africa* in July 2010.[22]

Local communities are also increasingly relying on the law as a means of resistance. Legally, the situation has evolved in opposing directions. On the one hand, Peru, Ecuador, Bolivia, and Colombia implemented friendly mining regulations granting a large number of mining titles in the 1990s. They also ratified dozens of investment treaties.[23] On the other hand, all four countries passed constitutional and legal reforms granting local communities competing rights—essentially procedural rights, such as free, prior, and informed consent (FPIC) and the option of holding referendums to organize the territory. They additionally adopted more stringent environmental standards, which challenged existing and planned investment projects.[24] Equally important, these countries have ratified international treaties recognizing indigenous and peasants' rights, including FPIC, and voted in favour of the UN Declaration on the Rights of Indigenous Peoples and the UN Declaration on the Rights of Peasants and Other People Working in Rural Areas (Colombia abstained, however).[25]

In this context, the Inter-American Court of Human Rights (IACtHR) has become an important forum for local communities.[26] After exhausting local

[21] Benedicte Bull and Mariel Aguilar-Støen, 'Changing Elites, Institutions and Environmental Governance' in Fabio De Castro, Barbara Hogenboom, and Michiel Baud (eds.), *Environmental Governance in Latin America* (Palgrave 2016) 137–63, 145, 147–8.

[22] David Schneiderman, *Resisting Economic Globalization: Critical Theory and International Investment Law* (Palgrave 2013) 103–12; A. Claire Cutler, 'Transformations in Statehood, the Investor-State Regime, and the New Constitutionalism' (2016) 23 Indiana Journal of Global Legal Studies 95–125, 118–19.

[23] Valencia (n. 18) 112–20; Van der Veen et al. (n. 17) 3–6.

[24] Merino (n. 19) 76, 80.

[25] See S. James Anaya, *Indigenous Peoples in International Law* (OUP 2004).

[26] Lorenzo Cotula, 'Land, Property and Sovereignty in International Law' (2016) 25 Cardozo Journal of International & Comparative Law 219–86, 240–1, 258–9; José E. Alvarez, 'The Human Right of Property' (2018) University of Miami Law Review (2018) 580–705, 606–14.

remedies, various indigenous groups have taken their complaints to the IACtHR, claiming that states were promoting extractivism in violation of their human rights, including their communal property rights. The court has recognized that indigenous peoples hold a special category of property rights, the protection of which is closely related to the recognition of their territory, lifestyle, and culture. This interpretation was the result of combining the protection of property with procedural rights such as FPIC. The IACtHR has developed a relatively extensive jurisprudence on communal property rights, emphasizing that states are expected to proactively protect these rights. Its judges have affirmed that the Inter-American Convention of Human Rights is a 'living instrument' that must respond to the changing circumstances in the 'current living conditions'.[27] Altogether, these decisions represent an important development of human rights law. For Alvarez, the IACtHR has needed 'to evolve its own creative property rights jurisprudence in response to claims made by distinctive indigenous peoples within the Americas'.[28]

International recognition of local rights, particularly property rights, has permitted local communities to resist investment projects not only through social mobilization but also via domestic and international litigation. The clash of interests is now also a clash of rights. Complex transnational litigation has uncovered the fact that there is more at stake in foreign investment relations than foreign investor rights and states' right to regulate. The case of Lago Agrio is probably the best example of this complexity. The dispute started in 1995 when the Ecuadorian authorities approved foreign investor Texaco/Chevron's poor remediation plan even though the company had caused an environmental tragedy—a prime example of national elites and foreign investors working together.[29] Unsurprisingly disappointed, the local community has tried to obtain compensation in several jurisdictions, in the US, Ecuador, Brazil, Argentina, Canada, and two international courts. Chevron has struck back using different fora, including ISDS.[30]

Since the post-World War II period, some influential international lawyers had predicted this multiplication of proprietary rights under international law. They argued that the internationalization of foreign investor rights was only a stage in international law's evolution, closely related to the emergence and consolidation

[27] *Mayangna (Sumo) Awas Tingni Cmty v. Nicaragua* (Inter-Am. Ct HR (ser. C) No. 79) Merits, Reparations and Costs Judgment, 31 August 2001, paras. 146, 145–9. Also, *Sawhoyamaxa Indigenous Cmty. v. Paraguay* (Inter-Am. Ct HR (ser. C) No. 146) Merits, Reparations and Costs Judgment, 29 March 2006, para. 120; *Yakye Axa Indigenous Cmty. v. Paraguay* (Inter-Am. Ct HR (ser. C) No. 125) Merits, Reparations and Costs Judgment, 17 June 2005, para. 125.

[28] Alvarez (n. 26) 649.

[29] Judith Kimerling, 'Indigenous Peoples and the Oil Frontier in Amazonia: The Case of Ecuador, Chevron Texaco, and Aguinda v. Texaco' (2006) 38 New York University Journal of International Law And Politics 413–664.

[30] See Lise Johnson, 'Case Note: How Chevron v. Ecuador is Pushing the Boundaries of Arbitral Authority' 13 April 2012, Investment Treaty News, available at https://www.iisd.org/itn/2012/04/13/case-note-how-chevron-v-ecuador-is-pushing-the-boundaries-of-arbitral-authority/ (last visited 6 June 2020).

of an international community.[31] The elevation of other human rights to the international terrain was therefore only a matter of time. As their prediction came true, foreign investor rights are no longer an exception to the rule but rather the 'most enforceable "human right" in the canon'.[32]

This situation creates structural and interpretative disadvantages for local communities. In terms of interpretation, the problem is that their demands are not only about distribution but also about recognition. Communities' rights are locally embedded and enable community life; inevitably, foreign investment disrupts this embeddedness. Extractive industries change the dynamics of a town, creating booms and busts, and preclude other activities such as agriculture or tourism. Privatization puts individualism and profitability over other values, such as solidarity and social cohesion, altering social relations. The interpretative question, then, is whether international arbitrators can strike a balance between the incommensurable interests of foreign investors, states, and local communities. As Fraser explains, demands of recognition call instead for political solutions and, crucially, this requires more participation and representation.[33]

In structural terms, moreover, the resolution of ISDS disputes involving local communities are irremediably shaped by the social dynamics that favour extractivism. Most large investment projects emerge from the common interests of foreign investors and states. Governments actively advertise locational advantages—indicating potential mineral sites through geological maps on which local communities are made invisible—and the benefits of the relevant sectoral regulation.[34] Foreign investors may rely on these sectoral regulations or ask for further assurances before investing, and negotiations may lead governments to ratify the benefits of the regulation or offer additional incentives. These negotiations do not have to be transparent, so local communities are rarely privy to them, and government assurances may give rise to legitimate expectations in ISDS irrespective of whether the authority had competences over that matter.

Eventually, there comes a stage at which foreign investors and states do need to involve local communities for legal and political reasons. This is especially so since new environmental and consultation rules require states and foreign investors to assess a project's environmental impact, consult the local community, and obtain

[31] Among others, this includes the international lawyers who drafted the Response to the Questionnaire of the International Committee on Nationalization on behalf of the American Branch of the International Law Association in 1958, as well as René-Jean Dupuis, Elihu Lauterpacht, and Orrego Vicuña. See the discussion in Introduction, Section B, and Chapter 2, Section D.7.

[32] Alvarez (n. 26) 663.

[33] Nancy Fraser, *Scales of Justice: Reimagining Political Space in a Globalizing World* (Columbia University Press 2010) 6–10, 15–16.

[34] In addition to traditional forms of regulatory givings, the way land and mineral resources are organized through maps, zoning rules, and divisions between private and communal public space play a fundamental role in embedding these resources into the needs of foreign investors and the global economy. See Nicholas Blomley, 'Landscapes of Property' (1998) 32 Law & Society Review 567–612, 588–93.

a social licence. However, this participation may come too late for local communities: at such a juncture the choice is often between accepting the project, alongside some redistribution in the form of corporate outreach, or resistance. Further, governments may not sympathize with local demands. Their satisfaction can result in fewer resources for the state or national elites and, more importantly, social resistance may be a negative signal for foreign investment, posing an obstacle to extractivism. Governments care about the reputational costs associated with project cancellation.[35] To minimize resistance and facilitate the project, state officials may propose some form of redistribution or use of force.

These strategies may or may not work. If the local community is divided, the government and foreign investor might aim to exploit this weakness. But such an approach may also coalesce the opposition, turning a local conflict into a national or international issue. Local communities may also turn to translocal mobilization and legal action. Domestic or international courts may order the state to respect their rights.[36] In these cases, particularly if the conflict escalates, the government may decide to delay, regulate, or even terminate the project. After all, national elites also want to remain in power.

Even then, such an outcome may be a pyrrhic victory for the local community. The cancellation of the project does not end the relationship between foreign investor, state, and community. Investors may take the dispute to ISDS. If the state loses the case, which is not unlikely, some of the taxes paid by the local community will be used to compensate the foreign investor, and this may also chill future regulation to protect local rights.

B. ISDS practice and local communities

ISDS tribunals are unfit to assess the whole fabric of facts and rights in investment disputes involving local communities. To a large extent, investment treaties are to be blamed for this. Not only do they contain no obligations for foreign investors, but they are also silent about local non-state actors and their rights. As we have seen, the arbitral mandate is limited to an examination of controversies between foreign investors and host states—the same states that facilitate these projects through regulatory givings in the first place, sometimes ignoring local

[35] Jonathan Bonnitcha, Lauge N. Skovgaard Poulsen, and Michael Waibel, *The Political Economy of the Investment Treaty Regime* (OUP 2017) 133.

[36] See, e.g., Colombian Constitutional Court, Judgment C-35, 8 February 2016, which gave rise to the claim in *Eco Oro v. Colombia* (ICSID Case No. ARB/16/41) Request for Arbitration, 8 December 2016, paras. 46–8; *Sawhoyamaxa Indigenous Cmty. v. Paraguay* (Inter-Am. Ct HR (ser. C) No. 146) Merits, Reparations and Costs Judgment, 29 March 2006 (The IACtHR noted that the enforcement of investment treaties 'should always be compatible with the American Convention, which is a multilateral treaty on human rights that stands in a class of its own and that generates rights for individual human beings and does not depend entirely on reciprocity among States', para 140).

communities' rights. With an ISDS dispute, the situation only gets worse for communities. They are not parties to the arbitration and can only submit *amicus curiae* briefings, which tribunals may or may not accept.

The actors and rights that investment treaties and ISDS make invisible are nonetheless central to foreign investment projects. Following a relational conception of foreign investment, they are as important as the rights of foreign investors and states.[37] For one thing, it can be argued that foreign investor rights serve a social function, like other property rights, and that fulfilling this function requires foreign investors to comply with certain ownership obligations to others within the local community. For another, the community may have competing rights over the resources emerging from property, a contract, or reliance. Local actors may have relied on foreign investors' promises to make significant life decisions. In ISDS, however, there is no space for foreign investor obligations or a relational interpretation of foreign investment. The combined effects of investment treaties and ISDS unplug foreign investment relations not only from domestic public imperatives, but also from the legitimate demands and rights of local actors. At this particular site of struggle, foreign investors may lose ISDS cases, but not their globally embedded rights, transactional relation with host states, or ability to make local communities invisible.

International law does not fix the problem. Most of the international rights belonging to local communities create correlative obligations for states, which are the primary actors responsible for protecting indigenous land or ensuring compliance with FPIC. While local communities have gained some rights under international law, foreign investors have resisted the creation of international corporate obligations. Following the models of the ICC and OECD Guidelines, the United Nations has developed a set of principles concerning business and human rights, but these create responsibilities rather than legally enforceable obligations. Overall they constitute 'trade-related, market-friendly human rights'.[38]

A systemic interpretation of investment treaties could help construe existing foreign investor obligations, but even in the best-case scenario these would likely be weak obligations and it is improbable that arbitrators would create new ones. In *Urbaser v. Argentina*, for instance, the arbitrators recognized that international human rights law can create obligations for foreign investors, but they characterized this legal relationship as a weak obligation 'on all parts, public and private parties, not to engage in an activity aimed at destroying such rights'.[39] Although

[37] Nicolás M. Perrone, 'The "Invisible" Local Communities: Foreign Investor Obligations, Inclusiveness, and the International Investment Regime' (2019) 113 American Journal of International Law Unbound 16–21.

[38] Upendra Baxi, *The Future of Human Rights* (OUP 2006) 234.

[39] *Urbaser v. Argentina* (ICSID Case No. ARB/07/26) Award, 8 December 2016, paras. 1199, 1194–9. Also, Partial Dissenting Opinion of Philippe Sands in *Bear Creek Mining v. Peru* (ICSID Case No. ARB/14/2) 30 November 2017, paras. 10–11.

certain ongoing initiatives are currently working to strengthen the link between foreign investment and human rights obligations, most notably the UN Binding Treaty on Transnational Corporations with respect to Human Rights, it remains to be seen whether they will be adopted and how effective they will be.[40] As discussed in Chapters 3 and 4, MNCs and Global North states oppose them.

The situation is no simpler procedurally, because ISDS is essentially a one-way street. Only foreign investors can file disputes. States may be able to bring foreign investor obligations into ISDS, as defences, claiming that an investor breached its obligations or contributed to the situation that led to the impossibility or termination of the project. The *MTD* and *Occidental 2* tribunals, for instance, accepted these defences, ordering a reduction in the compensation.[41] Counterclaims, however, are more difficult. They depend on the scope of the dispute settlement clause. In *Urbaser*, the arbitration clause in the relevant treaty was broadly worded, allowing the tribunal to resolve 'any dispute' between the parties related to the investment. Tribunals have been more restrictive when treaty wording refers to specific causes of action.[42]

Both a defence and a counterclaim, also, require showing the relevance of the obligation to the ISDS context. Tribunals may find that the scope and enforcement of an obligation is governed by a different law and should be determined by another tribunal—obligations emerging from domestic law or a contract, for example. This obstacle can only be surmounted if the foreign investor explicitly accepts the jurisdiction of the ISDS tribunal, as in *Burlington v. Ecuador*.[43]

The position of local communities in ISDS is worse than that of states. Most domestic legal systems allow third parties to participate in proceedings in which their rights are at stake. Yet this is not the case for investment treaties and ISDS, which make local communities invisible both substantively and procedurally. As discussed, local communities are not parties to these disputes and can only participate through *amicus curiae*, submissions which could inform the tribunal about facts and laws directly involved in the dispute but overlooked by investor and state. Some ISDS tribunals have welcomed these submissions; others have rejected them under the rationale that they do not bring anything new to the dispute or that the petitioners have not shown a significant interest.[44] Either way, an *amicus curiae*

[40] See Open-Ended Intergovernmental Working Group on Transnational Corporations and Other Business Enterprises With Respect to Human Rights, available at https://www.ohchr.org/en/hrbodies/hrc/wgtranscorp/pages/igwgontnc.aspx (last visited 18 June 2019).

[41] *MTD v. Chile* (ICSID Case No. ARB/01/7) Award, 25 May 2004, paras. 177–8, 242–3; *Occidental v. Ecuador 2* (ICSID Case No. ARB/06/11) Award, 5 October 2012, paras. 672–87.

[42] Compare *Urbaser v. Argentina* (ICSID Case No. ARB/07/26) Award, 8 December 2016, with *Rusoro Mining v. Venezuela* (ICSID Case No. ARB(AF)/12/5) Award, 22 August 2016.

[43] *Burlington v. Ecuador* (ICSID Case No. ARB/08/5) Decision on Ecuador's Counterclaims, 7 February 2017, para. 6. Also, see *Urbaser v. Argentina* (ICSID Case No. ARB/07/26) Award, 8 December 2016, para. 1206.

[44] ISDS practice concerning *amicus curiae* submissions is not consistent. They were accepted in various ISDS cases, e.g. *Methanex v. USA* (NAFTA—UNCITRAL) Decision of the Tribunal on Petitions from Third Persons to Intervene as 'amici curiae', 15 January 2001. Some rejections include *Von Pezold*

submission does not equal full participation because tribunals do not have to engage with it and it does not grant communities a way to enforce their rights.[45] While ISDS disputes directly affect the situation and rights of local communities, there is not much the latter can do about it under international investment law.

The other side of the story consists of the rights of foreign investors. As discussed in the previous chapters, foreign investors are entitled to receive compensation in cases of expropriation, disappointment of their legitimate expectations, and violations of due process. This treatment is in stark contrast with that granted to local communities in most instances, as they are rarely aware or consulted about the decision to open their area for business, support a project, or grant regulatory givings. These givings may even be the result of *ultra vires* representations and assurances. In arbitrating a conflict with the host state, ISDS tribunals determine whether the measure affecting the investment project was reasonable, proportionate, and consistent with international standards. Communities' expectations do not count here, and the technical and scientific language necessary to justify public regulation may not capture their distributive or recognition demands. A community may also need to employ social mobilization to make a conflict visible, which some arbitrators have negatively associated with arbitrary and political motivations, as in *Metalclad* and *TecMed*. Other tribunals have been more tolerant of political motives, but only as long as states can supply good technical and scientific reasons for the controversial measures.

As I show next, recent cases involving local communities against Ecuador, Peru, Bolivia, and Canada have shared common features. For most tribunals, the political decision to open an area to extractive business was made before any social opposition or unrest. The state was open for business, supported the project, and foreign investors were induced to invest through a hospitable business climate. Unless specific commitments or representations were granted, this decision does not equal regulatory stability or a right to extract the minerals—investors still need to obtain environmental and social licences, and technical and scientific evidence may indicate that the project is non-viable. Nonetheless, the reasoning in these awards shows that local opposition by itself is not sufficient to change states' attitude to a project. States have to act consistently irrespective of community acquiescence or opposition—and even if the community was never properly informed or consulted. This includes cases in which local communities could only resist the project outside institutional channels, as in Ecuador, Peru, and Bolivia, and in

& others v. Zimbabwe (ICSID Case No. ARB/10/15) Procedural Order No. 2, 26 June 2012, paras. 59–63 and, more recently, *Eco Oro v. Colombia* (ICSID Case No. ARB/16/41) Procedural Order No. 6 Decision on Non-Disputing Parties' Application, 18 February 2019.

[45] See *Pac Rim Cayman v. El Salvador* (ICSID Case No. ARB/09/12) Award, 14 October 2016, para. 3.30; *Biwater v. Tanzania* (ICSID Case No. ARB/05/22) Procedural Order No. 5, 2 February 2007, paras. 25–30, 71.

which opposition was articulated within the existing institutional framework, as in Canada.

1. *Copper Mesa v. Ecuador*

The facts relevant to the *Copper Mesa v. Ecuador* case date to the early 1990s, when the World Bank funded the mapping of subsoil minerals and significant copper reserves were confirmed in the Junín region, an area without much of a mining history.[46] Ecuador's mining laws did not require environmental impact assessments or community consultation; such mechanisms were only implemented in 1999 and 2000, and even then their review and approval were delegated to a division formally part of the Ministry of Mines.[47] The central role of this ministry suggests the government's pro-mining attitude, despite the allegedly progressive reforms implemented since the late 1990s. Meanwhile, the majority of Junín's local community expressed opposition to mining from the time that the reserves were confirmed. Between the 1990s and late 2000s, a Japanese and a Canadian investor, each enjoying governmental support, attempted to extract copper in the region. Neither project moved to the extraction phase, however, due to social unrest and popular protest.[48]

For the community of Junín, the choices posed by these mining projects had serious implications. The first environmental study conducted by Bishimetal, the Japanese investor, suggested that its project would involve 'massive deforestation [that] will give rise to an increase in dry conditions (known as "Desertification"), effects on the local climate and alternation of the vegetation'.[49] This study was leaked to the public unofficially, immediately creating controversy within the community. Bishimetal then desisted from the project. A few years later, Copper Mesa claimed that new technologies and a different plan would reduce these costs and risks. Yet the community was concerned that mining activities threatened not only the environment but also their way of life. During the discussions with this Canadian investor, it became clear that the community feared that these projects were 'trying to change [their] lifestyle for a few jobs'.[50] The local leaders affirmed that those forced to sell their land would have no option but to become employees of Copper Mesa.

46 Linda D'Amico 'El Agua es Vida/Water Is Life': Community Watershed Reserves in Intag, Ecuador, and Emerging Ecological Identities' in Barbara Rose Johnston, Lisa Hiwasaki, Irene J. Klaver, Ameyali Ramos Castillo, and Veronica Strang (eds.), *Water, Cultural Diversity, and Global Environmental Change: Emerging Trends, Sustainable Futures?* (Springer 2012) 433–43, 435.

47 *Copper Mesa v. Ecuador* (PCA Case No. 2012-02) Award, 15 March 2016, paras. 1.89-105.

48 D'Amico (n. 46) 435.

49 *Copper Mesa v. Ecuador* (PCA Case No. 2012-02) Award, 15 March 2016, paras. 4.25, 4.25–7.

50 Ibid., para. 4.82. The tension between jobs, environment, and the local way of life is frequent. For another ISDS case, see the dispute between The Renco Group (Doe Run), Peru and the community in La Oroya (ICSID Case No. UNCT/13/1). Valencia (n. 18) 24–31.

The *Copper Mesa* case revealed that protecting the local community was not a top priority for the foreign investor or the Ecuadorian government. Despite the controversy around Bishimetal's project, the government advertised the Junín region again in maps and documentation prepared by Ecuador Mining Development Project. Copper Mesa acquired the concessions later. These actions were challenged by the local community, but Ecuadorian authorities confirmed the validity of these concessions and helped the investor move on with the project.[51] Copper Mesa did not find an acquiescent environment in Junín, however, and its corporate strategy for dealing with this opposition was violence and illegality. At first, the government remained quiet about the situation; historically, the Ecuadorian state had a weak presence in the region.[52] Only after three years of violence, in mid-2006, did the Ministry of Mines react by announcing that the escalation of the conflict was 'deplorable' and that the investor was 'directly responsible'.[53]

This social unrest and violence posed problems for the investment project. Copper Mesa could not finalize its community consultation, which was required as part of the environmental impact study. The government pointed out that parts of the community had not been consulted, and Copper Mesa responded that entering into those areas was not possible.[54] In its analysis of the facts, the *Copper Mesa* tribunal concluded that by late 2006 the investor had 'acquired, irrevocably, a malign reputation for intimidation, threats, deception, mendacity and violence amongst members of the local communities in the Junín area'.[55] According to the arbitrators, though, the government of Ecuador was still willing to give a green light to the project if Copper Mesa managed to finalize the additional consultations.[56]

In 2007, after the election of a new president, the Ecuadorian government became more actively involved in pacifying the region. Ecuadorian officials travelled there, and a tripartite agreement was reached between the investor, the community, and the government. Copper Mesa was later accused of violating the agreement, however, and the government requested it to suspend all activities in Junín.[57] This order was later amended to prohibit any consultation with the communities, *de facto* impeding the finalization of the environmental impact study.[58] The impasse continued until 2008, when the government decided to terminate the concession—without hearing from the investor—due to the lack of an environmental impact study.[59] Remarkably, after decades of violence and unrest in the Junín region, in 2009 the government again listed the area as a potential site for a

[51] *Copper Mesa v. Ecuador* (PCA Case No. 2012-02) Award, 15 March 2016, paras. 4.108–97.
[52] Ibid., paras. 4.132, 4.149, 4.157–70, 4.95–115.
[53] Ibid., para. 4.186.
[54] Ibid., paras. 4.232–3.
[55] Ibid., para. 4.265.
[56] Ibid., para. 4.267.
[57] Ibid., paras. 4.286–92.
[58] Ibid., paras. 4.300–4.
[59] Ibid., paras. 4.307, 4.316–17.

mining project. In 2011, the National Mining Sector Development Plan 2011–2015 referred to Junín as having its largest copper reserves, and new investors showed interest in the project.[60]

Meanwhile Copper Mesa filed an ISDS case, under the Ecuador–Canada BIT, accusing the government of expropriating the investment and of unfair and inequitable treatment. No *amicus curiae* was submitted to this tribunal. Ecuador's main arguments related to the social unrest in Junín and Copper Mesa's 'malign reputation'. Concerning the claim of expropriation, the arbitrators observed that Ecuador was aware of Copper Mesa's actions and did nothing about it for several years. The foreign investor could not finalize the consultation process because Ecuador ordered the investor to stop any activity so to pacify the region. Moreover, Copper Mesa could not participate in the administrative process leading to the termination of the concession, or challenge that decision later. The arbitrators concluded that the termination of the concession was a disproportionate measure; the state had entirely sided with the local community. This may have been a response to social unrest, the tribunal accepted, but it was implemented 'in an arbitrary manner and without due process'.[61]

In relation to the FET claim, the tribunal discussed what behaviour Copper Mesa had been entitled to expect from Ecuador in the circumstances of this dispute. It noted that rather than preventing Copper Mesa from continuing with its activities in the Junín region, 'the Respondent should have attempted something to assist the Claimant in completing its consultations and other requirements for the EIS'.[62] Ecuador granted Copper Mesa a concession and was therefore required to facilitate the project. Tellingly, the arbitrators were unsure how Ecuador could have done this: 'Plainly, the Government in Quito could hardly have declared war on its own people. Yet, in the Tribunal's view, it could not do nothing.'[63] Making it legally impossible to carry out the consultations with the community, they concluded, had aggravated things for Copper Mesa.

The arbitrators also reflected on Copper Mesa's behaviour. They took into consideration the facts of the case and Ecuadorian law to conclude that the investor had contributed to the violence and social unrest in the region. The tribunal noted that no matter how serious the local opposition, investors 'should not resort to recruiting and using armed men [. . .] not as an accidental or isolated incident but as part of premeditated, disguised and well-funded plans to take the law into its own hands'.[64] Copper Mesa's senior personnel in Quito were guilty of orchestrating violent acts committed on its behalf, in violation of Ecuadorian criminal law. At the same time, the arbitrators preferred 'to base their decision on the Claimant's

60 Ibid., paras. 4.329, 4.349–50.
61 Ibid., paras. 6.66, 6.56–9.
62 Ibid., para. 6.83.
63 Ibid., paras. 6.83, 6.76–84.
64 Ibid., para. 6.99.

negligence, rather than the wilful conduct of its Canadian senior management'.[65] In practice, this preference meant that the foreign investor was not responsible for the crimes committed but merely for lack of due diligence. This translated into a reduction of only 30% of the compensation requested, which looks small even when compared to other reductions in cases of lack of due diligence. The potential violation of international human rights by Copper Mesa, which Ecuador raised during the arbitration, was not appropriately addressed by the tribunal.[66]

2. *Bear Creek v. Peru*

The *Bear Creek v. Peru* dispute goes back to the early 2000s. Peru had adopted a friendly environment for mining activities, granting a great number of mining titles. The sector was thinly regulated, and many titles overlapped with indigenous land and reserves.[67] While the requirement to consult with local communities was already in place in 2001, the central government embraced a passive attitude towards indigenous peoples and their rights. Firms were expected to carry out these consultations themselves, and the Ministry of Energy and Mines would only review and approve the process.[68] Pinto Herrera explains that this enabled many conflicts over land and water with local communities, one such conflict emerging from Canadian firm Bear Creek's plan to mine silver in Santa Ana, Puno.[69] The Peruvian government endorsed this project from the early stages; in 2007 it validated the concession situated in a border zone despite constitutional and legal objections. The investor initially gained some support from the local community, but opposition later became robust as locals grasped the implications of the project. In a matter of months, Santa Ana became a symbol of resistance against mining in the Puno region.[70]

The Aymara communities living near Bear Creek's project faced a difficult dilemma. They are poor and rural, and the prospect of jobs had led to their initial support for the investor, particularly among the communities directly impacted. The focus of resistance were those communities indirectly affected, mainly the residents of the districts of Huacullani and Kelluyo, who would suffer the negative consequences but receive no benefits.[71] This division vanished, however, when

[65] Ibid., para. 6.100.

[66] Ibid., paras. 2.12, 5.62–4.

[67] Honorio Pinto Herrera, 'Conflicto minero en Santa Ana (Puno)' (2013) 17 Investigaciones sociales 207–19, 208–10.

[68] Ibid., 210–12; *Bear Creek v. Peru* (ICSID Case No. ARB/14/2) Award, 30 November 2017, paras. 152–4, 159, 262 (*amicus curiae* submissions).

[69] Pinto Herrera (n. 67) 208.

[70] Ibid., 218–19.

[71] *Bear Creek v. Peru* (ICSID Case No. ARB/14/2) Award, 30 November 2017, paras. 218–20 (*amicus curiae* submissions).

people better understood the implications of the project in 2008. Bear Creek's consultations had focused on the benefits and downplayed the costs, misleading the community. The people of Puno had no experience of mining or knowledge of the technical aspects, and two *amicus curiae* submissions in the ISDS case confirm that information was manipulated and that the costs and risks of this project were significant.[72] They included water and environmental pollution, as well as impact on the Aymara way of life, culture, and the relationship with nature or *Pachamama*. The Aymara community in Puno had both distributive and recognition concerns, but over time the latter gained precedence.[73]

The *Bear Creek* dispute shows that neither government nor investor were particularly concerned about the community. The investor misled them and approached the consultation process in a formalistic way. Its strategy consisted of disregarding the communities indirectly impacted and using a language alien to the Aymara people.[74] Bear Creek expected to speed up the social licence process and quickly obtain the green light from the Ministry of Mines and Energy. Meanwhile, the government was absent from the territory, had limited dialogue with local authorities, and reacted only after the social crisis hit the national media. The ministry had no proactive role in the consultation process, no control over the foreign investor, and limited itself to approving and often endorsing Bear Creek's outreach activities without making objections.[75] The central government, most specifically the Ministry of Mines and Energy, was both party and judge in the question.

Opposition to the Santa Ana project led to a severe social crisis that was unforeseen by both the central government and the investor. Communities in Puno resorted to demonstrations and strikes to make the conflict visible. In 2008, Bear Creek responded by reducing activities for a year, but the situation did not calm down. Instead, opposition grew geographically and politically until, in May and June 2011, the demand was not only for the cancellation of the Santa Ana Project but also for the suspension of all mining in Puno.[76]

The government's first reaction was to confirm that Bear Creek's project was legal and complied with the regulation. Annulling the concession, for the Minister of Energy and Mines, would be 'unconstitutional'.[77] The severity of the situation, however, forced the government to make some efforts to pacify the region. The administration in Lima was prepared to make concessions, while the opposition party submitted a law to congress regulating FPIC as established under ILO Convention 169, which Peru had ratified in 1994. But the social conflict further escalated, more

[72] Ibid., paras. 218–23 (*amicus curiae* submissions), 405.
[73] Ibid., paras. 225–6 (*amicus curiae* submissions).
[74] Ibid., paras. 256, 260–1 (*amicus curiae* submissions), 407.
[75] Ibid., paras. 174–9, 409–12; Pinto Herrera (n. 67) 211–12.
[76] *Bear Creek v. Peru* (ICSID Case No. ARB/14/2) Award, 30 November 2017, paras. 155–203.
[77] Ibid., paras. 186, 191.

regions joined the demonstrations, several Aymara leaders were injured, and six people were killed by police.[78]

At this point, the government changed its position and terminated Bear Creek's concession. The rationale was that the consultation had not been finalized—the crisis prevented the investor from addressing some observations—and that the concession infringed legal and constitutional limitations for border zones. The measure was also necessary to bring peace to the region. Later, the Peruvian government passed a law on indigenous prior consultation, implemented a moratorium on new mining titles in the Puno region, and required existing projects to carry out consultation according to ILO Convention 169.[79]

Bear Creek responded by filing an ISDS case against Peru, claiming that the termination constituted indirect expropriation and violated the FET and other treaty standards. The tribunal accepted two *amicus curiae* submissions dealing with the situation of the local community. It started by observing that Bear Creek never acquired a right to mine in Santa Ana, as its environmental impact study was never approved. However, the investor had 'a right to seek a right to mine and pursue a mining project' that could have been the object of an expropriation.[80] As in *Copper Mesa*, Peru concentrated on Bear Creek's conduct, focusing on the acquisition of the mine in a border zone and its role in the social crisis in Puno. According to Peru, this left the government with no option but to cancel the concession.[81]

The arbitrators were not convinced that Peru had cancelled the concession legally. For one thing, Peru was aware that the concession was first granted to a Peruvian employee of Bear Creek and only later acquired by the foreign investor after the government approved the transfer through a public necessity decree. Peru never objected to this situation before cancelling the concession; it alleged the existence of new evidence concerning its illegality, but this evidence was never submitted to the tribunal.[82] For another thing, the arbitrators noted that the government not only knew about the local opposition in Santa Ana, at least since early 2011, but also approved and supported Bear Creek's outreach activities until the decision to cancel the concession three-and-a-half years later.[83]

The majority of the tribunal concluded that Bear Creek 'could take it for granted to have complied with all legal requirements with regard to its outreach to the local communities'.[84] Yet, Peru rushed to draft and issue the cancellation of the project in four hours, late at night, giving Bear Creek no opportunity to comment. Peru claimed that the cancellation was necessary to restore peace, but the majority

[78] Ibid., paras. 181, 183, 197; Pinto Herrera (n. 67) 214–17.
[79] *Bear Creek v. Peru* (ICSID Case No. ARB/14/2) Award, 30 November 2017, paras. 200–8, 276.
[80] Ibid., para. 295.
[81] Ibid., paras. 276, 387–8.
[82] Ibid., paras. 387, 395–9.
[83] Ibid., paras. 409–14.
[84] Ibid., paras. 412.

decided that there was no contributory fault or liability of Bear Creek for the social crisis in the Puno region.[85]

The arbitrators disagreed on the scope of Bear Creek's obligations, particularly under international law, and its contribution to the social crisis. The majority acknowledged that the local community did not trust Bear Creek, and accepted that the investor could have done more to improve its community relations.[86] Taking a relatively formalistic view, however, these arbitrators observed that Bear Creek was only required to show compliance with domestic law and the principle of good faith. Essentially, 'private companies cannot "fail to comply" with ILO Convention 169 because it imposes no direct obligations on them'.[87] The majority decided this question according to Peruvian law, as a result, in an interpretative turn at odds with the premise that domestic law is a source of political risk for foreign investors.

The dissenting arbitrator approached the issue differently. Following *Urbaser*, he noted that both foreign investors and local communities have rights under international law, and the latter's 'are not lesser rights'.[88] ILO Convention 169 may not impose direct obligations on foreign investors, but this does not 'mean that it is without significance or legal effects for them'.[89] Bear Creek's obligations under domestic law, in particular to obtain a social licence, had to be interpreted in light of ILO Convention 169. The dissenting arbitrator considered that this obligation requires obtaining the 'necessary understanding' among all parties involved in the project, whether directly or indirectly.[90] Relying extensively on the *amicus curiae* submissions, he concluded that Bear Creek did not comply with this obligation. The foreign investor was responsible for the lack of engagement with the communities indirectly impacted by the project, and for overlooking the Aymara language and the importance of the *Pachamama*. In this way, Bear Creek's conduct had contributed to the social crisis leading to the cancellation of the project, and the compensation should be reduced by 50%.[91]

3. *South American Silver v. Bolivia*

Although South American Silver (SAS) had been active in Bolivia since 1994, the Mallku Khota project was the result of ten mining titles acquired and consolidated between 2003 and 2008. In this period, Bolivia's government supported the firm

[85] Ibid., paras. 565–9.
[86] Ibid., paras. 403–8.
[87] Ibid., para. 664.
[88] Partial Dissenting Opinion of Philippe Sands in *Bear Creek v. Peru* (ICSID Case No. ARB/14/2) 12 September 2017, para. 36.
[89] Ibid., paras. 10, 37.
[90] Ibid., para. 6.
[91] Ibid., paras. 38–9.

and encouraged it to 'continue carrying out exploration projects in Bolivia'.[92] The governor of Potosí issued an exploration certificate in 2006, and received SAS to discuss the consultation process related to Mallku Khota in 2011. SAS conducted community outreach activities with limited or no governmental supervision despite ILO Convention 169, in force in Bolivia since 1991. Only external consultants were involved in reviewing its community programme.[93] A think tank report has deemed that the government was 'permissive' in handling this specific project; the state was essentially absent.[94] The election of Evo Morales as president of Bolivia in 2006 and his constitutional reforms had suggested that the country's friendly environment to foreign investment would change. However, this case shows that the Morales administration mainly had distributive demands in Mallku Khota. It was interested in increasing state participation in the benefits and operation of mining projects, but much less in addressing recognition claims.[95]

The Aymara and Quechua communities, on the other hand, were worried about their territory and way of life. They mainly live on agriculture and fishing, and displacement was a possibility under Bolivian laws.[96] Exploration activities had already affected sacred sites and polluted the area, including rivers and lakes. This led to active resistance, particularly from those communities directly affected. Aware of this opposition, SAS opted to try and divide the community to finalize the consultation process. It sought the support of the communities living further from the project so as to outnumber those resisting it.[97] Its outreach programme included road improvements, support for fishers, and scholarships. SAS also promised jobs and limited social and environmental impacts; its intention to fulfil these promises was challenged both before and during the ISDS case.[98] This divisive strategy created problems because the Aymara and Quechua communities make decisions by consensus, not majority. Although some people supported the Mallku Khota project, an important part of the community did not want to give up their territory or way of life. Gradually, this second group grew more influential.

The conflict between the local community and SAS escalated in 2010. Those living near the investment site accused SAS of abuse of authority, pollution, lack of respect to the indigenous authorities, fraud, threats, and 'the rape of women from the community'. A town hall declared SAS's presence illegal because it had violated

[92] *South American Silver v. Bolivia* (PCA Case No. 2013-15) Award, 22 November 2018, paras. 86, 86–9.

[93] Ibid., paras. 91–6, 104–9.

[94] Georgina Jiménez and Jorge Campanini, 'Mallku K: Breve cronología del conflicto minero en Mallku Khota' (29 August 2012) Petropress—CEDIB 24–37, 27, 24–5.

[95] Ibid., 35–7. Also, Claude Le Gouill, 'Mining Imaginaries and Social Conflicts in Bolivia: A Multilevel Approach to the Mallku Khota Conflict' (2016) 82 Cahiers des Amériques Latines 49–69, 50.

[96] Jiménez and Campanini (n. 94) 35–7.

[97] *South American Silver v. Bolivia* (PCA Case No. 2013-15) Award, 22 November 2018, paras. 491, 505.

[98] Ibid., paras. 107, 113. Jiménez and Campanini (n. 94) 32.

'the collective rights of the Indigenous Communities'.[99] The investor responded by asking the government to mediate, 'enforce [. . .] the legal order', and allow SAS to continue its activities.[100] Despite the seriousness of the allegations, the government continued to support the project in early 2011. Some communities responded by prohibiting mining in their territories. In the meantime, rumours spread that the government was evaluating the expropriation of the Mallku Khota project. A think tank report also suggests that SAS tried to rush the consultation process because obtaining the licences to extract silver would be more difficult after certain policy reforms and a Bolivian Constitutional Court decision.[101]

In 2012, social unrest increased rapidly. SAS's supporters abducted a community leader, the foreign investor asked the government to stop illegal mining in Mallku Khota, and police entered the communities' territory. The government suggested SAS pause exploration for three months, but the firm rejected this option. Subsequent community meetings turned violent, for which the community and SAS blamed each other.[102] The conflict became a national issue in mid-2012. There were riots in La Paz as demonstrators demanded the cancellation of the investment project and the release of an incarcerated community leader. They also complained that the government had infiltrated their protest with people supporting the creation of cooperatives in Mallku Khota.[103] Back in Potosí, those opposing the project had blocked access to the investment site. The community accused SAS of infiltrating a meeting using two SAS engineers 'dressed like members of the indigenous community'.[104] More social unrest followed these allegations, and a community member was killed by police. The government initially insisted on the legality of SAS's project, blaming a minority in the community for the violent clashes, but later signed a memorandum of understanding with the indigenous groups and expropriated the Mallku Khota project.[105]

SAS took the dispute to ISDS, arguing that Bolivia had unlawfully expropriated the investment, breached its legitimate expectations, and failed to comply with the full protection and security (FPS) standard by not militarizing the area. There was no *amicus curiae* submission. As in *Bear Creek*, Bolivia requested the tribunal examine the case in light of the international laws related to foreign investors—the UK–Bolivia BIT—and indigenous peoples, such as ILO Convention 169, the American Convention of Human Rights, and the United Nations Declaration on

[99] *South American Silver v. Bolivia* (PCA Case No. 2013-15) Award, 22 November 2018, paras. 114–15. Other groups continued to support the project.

[100] Ibid., para. 122.

[101] Ibid., paras. 98–103, 120–34; Jiménez and Campanini (n. 94) 33–4.

[102] *South American Silver v. Bolivia* (PCA Case No. 2013-15) Award, 22 November 2018, paras. 143–52.

[103] Jiménez and Campanini (n. 94) 26.

[104] Ibid., 27; *South American Silver v. Bolivia* (PCA Case No. 2013-15) Award, 22 November 2018, paras. 155–60.

[105] Ibid., paras. 162–3; Jiménez and Campanini (n. 94) 26, 33.

the Rights of Indigenous Peoples. For Bolivia, this request was consistent with a systemic interpretation of international law under Article 31.3.c) of the Vienna Convention on the Law of Treaties. The tribunal disagreed, noting that ILO Convention 169 is not customary international law, the UK is not a party to this treaty, and, ultimately, Bolivia failed to show 'how these rules conflicted with the [investment treaty] or why they should prevail over its provisions'.[106]

Bolivia attempted other legal strategies to bring SAS's conduct into the proceedings. It claimed that the tribunal had no jurisdiction to hear the case under the unclean hands doctrine or, alternatively, that the investment was not made according to Bolivian law. But the arbitrators rejected these arguments too. They stated that the unclean hands doctrine is not a general principle of international law and does not form part of international public policy. Further, Bolivia's allegation of illegality did not 'go to the essence of the investment'.[107]

The tribunal did accept that SAS's behaviour could be relevant for the merits of the dispute, concentrating on its community outreach programme. The arbitrators paid less attention to the serious allegations of rape and community infiltration, preferring to focus on SAS's overall strategy. In this regard, they concluded that its conduct was not 'the sole cause of the social conflict and the severe clashes in the area', but 'the actions it took upon seeing the first seeds of the conflict contributed to the divisiveness and more profound clashes among the Indigenous Communities'.[108] The tribunal identified serious shortcomings in SAS's community relations program, which ignored the recommendations of the consultants hired by the investor. SAS overlooked the consensus rule and the 'delicate social and cultural balance' of the Aymara and Quechua peoples.[109] The dissenting arbitrator partly disagreed with this, however, observing that Bolivia was also 'responsible for maintaining public order [. . .] Yet, public order was scarcely and on many occasions insufficiently maintained.'[110]

After determining the relevance of SAS's conduct, the tribunal moved on to discuss the expropriation, FET, and FPS claims. The expropriation decree and Bolivia's strategy in the ISDS litigation shaped the reasoning on the merits, as the country accepted that an expropriation had taken place and only challenged its unlawful character. Later, Bolivia argued that the measure was, in fact, an exercise of its police powers, and thus no compensation was required, but the arbitrators rejected this argument as inconsistent with its previous conduct and submissions.[111]

[106] *South American Silver v. Bolivia* (PCA Case No. 2013-15) Award, 22 November 2018, paras. 217, 214–18.

[107] Ibid., paras. 470, 453.

[108] Ibid., paras. 505, 491.

[109] Ibid., paras. 406–7.

[110] Separate Opinion of Francisco Orrego Vicuña in *South American Silver v. Bolivia* (PCA Case No. 2013-15) Award, 22 November 2018, para. 2.

[111] *South American Silver v. Bolivia* (PCA Case No. 2013-15) Award, 22 November 2018, paras. 622–30.

In relation to the legality of the expropriation, the arbitrators were convinced that the measure was for a public purpose. The expropriation decree mentioned the situation of social unrest as well as the need to protect lives and to 'preserve the peace and return to normalcy'.[112] Further, SAS had contributed to this situation, and militarizing the area, as it requested, was neither a reasonable alternative nor enough reason to find a violation of the FPS standard. However, the tribunal observed that Bolivia never offered SAS any compensation, turning the expropriation into an unlawful measure under the BIT. This was Bolivia's only breach.[113] The claim of legitimate expectations was dismissed because SAS operated 'in an area inhabited by indigenous communities, under specific political, social, cultural, and economic conditions'—communities that Bolivia had a duty to protect and oversee.[114]

The controversial conduct of SAS, in the end, had only a limited impact on the outcome of the case. Bolivia argued that its measure was excused by a state of necessity, that is, the necessity to protect human and indigenous rights. The tribunal acknowledged this, but reasoned that the state could not excuse its failure to compensate SAS under this exception.[115] Similarly, Bolivia asked for a reduction of the compensation due to SAS's contribution to the situation that prompted the social unrest. The arbitrators disagreed again, reasoning that SAS did not contribute to the non-payment of compensation. From the position of the investor, and as a supplementary justification for rejecting SAS's contributory fault, the arbitrators finally stated that Bolivia had deprived SAS of 'the possibility of continuing with the development of the Project and of receiving any benefit therefrom'.[116]

4. *Bilcon v. Canada*

In 2002, the Clayton Family Group and Bilcon (hereinafter Bilcon) entered into an agreement with Nova Stone exporters to develop the Whites Point project in Digby Neck, Nova Scotia, in Canada. The project consisted of building and operating a quarry and a marine terminal. The investment climate was fundamental to making this business decision. In addition to 'a rich history in industrial mineral production spanning a period of over 200 years', Nova Scotia's government had implemented a friendly investment environment for mining. Policy papers emphasized the benefits of mining, such as jobs and tax revenue, as well as the

[112] Ibid., para. 560. The tribunal noted, nonetheless, that 'the conduct of some Bolivian officials can be called into question, in particular the timing of their interventions to remedy the conflict and the absence of higher-ranking officials at certain fundamental meetings'. Ibid., para. 566.

[113] Ibid., para. 610.

[114] Ibid., para. 655.

[115] Ibid., paras. 618–21.

[116] Ibid., paras. 876, 875–6.

government's commitment to reconciling resource extraction with environmental protection and community development.[117] The provincial government also announced that Nova Scotia was 'very well situated' to ship goods to Europe and the US Eastern Seaboard and Gulf Coast.[118] In addition to the generally friendly environment, the Department of Natural Resources had actively encouraged Bilcon to invest in Digby Neck. Technical officers met with Bilcon employees more than a dozen times, providing technical information, while Bilcon received political support from the provincial premier and the minister of natural resources, who encouraged the project and underlined the need for jobs.[119]

While the government of Nova Scotia was open for business, the local Digby Neck community was concerned about the Whites Point project.[120] It was less optimistic about reconciling its values with mining. Some people supported the project based on the potential jobs, but the majority had reservations beyond the distribution of benefits, costs, and risks.[121] Contrary to the cases of *Copper Mesa*, *Bear Creek*, and *SAS*, local opposition in *Bilcon* was primarily channelled through institutional mechanisms. The Canadian government was present in Digby Neck, and the feasibility of the Whites Point project was examined by multiple agencies—not only the mining authority—and an independent panel.

Tensions between Bilcon and the Digby Neck community were evident throughout the entire review process. The project became a provincial and national issue, and a subject of discussion during Nova Scotia's 2003 election. Bilcon established a community liaison committee as part of its public information program early on, which already showed 'how engaged and opposed the local community was to the project'.[122] The investor insisted that an independent panel 'could only recommend modifications to the Project; it could not prevent the Project from going ahead'.[123] Bilcon also filed a defamation suit against a local newspaper for negative comments about the firm.

In view of the local opposition, provincial and federal authorities submitted the case to a joint review panel (JRP), which arguably signalled the end of their technical and political support for the Whites Point project.[124] This independent

[117] *Bilcon v. Canada* (PCA Case No. 2009-04) Award on Jurisdiction and Liability, 17 March 2015, paras. 461, 449, 453. Also, G. Prime, 'An Overview of the Industrial Mineral Potential of the North Mountain Basalt' in Nova Scotia Department of Natural Resources, Mineral Resources Branch, Report of Activities 2007(2008) 81–104.

[118] *Bilcon v. Canada* (PCA Case No. 2009-04) Award on Jurisdiction and Liability, 17 March 2015, para. 459.

[119] Ibid., paras. 456–66.

[120] Ibid., paras. 468–9.

[121] Ibid., paras. 509–10.

[122] Ibid., paras. 162, 467–8.

[123] Dissenting Opinion of Donald McRae in *Bilcon v. Canada* (PCA Case No. 2009-04) 10 March 2015, para. 18.

[124] *Bilcon v. Canada* (PCA Case No. 2009-04) Award on Jurisdiction and Liability, 17 March 2015, paras. 157, 162–3.

panel would produce a report for the consideration of the provincial and regional government, which would make the final decision on the project. From the start, the JRP hearings were not characterized by friendliness. Bilcon alleged demonstrations of anti-US sentiment, disregard for science, and a 'very public venting of criticism'.[125] The panel, in turn, concluded that Bilcon had 'undermined the willingness of local residents to enter into meaningful discussions with the Proponent and hardened local attitudes against the project'.[126] The JRP deliberations demonstrate that the community was worried about their 'sense of place, their desire for self-reliance, and the need to respect and sustain their surrounding environment'.[127]

Under federal and provincial regulations, the JRP had a relatively broad mandate. It was tasked with assessing the Whites Point project considering 'likely significant adverse effects after mitigation', and 'socio-economic conditions, on environmental health, physical and cultural heritage'. The panel supplemented these guidelines with 'social and cultural patterns'.[128] An important feature of this review process also consisted of the preparation of a mitigation plan, the implementation of which should eventually allow the project to proceed. These various guidelines indicate some tension between distribution and recognition concerns. Benefits, costs, and risks can be increased, reduced, or allocated differently, but broader recognition issues can rarely be mitigated or compensated.

In the case of Whites Point, the JRP focused on all the dimensions of the project but paid particular attention to 'community core values'.[129] This category had not been used in Canada before. For the panellists, these values referred to the community's self-determination, self-reliance, history, character, and attitudes. The view from Digby Neck contrasted with the federal and provincial assumption that issues of distribution and recognition could be reconciled. Those in the locality spoke of their right to decide, their right to block the project, and to maintain their livelihood and traditions. The panellists did not think that the costs and risks of the project were irreconcilable—'other impacts of the project [...] should not be judged "significant"'—but they were of the view that 'community core values' could not be mitigated. Put simply, the community wanted 'to take a different development path'.[130]

For these reasons, the JRP recommended the rejection of the Whites Point project without suggesting a mitigation plan—yet another novel move for a review panel. The federal and provincial governments accepted this specific recommendation and rejected Bilcon's project.[131] Interestingly, the JRP also took issue with

125 Ibid., paras. 514, 566.
126 Dissenting Opinion of Donald McRae in *Bilcon v. Canada* (PCA Case No. 2009-04) 10 March 2015, para. 18.
127 Ibid., para. 16.
128 *Bilcon v. Canada* (PCA Case No. 2009-04) Award on Jurisdiction and Liability, 17 March 2015, paras. 478, 487, 497.
129 Ibid., para. 503.
130 Ibid., paras. 503, 521, 507–47.
131 Ibid., para. 577.

Nova Scotia's natural resource policy. It suggested a moratorium on new projects in the area, higher environmental standards, and 'more effective mechanisms than those currently in place for consultation with local governments'.[132]

As with the previous cases discussed in this chapter, the dispute did not end there. Bilcon filed an ISDS case against Canada under NAFTA's Chapter 11, claiming that the Whites Point project review was arbitrary, unfair, and discriminatory. The majority of the tribunal looked at the facts of this case through the expectations that Bilcon could reasonably have entertained after relying on 'specific encouragements at the political and technical level'.[133] The arbitrators said the investor was not entitled to have the project approved, but could legitimately expect that it 'would be assessed on the merits of its environmental soundness in accordance with the same legal standards applied to applicants generally'.[134] The dissenting arbitrator opined that this reasoning was unhelpful. Every investor can expect that the authorities will apply the law, he concluded, and portraying the facts as the majority did only served to create an 'aura of mistreatment of the claimant'.[135] Storytelling plays a fundamental role in every investment dispute, as arbitrators admit, but in the *Bilcon* case this role was clear.

Looking at the deliberations and the report of the JRP, the majority of the tribunal decided that the procedure and outcome were unfair to Bilcon. The regulatory process followed an 'unprecedented approach' and was 'unwinnable' for the investor.[136] The arbitrators felt that the 'core community values' concept was neither explained to Bilcon, nor was it allowed to request a clarification or respond to that concept. Equally important, the concept was vague and ambiguous. The majority identified four different interpretations within the report. Some of these interpretations permitted a reconciliation of the costs and risks with the community's expectations; others put things as if they were matters of 'philosophical belief', which could not be assessed or mitigated.[137] The majority also noted that the inhabitants of Digby Neck were hostile to Bilcon, a suggestion that the dissenting arbitrator found was another way of building an 'aura' of mistreatment.[138]

For the majority, the main flaw of the JRP was not providing a mitigation plan that could have allowed the project to proceed to the next phase. This turned the Digby Neck area into a *de facto* 'no go' zone.[139] The arbitrators observed that

[132] Ibid., paras. 188, 570.

[133] Ibid., paras. 448, 455.

[134] Ibid., paras. 447, 470.

[135] Dissenting Opinion of Donald McRae in *Bilcon v. Canada* (PCA Case No. 2009-04) 10 March 2015, para. 5.

[136] *Bilcon v. Canada* (PCA Case No. 2009-04) Award on Jurisdiction and Liability, 17 March 2015, paras. 450, 453, 590, 739–40.

[137] Ibid., paras. 528, 507–47.

[138] Dissenting Opinion of Donald McRae in *Bilcon v. Canada* (PCA Case No. 2009-04) 10 March 2015, para. 6.

[139] *Bilcon v. Canada* (PCA Case No. 2009-04) Award on Jurisdiction and Liability, 17 March 2015, paras. 571, 589.

this conduct violated the national treatment standard, as investors in similar circumstances were given the possibility to mitigate damages. Also, it was arbitrary and inconsistent with Canada's legislation, including Nova Scotia's laws and NAFTA itself, all of which 'expressly acknowledge that economic development and environmental integrity can not only be reconciled, but can be mutually reinforcing'.[140]

The dissenting arbitrator approached the facts and the work of the JRP differently. First, he said that 'core community values' was not a novel or unprecedented concept. It was rather a proxy or name given to 'the human environment effects'.[141] Secondly, he found that the problem of the review process was not the hostility to the foreign investor, but the lack of community engagement on Bilcon's part. The latter created a sense of distrust among the community. His analysis of the report paid less attention to Nova Scotia's actions and legislation, and instead privileged Digby Neck's community core values. The dissenting arbitrator also gave little weight to the JRP's more general recommendations, concerning the need to strengthen environmental standards and implement a general moratorium. The issue, in his view, was much less about reconciling different interests. It was about Bilcon's failure to 'satisfy the Panel that the project could operate consistently with those core values'.[142]

The dissenting arbitrator further criticized the majority for promoting regulatory chill and downplaying recognition concerns. In his view, the majority found that a controversial issue of domestic law, namely the use of the 'core community values' concept, amounted to a violation of the minimum standard of treatment, although this was neither a grossly unfair nor an egregious behaviour of Canada. This conclusion, he opined, went beyond the interpretation of the minimum standard of treatment, as defined in *Waste Management 2*, and equalled an intrusion into domestic law. An approach that could chill environmental reviews.[143] Lastly, the dissenter reproved the majority for privileging scientific and technical aspects over human environment concerns. In a short passage, the majority responded to these criticisms by noting that Canada could implement any level of protection; the problem was that the JRP did not discharge its legal obligations appropriately.[144]

[140] Ibid., para. 597.

[141] Dissenting Opinion of Donald McRae in *Bilcon v. Canada* (PCA Case No. 2009-04) 10 March 2015, paras. 15–16. For a detailed critique of the majority's findings, see Meinhard Doelle, 'The Bilcon NAFTA Tribunal: A Clash of Investor Protection and Sustainability-Based Environmental Assessments' in Stanley D Berger (ed.), *Key Developments in Environmental Law* (Thomson Reuters 2017) 99–123.

[142] Dissenting Opinion of Donald McRae in *Bilcon v. Canada* (PCA Case No. 2009-04) 10 March 2015, para. 26.

[143] Ibid., paras. 35, 48–51.

[144] *Bilcon v. Canada* (PCA Case No. 2009-04) Award on Jurisdiction and Liability, 17 March 2015, para. 598. The majority also observed that this approach 'does not place economics or technology above human concerns', ibid., para. 736.

Conclusion

Investment disputes involving local communities and the extractive sector challenge certain basic premises of investment treaties and ISDS. States frequently support such investments before and during a project, and when support obsolesces it is often because governments have no other choice. In the cases analysed in this chapter, cancellation was necessary to avoid a much larger social conflict that would have threatened the ruling elite as well as other investment projects and the extractivist economic model itself. Foreign investors, in general, should be grateful for these measures. But investment treaties and ISDS make a large part of this complexity invisible, and arbitrators downplay claims of recognition and the embeddedness of local rights. Demands of recognition are articulated in a language that arbitrators distrust: a language of politics, values, and aspirations that relate not to the global economy but to the local community.[145] Storytelling plays an important role in this reasoning by focusing primarily on states' inconsistent behaviour. Locals are not expected to have much of a voice, but to adapt to the demands of the global natural resource sector. The *Bilcon* award also shows that channelling local claims of recognition through established institutional mechanisms may not make a difference.

Local communities may ultimately manage to block projects, or other international courts may protect their rights, but this counts for little in ISDS. One reason is that foreign investors can look for protection in unexpected places. If the risk comes from international law they can find shelter in domestic law, as in *Bear Creek*. In reality, there is nothing unexpected in this because some states—and their national elites—have promoted extractivism for decades, or even centuries. Another reason is that the recognition of local communities in international law (FPIC, for example) is modest when compared to the protection enjoyed by foreign investors, who have substantive and procedural rights over a project and a right to participate in the host country's regulatory process. Rather than a radical rethinking of international investment law, then, these developments are consistent with the legal imagination of the norm entrepreneurs of the 1950s and 1960s.

[145] There is some consensus in investment law literature that ISDS arbitrators distrust politics, although the extent and reasons for this distrust remains debated. See, e.g., Jonathan Bonnitcha and Zoe Phillips Williams, 'State Liability for "Politically" Motivated Conduct in the Investment Treaty Regime' (2020) 33 Leiden Journal of International Law 77–100; David Schneiderman, 'Hayek's Dream: International Investment Law and the Denigration of Politics' (2019) available at SSRN: https://ssrn.com/abstract=3397624 (last visited 29 September 2020).

Conclusion

Towards a New Legal Imagination

For the norm entrepreneurs of the 1950s and 1960s, investment treaties and ISDS were always intended to be more than a dispute settlement mechanism. They also provided a platform to ground ideas about the role of foreign investors and foreign investment. The discussions, lobbying, and networking of these individuals and their professional associations gave shape to an imagination of international investment law as revolving around one fundamental purpose: the calculability of foreign investors. Put differently, investment treaties and ISDS were conceived as an antidote to claims of redistribution, recognition, and attempts to embed foreign investor rights into the relevant locality. Whether the legal reasoning concentrates on foreign investor rights or on states' right to regulate, it always aims to ensure that the exercise of public authority remains consistent with the original investment decision. It is difficult to think about international investment law outside this box, even as the world faces the COVID-19 pandemic or the climate change crisis.

Today this legal imagination occupies the space of international investment law, but its evolutionary path was not straightforward. In the post-World War II period, the norm entrepreneurs faced resistance from the Global South as much as from those who believed in state economic intervention and development aid. Their initiatives are well-documented, as much as their efforts to resist competing imaginations in the 1970s. The Geneva Association was still active during this decade, but it was the International Chamber of Commerce that took the protagonist's role by elaborating and promoting the ICC Guidelines and a voluntary approach to foreign investor obligations. Large MNCs, such as Royal Dutch Shell and Exxon, all lined up behind this initiative as a complement to investment treaties and ISDS.

The norm entrepreneurs of the 1950s and 1960s were aware of the significance of ISDS beyond the resolution of cases, envisioning this direct private remedy as a fertile site for consolidating and progressively developing the law in accordance with their vision of foreign investment relations. The similarity between the interpretations they promoted and contemporary ISDS practice is remarkable. This includes a broad interpretation of foreign investor rights and indirect expropriation, the protection of reliance, and an emphasis on a case-by-case analysis. The only minor, formal distinction is that ISDS arbitrators protect foreign investors' legitimate expectations under the FET standard instead of under the umbrella clause. The resemblance between the views of the norm entrepreneurs and international

Investment Treaties and the Legal Imagination. Nicolás M. Perrone, Oxford University Press (2021). © Nicolás M. Perrone.
DOI: 10.1093/oso/9780198862147.003.0009

investment law today is even more significant if we consider that the dominant approach to foreign investor obligations continues to follow the ICC Guidelines. Effectively, the current canon of imagination of foreign investor rights and obligations remains theirs.

In the last chapters, I have shown that arbitrators do defer sometimes to public authority when reviewing public measures aimed at curbing the costs and risks associated with investment projects. Their interpretation of the right to regulate, however, is embedded into global institutions. ISDS tribunals talk about balance and reasonableness, but these criteria are dictated by global knowledge and standards. This approach to public regulation benefits foreign investors, as they are globally embedded subjects and often have more leverage over the standard-setting process than most governments. Most of the population lacks the means or capacity to participate in such sites of norm production. Some Global North states may be more influential than MNCs in the elaboration of these global standards, but most Global South countries are rule-takers—and local communities even more so. The global terrain is global to the extent that those who are globally powerful can participate in norm creation.[1]

MNCs' prominent role in the global terrain of standards-setting and knowledge creation is consistent with the vision of the norm entrepreneurs. For them, 'enlightened business' was destined to write the rules of the world economy. Unlike classical liberals and neoliberals, who insist on the importance of the invisible hand or the anonymous market, the norm entrepreneurs predicted a significant role for business in rule creation. Consolidating this role under national democracies was difficult, but the intricacies of global governance provided 'enlightened business' with a great opportunity, which they have not wasted. In this account, investment treaties and ISDS play a fundamental role: they embody the last resort to interpret and enforce global standards when states—or local communities—attempt to deviate from these norms.

Importantly, the way ISDS practice treats states' right to regulate overlooks the fact that governments face far more difficult choices than international investment law acknowledges. They must strike an all but impossible balance between regulatory givings and the need to regulate for the public interest. Foreign investors and international organizations recommend states implement incentives and friendly business regulations to attract foreign investment, but quite often they are nowhere to be seen when these regimes prove unsustainable and governments are left with no choice but to reform or terminate the givings. A serious problem is that the Global South countries required to grant more givings are often those that lack the institutional capacity to fully understand the potential consequences of these

[1] I have discussed this argument in more detail elsewhere. Nicolás M. Perrone, 'The International Investment Regime after the Global Crisis of Neoliberalism: Rupture or Continuity' (2016) 23 Indiana Journal of Global Legal Studies 603–27.

measures until it is too late. Where sustainable development requires adjustment and renegotiation, investment treaties and ISDS only offer rigidity and *pacta sunt servanda*.

Many of the ISDS cases discussed in this book resulted from generous givings that turned out to be environmentally, socially, and economically unsustainable. ISDS practice consistently marginalizes the circumstances leading to this initial distributive outcome, including the requests of the foreign investors or the policy advice of international organizations. Silencing the origin of givings is necessary to facilitate foreign investors' calculability. The narrative that states entice foreign investors enables the enforcement of givings that were sometimes unsustainable from the start. If arbitrators were to instead associate foreign investors—either individually or as a category—with the creation of the original legal framework, their storytelling would open up a space to challenge investors' reliance on the givings or to focus on the fulfilment of states' expectations. Arguably, governments also trusted that foreign investors would benefit the domestic economy when implementing the schemes that soured. Perhaps ISDS practice would appear more balanced if some states, at least those lacking institutional capacity and information, could benefit from the representations and assurances granted by foreign investors and international organizations. Yet this is not the case: reliance is protected only in a one-way sense.

While it can be argued that ISDS practice is based on a transactional model, where foreign investors and states are placed at the same level, this ignores the fact that awards have not only recognized but also recalibrated states' right to regulate, particularly when foreign investors do not have legitimate expectations. Those defending ISDS insist on this recalibration as evidence of how things have evolved since the times of *Metalclad* and *TecMed*, but such an optimistic view overlooks the way ISDS practice treats regulatory givings and embeds the right to regulate into the global terrain. States' ability to pass measures for the public interest is undermined from above, from global standards and institutions, as well as from a transactional model that protects investors' reliance. Under investment treaties and ISDS, the relationship between foreign investors and states is interpreted through a regulatory model unless the investor has a legitimate expectation, but this legal regime always plugs foreign investor rights and states' right to regulate into global institutions, and it does so by excluding public domestic imperatives. In several cases, moreover, arbitrators describe the facts of the dispute in a transactional manner, despite a lack of legitimate expectations, creating an aura of mistreatment of the investor. *Bilcon* is a paradigmatic example here.

The consequences of this legal imagination go beyond the relationship between foreign investors and states. Investment treaties and ISDS make local communities invisible. They create a legal regime that puts communities in tragic situations, as their lifestyles, values, and cultures are put on trial in disputes they are not party to. Not only can they not participate in the arbitrations, but ISDS practice has been unwilling to take recognition claims seriously, treating them as unreasonable or unpredictable. The premise that the resources that make an investment project can—and sometimes must—serve different purposes has been marginalized by international investment law.

In this way, arbitrators favour a political economy that silences local communities before, during, and after foreign investment projects. Their awards reinforce the premise that foreign investors are safe as long as they have the state on their side, confirming their actions either explicitly or implicitly. When things go wrong, as seen in *Copper Mesa* or *Bear Creek*, investors can tell tribunals that they were entitled to rely on states' reassurances: it was the state that was inconsistent by first supporting and then terminating the project. My argument is not that investment treaties and ISDS are to blame for the attitude of some governments or national elites, but that this regime gives too much legal relevance to public measures in favour of foreign investors, facilitating projects that can be detrimental to local communities. These communities are asked to make large sacrifices to adapt to investment projects, while states remain absent and foreign investors have no intention of recognizing local values or traditions.

Finally, there is also the long-term impact of investment treaties and ISDS. The norm entrepreneurs envisioned that this legal regime would facilitate the continuation of a natural resource-based model for the Global South. This model was particularly convenient for this coalition, as many of its members were executives and lawyers of MNCs involved in the oil and mineral sector. Creating the conditions to enable foreign investors to extract natural resources in the Global South was more important for the investors than for the countries themselves. States could obtain capital and technology from other sources, such as development aid or technology transfer, and decide whether to launch an industrialization programme, focus on their natural wealth, or both. MNCs such as Royal Dutch Shell or Rio Tinto, however, depended on these opportunities to stay in business.

Unsurprisingly, investment treaties and ISDS have attracted a lot of critique and discussions about reform. Most of these discussions, however, continue to be shaped by the legal imagination of the norm entrepreneurs of the 1950s and 1960s. This imagination has contributed to blocking a broad debate about the role of foreign investment in sustainable development. The natural resource model, which closely intersects with investment treaties and ISDS, has proved deleterious for the Global South and the environment more generally. Similarly, some privatizations have not been successful and foreign investment projects, generally speaking, do not always unfold as expected by the host country and local community. Yet the Global North and, more counterintuitively, the Global South both seem more concerned about discussing whether to establish a permanent court and other procedural innovations rather than re-examining the ground rules governing foreign investment relations.[2] The current debate resembles more the deliberations within the International Chamber of Commerce or the Geneva Association than diplomatic negotiations during the post-World War II or the 1970s.

The excessive focus on ISDS in international discussions and negotiations has also served to silence other issues, such as development aid and technology transfer—exactly the issues that the norm entrepreneurs criticized and sought to remove from the policy agenda. The developmental dimension of the debate remains bracketed even though empirical evidence, at least since the 1970s, shows that foreign investment can be detrimental to host countries. More than sixty years after Abs's Magna Carta, international investment lawyers and policy makers continue to work on the problems of foreign investment in terms of the premises set by the norm entrepreneurs. This is the most remarkable achievement of Abs, Shawcross, and their coalition.

Crucially, this influence occurs irrespective of who wins or loses each ISDS case. The job of the law is not only to resolve disputes, but also to shape conduct and expectations, and the outcome of ISDS cases is as relevant as the arbitrators' reasoning in this respect. Arbitrators have adapted to changes and critique without undermining the legal imagination of the norm entrepreneurs. The shift to proceduralism has not entailed a markedly different approach to legitimate expectations, and arbitrators now consider the importance of foreign investor rights to information and to participate in host-state regulatory processes. This participation adds to investors' global influence, strengthening their position at all levels of governance.

It is true that the increasing relevance of local communities under international law poses a new challenge for ISDS practice, but so far this question has taken the shape foreseen by the norm entrepreneurs and arbitrators. International law has recognized that local communities have rights over their territory, but they can only enforce these rights against states. Taking local communities seriously would require rethinking international investment law, for instance, by allowing these communities to sue foreign investors before human rights courts with the expectation that these judges would be able to resolve cases involving distributive as well as recognition claims. But if these two international property regimes operate separately, ISDS arbitrators can continue blaming states for giving ambivalent signals to investors, not finding alternatives consistent with the rights of both investors and communities, or coming up with new unexpected criteria when reviewing an investment project.

[2] UNCITRAL Working Group III, tasked with investor-state dispute settlement reform, has decided to focus on procedural matters only, including the potential creation of an appeal mechanism or a permanent investment court. See Anthea Roberts and Taylor St John, 'UNCITRAL and ISDS Reform: Visualising a Flexible Framework' (2019) EJIL Talk, 24 October 2019.

A common critique against seeing foreign investor rights as social relations is that such a view distorts the goal of ISDS. The job of arbitrators is to focus on the resolution of disputes arising from an investment, not on the multiple social relations associated with it. This critique insists on the usefulness of investment treaties and ISDS to settle disputes peacefully according to the rule of law, preventing the return of gunboat diplomacy, and may go as far as accepting that the resolution of ISDS cases may create regulatory chill and moral hazard. This position denies that international investment law is involved in the problems created by hazardous waste management in Mexico or privatizations in Argentina. As Paulsson says, if a policy goes wrong and fails to meet the expectations of the population, we should blame the policy rather than the legal regime.

The problem is that policy and law are inevitably intertwined. The norm entrepreneurs were interested in investment treaties and ISDS not only as a mechanism to resolve disputes but also as a platform from which to channel conduct and expectations. They used law to discuss and advance their views on policy, and drew on policies to justify a specific legal regime for foreign investment. The outcome of this project is a set of rules and principles that promote the calculability of foreign investors but at the cost of excluding certain issues and rendering some actors invisible. This is of significant policy relevance, and from a legal standpoint what is excluded is as important as what we protect. Our understanding of the latter remains limited unless we also concentrate on the former.

Ultimately, these exclusions serve the purpose of making states 'calculable, regular' so they are able to stand security for their own future, 'which is what one who promises does!'[3] But not all state promises are equally important for investment treaties and ISDS. In a recent dissent, Gary Born notes that 'if Czech legislation can be ignored or rewritten here, then the same can happen in other cases. Neither future investors nor others will ignore that unfortunate fact.'[4] This observation evokes the central core of the legal imagination, but also leaves us with the question: who are the *others* in this story? The rest of the population does not trust states much, but they cannot use ISDS. A famous song by Violeta Parra, a Chilean folk singer, reminds us how little the promises of politicians are worth for common people: 'look how presidents smile; when they make promises to the innocent' [*Miren como sonríen los presidentes; cuando le hacen promesas al inocente*]. Investment treaties and ISDS may not be directly responsible for *devaluat*ing the promises of presidents and prime ministers, but by granting foreign investors 'extraordinary citizenship' status they have not done democracy a great favour either.

* * *

[3] Friedrich Nietzsche, *The Genealogy of Morals: A Polemic* (trans. W. Kaufmann) (Modern Library 1888 [2000]) 494. Cited in Roy Kreitner, *Calculating Promises: The Emergence of Modern American Contract Doctrine* (Stanford University Press 2006) ii.

[4] Dissenting Opinion of Gary Born in *JSW Solar v. Czech Republic* (PCA Case No. 2014-03) 11 October 2017, para. 110.

The objective of this book is not to advocate for a correct interpretation of investment treaties, or propose an ideal model to govern foreign investment relations. There is a constructive side of its argument, still, as I have discussed moral and legal reasons for including the issues that have been silenced and to hear the actors who have been made invisible. Empirical evidence likewise indicates that we should rethink the way we approach foreign investment relations and international investment law. The obsolescing bargain model distorts reality, investment treaties rarely attract foreign investment, and the development question is missing from this field. But the analysis I have presented suggests that rethinking international investment law requires more than normative arguments or empirical evidence. We should also engage in constructive discussions and debates about where foreign investors, states, and local communities want to take foreign investment relations in the future.

The creativity of those who defend and those who criticize investment treaties, however, seems trapped in a binary discussion, restricted to approving or rejecting investment treaties and ISDS. Even those who criticize this legal regime rarely propose a different set of international rules for foreign investment. This negative approach contrasts with the position taken by the UN Group of Eminent Persons, who believed that the measures to ensure that foreign investment contributes to sustainable development would be 'ineffective and frustrated' without an appropriate international framework. Emphasizing the binary character of the discussion probably resonates with the heirs of Abs, Shawcross, Rhyne, and Haight.[5] The idea of a legal vacuum prompts fears of disorder, anarchy, or gunboat diplomacy. This position is more perplexing when it comes from some critics.

For those who believe the current regime cannot be fixed, but an international framework is necessary to coordinate domestic action, the post-World War II efforts of the norm entrepreneurs provide some lessons on how to re-imagine international investment law. Our efforts must be ambitious, like theirs, and ideas alone are not enough. The Geneva Association, the International Chamber of Commerce, and other members of the coalition of norm entrepreneurs insisted on their imaginary of foreign investment relations although it was described as too favourable to foreign investors. They answered back by asserting the practical character of their proposals, while showing conviction that their approach to the law was the correct one. My argument is that their success lay not

[5] There is some continuity between the 1950s and the present norm entrepreneurs for international investment protection. The current ones include the International Bar Association, Charles N. Brower, and Stephen M. Schwebel. David Schneiderman, 'The Paranoid Style of Investment Lawyers and Arbitrators: Investment Law Norm Entrepreneurs and their Critics' in C. L. Lim (ed.), *Alternative Visions of the International Law on Foreign Investment: Essays in Honour of Muthucumaraswamy Sornarajah* (CUP 2016) 131–55.

in their ideas *per se* but in how they collated them into the larger frame of foreign investment relations.

The challenges to replace this way of thinking about foreign investment should not be underestimated. The norm entrepreneurs relied on a network of like-minded individuals, and had influential contacts with governments and international organizations. At the same time, history shows that their project was more fragile when there were other serious contenders on the horizon. These were not just the Global South and labour unions. In the 1970s, many people considered that the world needed a GATT—a compromise of embedded liberalism—for foreign investment. The political context of the 1970s probably fostered these competing imaginations, but so do the decay of the neoliberal consensus and the crisis of international organizations today.

In this context of crisis and uncertainty about the future, it is worth considering what a competing imagination would look like if it included as many claims of distribution and recognition as possible while being receptive to the tensions between global and local embeddedness. I see the starting point as quite the opposite of what Elihu Lauterpacht[6] or Wälde[7] suggested as the solution to fix international investment law. The idea of an international legal regime or regimes capable of protecting everybody's rights from states—foreign investors, domestic investors, and local communities—is unrealistic. This is because investment treaties and ISDS work on the basis of exclusion: for this approach to governance to work, somebody or something needs to be excluded. Constructing a regime based on *inclusion* poses different challenges. The work of Jennifer Nedelsky suggests we should not begin by reconceptualizing foreign investor rights, or states' right to regulate, but rather by asking ourselves 'what patterns of relationship among people and the material world we want'.[8] This starting point is markedly different from political risk, and requires shifting the focus from *investments* to *social relations*. In this competing imagination, it would be reasonable to ask foreign investors to behave as members of the host country and local community, with rights as well as obligations. There might be good reason, in specific circumstances, to treat certain foreign investors differently, but there is no justification for exempting them from the sacrifices people make to promote a better communal and individual life for everyone. There is nothing extraordinary about foreign investors.

[6] Elihu Lauterpacht, 'International Law and Private Foreign Investment' (1997) 4 Indiana Journal of Global Legal Studies 259–76, 275–6.

[7] Thomas Wälde, 'The Specific Nature of Investment Arbitration' in Philippe Kahn and Thomas Wälde (eds.), *Les Aspects Nouveaux du Droit des Investissements Internationaux/New Aspects of International Investment Law* (Martinus Nijhoff Publishers 2007) 43–120, 44, 93, 99, 111, 119.

[8] Jennifer Nedelsky, 'Law, Boundaries, and the Bounded Self' (1990) 30 Representations 162–89, 184.

Documents from International Organizations, Professional Associations, and Research Institutions

American Bar Association, *The Protection of Private Property Invested Abroad. A Report by the Committee on International Trade and Investment. Section of International and Comparative Law* (1963).

American Branch of the International Law Association, 'Response to the Questionnaire of the International Committee on Nationalization, 1958' in Society to Advance the Protection of Foreign Investments, *Convention on Investments Abroad with Comments, Speeches and New Literature*, Publication No. 3 (Bergisch Gladbach, J. Heider 1960) 81–96.

Bilderberg Meetings, 'Buxton Conference' 13–15 September 1958, available at https://info.publicintelligence.net/bilderberg/BilderbergConferenceReport1958.pdf (last visited 3 July 2020).

Business and Industry Advisory Committee, 'Observations on the note by the Secretariat of the OECD Development Assistance Committee related to the International Chamber of Commerce Guidelines for International Investment' Meeting on 25 June 1973 (Edwin Martin Personal Papers, The John F. Kennedy Library, Box 37).

Central Intelligence Agency, 'Abs, Hermann Josef' 1970 Current Biography (Disclosed under the Nazi War Crimes Disclosure Act), available at https://www.cia.gov/library/readingroom/docs/ABS%2C%20HERMANN%20J._0051.pdf (last visited 2 July 2020).

Council of Europe, 'Opinion on the OECD Draft Convention on the Protection of Foreign Property' (1964) 3 International Legal Materials 133–50.

HSBC, 'A Climate for Recovery: The Colour of Stimulus Goes Green' 25 February 2009, available at https://www.globaldashboard.org/wp-content/uploads/2009/HSBC_Green_New_Deal.pdf (last visited 4 June 2019).

IISD and The Royal Institute of International Affairs, 'Investment, Doha and the WTO: Background Paper to the Chatham House Meeting convened by RIIA and IISD Trade and Sustainable Development Priorities Post-Doha' London, April 7–8, 2003, available at https://www.iisd.org/sites/default/files/publications/investment_riia_iisd.pdf (last visited 25 May 2020).

International Association for the Promotion and Protection of Private Foreign Investments, 'Note: Reunion de l'APPI à Zurich,' Berne 15 November 1965 (Swiss Diplomatic Documents, dodis.ch/31990).

International Association for the Promotion and Protection of Private Foreign Investments, 'A.P.P.I.' (1966).

International Association for the Promotion and Protection of Private Foreign Investments, 'Fourth half-yearly report on events affecting private foreign investment in some capital-receiving countries', 35/72, August 1972.

International Association for the Promotion and Protection of Private Foreign Investments, 'Fifth Biannual report on events affecting private foreign investment in some capital-receiving countries', 13/73, May 1973.

International Bar Association, 'Cologne Conference Resolution 1958' in Society to Advance the Protection of Foreign Investments, *Convention on Investments Abroad with Comments, Speeches and New Literature*, Publication No. 3 (Bergisch Gladbach, J. Heider 1960) 35.

International Chamber of Commerce, 'Intelligent International Investment' A Report of the Committee on Business Participation in Foreign Economic Development, April 1949.

International Chamber of Commerce, 'Attracting Foreign Investment' Statement adopted by the Executive Committee of the ICC, February 1959.

International Chamber of Commerce, 'Biennial Report 1957/1958' in Society to Advance the Protection of Foreign Investments, *Convention on Investments Abroad with Comments, Speeches and New Literature*, Publication No. 3 (Bergisch Gladbach, J. Heider 1960) 44–5.

International Chamber of Commerce, 'Statements and resolutions of the ICC, 1963–1965. 20th Congress' (1965).

International Chamber of Commerce, '1949 International Code of Fair Treatment for Foreign Investments' in UNCTAD, *International Investment Instruments: A Compendium*, vol. 3 (United Nations 1996) 273–8.

International Chamber of Commerce, '1972 Guidelines for International Investment' in UNCTAD, *International Investment Instruments: A Compendium*, vol. 3 (United Nations 1996) 279–91.

International Chamber of Commerce, United States Council, 'A New Challenge to Private Enterprise' (1975).

International Chamber of Commerce, 'ICC Dispute Resolution 2018 Statistics' (2019), available at https://nyiac.org/wp-content/uploads/2019/08/icc_disputeresolution2018statistics.pdf. (last visited 20 November 2020)

International Law Association, 'Washington Congress Resolution 1959' in Society to Advance the Protection of Foreign Investments, *Convention on Investments Abroad with Comments, Speeches and New Literature*, Publication No. 3 (Bergisch Gladbach, J. Heider 1960) 34.

International Law Association, 'Draft Statutes of the Arbitral Tribunal for Foreign Investment' included in UNCTAD, *International Investment Instruments: A Compendium*, vol. 3 (United Nations 1996) 259–72.

OECD Development Assistance Committee, 'Review of OECD/DAC Activities in the Field of Private Investment' Background document for the UN Panel Meeting in Amsterdam on Foreign Private Investment and the Development Process, 7 February 1969 (Edwin Martin Personal Papers, The John F. Kennedy Library, Box 37).

OECD, 'OECD Draft Convention on the Protection of Foreign Property' (1968) 2 The International Lawyer 331–53.

OECD, 'Green Growth: Overcoming the Crisis and Beyond' (OECD 2009).

OECD, Secretariat of the Development Assistance Committee, 'Comments on the ICC Guidelines for International Investment' DAC(73)19, 22 March 1973 (Edwin Martin Personal Papers, The John F. Kennedy Library, Box 37).

Society to Advance the Protection of Foreign Investments, 'International Convention for the Mutual Protection of Private Property Rights in Foreign Countries: draft' (1957).

Society to Advance the Protection of Foreign Investments, 'Introduction' in Society to Advance the Protection of Foreign Investments, *Convention on Investments Abroad with Comments, Speeches and New Literature*, Publication No. 3 (Bergisch Gladbach, J. Heider 1960) 5–6.

UNCTAD, *World Investment Report 1991: The Triad in Foreign Direct Investment* (United Nations 1991).

UNCTAD, *World Investment Report 1992: Transnational corporations as engines of growth* (United Nations 1992).

UNCTAD, *World Investment Report 1993: Transnational corporations and integrated international production* (United Nations 1993).

UNCTAD, *World Investment Report 1994: Transnational Corporations, Employment and the Workplace* (United Nations 1994).

UNCTAD, *World Investment Report 1996: Investment, trade and international policy agreements* (United Nations 1996).

UNCTAD, *World Investment Report 1998: Trends and Determinants* (United Nations 1998).

UNCTAD, *World Investment Report 1999: Foreign Direct Investment and the Challenge of Development* (United Nations 1999).

UNCTAD, *Fair and Equitable Treatment. UNCTAD Series on Issues in International Investment Agreements* (United Nations 1999).

UNCTAD, *Taking of Property. UNCTAD Series on Issues in International Investment Agreements* (United Nations 2000).

UNCTAD, *World Investment Report 2001: Promoting Linkages* (United Nations 2001).

UNCTAD, *World Investment Report 2003: FDI Policies for Development: National and International Perspectives* (United Nations 2003).

UNCTAD, *World Investment Report 2008: Transnational Corporations, and the Infrastructure Challenge* (United Nations 2008).

UNCTAD, *World Investment Report 2010: Investing in a Low-Carbon Economy* (United Nations 2010).

UNCTAD, *Investment Policy Framework for Sustainable Development* (United Nations 2012).

UNCTAD, *World Investment Report 2013: Global Value Chains—Investment and Trade for Development* (United Nations 2013).

UNCTAD, *World Investment Report 2015: Reforming International Investment Governance* (United Nations 2015).

United Nations Department of Economic and Social Affairs, *The Impact of Multinational Corporations on Development and on International Relations*, ST/ESA/6 (United Nations 1974).

United Nations Department of Economic and Social Affairs, *Summary of the Hearings Before the Group of Eminent Persons to Study the Impact of Multinational Corporations on Development and International Relations*, ST/ESA/15 (United Nations 1974).

United Nations Department of Economic and Social Affairs, *Privatization in Latin America in the early 1990s*, ST/ESA/PAD/SER.E/17 (United Nations 1999).

United Nations Environment Programme, 'Global Green New Deal: Policy brief' March 2009, available at https://www.greengrowthknowledge.org/resource/global-green-new-deal-policy-brief (last visited 17 June 2020).

United Nations GA Official Records, 29th Session, A/C.2/SR.1638 (25 November 1974).

United Nations, Charter of Economic Rights and Duties of States, General Assembly Resolution 3281 (xxix), 29th Session (12 December 1974).

United Nations, Declaration and Programme on the Establishment of a New International Economic Order, UN General Assembly Resolution 3201/2, 6th Special Session, A/RES/3201-2(S-VI) (1 May 1974).

United Nations, Permanent Sovereignty over Natural Resources, General Assembly Resolution 1803(xvii), 17th Session (14 December 1962).

United States Embassy in Quito, 'GOE negotiating oil contracts—again: firms agree to use services model' 19 August 2008, available at https://wikileaks.org/plusd/cables/08QUITO764_a.html (last visited 26 May 2020).

United States Embassy in Quito, 'Oil companies considering options under Ecuador's 99 percent revenue sharing decree' 25 October 2007, available at https://wikileaks.org/plusd/cables/07QUITO2373_a.html (last visited 26 May 2020).

United States Embassy in Quito, 'Progress on Occidental case' 27 August 2004, available at http://wikileaks.org/plusd/cables/04QUITO2380_a.html (last visited 26 May 2020).

United States Embassy in Quito, 'Spanish Repsol agrees to new oil contract with GOE; U.S. partner murphy resists' 13 November 2008, available at https://wikileaks.org/plusd/cables/08QUITO1058_a.html. (last visited 26 May 2020).

United States Senate, Multinational corporations a compendium of papers submitted to the Subcommittee on International Trade of the Committee on Finance of the United States (US Govt Print. Off., 1973).

United States Senate, Multinational corporations and United States foreign policy. Hearings before the Subcommittee on Multinational Corporations of the Committee on Foreign Relations, Ninety-third Congress. Part I (US Govt Print. Off., 1973–1976).

World Bank Consultative Meeting of Legal Experts, Addis Ababa, December 16–20, 1963, Summary Record of Proceedings in ICSID, *Convention on the Settlement of Investment Disputes between States and Nationals of other States, Documents concerning the origin and formulation of the convention*, vol. II (World Bank 1968).

World Bank, *World Development Report 1985: International Capital and Economic Development* (World Bank 1985).

World Bank, *Legal Framework for the treatment of Foreign Investment, Volume II: Guidelines* (World Bank 1992).

World Bank, *World Development Report 2005: A Better Investment Climate for Everyone* (World Bank 2005).

World Bank, *World Bank Group Archivists' Chronology 1944-2013* (World Bank 2014).

Bibliography

Abs, Hermann J., 'The Safety of Capital' in James Daniel (ed.), *Private Investment: The Key to International Industrial Development: A Report of the San Francisco Conference, October 14–18, 1957* (McGraw Hill 1958) 69–77.

Abs, Hermann J., *Proposals for Improving the Protection of Private Foreign Investments* (Institut International D'Etudes Bancaires 1958).

Abs, Hermann J., 'Die Konjunktur bleibt ruhig' (1959) 32 Vortragsreihe des Deutschen Industrieinstituts 1–4.

Abs, Hermann J., *Die rechtliche Problematik privater Auslandsinvestitionen*. Vortrag gehalten vor der Juristischen Studiengesellschaft in Karlsruhe, am 16. Dezember 1968 (Müller 1969).

Abs, Hermann J. and Hartley Shawcross, 'The Proposed Convention to Protect Private Foreign Investment: Introduction' (1960) 9 Journal of Public Law 115–24.

Abs, Hermann J., Oliver Franks, and Allan Sproul, 'Bankers' Mission to India and Pakistan February-March, 1960: A Letter to Eugene R. Black, President, International Bank for Reconstruction and Development' (World Bank 1960).

Aisbett, Emma and Carol McAusland, 'Firm Characteristics and Influence on Government Rule-Making: Theory and Evidence' (2013) 29 European Journal of Political Economy 214–35.

Aitken, Thomas, *The Multinational Man: The Role of the Manager Abroad* (Routledge 2012 [1973]).

Akinsanya, Adeoye, 'International Protection of Direct Foreign Investments in the Third World' (1987) 36 International & Comparative Law Quarterly 58–75.

Aldrich, George H., 'What Constitutes a Compensable Taking of Property? The Decisions of the Iran-United States Claims Tribunal' (1994) 88 American Journal of International Law 585–610.

Alexander, Gregory S., *Commodity & Propriety: Competing Visions of Property in American Legal Thought, 1776-1970* (University of Chicago Press 1997).

Alexander, Gregory S., *The Global Debate over constitutional Property: Lessons for American Takings Jurisprudence* (University of Chicago Press 2006).

Alexander, Gregory S. and Eduardo M. Peñalver, *An Introduction to Property Theory* (CUP 2012).

Alexander, Gregory S., Eduardo M. Peñalver, Joseph William Singer, and Laura S. Underkuffler, 'A Statement of Progressive Property' (2009) 94 Cornell Law Review.

Allen, Danielle, *Talking to Strangers: Anxieties of Citizenship since Brown v. Board of Education* (University of Chicago Press 2004).

Alter, Karen J., 'Private Litigants and the New International Courts' (2006) 39 Comparative Political Studies 22–49.

Alvarez, José E., 'Why are we "Re-calibrating" our Investment Treaties?' (2010) 4 World Arbitration and Mediation Review 143–61.

Alvarez, José E. 'Is Investor-State Arbitration "Public"?' (2016) 7 Journal of International Dispute Settlement 534–76.

Alvarez, José E., 'The Human Right of Property' (2018) 72 University of Miami Law Review 580–705.

Alvarez, José E. and Kathryn Khamsi 'The Argentine Crisis and Foreign Investors. A Glimpse into the Heart of the Investment Regime' in Karl P. Sauvant (ed.), *Yearbook on International Investment Law and Policy 2008/2009* (OUP 2009) 379–478.

Alvarez, José E. and Tegan Brink, 'Revisiting the Necessity Defense: Continental Casualty v. Argentina' in Karl P. Sauvant (ed.), *Yearbook on International Investment Law & Policy 2010-2011* (OUP 2012) 319–62.

Alvik, Ivar, *Contracting with Sovereignty: State Contracts and International Arbitration* (Hart 2011).

Alvord, Ellsworth C., Letter to Theodore Francis Green, Chairman, Senate Committee on Foreign Relations, 30 July 1957, in The Joint Committee on Internal Revenue Taxation, Legislative History of United States Tax Conventions (1962).

Anaya, James, *Indigenous Peoples in International Law* (OUP 2004).

Anderson, Chandler P., 'Basis of the Law against Confiscating Foreign-Owned Property' (1927) 21 American Journal of International Law 525–33.

Andrade A., Pablo, 'The Government of Nature: Post-Neoliberal Environmental Governance in Bolivia and Ecuador' in Fabio De Castro, Barbara Hogenboom, and Michiel Baud (eds.), *Environmental Governance in Latin America* (Palgrave 2016) 113–36.

Anghie, Anthony, *Imperialism, Sovereignty and the Making of International Law* (CUP 2005).

Arato, Julian, 'Corporations as Lawmakers' (2015) 56 Harvard International Law Journal 229–95.

Arato, Julian, 'The Private Law Critique of International Investment Law' (2019) 113 American Journal of International Law 1–53.

Assies, Willem and Emilio Duhau, 'Land Tenure and Tenure Regimes in Mexico: An Overview' in Janine M. Ubink, André J. Hoekema, and Willem J. Assies (eds.), *Legalising Land Rights. Local Practices, State Responses and Tenure Security in Africa, Asia and Latin America* (Leiden University Press 2009) 355–86.

Baer, Werner and Gabriel Montes-Rojas, 'From Privatization to Re-nationalization: What Went Wrong with Privatizations in Argentina?' (2008) 36 Oxford Development Studies 323–37.

Baker, Edgar R., 'Preface' in James Daniel (ed.), *Private Investment: The Key to International Industrial Development: A Report of the San Francisco Conference, October 14–18, 1957* (McGraw Hill 1958).

Baker, Robert L. (ed.), *Business Leadership in a Changing World; a report of the International Industrial Conference in San Francisco, September 11–15, 1961* (McGraw Hill 1962).

Bakker, Karen, *Privatizing Water: Governance Failure and the World's Urban Water Crisis* (Cornell University Press 2010).

Baldwin, Richard, *The Great Convergence: Information Technology and the New Globalization* (Harvard University Press 2016).

Ball, George W., 'The Role of Lawyers in the International Investment Field' (1959–1960) 11 Virginia Law Weekly 1–9.

Bant, Elise and Michael Bryan, 'Fact, Future and Fiction: Risk and Reasonable Reliance in Estoppel' (2015) 35 Oxford Journal of Legal Studies 427–52.

Barnet, Richard and Ronald Muller, 'Global Reach: The Power of the Multinational Corporations' (Simon and Schuster 1974).

Barnett, Randy E., 'The Death of Reliance' (1996) 46 Journal of Legal Education 518–36.

Barrère, Christian, 'Judicial System and Property Rights' in Enrico Colombatto (ed.), *The Elgar Companion to the Economics of Property Rights* (Edward Elgar Publishing 2006) 129–53.

Battle, Gordon, 'The Two Fundamental Concepts of Arbitration and Their Relation to Rules of Law' (1930) 16 Virginia Law Review 255–60.

Baxi, Upendra, *The Future of Human Rights* (OUP 2006).

Bebbington, Anthony, 'Extractive industries, socio-environmental conflicts and political economic transformations in Andean America' in Anthony Bebbington (ed.), *Social Conflict, Economic Development and Extractive Industry: Evidence from South America* (Routledge 2012) 3–26.

Becker, Loftus, 'Just Compensation in Expropriation Cases: Decline and Partial Recovery' Speech before the American Society of International Law, 1958, in Society to Advance the Protection of Foreign Investments, Convention on Investments Abroad with Comments, Speeches and New Literature, Publication No. 3 (Bergisch Gladbach, J. Heider 1960) 68–80.

Bejarano González, Fernando, 'El conflicto del basurero tóxico de Metalclad en Guadalcázar, San Luis Potosí' in Laura Carlsen, Timothy A. Wise, and Hilda Salazar (eds.), *Enfrentando la globalización: respuestas sociales a la integración económica de México* (Porrúa 2003) 27–54.

Bell, Abraham and Gideon Parchomovsky, 'Givings' (2001) 111 Yale Law Journal 547–618.

Bentham, Jeremy, *The Theory of Legislation* (Trübner & Co. 1864).

Bergsten, C. Fred, 'Globalizing Free Trade' (1996) 75 Foreign Affairs 105–20.

Berkeley, Bill, 'Zaire: An African Horror Story' The Atlantic, August 1993.

Bjorklund, Andrea K., 'Improving the International Investment Law and Policy System. Report of the Rapporteur. Second Columbia International Investment Conference: What's Next in International Investment Law and Policy?' in José E. Alvarez, Karl P. Sauvant with Kamil Ahmed and Gabriela Vizcaino (eds.), *The Evolving International Investment Regime: Expectations, Realities, Options* (OUP) 213–46.

Black, Eugene R., 'The World Bank, An Appraisal of its Activities' (1959–1960) 11 Virginia Law Weekly 16–20.

Black, Eugene R., 'Address to the Annual Meeting of the Board of Governors, September 1961' in ICSID, Convention on the Settlement of Investment Disputes between States. Documents Concerning the Origin and the Formulation of the Convention, vol. II, Part 1 (World Bank 1968).

Black, F. M., 'Memorandum: Roundtable of Private Foreign Investment in Latin America' OECD FMB/878, 27 February 1973 (Edwin Martin Personal Papers, The John F. Kennedy Library, Box 37).

Blanpain, Roger, *The OECD Guidelines for Multinational Enterprises and Labour Relations, 1976-1979: Experience and Review* (Springer 1979).

Blomley, Nicholas, 'Landscapes of Property' (1998) 32 Law & Society Review 567–612.

Bonnitcha, Jonathan, *Substantive Protection under Investment Treaties* (CUP 2014).

Bonnitcha, Jonathan, Lauge N. Skovgaard Poulsen, and Michael Waibel, *The Political Economy of the Investment Treaty Regime* (OUP 2017).

Bonnitcha, Jonathan and Zoe Phillips Williams, 'State Liability for "Politically" Motivated Conduct in the Investment Treaty Regime' (2020) 33 Leiden Journal of International Law 77–100.

Boumédiène, Houari 'Declaration and Programme of Action on the Establishment of a New International Economic Order' UN General Assembly Official Record, 6th Special Sess., prov. verbatim rec. A/PV.2208 (10 April 1974).

Brierly, James Leslie, *The Law of Nations* (OUP 1963).

Brinkley, Alan, *The Publisher: Henry Luce and his American century* (Knopf 2010).

Broad, Robin, 'Corporate Bias in the World Bank Group's International Centre for Settlement of Investment Disputes: A Case Study of a Global Mining Corporation

Suing El Salvador' (2014) 36 University of Pennsylvania Journal of International Law 851–74.

Broches, Aron, 'Problems of Private Foreign Investment' Speech before the Third Annual Institute on Corporate Counsel, devoted to foreign Operations of American Enterprises, Fordham University School of Law, 8 December 1961 (Broches, M. Aron—Articles and Speeches (1951–1982)—vol. 1) (1651418) World Bank Group Archives, Washington, DC, United States.

Broches, Aron, 'The Present Need for a Permanent Arbitral Tribunal' Address at the Institute on Permanent International Courts organized by the Minnesota State Bar Association, 13 June 1962 (Broches, M. Aron—Articles and Speeches (1951–1982)—vol. 1) (1651418) World Bank Group Archives, Washington DC, United States.

Broches, Aron, *Selected Essays: World Bank, ICSID and other Subjects of Public and Private International Law* (Martinus Nijhoff Publishers 1995).

Brower, Charles N. and John B. Tepe, 'The Charter of Economic Rights and Duties of States: A Reflection or Rejection of International Law?' (1975) International Lawyer 295–318.

Brower, Charles N. and Sarah Melikian, '"We Have Met The Enemy And He Is US!" Is the Industrialized North "Going South" on Investor-State Arbitration?' (2015) Arbitration International 19–26.

Brown, Wendy, *Undoing the Demos: Neoliberalism's Stealth Revolution* (Zone Books 2015).

Bull, Benedicte and Mariel Aguilar-Støen, 'Changing Elites, Institutions and Environmental Governance' in Fabio De Castro, Barbara Hogenboom, and Michiel Baud (eds.), *Environmental Governance in Latin America* (Palgrave 2016) 137–63.

Busse, Matthias, Jens Königer, and Peter Nunnenkamp, 'FDI Promotion through Bilateral Investment Treaties: More than a BIT?' (2010) 146 Review of World Economics 147–77.

Cameron, Peter D. and Michael C. Stanley, *Oil, Gas, and Mining: A Sourcebook for Understanding the Extractive Industries* (World Bank 2017).

Cantegreil, Julien, 'The Audacity of the Texaco/Calasiatic Award: René-Jean Dupuy and the Internationalization of Foreign Investment Law' (2011) 22 European Journal of International Law 441–58.

Capling, Ann and Kim R. Nossal, 'The Rise and Fall of Chapter 11: Investor-State Dispute Mechanisms in the North American Free Trade Agreement and the Australia–United States Free Trade Agreement' Paper prepared for the Oceanic Conference on International Studies, Australian National University, July 2004, 26–7.

Cavallo, Domingo F., 'Lessons from Argentina's Privatization Experience' (1997) 50 Journal of International Affairs 459–74.

Chang, Ha-Joon, 'Intellectual Property Rights and Economic Development: Historical Lessons and Emerging Issues' (2001) 2 Journal of Human Development 287–309.

Chang, Ha-Joon, 'Regulation of Foreign Investment in Historical Perspective' (2004) 16 European Journal of Development Research 687–715.

Chang, Seung Wha, Farewell Speech at the WTO Dispute Settlement Body, 26 September 2016, available at https://www.wto.org/english/news_e/news16_e/changfarwellspeech_e.pdf (last visited 29 September 2020).

Charlotin, Damien, 'In Now-Public Isolux v. Spain Award, Measures That Later Breached Investor Protections in Eiser Case Were not Deemed to Breach Isolux's Legitimate Expectations' IAReporter, 29 June 2017.

Chernykh, Yuliya, 'The Gust of Wind: the Unknown Role of Sir Elihu Lauterpacht in the Drafting of the Abs-Shawcross Draft Convention' in Stephan W. Schill, Christian J. Tams,

and Rainer Hofmann (eds.), *International Investment Law and History* (Edward Elgar Publishing 2018) 241–85.
Chimni, Bhupinder, 'International Institutions Today: An Imperial Global State in the Making' (2004) 15 European Journal of International Law 1–37.
Clapp, Jennifer, 'Seeping through the Regulatory Cracks' (2002) 22 SAIS Review 141–55.
Cohen, Morris, 'Property and Sovereignty' (1927) 13 Cornell Law Quarterly 8–30.
Cohen, Stephen, *Multinational Corporations and Foreign Direct Investment: Avoiding Simplicity, Embracing Complexity* (OUP 2007).
Cointe, Béatrice and Alain Nadaï, *Feed-in Tariffs in the European Union: Renewable Energy Policy, the Internal Electricity Market and Economic Expertise* (Palgrave 2018).
Cole, Daniel H. and Peter Z. Grossman, 'The Meaning of Property Rights: Law Versus Economics?' (2002) 78 Land Economics 317–30.
Colen, Liesbeth and Andrea Guariso, 'What Type of FDI is Attracted by BITs' in Olivier de Schutter, Johan Swinnen, and Jan Wouters (eds.), *Foreign Direct Investment and Human Development: The Law and Economics of International Investment Agreements* (Routledge 2013) 138–56.
Colen, Liesbeth, Miet Maertens, and Johan Swinnen, 'Foreign Direct Investment as an Engine for Economic Growth and Human Development: A Review of the Arguments and Empirical Evidence' in Olivier De Schutter, Johan Swinnen, and Jan Wouters (eds.), *Foreign Direct Investment and Human Development* (Routledge 2012) 70–115.
Collins, Hugh, 'Regulating Contract Law' in Christine Parker, Colin Scott, Nicola Lacey, and John Braithwaite (eds.), *Regulating Law* (OUP 2004) 13–32.
Comeaux, Paul E. and N. Stephen Kinsella, 'Reducing Political Risk in Developing Countries: Bilateral Treaties, Stabilization Clauses and MIGA and OPIC Investment Insurance' (1994) 15 New York Law School Journal of International and Comparative Law 1–48.
Correa, Carlos M., 'Public Health and Intellectual Property Rights' (2002) 2 Global Social Policy 261–78.
Cotula, Lorenzo, *Human Rights, Natural Resource and Investment Law in a Globalised World: Shades of Grey in the Shadow of the Law* (Routledge 2012).
Cotula, Lorenzo, 'The New Enclosures? Polanyi, International Investment Law and the Global Land Rush' (2013) 34 Third World Quarterly 1605–29.
Cotula, Lorenzo, 'Land, Property and Sovereignty in International Law' (2016) 25 Cardozo Journal of International & Comparative Law 219–86.
Cotula, Lorenzo, 'The State of Exception and the Law of the Global Economy: A Conceptual and Empirico-Legal Inquiry' (2017) 8 Transnational Legal Theory 424–54.
Cotula, Lorenzo and Mika Schröder, 'Community Perspectives in Investor-State Arbitration' (2017) International Institute for Environment and Development, available at https://pubs.iied.org/12603IIED/ (last visited 16 May 2020).
Craig, Paul P., 'Substantive Legitimate Expectations in Domestic and Community Law' (1996) 55 Cambridge Law Journal 289–312.
Crawford, James, *Brownlie's Principles of Public International Law* (OUP 2012).
Crosbie, Eric, Particia Sosa and Stanton A. Glantz, 'Defending Strong Tobacco Packaging and Labelling Regulations in Uruguay: Transnational Tobacco Control Network Versus Philip Morris International' (2018) 27 Tobacco Control 185–194.
Cutler, Claire, 'Artifice, Ideology and Paradox: The Public/Private Distinction in International Law' (1997) 4 Review of International Political Economy 261–85.
Cutler, Claire A., *Private Power and Global Authority: Transnational Merchant Law in the Global Political Economy* (CUP 2003).

Cutler, Claire A., 'Transformations in Statehood, the Investor-State Regime, and the New Constitutionalism' (2016) 23 Indiana Journal of Global Legal Studies 95–125.

D'Amico, Linda 'El Agua es Vida/Water Is Life': Community Watershed Reserves in Intag, Ecuador, and Emerging Ecological Identities' in Barbara Rose Johnston, Lisa Hiwasaki, Irene J. Klaver, Ameyali Ramos Castillo, and Veronica Strang (eds.), *Water, Cultural Diversity, and Global Environmental Change: Emerging Trends, Sustainable Futures?* (Springer 2012) 433–43.

Dagan, Hanoch, 'Reimagining Takings Law' in Gregory S. Alexander and Eduardo M. Peñalver (eds.), *Property and Community* (OUP 2010) 39–56.

Dagdeviren, Hulya, 'Political Economy of Contractual Disputes in Private Water and Sanitation: Lessons from Argentina' (2011) 82 Annals of Public and Cooperative Economics 25–44.

De Schutter, Olivier, 'The Challenge of Imposing Human Rights Norms on Corporate Actors' in Olivier De Schutter (ed.), *Transnational Corporations and Human Rights* (Hart 2006) 1–40.

De Zwart, Pim, *Globalization and the Colonial Origins of the Great Divergence: Intercontinental Trade and Living Standards in the Dutch East India Company's Commercial Empire, c. 1600-1800* (Brill 2016).

Del Rio, Jorge, *Política argentina y monopolios eléctricos* (Cátedra Lisandro de la Torre 1957).

Del Rio, Jorge, *Electricidad y liberación nacional. El caso S.E.G.B.A.* (Peña Lillo 1960).

Desbordes, Rodolphe and Julien Vauday, 'The Political Influence of Foreign Firms in Developing Countries' (2007) 19 Economics & Politics 421–51.

Desierto, Diane A., 'Necessity and Supplementary Means of Interpretation for Non-Precluded Measures in Bilateral Investment Treaties' (2009) University of Pennsylvania Journal of International Law 31 (2009) 827–934.

Dezalay, Yves and Bryant G. Garth, *Dealing in Virtue: International Commercial Arbitration and the Construction of a Transnational Legal Order* (University of Chicago Press 1996).

Dezalay, Yves and Bryant G. Garth, 'Introduction: Lawyers, Law, and Society' in Yves Dezalay and Bryant G. Garth (eds.), *Lawyers and the Rule of Law in an Era of Globalization* (Routledge 2011) 1–16.

Die Zeit, 'Vermögensschutz' (5 April 1956).

Die Zeit, 'Eigentum ist auch bei uns nicht sicher' (13 July 1979).

Diebold, Nicolas F., *Non-Discrimination in International Trade in Services: 'Likeness' in WTO/GATS* (CUP 2010).

Dillon, Douglas, 'The Role of Private Capital in US Foreign Policy' (1959–1960) 11 Virginia Law Weekly 10–15.

Doelle, Meinhard, 'The Bilcon NAFTA Tribunal: A Clash of Investor Protection and Sustainability-Based Environmental Assessments' in Stanley D Berger (ed.), *Key Developments in Environmental Law* (Thomson Reuters 2017) 99–123.

Dolzer, Rudolf and Margrete Stevens, *Bilateral Investment Treaties* (Martinus Nijhoff Publishers 1995).

Dolzer, Rudolf, 'Indirect Expropriations: New Developments' (2002) 11 New York University Environmental Law Journal 64–93.

Dolzer, Rudolf and Christoph Schreuer, *Principles of International Investment Law* (OUP 2012).

Donaldson, David J. and Dileep M. Wagle, *Privatization: Principles and Practice* (International Finance Corporation—World Bank 1995).

Douglas, Zachary, 'The Hybrid Foundations of Investment Treaty Arbitration' (2003) 74 British Yearbook of International Law 151–289.

Douglas, Zachary, 'Nothing if not Critical for Investment Treaty Arbitration: Occidental, Eureko and. Methanex' (2006) 22 Arbitration International 27–52.
Drahos, Peter and John Braithwaite, 'Intellectual Property, Corporate Strategy, Globalisation: TRIPS in Context' (2001) 20 Wisconsin International Law Journal 451–80.
Drahos, Peter and John Braithwaite, *Information Feudalism: Who Owns the Knowledge Economy?* (Earthscan 2002).
Drajem, Mark and Christopher Donville, 'Methanex Says California Additive Ban Illegal under NAFTA Rules' (2004) Institute for Agriculture and Trade Policy, 7 June 2004, available at https://www.iatp.org/news/methanex-says-california-additive-ban-illegal-under-nafta-rules (last visited 25 May 2020).
Duarte Tagles, Héctor F., 'CYTRAR: Detrás de los Residuos Peligrosos en Sonora' (2003) 13 Acta Universitaria (2003) 14–21.
Duncan, Val, 'The International Company and Overseas Investment' in The Institute of Economic Affairs, 'Overseas Investment or Economic Nationalism?' (1967) Occasional paper No. 15, 18–25.
Dupuy, Pierre-Marie and Julie Maupin, 'Of Wit, Wisdom, and Balance in International Law. Reflections on the Tokyo Resolution of the Institut de Droit International' in David Caron, Stephan W. Schill, Abby Cohen Smutny, and Epaminontas E. Triantafilou (eds.), *Practising Virtue: Inside International Arbitration* (OUP 2016) 706–21.
Dupuy, René-Jean, *Dialectiques du droit international: souveraineté des États, communauté internationale et droits de l'humanité* (Pedone 1999).
Eden, Lorraine, Stefanie Lenway, and Douglas A. Schuler, 'From the Obsolescing Bargain to the Political Bargaining Model' in Robert Grosse (ed.), *International Business and Government Relations in the 21st Century* (CUP 2005) 251–72.
Eisenhower, Dwight D., 'A World of Growth, a World of Law' Speech at Delhi University 1959, in Society to Advance the Protection of Foreign Investments, Convention on Investments Abroad with Comments, Speeches and New Literature, Publication No. 3 (Bergisch Gladbach, J. Heider 1960) 31–2.
Evans, Peter B., *Embedded Autonomy: States and Industrial Transformation* (Princeton University Press 2012).
Evans, Sterling, *The Green Republic: A Conservation History of Costa Rica* (University of Texas Press 2010).
Faber, Daniel, *Capitalizing on Environmental Injustice: The Polluter-Industrial Complex in the Age of Globalization* (Rowman & Littlefield Publishers 2008).
Fanon, Franz, *A Dying Colonialism* (Haakon Chevalier, trans) (Grove Press 1965 [1959]).
Fanon, Franz, *The Wretched of the Earth* (C. Farrington, trans) (Grove Press 1968 [1961]).
Fatouros, A. A., 'An International Code to Protect Private Investment-Proposals and Perspectives' (1961) 14 University of Toronto Law Journal 77–102.
Fischel, William, *Regulatory Takings: Law, Economics, and Politics* (Harvard University Press 1995).
Fitzmaurice, Andrew, *Sovereignty, Property and Empire, 1500–2000* (CUP 2014).
Forsyth, Christopher, 'Legitimate Expectations Revisited' (2011) 16 Judicial Review 429–39.
Foucault, Michel, *The Birth of Biopolitics: Lectures at The Collège de France, 1978–1979* (Palgrave 2010).
Fraser, Nancy, *Scales of Justice: Reimagining Political Space in a Globalizing World* (Columbia University Press 2010).
Fraser, Nancy and Axel Honneth, *Redistribution or Recognition?: A Political-Philosophical Exchange* (Verso 2003).

Fredriksson, Per G. (ed.), 'Trade, Global policy, and the Environment' (1999) World Bank Discussion Paper No. 402, available at http://documents.worldbank.org/curated/en/581201468277743126/pdf/multi-page.pdf (last visited 25 May 2020).

Gaillard, Emmanuelle, 'Chronique des sentences arbitrales—Centre International pour le Règlement des Différends Relatifs aux Investissements (CIRDI)' (2008) 1 Journal du droit international 311–64.

García Amador, F. V., 'Fourth Report on State Responsibility by Mr F.V. Garcia-Amador, Special Rapporteur' [1959] Yearbook of the International Law Commission, vol. 2 (A/CN.4/119, 1959) 1–35.

Gaud, William S., 'Private Foreign Investment in the 70s' (1972) Annual Meeting of the Association Internationale pour la Promotion et la Protection des Investissements Privés en Territoires Étrangers, Munich, 31 October 1972 (Gaud William S.—Articles and Speeches (1969–1973)—vol. 02) (1651742) World Bank Group Archives, Washington, DC, United States.

Gazzini, Tarcisio, 'Bilateral Investment Treaties and Sustainable Development' (2014) 15 Journal of World Investment & Trade 929–63.

Geppert, Mike and Christoph Dörrenbächer 'Politics and Power in the Multinational Corporation: An Introduction' in Mike Dörrenbächer and Mike Geppert (eds.), *Politics and Power in the Multinational Corporation: The Role of Institutions, Interests and Identities* (CUP 2011) 3–38.

Gilens, Martin and Benjamin I. Page, 'Testing Theories of American Politics: Elites, Interest groups, and Average Citizens' (2014) 12 Perspectives on Politics 564–81.

Ginsburg, Tom, 'International Substitutes for Domestic Institutions: Bilateral Investment Treaties and Governance' (2005) 25 International Review of Law and Economics 107–23.

Gold, Andrew, 'A Property Theory of Contract' (2009) 103 Northwestern University Law Review 1–62.

Goldberg, Paul M. and Charles P. Kindleberger, 'Toward a GATT for Investment: A Proposal for Supervision of the International Corporation' (1970) 2 Law and Policy in International Business 295–325.

Goodman, Nelson, *Ways of Worldmaking* (Hackett Publishing 1978).

Greene, James, *The Search for Common Ground; A Survey of Efforts to Develop Codes of Behavior in International Investment: A Special Report to the U.S. Committee*, Pacific Basin Council (The Conference Board 1971).

Haight, George W. 'Activities of the International Chamber of Commerce and other Business Groups' (1960) 54 Proceedings of the American Society of International Law at Its Annual Meeting 200–205.

Haight, G. W., 'The New International Economic Order and the Charter of Economic Rights and Duties of States' (1975) 9 International Lawyer 591–604.

Hale, Thomas, *Between Interests and Law: The Politics of Transnational Commercial Disputes* (CUP 2015).

Hamilton, Lee H. and Daniel K. Inouye, *Report of the Congressional Committees Investigating the Iran/Contra Affair* (U.S. House of Representatives Select Committee to Investigate Covert Arms Transactions with Iran, U.S. Senate Select Committee on Secret Military Assistance to Iran and the Nicaraguan Opposition 1987).

Hann, C. M., 'Introduction: The Embeddedness of Property' in C. M. Hann (ed.), *Property Relations: Renewing The Anthropological Tradition* (CUP 1998) 1–47.

Harvey, David, *The New Imperialism* (OUP 2003).

Haselip, James, 'Renegotiating Electricity Contracts after an Economic Crisis and Currency Devaluation: The Case of Argentina' (2005) 18 Electricity Journal 78–88.

Haselip, James, Isaac Dyner, and Judith Cherni, 'Electricity Market Reform in Argentina: Assessing the Impact for the Poor in Buenos Aires' (2005) 13 Utilities Policy (2005) 1–14.
Hayek, Friedrich A., *The Constitution of Liberty* (University of Chicago Press 1978 [1960]).
Heidenreich, Martin, 'The Social Embeddedness of Multinational Companies: A Literature Review' (2012) 10 Socio-Economic Review 549–79.
Henckels, Caroline, *Proportionality and Deference in Investor-State Arbitration* (CUP 2015).
Hepburn, Jarrod, 'Argentina Re-opens Arbitrator Ethics Issues in Bid to Set-Aside Water Concessions Award' IAReporter, 3 August 2015.
Hirsch, Moshe, 'Investment Tribunals and Human Rights Treaties: A Sociological Perspective' in Freya Baetens (ed.), *Investment Law within International Law: Integrationist Perspectives* (CUP 2013) 85–105.
Ho, Jean, *State Responsibility for Breaches of Investment Contracts* (CUP 2018).
Hodgson, Mélida and Melissa Stewart, 'Experts in Investor-State Arbitration: The Tribunal as Gatekeeper' 9 (2018) Journal of International Dispute Settlement 453–463.
Horwitz, Morton J., *The Transformation of American Law, 1780-1860* (Harvard University Press 1977).
Hufbauer, Gary Clyde and Jeffrey J. Schott, *NAFTA Revisited: Achievements and Challenges* (Peterson Institute 2005).
Huhtanen, Tomi, 'Europe and Green Growth: the Key to Recovery?' in Robert Schuman Foundation (ed.), *State of the Union 2010: Schuman Report on Europe* (Springer 2010) 91–8.
Hyde, Charles C., *International Law Chiefly as Interpreted and Applied by the United States* (Fred B. Rothman & Co 1983 [1947]), vol. 1, 650.
Hynning, Clifford J., 'The World Banks' plan for the Settlement of International Investment Disputes' (1965) 51 American Bar Association Journal 558-63.
Idrovo, Alvaro J., 'Cerro Matoso Mine, Chemical Mixtures, and Environmental Justice in Colombia' (2018) 391 The Lancet 2320.
Jacobs, David, *Renewable Energy Policy Convergence in the EU: The Evolution of Feed-in Tariffs in Germany, Spain and France* (Ashgate 2012).
Jacott, Marisa, Cyrus Reed, and Mark Winfield. 'The Generation and Management of Hazardous Wastes and Transboundary Hazardous Waste Shipments between Mexico, Canada and the United States Since NAFTA: A 2004 Update' (2004) Texas Center for Policy Studies, available at http://www.texascenter.org/publications/hazwaste04.pdf (last visited 2 July 2020).
James, Paul, 'The Social Imaginary in Theory and Practice' in Chris Hudson and Erin K. Wilson (eds.), *Revisiting the Global Imaginary* (Palgrave 2019) 33–48.
Jandhyala, Srividya, Witold J. Henisz, and Edward D. Mansfield, 'Three Waves of BITs: The Global Diffusion of Foreign Investment Policy' (2011) 55 Journal of Conflict Resolution 1047–73.
Jenner, Steffen, Gabriel Chan, Rolf Frankenberger, and Mathias Gabel, 'What Drives States to Support Renewable Energy?' (2012) 33 Energy Journal 1–12.
Jennings, Robert Y., 'State Contracts in International Law' (1961) 37 British Yearbook of International Law 156–82.
Jiménez, Georgina and Jorge Campanini, 'Mallku K: Breve cronología del conflicto minero en Mallku Khota' (29 August 2012) Petropress–CEDIB 24–37.
Johnson, Lise, 'Case Note: How Chevron v. Ecuador is Pushing the Boundaries of Arbitral Authority' 13 April 2012, Investment Treaty News, available at https://www.iisd.org/itn/

2012/04/13/case-note-how-chevron-v-ecuador-is-pushing-the-boundaries-of-arbitral-authority/ (last visited 6 June 2020).

Kaufmann-Kohler, Gabrielle, 'Arbitral Precedent: Dream, Necessity or Excuse?: The 2006 Freshfields Lecture' (2007) 23 Arbitration International 357–78.

Kennedy, David, 'The "Rule of Law," Political Choices, and Development Common Sense' in David M. Trubek and Alvaro Santos (eds.), *The New Law and Economic Development: A Critical Appraisal* (CUP 2006) 95–173.

Kennedy, David, 'Some Caution about Property Rights as a Recipe for Economic Development' (2011) 1 Accounting, Economics, and Law (article 3).

Kennedy, David, *A World of Struggle: How Power, Law, and Expertise Shape Global Political Economy* (Princeton University Press 2016).

Kennedy, Duncan, 'The Stakes of Law, or Hale and Foucault!' (1991) 15 Legal Studies Forum 327–66.

Kennedy, Duncan, *A Critique of Adjudication [fin de siècle]* (Harvard University Press 1997).

Kennedy, Duncan, 'The Political Stakes in "Merely Technical" Issues of Contract Law' (2001) 1 European Review of Private Law 7–28.

Kiguel, Miguel, 'Argentina's 2001 Economic and Financial Crisis: Lessons for Europe' in (2011) Beyond Macroeconomic Policy Coordination Discussions in the G-20, 7–9, 7, available at https://www.brookings.edu/wp-content/uploads/2016/06/11_think_tank_20.pdf (last visited 4 June 2020).

Kimerling, Judith, 'Indigenous Peoples and the Oil Frontier in Amazonia: The Case of Ecuador, Chevron Texaco, and Aguinda v. Texaco' (2006) 38 New York University Journal of International Law And Politics 413–664.

Kingsbury, Benedict, '"Indigenous Peoples" in International Law: A Constructivist Approach to the Asian Controversy' (1998) 92 American Journal of International Law 414–57.

Korngold, Gerald and Andrew Morriss, 'Introduction: The Story of Property Stories' in Gerald Korngold and Andrew Morriss (eds.), *Property Stories* (Foundation Press 2009) 1–8.

Koskenniemi, Martti, 'International Law and the Emergence of Mercantile Capitalism: Grotius to Smith' in Pierre-Marie Dupuy and Vincent Chetail (eds.), *The Roots of International Law/Les fondements du droit international: Liber Amicorum Peter Haggenmacher* (Martinus Nijhoff Publishers 2013) 3–37.

Koskenniemi, Martti, 'It's Not the Cases, It's the System' (2017) 18 Journal of World Investment & Trade 343–53.

Kostova, Tatiana and Kendall Roth 'Adoption of Organizational Practice by Subsidiaries of Multinational Corporations: Institutional and Relational Effects' (2002) 45 Academy of Management Journal 215–33.

Kraske, Jochen, *Bankers with a Mission: The Presidents of the World Bank, 1946-91* (World Bank 1996).

Kreitner, Roy, *Calculating Promises: The Emergence of Modern American Contract Doctrine* (Stanford University Press 2006).

Kurtz, Jürgen, 'Adjudging the Exceptional at International Investment Law: Security, Public Order and Financial Crisis' (2010) 59 International & Comparative Law Quarterly 325–71.

Kurtz, Jürgen, *The WTO and International Investment Law: Converging Systems* (CUP 2016).

Lalive, Pierre A., 'The Doctrine of Acquired Rights' in International and Comparative Law Center, Southwester Legal Foundation, *Rights and Duties of Private Investors Abroad* (M. Bender 1965) 145–200.

Lando, Ole, 'The Law Applicable to the Merits of the Dispute' in Peter Šarčević (ed.), *Essays on International Commercial Arbitration* (Martinus Nijhoff Publishers 1989) 129–59.

Lang, Andrew, *World Trade Law After Neoliberalism: Re-imagining the Global Economic Order* (OUP 2011).

Langford, Malcolm and Daniel Behn, 'Managing Backlash: The Evolving Investment Treaty Arbitrator?' (2018) 29 European Journal of International Law 551–80.

Latif, Mohamed Bin Abdul and Bin Mohamed Almulhim, *Middle East Oil: A Redistribution of Values Arising from the Oil Industry* (University Press of America 2009).

Lauterpacht, Elihu, 'Organisation for European Economic Co-operation. Summary of Mr Lauterpacht's Explanations' in Society to Advance the Protection of Foreign Investments, Convention on Investments Abroad with Comments, Speeches and New Literature, Publication No. 3 (Bergisch Gladbach, J. Heider 1960) 19–28.

Lauterpacht, Elihu, 'International Law and Private Foreign Investment' (1997) 4 Indiana Journal of Global Legal Studies 259–76.

Lauterpacht, Hersch, *The Function of Law in the International Community* (OUP 2011 [1933]).

Le Gouill, Claude, 'Mining Imaginaries and Social Conflicts in Bolivia: A Multilevel Approach to the Mallku Khota Conflict' (2016) 82 Cahiers des Amériques Latines 49–69.

Lehavi, Amnon, 'The Global Law of The Land' (2010) 81 University of Colorado Law Review 425–71.

Leiter-Bockley, Andrea, *Making the World Safe for Investment: The Protection of Foreign Property 1922-1959* (2019) Doctoral thesis, University of Melbourne & University of Vienna.

Leonhardsen, Erlend, 'Looking for Legitimacy: Exploring Proportionality Analysis in Investment Treaty Arbitration' (2012) 3 Journal of International Dispute Settlement 95–136.

Lew, Julian D. M., 'Achieving the Dream: Autonomous Arbitration' (2006) 22 Arbitration International 179–203.

Li, Quan, 'Outlier, Measurement, and the Democracy-FDI Controversy' (2009) 4 Quarterly Journal of Political Science 167–81.

Li, Quan and Adam Resnick, 'Reversal of Fortunes: Democratic Institutions and Foreign Direct Investment Inflows to Developing Countries' (2003) 57 International organization 175–211.

Life Magazine, 'Editorial: A Good Idea for Foreign Investment' 28 October 1957.

Lim, Chin Leng, Jean Ho, and Martins Paparinskis, *International Investment Law and Arbitration: Commentary, Awards and other Materials* (CUP 2018).

Linarelli, John, Margot Salomon, and Muthucumaraswamy Sornarajah, *The Misery of International Law: Confrontations with Injustice in the Global Economy* (OUP 2018).

Llewellyn, Karl, *Jurisprudence: Realism in Theory and Practice* (Transaction Publishers 2000).

Love, James, 'Access to Medicine and Compliance with the WTO TRIPS Accord: Models for State Practice in Developing Countries' in Peter Drahos and Ruth Mayne (eds.), *Global Intellectual Property Rights: Knowledge, Access and Development* (Palgrave 2002) 74–89.

Luce, Henry R., 'The Way of the Law: The Road to the Mountain of Vision' (1959) 45 American Bar Association Journal 482-525.

Luce, Henry, 'Peace through Law' Speech before the International Chamber of Commerce, 1959 Washington Congress, in Society to Advance the Protection of Foreign Investments, Convention on Investments Abroad with Comments, Speeches and New Literature, Publication No. 3 (Bergisch Gladbach, J. Heider 1960) 36–40.

Luna, Félix, *Alvear: Las luchas populares en la década del 30* (Schapire 1975).

Luo, Yadong, 'Toward a Cooperative View of MNC–Host Government Relations: Building Blocks and Performance Implications' (2001) 32 Journal of International Business Studies 401–19.

Macpherson, C. B., 'The Meaning of Property' in C. B. Macpherson (ed.), *Property, Mainstream and Critical Positions* (University of Toronto Press 1978) 1–14.

Mahr, Krista, 'Sri Lanka to Start Tally of Civil-War Dead' *Time Magazine*, 28 November 2013.

Maine, Henry Sumner, *Ancient Law: Its Connection with the Early History of Society and its Relation to Modern Ideas* (J. M. Dent & Sons Ltd. 1917 [1861]).

Mann, F. A., 'State Contracts and State Responsibility' (1960) 54 American Journal of International Law 572–91.

Mann, Howard, 'The Final Decision in Methanex v. United States: Some New wine in Some New Bottles' (2005) International Institute for Sustainable Development, available at https://www.iisd.org/sites/default/files/publications/commentary_methanex.pdf (last visited 25 May 2020).

Manning, Paul, *Martin Bormann, Nazi in Exile* (Stuart 1981).

Marcoux, Jean-Michel, *International Investment Law and Globalization: Foreign Investment, Responsibilities and Intergovernmental Organizations* (Routledge 2018).

Marsh, Norman S., 'A Note on the European Convention for the Protection of Human Rights and Fundamental Freedoms, 1950, in Relation to the Protection of Property' in Joseph G. Starke (ed.), *The Protection and Encouragement of Private Foreign Investment* (Butterworths 1966) 137–40.

Mathur, Aparna and Kartikeya Singh, 'Foreign Direct Investment, Corruption and Democracy' (2013) 45 Applied Economics 991–1002.

McKern, Bruce, 'Transnational Corporations and the Exploitation of Natural Resources' in UNCTAD, *Transnational Corporations and World Development* (Thomson Business Press 1996) 327–58.

McLachlan, Campbell, 'Investment Treaties and General International Law' (2008) 57 International and Comparative Law Quarterly 361–401.

Mendonça, Miguel, *Feed-in Tariffs: Accelerating the Deployment of Renewable Energy* (Earthscan 2007).

Merino, Roger, 'Re-politicizing Participation or Reframing Environmental Governance? Beyond Indigenous' Prior Consultation and Citizen Participation' (2018) 111 World Development 75–83.

Merino, Roger, 'The Cynical State: Forging Extractivism, Neoliberalism and Development in Governmental Spaces' (2020) 41 Third World Quarterly 58–76.

Merkel, Wolfgang, 'Is There a Crisis of Democracy?' (2014) 1 Democratic Theory 11–25.

Merrill, Thomas W. and Henry E. Smith, 'Optimal Standardization in the Law of Property: The Numerus Clausus Principle' (2000) 110 Yale Law Journal 1–70.

Merrill, Thomas W. and Henry E. Smith, 'What Happened to Property in Law and Economics?' (2001) 111 Yale Law Journal 357–98.

Metzger, Stanley D., 'Multilateral Conventions for the Protection of Private Foreign Investment' (1960) 9 Journal of Public. Law (1960) 133–46.

Meyer, Klaus E., Ram Mudambi, and Rajneesh Narula 'Multinational Enterprises and Local Contexts: The Opportunities and Challenges of Multiple Embeddedness' (2011) 48 Journal of Management Studies 235–52.

Michaels, Ralf, 'Dreaming law without a state: scholarship on autonomous international arbitration as utopian literature' (2013) 1 London Review of International Law 35–62.

Michelman, Frank I., 'Property, Utility, and Fairness: Comments on the Ethical Foundations of "Just Compensation" Law' (1967) 80 Harvard Law Review 1165–258.

Miller, Arthur S., 'Protection of Private Foreign Investment by Multilateral Convention' (1959) 53 American Journal of International Law 371–78.

Minteer, Ben A. and Thaddeus R. Miller, 'The New Conservation Debate: Ethical Foundations, Strategic Trade-offs, and Policy Opportunities' (2011) 144 Biological Conservation 945–47.

Miraftab, Faranak, 'Public-Private Partnerships: The Trojan Horse of Neoliberal Public-Private Partnerships: The Trojan Horse of Neoliberal Development?' (2004) 24 Journal of Planning Education and Research 89–101.

Montt, Santiago, *State Liability in Investment Treaty Arbitration: Global Constitutional and Administrative Law in the BIT Generation* (Hart 2009).

Möslein, Florian and Karl Riesenhuber, 'Contract Governance—A Draft Research Agenda' (2009) 5 European Review of Contract Law 248–89.

Nedelsky, Jennifer, 'Law, Boundaries, and the Bounded Self' (1990) 30 Representations 162–89.

Newcombe, Andrew and Lluís Paradell, *Law and Practice of Investment Treaties: Standards of Treatment* (Wolters Kluwer 2009).

Nietzsche, Friedrich, *The Genealogy of Morals: A Polemic* (trans. W. Kaufmann) (Modern Library 1888 [2000]).

Nordström, Håkan and Scott Vaughan, 'Trade and the Environment' (1999) WTO Special Studies No. 4, available at https://www.econstor.eu/bitstream/10419/107057/1/wto-special-study_4_e.pdf (last visited 25 May 2020).

North, Douglas, *Structure and Change in Economic History* (W. W. Norton 1981).

Nwogugu, Edwin I., *The Legal Problems of Foreign Investment in Developing Countries* (Manchester University Press 1965).

O'Brien, James E., 'James E. O'Brien: Odyssey of a Journeyman Lawyer' Interview by Carole Hicke in 1987-1990, Oral History Center, The Bancroft Library, University of California, Berkeley, 1991.

O'Donnell, Guillermo A., *Bureaucratic Authoritarianism: Argentina, 1966-1973, in Comparative Perspective* (University of California Press 1988).

Oppenheim, Lassa and Hersch Lauterpacht, *International Law: A Treatise* (Longmans 1948).

Orrego Vicuña, Francisco, *International Dispute Settlement in an Evolving Global Society: Constitutionalization, Accessibility, Privatization* (CUP 2004).

Ortino, Federico, 'Refining the Content and Role of Investment "Rules" and "Standards": A New Approach to International Investment Treaty Making' (2013) 28 ICSID Review 152–68.

Ostrom, Elinor, *Governing the Commons: The Evolution of Institutions for Collective Action* (CUP 1990).

Owusu, Francis, 'Pragmatism and the Gradual Shift from Dependency to Neoliberalism: The World Bank, African Leaders and Development Policy in Africa' (2003) 31 World Development 1655–72.

OXFAM, 'Glamis Gold: A Case Study of Investing in Destruction' (2003) Briefing Paper, 2, available at https://www.oxfamamerica.org/explore/research-publications/investing-in-destruction-glamis-gold/ (11 June 2020).

Pahuja, Sundhya, *Decolonising International Law: Development, Economic Growth and the Politics of Universality* (CUP 2011).

Pahuja, Sundhya and Anna Saunders, 'Rival Worlds and the place of the Corporation in International Law' in Jochen von Bernstorff, Philipp Dann (eds.), *The Battle for International Law in the Decolonization Era* (OUP 2018) 141–67.

Paparinskis, Martins, 'Limits of Depoliticisation in Contemporary Investor-State Arbitration' in James Crawford and Sarah Nouwen (eds.), *Select Proceedings of the European Society of International Law*, vol. 3 (Hart 2010) 271–82.

Paparinskis, Martins, *The International Minimum Standard and Fair and Equitable Treatment* (OUP 2013).

Paulsson, Jan, 'Arbitration without Privity' (1995) 10 ICSID Review 232–57.

Paulsson, Jan, *Denial of Justice in International law* (CUP 2005).

Paulsson, Jan, 'International Arbitration and the Generation of Legal Norms: Treaty Arbitration and International Law' in Albert Jan van den Berg (ed.), *International Arbitration 2006: Back to Basics?* (Kluwer Law International 2007) 879–89.

Paulsson, Jan, 'The Power of States to Make Meaningful Promises to Foreigners' (2010) 1 Journal of International Dispute Settlement 341–52.

Peck, Jamie, *Constructions of Neoliberal Reason* (OUP 2010).

Perrone, Nicolás M., 'The International Investment Regime after the Global Crisis of Neoliberalism: Rupture or Continuity' (2016) 23 Indiana Journal of Global Legal Studies 603–27.

Perrone, Nicolás M., 'UNCTAD's World Investment Reports 1991–2015: 25 Years of Narratives Justifying and Balancing Foreign Investor Rights' (2018) 19 Journal of World Investment & Trade 7–40.

Perrone, Nicolás M., 'Making Local Communities Visible: A Way to Prevent the Potentially Tragic Consequences of Foreign Investment?' in Alvaro Santos, Chantal Thomas, David Trubek (eds.), *World Trade and Investment Law Reimagined A Progressive Agenda for an Inclusive Globalization* (Anthem Press 2019) 171–82.

Perrone, Nicolás M., 'The "Invisible" Local Communities: Foreign Investor Obligations, Inclusiveness, and the International Investment Regime' (2019) 113 American Journal of International Law Unbound 16–21.

Perrone, Nicolás M., 'International Investment Law as Transnational Law' in Peer Zumbansen (ed.), *Oxford Handbook of Transnational Law* (OUP forthcoming).

Perrone, Nicolás M. and David Schneiderman, 'International Economic Law's Wreckage: Depoliticization, Inequality, Precarity' in Emilios Christodoulidis, Ruth Dukes, and Marco Goldoni (eds.), *Research Handbook on Critical Legal Theory* (Edward Elgar Publishing 2019) 446–72.

Petrini, Francesco, 'Who'll Stop the Runaway Shop? The Battle to Regulate Multinationals' Activities Inside the EEC at the Dawn of Globalization', paper presented at EUSA Twelfth Biennial International Conference, Boston, 2011.

Petrini, Francesco, 'Capital Hits the Road: Regulating Multinational Corporations During the Long 1970s' in Knud Andresen and Stefan Müller (eds.), *Contesting Deregulation: Debates, Practices and Developments in the West Since the 1970s* (Berghahn Books 2017) 185–98.

Pinto Herrera, Honorio, 'Conflicto minero en Santa Ana (Puno)' (2013) 17 Investigaciones sociales 207–19.

Pistor, Katharina, *The Code of Capital: How the Law Creates Wealth and Inequality* (Princeton University Press 2019).

Pohl, Joachim, 'Societal Benefits and Costs of International Investment Agreements: A Critical Review of Aspects and Available Empirical Evidence' (2018) OECD Working Papers on International Investment, No. 2018/01.

Polanyi, Karl, *The Great Transformation: The Political and Economic Origins of our Time* (Beacon Press 2001 [1957]).

Porterfield, Matthew C., 'Exhaustion of Local Remedies in Investor-State Dispute Settlement: An Idea Whose Time Has Come?' (2015) 41 Yale Journal of International Law Online 1–12.

Prime, G., 'An Overview of the Industrial Mineral Potential of the North Mountain Basalt' in Nova Scotia Department of Natural Resources, Mineral Resources Branch, Report of Activities 2007 (2008) 81–104.

Puig, Sergio, 'Social Capital in the Arbitration Market' (2014) 25 European Journal of International Law 387–424.

Puig, Sergio, 'Tobacco Litigation in International Courts' (2016) 57 Harvard International Law Journal 383–432.

Purdy, Jedediah, *The Meaning of Property: Freedom, Community, and the Legal Imagination* (Yale University Press 2010).

Quijano, Aníbal, 'Coloniality of Power, Eurocentrism, and Latin America,' (2000) 1 Nepantla: Views from South 533–80.

Rabasa Mishkin, Emilio Óscar, Speech of the Mexican Ambassador before the General Assembly of the United Nations, UNGA Official Records, 29th Session, A/PV.2315 (12 December 1974) 1378.

Radin, Margaret Jane, 'Property and Personhood' (1982) 34 Stanford Law Review 957–1015.

Rajagopal, Balakrishnan, *International Law from Below: Development, Social Movements, and Third World Resistance* (CUP 2003).

Reed, Cyrus, Marisa Jacott and Alejandro Villamar, 'Hazardous waste management in the United States-Mexico border states: more questions than answers' (2000) Texas Center for Policy Studies, available at http://www.texascenter.org/publications/haz2000.pdf (last visited 25 May 2020).

Reich, Charles A., 'The New Property' (1964) 73 Yale Law Journal 733–87.

Reinhardt, Eberhard, Letter to Prof. Dr F. Wahlen, Swiss Federal Council, Political Department, 23 January 1964 (Swiss Diplomatic Documents, dodis.ch/31989).

Reisman, Michael W., '"Case Specific Mandates" Versus "Systemic Implications": How Should Investment Tribunals Decide?' (2013) 29 Arbitration International 131–52.

Reisman, Michael W. and Rocio Digón, 'Eclipse of Expropriation?' in Arthur Rovine (ed.), *Contemporary Issues in International Arbitration and Mediation, The Fordham Papers* (Martinus Nijhoff Publishers 2009) 27–46.

Retinger, J. H., 'The Bilderberg Group' (1956), available at https://info.publicintelligence.net/bilderberg/BilderbergGroupRetinger.pdf (last visited 3 July 2020).

Reynolds, Paul, 'Legitimate Expectations and the Protection of Trust in Public Officials' (2011) 2 Public Law 330–52.

Rhyne, Charles S., 'World Law to Protect World Investment' Speech before the American Bankers Association, New York 1958, in Society to Advance the Protection of Foreign Investments, Convention on Investments Abroad with Comments, Speeches and New Literature, Publication No. 3 (Bergisch Gladbach, J. Heider 1960) 61–7.

Riles, Annelise, 'Property as Legal Knowledge: Means and Ends' (2004) 10 Journal of the Royal Anthropological Institute 775–95.

Robbins, Peter T., 'Transnational Corporations and the Discourse of Water Privatization' (2003) 15 Journal of International Development 1073–82.

Roberts, Anthea, 'Power and Persuasion in Investment Treaty Interpretation: The Dual Role of States' (2010) 104 American Journal of International Law 179–225.

Roberts, Anthea and Taylor St John, 'UNCITRAL and ISDS Reform: Visualising a Flexible Framework' (2019) EJIL Talk, 24 October 2019.

Robertson, Lindsay G., *Conquest by Law: How the Discovery of America Dispossessed Indigenous Peoples of their Lands* (OUP 2005).

Robinson, Joanna L., *Contested Water: The Struggle Against Water Privatization in the United States and Canada* (The MIT Press 2013).

Rockefeller, David 'The Aspirations of Mankind in a Troubled World' Address at the International Industrial Conference, San Francisco, 17 September 1965.

Rockefeller, David, 'What Private Enterprise Means to Latin America' (1966) 44 Foreign Affairs 403–16.

Rockefeller, Nelson A., 'Why not a Wider Consensus among Nations?' in James Daniel (ed.), *Private Investment: The Key to International Industrial Development: A Report of the San Francisco Conference, October 14–18*, 1957 (McGraw Hill 1958) 78–80.

Rodotà, Stefano, *El terrible derecho: estudios sobre la propiedad privada* (trans. Luis Diez-Picazo) (Civitas 1986).

Rodríguez-Boetsch, Leopoldo, 'Public Service Privatisation and Crisis in Argentina' (2005) 15 Development in Practice 302–15.

Rodrik, Dani, 'The New Development Economics: We Shall Experiment, but How Shall We Learn?' in Jessica Cohen, and William Easterly (eds.), *What Works in Development?: Thinking Big and Thinking Small* (Brookings Institution Press 2010) 24–47.

Rodrik, Dani, 'Rethinking Growth Policies in the Developing World' 2004 Luca d'Agliano Lecture, available at https://j.mp/2o5o9H1 (last visited 21 May 2020).

Röpke, Wilhelm, *International Order and Economic Integration* (D. Reidel 1959).

Rosanvallon, Pierre, *La contre-démocratie: la politique à l'âge de la défiance* (Groupe Seuil 2006).

Rose, Carol M., 'Mahon Reconstructed: Why the Takings Issue is Still a Muddle' (1984) 57 Southern California Law Review 561–99.

Rose, Carol M., 'Property as Storytelling: Perspectives from Game Theory, Narrative Theory, Feminist Theory' (1990) 2 Yale Journal of Law & the Humanities 37–58.

Rowe, James K., 'Corporate Social Responsibility as Business Strategy' in Ronnie D. Lipschutz with James K. Rowe (eds.), *Globalization, Governmentality and Global Politics: Regulation for the Rest of Us?* (Routledge 2005) 122–60.

Ruggie, John Gerald, 'International Regimes, Transactions, and Change: Embedded Liberalism in the Postwar Economic Order' (1982) 36 International Organization 379–415.

Sagafi-nejad, Tagi and John Dunning, The *UN and Transnational Corporations: From Code of Conduct to Global Compact* (Indiana University Press 2008).

Salacuse, Jeswald W., 'The Emerging Global Regime for Investment' (2010) 51 Harvard International Law Journal 427–73.

Salacuse, Jeswald W., *The Three Laws of International Investment: National, Contractual, and International Frameworks for Foreign Capital* (OUP 2013).

Salacuse, Jeswald W., *The Law of Investment Treaties* (OUP 2015).

Salacuse, Jeswald W. and Nicholas P. Sullivan, 'Do BITs Really Work: An Evaluation of Bilateral Investment Treaties and their Grand Bargain' (2005) 46 Harvard International Law Journal (2005) 67–130.

Sally, Razeen, *Classical Liberalism and International Economic Order: Studies in Theory and Intellectual History* (Routledge 2002).

Santos, Boaventura de Sousa, *Toward a New Legal Common Sense: Law, Globalization, and Emancipation* (CUP 2002).

Sassen, Saskia, *Losing Control? Sovereignty in an age of Globalization* (Columbia University Press 1996).

Sattorova, Mavluda, *The Impact of Investment Treaty Law on Host States: Enabling Good Governance?* (Bloomsbury Publishing 2018).
Sauvant, Karl P., 'The Negotiations of the United Nations Code of Conduct on Transnational Corporations: Experience and Lessons Learned' (2015) 16 Journal of World Investment & Trade 11–87.
Scheiber, Harry N., 'Introduction' in Harry N. Scheiber (ed.), *The State and Freedom of Contract* (Stanford University Press 1998) 1–12.
Scheppele, Kim Lane, 'Facing Facts in Legal Interpretation' (1990) 30 Representations 42–77.
Schill, Stephan, 'W(h)ither Fragmentation? On the Literature and Sociology of International Investment Law' (2011) 22 European Journal of International Law 875–908.
Schill, Stephan W., 'Deference in Investment Treaty Arbitration: Re-conceptualizing the Standard of Review' (2012) 3 Journal of International Dispute Settlement 577–607.
Schill, Stephan W. and Kerem Gülay, 'Approaches to Foreign Direct Investment in Legal Research' in Markus Krajewski and T. Rhea Hoffmann (eds.), *Research Handbook On Foreign Direct Investment* (Edward Elgar Publishing 2019).
Schneiderman, David, *Constitutionalizing Economic Globalization. Investment Rules and Democracy's Promise* (CUP 2008).
Schneiderman, David, 'Legitimacy and Reflexivity in International Investment Arbitration: A New Self-Restraint?' (2011) 2 Journal of International Dispute Settlement 471–95.
Schneiderman, David, *Resisting Economic Globalization: Critical Theory and International Investment Law* (Palgrave 2013).
Schneiderman, David, 'Judging in Secular Times: Max Weber and the Rise of Proportionality' (2013) 63 Supreme Court Law Review 557–77.
Schneiderman, David, 'The Global Regime of Investor Rights: Return to the Standards of Civilised Justice?' (2014) 5 Transnational Legal Theory 60–80.
Schneiderman, David, 'Constitutional Property Rights and Elision of the Transnational: Foucauldian Misgivings' (2015) 24 Social & Legal Studies 65–87.
Schneiderman, David, 'The Paranoid Style of Investment Lawyers and Arbitrators: Investment Law Norm Entrepreneurs and their Critics' in C. L. Lim (ed.), *Alternative Visions of the International Law on Foreign Investment: Essays in Honour of Muthucumaraswamy Sornarajah* (CUP 2016) 131–55.
Schneiderman, David, 'Hayek's Dream: International Investment Law and the Denigration of Politics' (2019) available at SSRN: https://ssrn.com/abstract=3397624 (last visited 29 September 2020).
Schreuer, Christoph, 'Unjustified Enrichment in International Law' (1974) 22 American Journal of Comparative Law 281–301.
Schreuer, Christoph, 'Fair and Equitable Treatment in Arbitral Practice' (2005) 6 Journal of World Investment & Trade 357–86.
Schreuer, Christoph, 'Investment Arbitration' in Cesare Romano, Karen Alter, and Yuval Shany (eds.), *The Oxford Handbook of International Adjudication* (OUP 2014) 295–315.
Schwarzenberger, Georg, 'Decolonisation and the Protection of Foreign Investments' (1967) 20 Current Legal Problems 213–31.
Schwarzenberger, Georg, *Foreign Investments and International Law* (Stevens & Sons 1969).
Schwebel, Stephen M., 'On Whether the Breach by a State of a Contract with an Alien is a Breach of International law' in Stephen M. Schwebel, *Justice in International Law: Selected Writings* (CUP 1994) 425–35.
Scranton, Philip and Patrick Fridenson, *Reimagining Business History* (John Hopkins University Press 2013).

Segnini, Giannina, 'Fijan pago por Santa Elena' La Nación, 18 February 2000, available at http://wvw.nacion.com/ln_ee/2000/febrero/18/pais1.html (last visited 25 May 2020).

Sell, Susan K., 'TRIPS was Never Enough: Vertical Forum Shifting, FTAs, ACTA, and TPP' (2010) 18 Journal of Intellectual Property Law 447–78.

Serra, Narcis, Shari Spiegel and Joseph E. Stiglitz, 'Introduction: From the Washington Consensus Towards a New Global Governance' in Narcis Serra and Joseph E. Stiglitz (eds.), *The Washington Consensus Reconsidered: Towards a New Global Governance* (OUP 2008) 3–13.

Servan-Schreiber, Jean Jacques, *The American Challenge* (Penguin Books 1969 [1967]).

Shaikh, Anwar, *Capitalism: Competition, Conflict, Crises* (OUP 2016).

Shaikh, Hafeez and Manuel Angel Abdala, *Argentina Privatization Program: A Review of Five cases* (World Bank 1996).

Shapiro, Daniel, Bersant Hobdari, and Chang Hoon Oh, 'Natural Resources, Multinational Enterprises and Sustainable Development' (2018) 53 Journal of World Business 1–14.

Shapiro, Harvey D., 'Multinationals' *New York Times*, 18 March 1973.

Shawcross, Hartley, 'The Promotion of International Investment' Speech before the Society to Advance the Protection of Foreign Investments, Cologne 1959, in Society to Advance the Protection of Foreign Investments, Convention on Investments Abroad with Comments, Speeches and New Literature, Publication No. 3 (Bergisch Gladbach, J. Heider 1960) 46–60.

Shawcross, Hartley, 'Problems of Foreign Investment,' (1961) 102 Recueil des Cours 339–63.

Shawcross, Hartley, 'Introductory Address' in The Institute of Economic Affairs, 'Overseas Investment or Economic Nationalism?' (1967) Occasional paper No. 15, 9.

Shawcross, Hartley, 'A Warmer Welcome from the Developing Countries' in The Institute of Economic Affairs, 'Overseas Investment or Economic Nationalism?' (1967) Occasional paper No. 15, 26–9.

Shawcross, Hartley, *Life Sentence: The Memoirs of Hartley Shawcross* (Constable 1995).

Shihata, Ibrahim, 'Toward Greater Depoliticization of Investment Disputes: The Roles of ICSID and MIGA' (1986) 1 ICSID Review 1–25.

Shihata, Ibrahim, 'Factors Influencing the Flow of Foreign Investment and the Relevance of a Multilateral Investment Guarantee Scheme,' (1987) 21 International Lawyer 671–94.

Sierra Camargo, Ximena, *Derecho, Desarrollo y Extractivismo: La disputa por el oro en Colombia en un contexto de colonialidad global.* (2018) Doctoral thesis, Universidad del Rosario (Colombia).

Singer, Joseph William, 'The Reliance Interest in Property' (1988) 40 Stanford Law Review 611–751.

Singer, Joseph William, 'Sovereignty and Property' (1991) 86 Northwestern University Law Review 1–56.

Singer, Joseph William, *Entitlement: The Paradoxes of Property* (Yale University Press 2000).

Singer, Joseph William, *No Freedom Without Regulation: The Hidden Lesson of the Subprime Crisis* (Yale University Press, 2015)

Skovgaard Poulsen, Lauge N., *Bounded Rationality and Economic Diplomacy: The Politics of Investment Treaties in Developing Countries* (CUP 2015).

Slobodian, Quinn, *Globalists: The End of Empire and the Birth of Neoliberalism* (Harvard University Press 2018).

Smith, Stephen A., *Contract Theory* (OUP 2004).

Sornarajah, Muthucumaraswamy, *Resistance and Change in the International Law on Foreign Investment* (CUP 2015).

Sornarajah, Muthucumaraswamy, *The International Law on Foreign Investment* (CUP 2017).

Sprankling, John G., *The International Law of Property* (OUP 2014).
Spühler, Willy, Letter to Eberhard Reinhardt, 16 August 1967 (Swiss Diplomatic Documents, dodis.ch//32862).
St John, Taylor, *The Rise of Investor-State Arbitration: Politics, Law, and Unintended Consequences* (OUP 2018).
Steringa, Hendrik, 'Energy Companies Divided over Renewable Energy in Brussels' Energy Post, 22 October 2015, available at https://energypost.eu/energy-companies-divided-renewable-energy-lobby-brussels/ (last visited 4 June 2020).
Stigson, Björn, 'Moving Ahead on Climate' in UN Environment Programme, *Climate Action: Getting Greener, Getting Slimmer, and Going Digital* (UN 2008).
Stopford, John M. and Susan Strange with John S. Henley, *Rival States, Rival Firms: Competition For World Market Shares* (CUP 1991).
Stopford, John M., 'The Growing Interdependence between Transnational Corporations and Governments' (1994) 3 Transnational Corporations 53–76.
Sunstein, Cass, 'Social Norms and Social Roles' (1996) 96 Columbia Law Review (1996) 903–68.
Taylor, Charles, *Modern Social Imaginaries* (Duke University Press 2004).
Taylor, Charles, *A Secular Age* (Harvard University Press 2007).
Tienhaara, Kyla 'Regulatory Chill and the Threat of Arbitration: A View from Political Science' in Chester Brown and Kate Miles (eds.), *Evolution in Investment Treaty Law and Arbitration* (CUP 2011) 606–28.
Titi, Catharine, *The Right to Regulate in International Investment Law* (Bloomsbury 2014).
Trachtenberg, Alan, *The Incorporation of America: Culture and Society in the Gilded Age* (Hill and Wang 1982).
Tucker, Todd N., *Judge Knot: Politics and Development in International Investment Law* (Anthem Press 2018).
Twining, William, *Globalisation and Legal Theory* (Butterworths 2000).
Tzouvala, Ntina, 'The Ordo-Liberal Origins of Modern International Investment Law: Constructing Competition on a Global Scale' in John D. Haskell and Akbar Rasulov (eds.), *European Yearbook of International Economic Law. Special Issue: New Voices and New Perspectives in International Economic Law* (Springer 2019) 37–54.
Umaña Quesada, Álvaro Francisco, *El Aeropuerto de Santa Elena: la historia política del Parque Nacional de Guanacaste* (Fundación CRUSA 2016).
Upham, Frank K., *The Great Property Fallacy: Theory, Reality, and Growth in Developing Countries* (CUP 2018).
Vagts, Detlev F., 'The Multinational Enterprise: A New Challenge for Transnational Law' (1970) 83 Harvard Law Review 739–92.
Valencia, Areli, *Human Rights Trade-Offs in Times of Economic Growth: The Long-Term Capability Impacts of Extractive-Led Development* (Palgrave 2016).
Van den Bossche, Peter, Farewell Speech at the WTO Dispute Settlement Body, 28 May 2019, available at https://www.wto.org/english/tratop_e/dispu_e/farwellspeech_peter_van_den_bossche_e.htm (last visited 29 September 2020).
Van der Meulen Rodgers, Yana, Anthony Bebbington, Catherine Boone, Jampel Dell'Angelo, Jean-Philippe Platteau, and Arun Agrawal, 'Experimental Approaches in Development and Poverty Alleviation' (2020) 127 World Development 1–6.
Van der Veen, Peter, Felix Remy, and John P. Williams, *A Mining Strategy for Latin America and the Caribbean: Estrategia minera para América Latina y El Caribe* (World Bank 1997).
Van Harten, Gus, *Investment Treaty Arbitration and Public Law* (OUP 2007).

Van Harten, Gus, *Sovereign Choices and Sovereign Constraints: Judicial Restraint in Investment Treaty Arbitration* (OUP 2013).

Van Harten, Gus and Martin Loughlin, 'Investment Treaty Arbitration as a Species of Global Administrative Law' (2006) 17 European Journal of International Law 121–50.

Veeder, V. V., 'The Lena Goldfields Arbitration: The Historical Roots of Three Ideas' (1998) 47 International and Comparative Law Quarterly 747–92.

Veeder, V. V., 'Chancellor Wirth and the Mologoles Concession 1923-1927: The German-Speaking Origins of the ICSID Convention' in Christina Binder, Ursula Kriebaum, August Reinisch, and Stephan Wittich (eds.), *International Investment Law for the 21st Century: Essays in Honour of Christoph Schreuer* (OUP 2009).

Verdross, Alfred, 'Quasi-International Agreements and International Economic Transactions' (1964) 18 Yearbook of World Affairs 230–47.

Vijgen, John, Li Fan Yi, Martin Forter, Rup Lal, and Roland Weber, 'The Legacy of Lindane and Technical HCH Production' (2006) 68 Organohalog Comp 899–904.

Vincent, M. André, 'Memorandum: International Chamber of Commerce Guidelines for International Investment' DAC/FPD(72)791, 27 December 1972 (Edwin Martin Personal Papers, The John F. Kennedy Library, Box 37).

Vincent, A., 'Memorandum: International Chamber of Commerce: Guidelines for International Investment' OECD AV-1446, 4 January 1973 (Edwin Martin Personal Papers, The John F. Kennedy Library, Box 37).

Viñuales, Jorge E., 'Sovereignty in Foreign Investment Law' in Zachary Douglas, Joost Pauwelyn, and Jorge E. Viñuales (eds.), *The Foundations of International Investment Law: Bringing Theory into Practice* (OUP 2014) 318–62.

Vittor, Luis, 'Las consultas vecinales sobre la minería: experiencias y desafíos' in Raphael Hoetmer, Miguel Castro, Mar Daza, José De Echave C., and Clara Ruiz, *Minería y movimientos sociales en el Perú Instrumentos y propuestas para la defensa de la vida, el agua y los territorios* (CooperAcción 2013) 503–11.

von Benda-Beckmann, Franz, Keebet von Benda-Beckmann, and Melanie Wiber, 'The Properties of Property' in Franz von Benda-Beckmann, Keebet von Benda-Beckmann, and Melanie Wiber (eds.), *Changing Properties of Property* (Berghahn Books 2006) 1–39.

von Moltke, Konrad, *An International Investment Regime?: Issues of Sustainability* (IISD 2000).

Wahlen, F., Answer to Eberhard Reinhardt's letter dated 23 January, 28 January 1964 (Swiss Diplomatic Documents, dodis.ch/31413).

Wälde, Thomas, 'Environmental Policies towards Mining in Developing Countries' (1992) 10 Journal of Energy & Natural Resources Law 327–57.

Wälde, Thomas, 'The Specific Nature of Investment Arbitration' in Philippe Kahn and Thomas Wälde (eds.), *Les Aspects Nouveaux du Droit des Investissements Internationaux/New Aspects of International Investment Law* (Martinus Nijhoff Publishers 2007).

Wälde, Thomas and Abba Kolo, 'Environmental Regulation, Investment Protection and "Regulatory Taking" in International Law' (2001) 50 International & Comparative Law Quarterly 811–48.

Waldron, Jeremy, *The Right to Private Property* (Clarendon Press 1988).

Waldron, Jeremy, 'Nozick and Locke: Filling the Space of Rights' (2005) 22 Social Philosophy and Policy 81–110.

Waldron, Jeremy, *The Rule of Law and the Measure of Property* (CUP 2012).

Wallenberg, Marcus, 'Evaluation of Structures in International Finance' in Robert L. Baker (ed.), *Business Leadership in a Changing World; a report of the International Industrial Conference in San Francisco, September 11–15, 1961* (McGraw Hill 1962) 137–45.

Weber, Max, *Economy and Society: An Outline of Interpretive Sociology*, Guenther Roth and Claus Wittich (eds.) (University of California Press 1978 [1922]).

Wells, Louis T. and Rafiq Ahmed, *Making Foreign Investment Safe: Property Rights and National Sovereignty* (OUP 2007).

White, Gillian, 'A New International Economic Order?' (1976) 16 Virginia Journal of International Law 323–45.

Whitehead, Lawrence, 'La política económica del sexenio de Echeverría: ¿qué salió mal y por qué?' (1980) 20 Foro internacional 484–513.

Whitman Rostow, Walt, *Concept and Controversy: Sixty Years of Taking Ideas to Market* (University of Texas Press 2010).

Wike, Richard, Katie Simmons, Bruce Stokes, and Janell Fetterolf, 'Globally, Broad Support for Representative and Direct Democracy. But Many also Endorse Nondemocratic Alternatives' October 2017, Pew Research Center.

Wilkins, Mira, *The History of Foreign Investment in the United States, 1914-1945* (Harvard University Press 2009).

Williams, John Fischer, 'International Law and the Property of Aliens,' (1928) 9 British Yearbook of International Law 1–30.

Williamson, Oliver E., *The Economic Institutions of Capitalism Firms, Markets, Relational Contracting* (Macmillan 1985).

Wolff von Amerongen, Otto, 'Need for World Investment Charter' Speech before the International Chamber of Commerce, 1959 Washington Congress, in Society to Advance the Protection of Foreign Investments, Convention on Investments Abroad with Comments, Speeches and New Literature, Publication No. 3 (Bergisch Gladbach, J. Heider 1960) 41–3.

Wongkaew, Teerawat, *Protection of Legitimate Expectations in Investment Treaty Arbitration* (CUP 2019).

Woods, George D., 'Annual Address by the President of the Bank and its affiliates,' 30 September 1963.

Zeyl, Trevor, 'Charting the Wrong Course: The Doctrine of Legitimate Expectations in Investment Treaty Law' (2011) 49 Alberta Law Review 203–35.

Zumbansen, Peer, 'Transnational Law' in Jan Smits (ed.), *Encyclopedia of Comparative Law* (Edward Elgar Publishing 2006) 738–54.

Zumbansen, Peer, 'The Law of Society: Governance through Contract' (2007) 14 Indiana Journal of Global Legal Studies (2007) 191–233.

Zumbansen, Peer, 'Defining the Space of Transnational law: Legal Theory, Global Governance, and Legal Pluralism' (2012) 21 Transnational Law & Contemporary Problems 305–36.

Index

For the benefit of digital users, indexed terms that span two pages (e.g., 52–53) may, on occasion, appear on only one of those pages.

Footnotes are indicated by n. after the paragraph number.